Palgrave Studies in the Theory and History of Psychology

Series Editor
Jack Martin
Simon Fraser University
Burnaby, British Columbia, Canada

Palgrave Studies in the Theory and History of Psychology publishes scholarly books that use historical and theoretical methods to critically examine the historical development and contemporary status of psychological concepts, methods, research, theories, and interventions. The books in the series are characterised by an emphasis on the concrete particulars of psychologists' scientific and professional practices, together with a critical examination of the assumptions that attend their use. These examinations are anchored in clear, accessible descriptions of what psychologists do and believe about their activities. All the books in the series share the general goal of advancing the scientific and professional practices of psychology and psychologists, even as they offer probing and detailed questioning and critical reconstructions of these practices.

More information about this series at
http://www.springer.com/series/14576

Vanessa Lux • Sigrid Weigel
Editors

Empathy

Epistemic Problems and Cultural-Historical Perspectives of a Cross-Disciplinary Concept

palgrave
macmillan

Editors
Vanessa Lux
Faculty of Psychology
Ruhr University Bochum
Bochum, Germany

Sigrid Weigel
ZfL Berlin
Berlin, Germany

Palgrave Studies in the Theory and History of Psychology
ISBN 978-1-137-51298-7 ISBN 978-1-137-51299-4 (eBook)
DOI 10.1057/978-1-137-51299-4

Library of Congress Control Number: 2017950557

Cover illustration: Lucio Fontana, "Concetto Spaziale, Attesa, 1960" (water-based paint on canvas, 81 x 65 cm), picture courtesy by Robilant+Voena, with the kind permission of Fondazione Lucio Fontana

This Palgrave Macmillan imprint is published by Springer Nature
The registered company is Macmillan Publishers Ltd.
The registered company address is: The Campus, 4 Crinan Street, London, N1 9XW, United Kingdom

Contents

List of Contributors

Christian G. Allesch, Assoc. Professor emeritus, Department of Psychology, University of Salzburg, Salzburg, Austria

David Freedberg, Pierre Matisse Professor of the History of Art at Columbia University; Director of The Italian Academy for Advanced Studies in America, Columbia University, Columbia, USA

Thomas Fuchs, MD, PhD, Karl Jaspers Professor of Philosophy and Psychiatry, Psychiatric Department, University of Heidelberg, Heidelberg, Germany

Vittorio Gallese, MD, Professor of Physiology at the Department of Neuroscience, University of Parma, Parma, Italy

Susan Lanzoni, PhD, historian of science, Division of Continuing Education, Harvard University, Boston, MAUSA

Marianne Leuzinger Bohleber, Prof. Dr., Director of the Sigmund Freud Institute, Frankfurt a.M, Germany

Vanessa Lux, PhD, Research fellow at the Department of Genetic Psychology, Faculty of Psychology, Ruhr University Bochum, Bochum, Germany

Patrizia Manganaro, Professor of History of Contemporary Philosophy and Philosophy of Language, Lateran University, Vatican City, Italy

Andrea Pinotti, Professor in Aesthetics, Università degli Studi di Milano, Milano, Italy

Helmut J. Schneider, Professor emeritus of German Literature, University of Bonn, Bonn, Germany

Mark Solms, Professor of Neuropsychology, University of Cape Town and Groote Schuur Hospital, Cape Town, South Africa

Sigrid Weigel, Prof. Dr. Dr. h.c. mult., former Director of the Zentrum für Literatur- und Kulturforschung Berlin, Permanent Visiting Professor at the German Department of Princeton University, New Jersey, USA

List of Figures

1

The Heterogeneity of Empathy
An Archaeology of Multiple Meanings and Epistemic Implications

Sigrid Weigel

Over the last two decades, the concept of "empathy" has secured a rather prominent place both within scholarship and in public discourse. Initiated – or at least fostered – by the discovery of the mirror neurons, empathy has come to play a central role, especially in psychology, psychoanalysis, evolutionary anthropology, and biology, as well as in different fields of social and cultural research. Indeed, in neuroscience, empathy studies "make up a relatively new subdiscipline" (Panksepp & Panksepp, 2013, p. 1). In the light of the fact that our neuronal system is activated whether we enact a sensorimotor action ourselves or whether we only perceive it as the movement of the other, the mirror paradigm has led to a re-conceptualization of the relationship between "self" and "other" and has driven scientific attention to their shared emotional system. This turn to a relational perspective not only triggered a withdrawal of the cognitive bias in neuroscience and its orientation towards emotions but also attracted the interest of disciplines traditionally

S. Weigel (✉)
Zentrum für Literatur- und Kulturforschung Berlin, Berlin, Germany
e-mail: weigel@zfl-berlin.org

V. Lux, S. Weigel (eds.), *Empathy*, Palgrave Studies in the Theory and History of Psychology, DOI 10.1057/978-1-137-51299-4_1

occupied with questions of inter-subjectivity. As a consequence, the scholarship on empathy has managed to bridge the long existing abyss between those research fields that are determined by experimental methods (like empirical psychology and the neurosciences) on the one hand and psychoanalysis on the other. In addition, this body of scholarship has initiated a growing, fruitful exchange between scholars of the life sciences and the humanities, and has thus partly overcome the habitual hostility of the "two cultures" towards one another. Jean Decety and William Ickes, in their study *The Social Neuroscience of Empathy*, even speak of an "explosion of empathy research" (Decety & Ickes, 2011, p. VII). If we take the increasing number of articles in journals like *Psychoanalytical Dialogues, Neuroscience Letters, Social Neuroscience, Neuropsychoanalysis, Psychological Research, Journal of Consciousness Studies* and many others as an indicator, the metaphor of explosion has by now indeed come into its own: empathy is today one of the hottest topics of research.

1 Between the "Two Cultures" – Chances and Problems

The shift to inter-subjectivity and the recent discussion of concepts such as simulation, imitation, and imagination are of special interest for scholars from the humanities because those terms belong to their long-standing concerns and vocabulary (Weigel, 2016). However, although the notion of shared feeling and related ideas such as pity, compassion, or sympathy are part of the established canon of key terms in philosophy, aesthetics, and poetics, the scientific carrier of empathy has brought the term and its conceptual relatives back into the centre of scholarship in philology, art, and media and film studies. Thus, the discovery of empathy in the field of experimental research has initiated a re-discovery of it in the field of hermeneutic disciplines – where traditional ideas now appear in a slightly altered guise after their engagement with the neuropsychological metamorphosis. Since topics such as the eighteenth-century theory of pity [*Mitleid*] or the nineteenth-century aesthetic theory of *Einfühlung* were somewhat marginalized in philosophy, art, and literary history during the last decades (dominated by deconstructivism, the "cultural turn" in Europe, and "Cultural Studies" in the Anglo-American discourse), the so-called emotional turn partly bears the character of the return of the repressed.

Today, empathy appears to be of similar relevance in both research cultures,[1] in this way making the exchange – sometimes even integration – of experimental and hermeneutic insights possible. Yet, as is often the case with interdisciplinary concepts that belong to various bodies of knowledge (see Müller, 2011),[2] one has to bear in mind that the idea of empathy can carry quite diverse connotations which are based on very different explanations of human affects, the psychic structure of the individual, and the emotional behaviour towards other fellow beings and outer worlds. Thus, when we use the term empathy it is by no means clear whether this refers to the same concept, capacity, or attitude. It makes an enormous difference whether an evolutionary approach – that regularly interprets the skills of a species as a function of survival – understands empathy, along with altruism, as part of the inter*dependence* of the members of a certain species or whether empathy is regarded as a human attitude of individuals towards the emotional state of the "other", that is, as a mode of inter-*subjectivity*. Therefore, this volume is dedicated to the attempt to illuminate the multiple semantics of empathy and related concepts, its epistemic problems, its disciplinary, cultural, and historical foundations as well as the intersections between them. It makes a difference whether one talks about sympathy, fellow feeling, pity, *Einfühlung*, or empathy, although these terms are often used as synonyms. Different words can be interpreted as symptoms – as symbols of memory [*Erinnerungssymbole*] (Freud, 1986/1925, p. 404) – of a conceptual history with multiple origins and paths.

[1] Although scholarship is today segmented in a much more complex and heterogeneous way than portrayed in 1959 in *The Two Cultures* by Charles Percy Snow (Snow, 1959/2001), it is still separated in research either based on empirical or experimental methods and oriented to findings or historic-hermeneutic approaches occupied with interpretation.

[2] For the special problem of interdisciplinary concepts as a new approach in the history of ideas see the e-journal *Forum interdisziplinärer Begriffsgeschichte* of the *Zentrum für Literatur- und Kulturforschung* Berlin (Research Center for Literature and Culture).

Yet, the snares of an interdisciplinary exchange on empathy are not limited to the heterogeneous meaning of the term. As regards the history of ideas and knowledge, the conceptual relatives of empathy are actually forerunners; each of them is coined by quite a different historical index, each of them being the offspring of a certain origin and genealogy. The current neurobiological term "empathy" is a product of modernity, more precisely of twentieth-century empirical psychology; it goes back to the British psychologist Edward Titchener (see Chapter 12, in this volume), who in 1908 used it to translate the German word *Einfühlung* (literally: "feeling in/into") that itself is far from having an unambiguous definition (see Chapters 9 and 11). *Einfühlung* stems from the field of aesthetic theory formulated in the second half of the nineteenth century (Robert Vischer, Friedrich Theodor Vischer, Theodor Lipps, and others) and gained a prominent place in psychology around 1900. Thus, the question arises in what way and to what extent the meaning of *Einfühlung*, and the epistemic foundation of the idea in a psychology-driven aesthetics, got transferred to the concept of empathy within empirical psychology, that is to say, on its way from experience-based reflections to laboratories and their quantitative methods (see Chapter 5). Likewise, which moments have been lost in translation for the purpose of scientific use since then? These paths of multiple translations – that is, translation between languages, disciplines, and times – form a paradigmatic constellation of the interplay as well as the tensions between cultural and scientific ways to approach the specific character of the human being. They include the possibility of examining the differences as well as the hidden or forgotten traces of exchange or circulation between the two scholarly thought styles [*Denkstile*] (Fleck, 1935/1979). This volume is an archaeology of empathy, one that hopes to illuminate the controversies, epistemic problems, and open questions encapsulated within the heterogeneous meaning of the idea and its various layers.

An archaeological perspective on the history of science may reveal correspondences between crucial controversial questions in current scholarship and certain moments in the history of focal ideas and their conceptual relatives. For example, the question whether empathy is conceptualized as an innate capacity of mutual perception on a mere neurobiological level or whether it is evaluated as an attitude to "feel in" or "feel with" another individual's emotional state – one of the fundamental inconsistencies of the current usage of the term –corresponds with the invention of "sympathy" by eighteenth-century Moral Philosophy. David Hume and Adam Smith, for instance attempted to single out a more basic quality of "human nature" from the traditional canon of passions (pity being one of them) handed down from classical knowledge. This controversy – that in the present popularity of empathy remains to a great extent implicit – has enormous impact on the discussion of the developmental function of empathy, on its relevance for care-giving, and in psychoanalysis in general (see Chapter 3). In relation to this dispute, the question arises in which way or at what stage the neurobiological capacity of a relational emotional system becomes charged with certain qualities. At issue is whether empathy conceptualized as a primary level of neurological-emotional exchange (or even as mere contagion) develops into the cognitive capacity of perspective taking or whether empathy regarded as a basic emotional resonance mechanism gets charged with a distinct emotional colour, with specific moral or social values. Through these operations empathy transforms into a human resource for communal and social purposes, in this way returning to a historical primal scene of ideas preceding empathy, namely "sympathy" and compassion/pity [*pieté, Mitleid* (Weigel 2012)], discussed in the eighteenth century as a means to foster sociality (see Chapter 8).

Another central controversy concerns the way the relationship between the Self and other minds is conceptualized. Here, the role of the unconscious (see Chapter 4) and of imagination come into play, for example in the question whether an empathic relation to the other operates through the imagination of his/her emotional state – through so-called perspective taking, adopting the perspective of another person – or whether empathy functions as a non-conscious, mutual resonance mechanism that needs no imaginative power (see Chapter 2). This dispute takes place in the aftermath of the imagination's powerful position in the long history of ideas; imagination played an important role in the theories of pity, compassion, and sympathy, alongside the topics of similarity and identification. "Is it possible to feel pity with a creature different from the Self?" Or moreover, "Is it necessary to imagine that the same adversity may also happen to me to let me feel pity with my neighbor?" Such questions already occupied Aristotle's considerations of affects [*pathé*] and pity [*eleos*], and they were repeatedly discussed at several points in the history of empathy. They reappear in current labs of Psychology Departments in the guise of technical terms: such as "ingroup/outgroup membership" (see, e.g., Hein, Silani, Preuschoff, Batson, & Singer, 2010) or the "Emotional Egocentricity Bias" (see, e.g., Riva, Triscoli, Lamm, Carnaghi, & Silani, 2016).

A third crucial issue concerns the character of the "other" with whom or which we empathize. On the one hand, this includes the question whether the empathic relation to other creatures is similar to that to the outer world, for example to landscapes, architecture, images, or other artefacts – or, in case it is not, how the former is distinct form the latter. At the centre of this debate is the concept of "animation", which is the idea that the empathic perception of inorganic things is the product of projecting or transferring our own feelings, our own emotional state, onto the inanimate world, even onto forms or colours. The fact that the figures of projection and animation presuppose an opposition of human beings versus the inanimate world of matter, empty of any character or emotional meaning, has produced critical reflections in the history of *Einfühlung* (see Chapter 10). On the other hand, the question of the "other" concerns the strong connection between theories of empathy and movement. The harshest opponents of the mirror neurons theory argue that the relevance of movement in empathy studies is due to the influential tradition of "motor theories of cognition" (Hickok, 2009). On the conceptual level this explanation fails to take into consideration that any emotional interrelationship between two individuals functions via visual indicators, that is, through such corporeal or sensual expressions of the affective state of the subject as gestures, facial, and corporeal movements. In addition, in view of theoretical influences, it is also a too short-sighted perspective. In the light of a broader history of knowledge, the interrelation of movement and empathy results from the fact that aesthetics and the arts, along with theatre, were influential fields in which the conceptual forerunners of empathy emerged. In these fields, the actual primary aspect is visuality, that is, the perceived bodily movement that indicates others' affects. At stake here is the role of kinaesthetics, or to put it in neuroscientific terminology, the role of "action understanding" and the sensorimotor system in the production of empathy: Is the resonance mechanism first and foremost activated by the perception of bodily movements and facial and corporeal gestures (Gallese et. al. 1996)? This kind of emotional activation by visually perceptible expressions of the other's emotions has long since been studied in relation to images (see Chapter 6). Moreover, are our feelings equally aroused through the perception of visual traces of human movements or human manufacturing alone, that is to say, even by traces of human hands or of man-made labour engaged with the effects of the producer, as several experiments of the Parma neuroscience group prompt (e.g., Umilità, Berchio, Sestito, Freedberg, & Gallese, 2012)? If the latter is the case, if human beings show empathic reactions to traces of artificial practices, then art provides a prominent means of experimental research on these specific traits of human nature (see Chapter 7).

In what follows, I am presenting four short constellations from the history of empathy and its relatives. This description will not follow a developmental narrative but rather an archaeological one, taking a different concept from the terminology of empathy as a point of entry in each part.

2 Empathy – In the Laboratories of Neurosciences and Psychology

In the laboratories of contemporary experimental and empirical research, where empathy has become a central subject in the wake of the discovery of mirror neurons in the brain (Rizzolatti, Fadiga, Gallese, & Fogassi, 1996; Rizzolatti, Fogassi, & Gallese, 2002, 2006), empathy is conceptualized in distinct ways. In a broader neurobiological paradigm "empathy" stands for a general low-level skill of humans and some animal species, namely "a capacity of one animal to express the emotional feelings of another" which is based on "emotional contagion" and is described as an "affect machine" (Panksepp & Panksepp, 2013, p. 1, 4). However, the majority of the field perceives empathy as a human skill of perceived (inter) action, as the capacity for understanding the actions of others – and in this way somehow also their intentions. In this context, the capacity is not yet linked to qualitative characteristics, but is rather a quasi-neutral trait in terms of any qualitative meaning. Described as the neurophysiological foundation of empathy, the mirror neurons here provide the prerequisite of mental imitation, that is, a neuronal-based resonance mechanism to engender embodied simulations (Gallese, 2009). Arguably, this idea has turned brain studies upside down, since the epistemological shift to affective resonance between the Self and others, to inter-subjectivity and related topics such as embodiment, has liberated the field from the long enduring dominance of a cognitive bias. Due to the emphasis on empathy, the computer-model of the brain, which regarded it as the central control system of any sensual, motoric, and cognitive function, is out of date. Whereas the brain was previously described as a mere cognitive system, recent brain research regards the emotional quality of brain functions as primal, older in terms of evolution, and in this way fundamental for developing higher mental skills like perspective taking, memory, and ethical evaluation. The impact of this shift for developmental psychology cannot be underestimated: the mental and social development of an individual depends on the successful, preceding formation of primal empathy, attained within an interactive, emotionally functional relation. As a consequence, psychoanalysis has re-entered the field.

Even approaches to the concept of empathy that do not refer to the mirror neurons presuppose a mechanism of shared feelings or a shared neuronal network, a mirror mechanism of sorts that is based on the neurobiological system (Decety & Meyer 2008). Other alternatives sketch a basic, non-conscious resonance mechanism which connects individuals through a kind of inter-subjectivity, inter-corporeality, or corresponding empathy. Despite the dispute over the correct neurological explanation, the model of mutual resonance provides a biological foundation that can be "loaded" with specific content. As a result, empathy is modelled in terms of certain attitudes or features of human behaviour, and is intertwined with specific psychological, social, or moral meanings, be it *attachment, care taking, altruism, pro-social behaviour,* or others. Indeed, such conceptualizations of empathy have triggered the emergence of whole new fields of research, first and foremost the field of *Social Neuroscience* (Decety & Ickes, 2011; Singer, 2012), and revived existing theories of pro-social behaviour such as Daniel Batson's "empathy-altruism-hypothesis" (Batson, 1991, 2011). These theories regard empathy as a basic social ability. Interpreted as a qualitative property, empathy seems to provide a means to remodel the image of men and their evolution – or even to use it as a blueprint for civilization, as Jeremy Rifkin has done in *The Empathic Civilisation* (Rifkin, 2009).

The bridges between neuroscientific approaches and psychoanalysis take a different route. From the point of view of individual psychology, the relational and the developmental perspectives in psychology function as an intersection where findings in brain development and the study of the psychic phenomena of individuals meet. Since clinical psychoanalysis is *ab ovo* based in an inter-subjective constellation, the neuroscientific shift to mutual resonance makes collaboration much easier. On a metapsychology level, however, things are more complicated; here it is still unclear in which way the idea of a "non-conscious" resonance mechanism relates to Sigmund Freud's concept of the "un-conscious". This problem concerns Freud's concept of narcissism and the relation to other minds (see Chapter 4) as well as the position of the "other" in object-relations theory.

This recent research evokes general questions about the meaning of the term empathy today. One is, as already mentioned, whether empathy is a primary neurobiological capacity, a shared neuronal network that enables mutual mental resonance, or whether it is a specific emotional attitude towards the other that holds the potential for social capacities. Even more complicated is the question as to how exactly the capacity of mirroring the affective state of the other (be it joy or pain) is enhanced so that it can provide a means of psycho-social behaviour (e.g. an awareness of the other's need for help). To answer these questions, there are currently different conceptual suggestions on the table. There is, for example the effort to differentiate the *levels* of empathy, as in Thomas Fuchs' philosophically informed psychological distinction between primary, extended, and reiterated empathy (see Chapter 2), which corresponds more or less with the *stages* of the infant as described from a developmental approach in psychology/psychoanalysis (Chapter 3). This approach also provides a bridge to the neuroevolutionary hierarchy of primary, secondary, and tertiary processes of empathy (Panksepp & Panksepp, 2013). And there is the attempt to differentiate several *types* of empathy, for example a negative kind, that is "empathic distress", in contrast to compassion defined as "feeling for" and as "positive, other related feelings" (Singer & Klimecki, 2014, R878). The latter seems to be an attempt to eventually rid empathy of the ambivalence that runs like a thread through the entire history of philosophical reflections on compassion/pity. That ambivalence has divided the discourse into two opposing camps: the apologists (such as the Earl of Shaftesbury, David Hume, Johann Gottfried Herder, Jean-Jacques Rousseau, and others), and the sceptics or critics (such as Thomas Aquinas, Baruch de Spinoza, Friedrich Nietzsche, and others) (see Hamburger, 1985).

However, what is still lacking, with respect to all the theories and versions of the concept, is actual evidence. While research studies based on clinical findings – whether they pertain to certain medical damages, observations of child development, or therapeutic relations to patients – deal with *in vivo* phenomena of empathy, the innumerable experiments in psychology and neuroscience laboratories are based on the *simulation* of certain social situations. In addition, they take single measurable reactions or scanned brain activities as indicators, for example as an indicator of the grades of empathic attitudes, or of different modes of behaving towards others, and the like. In this respect, one not only encounters the problem of quantifying qualities (Chapter 5) but also the problem that the experiment remains an "as if" situation. It is by no means clear how a proband who shows a "high helping rate towards strangers in a computer game" (Singer & Klimecki, 2014, R876) will actually react in reality, whether he/she will be ready and willing to help a stranger in actual life. In other words, and regarding the epistemic problems involved, any experimental set-up in empathy laboratory research has to cope with a double "as if" constellation: the experimental "as if" simulation of a mental stage that is itself conceptualized as an "as if" figure.

For current empirical research on empathy, the exchange with scholars from the humanities is promising in view of its cultural and conceptual pre-history, as explained above. Also, the increasing importance of concepts like imitation, simulation, imagination, or mimesis, as well as the growing relevance of embodiment and facial-corporeal gestures, should point current empirical research to the rich body of knowledge on these topics, produced and collected during at least 2000 years of thought. In the humanities, mimesis and imagination count among the basic presuppositions for understanding the enormous variety of different religious, social, cultural, and artistic practices (Benjamin 1933/1999). The fact that the current neuroscientific recognition of the role of simulated imitation is interpreted as a discovery can only be explained through the preceding underestimation, in brain research, of imagination for mental activities (which was probably due to the long-lasting constriction of the field to a mere cognitive process, and its focus on action neurons). For the humanities, in contrast, there exists nearly no exchange, communicative or active, without imagination, since imagination is considered a means to relate one's own feelings and thoughts to anything else, that is, to other individuals as well as to the material world, to ideas and wishes. In other words, imagination is regarded as the basic capacity to process and mediate sensual, mental, and corporeal perceptions as experiences.

3 *Einfühlung* – Animation of Art, the Outer World, and Other Selves

"The kinesthetic stimulus does not always and necessarily lead to actual movement, but always to the idea of it." This statement is not a description of the mirror neurons in a recent scientific article; rather, it stems from a 140-year-old text. It is a citation from Robert Vischer's conceptualization of the idea of *Einfühlung* in his dissertation of 1873, *Über das optische Formgefühl. Ein Beitrag zur Äshtetik*, translated into English as *On the Optical Sense of Form: A Contribution to Aesthetics* (R. Vischer, 1873/1927; 1873/1994, p. 99). As Mark Solms in this volume calls to our attention, the idea of "feeling in" has not only to do with feeling but also contains a spatial aspect (see Chapter 4). Actually, space stands at the origin of *Einfühlung*, since the "spatial understanding of forms" was the very site from which the concept of *Einfühlung* emerged in Vischer's work. Here he develops *Einfühlung* as an active human approach to the outer world, namely as a sort of involuntary emotional and imaginative transferral of the Self onto an object. This idea is founded in the interaction of emotion and imagination. Whereas "imagination" is regarded by him as a mental activity that shapes a vague feeling by turning it into an eidetic sensual form positioned vis-à-vis the inner Self, "emotion" [*Gefühl*] is considered an individual vital energy of the human being that relates to its own species, a sort of compassion [*Mitleidenschaft*] for all living nature. Against this background, *Einfühlung* is conceptualized as a capacity of the imagination that leads us to behave towards objects in the same way we would behave if they were living beings. In this respect, *Einfühlung* can be regarded as a revival and a psychological reconceptualization of the older idea of the "animation"[3] of nature and things, a main feature of magic and mythic thinking – which attracted the cultural-historical curiosity of so many scholars in the humanities around 1900, such as Tito Vignoli, Aby Warburg, Ernst Cassirer, and many contemporaries. In *Einfühlung* theory, the idea of animation advanced to a crucial term of aesthetic theory: it designates a specific attitude towards objects of art, images, architecture, etc. Robert Vischer's text seeks to answer how it is possible that we invest the outer world with emotions: How after all can we behave towards objects, forms, buildings, and other artefacts as if they were animated and were equipped with feelings?

When Robert's father Friedrich Theodor Vischer adopted the term in an essay on *The Symbol* (1887/1889) and integrated it in his aesthetic ideas, he described *Einfühlung* as involved in a constellation in which one's own emotions seem to look back at us, in which "the viewer lets his soul's moods and passions look back [*entgegenblicken*] to himself from nature's appearances and movements" (F. Th. Vischer, 1887/1889, p. 318–319). In this way, Vischer already sketched *Einfühlung* as a sort of mirror scene. It is based on an imaginative simulation of a corporeal movement perceived through the eye – "The eye follows the contours linearly as it were, as if one displays them with the finger tips" (F. Th. Vischer, 1887/1889, p. 307) – that is, as a sort of embodied simulation. In contrast to Robert Vischer, he did not consider this to be an involuntary act; instead, he outlined a state of cognition in which the conscious and the unconscious

[3] For the role of animation in nineteenth century see Papapetros, 2012.

seem to overlap or telescope in some way. For this purpose he invented a third cultural–historical stage of thinking between the poles of mere mythic thinking on the one hand and enlightened insight on the other, that is, the knowledge that individuals themselves ascribe meanings to the things they perceive and interact with. This third stage was named "poetic faith" [*poetischer Glaube*]; it implied interaction with and response to the character of things in spite of knowing that such meaningful interaction originates in our own emotions (F. Th. Vischer, 1887/1889, p. 296–301).

In numerous texts that followed Robert Vischer's introduction of the term, *Einfühlung* became a key concept of a whole body of psychological aesthetics. Yet in these texts the difference between the aesthetic perception of art and the understanding of the "other" plays an astonishingly marginal role. It was not the case, as one would expect, that an understanding of the human empathic relation to art or objects was derived from the insight into mutual human empathy; it went the other way round: the question of the other as another Self similar to one's own arose from the discourse on *Einfühlung* in art. It was Theodor Lipps, the translator of David Hume's *Treatise of Human Nature*, who in 1907 created the formula *Das Wissen von fremden Ichen* ("The knowledge of other Is") for the emerging consciousness of the psychic character of inter-subjectivity. In his essay, he addresses the question of how "me" or "the" I turns into "an" I, that is, one of multiple Is, and how the consciousness of another individual beyond myself may emerge and turn into a special sort of object (Lipps, 1907, p. 709). In his explanation, bodily movements and gestures play an important role. On a phenomenological level, he focuses on the interplay between the optical gesture and the kinaesthetic gesture, or in other words between the visible, perceivable, and the inner or felt gesture. In doing so, his description is not far from anticipating a scene of embodied simulation, either. In this respect, Lipps speaks of an immediate consciousness that does not result from experience but is rather based on the "instinct" of *Einfühlung*. The latter itself is described as having two sides, or as being the product of two factors, the instinct of vital expression [*Lebensäußerung*] and the instinct of imitation [*Nachahmung*]. Thus, *Einfühlung* is conceptualized by Lipps as an "original and at the same time most wonderful fact that cannot be traced further back, a fact different from a conclusion and not comparable to it" (1907, p. 713, transl. mine, S. W.), that is, as it were, a kind of "primary empathy". This original human capacity that bears no further explanation is in contemporary sciences termed "a product of evolution". For example, Michael Tomasello in his book on the *Cultural Origins of Human Cognition* (1999) describes the human capacity for perceiving the other as a human being invested with emotions and thus similar to myself as a product of evolution, or, in his words, "as a biological inheritance of the species Homo sapiens" (Tomasello, 1999, p. 90).

However, the question of empathic behaviour towards objects and the outer world and its relation to empathy towards other Selves became an issue of intense and critical discussion in the reception of *Einfühlung* theory (see Chapter 10). This problem remains a challenging theoretical controversy that needs to be re-addressed using the research tools of today. In what way does empathy with objects, or the imagination of "dead forms as living" [*die todte Form wie etwas Lebendiges*] (R. Vischer, 1873/1994, p. 104), function in comparison to inter-subjectivity? This question concerns highly relevant correspondences between ontogenetic and phylogenetic stages of the development of the mental/psychic apparatus (Decety & Svetlova 2012) – in other words, the cultural development of human mental capacities.

4 Sympathy – Implementation of a Natural Capacity into the Canon of Affects

Within the critical discussion of *Einfühlung*, the empathic attitude towards the other was the subject of another controversy, namely whether our understanding of the other must be understood as a secondary operation, interpreted in analogy to the understanding of the Self. It was Max Scheler who, in his book on *Wesen und Formen der Sympathie* (engl. *The Nature of Sympathy* (1923/1954), rejected this argument in a remarkable way, stating that the difficulties of the perception of the Self had as much been underestimated as those of the perception of the other had been overrated. Scheler entitled his book

Sympathy because his phenomenological approach to a universal vital expression goes far beyond aesthetics; he defined "sympathy", or the capacity of fellow feelings, as a "dowry of every living being" [*Mitgift allen Lebendigen*] (Scheler, 1923/1954, p. 134), thus using a similar metaphor as Tomasello about eight decades later.

Nevertheless, Scheler's reflections were motivated by a critical approach to *Einfühlung* and his attempt to distinguish different forms of fellow feelings [*Mitgefühl*]: (1) feeling together [*Mit-einanderfühlen*], (2) compassion with the sorrow and joy of the other, (3) emotional infection, and (4) *Einsfühlung* (literally feeling as one), that is, a sort of total identification of the Self with the other, with nature or something else, comparable to "primitive thinking". With the concept of *EinSfühlung*, Scheler explicitly outlined the phylogenetic perspective that already underlies the aesthetics of *Einfühlung* in F. Th. Vischer, Lipps, and others. In Scheler's book, the process of civilization entails a loss of animated nature, a continuous process of disenchantment: "Learning, in this sense, is not *animation*, but a continual '*de-animation*'". (Scheler, 1923/1954, p. 239) Seen against this cultural-historical horizon, the concept of *Einfühlung* as devised by aesthetic theory may be interpreted as a re-appropriation of a human capacity that humans lost and are still losing in the course of their phylogenetic and ontogenetic development, whereas art provides a field of re-gaining animation. This pertains to an underlying dialectics of empathy that is of special relevance, from an ontogenetic perspective, for the child's developmental psychology.

Another central concern of Scheler's book was to liberate the concept of sympathy from the burden of moral judgements and ethics inherited from its origin in moral philosophy. He argues that all fellow feelings are principally, that is, in any of their possible forms, "blind to values" [*wertblind*], in this way anticipating the idea of a human skill of mutual emotional resonance that is not yet charged with specific content. In this respect, his book positions itself in opposition especially to Adam Smith's *Theory of Moral Sentiments* (1759/2006), from which he adopted the term "sympathy". When sympathy was introduced and outlined by Hume and Smith in the eighteenth century, it had to guarantee the notion that human nature is principally a good one. Although Hume's *Treatise of Human Nature* (1738–40) in its main parts still follows the discourse on the catalogue of affects that stems from Aristotle's *Rhetorik, Ethiká Nikomácheiae,* and *Poietike* (Aristotle 2004, 2002, 2013) the chapter on sympathy interrupts this discursive order. For the chapter on sympathy forms a sort of excursion in his *Treatise* and introduces quite a different approach with its focus on basic human skills: indeed, Hume pens sympathy as a quality of human nature. This capacity is based on a fundamental resemblance among all human creatures, a resemblance amidst all their variety that enables us to enter into the sentiments of others and to embrace them with facility and pleasure. Hume describes sympathy as the propensity to sympathize with others and to receive by interaction their inclinations and sentiments, however, different, or even contrary to our own this particular other might be (Hume, 1738–40/2003, p. 225–226). Thus, the term sympathy marks a caesura in the history of knowledge on shared feelings and forms a step of transition towards the idea of empathy in modernity.

Beginning with Aristotle, and up to early modern philosophy (René Descartes, Baruch de Spinoza), the conceptual forerunner of sympathy, *compassion* [gr. *eleos*, lat. *commpassio*, *commiseratio*], is defined as one of the affects within a catalogue of ten or more affects but not as a basic, underlying capacity and means for shared feelings. In ancient theory, affect [gr. *pathê*] was considered as arousal, connected either with pleasure [*hêdonê*] or aversion [*lýpe*], which causes changes in the tempers and judgements of humans (*Rhetoric* II.1.1378a). Here, Aristotle adds that one has to address three questions as regards each of the affects, in the case of anger for example (1) what the state of mind of angry people is, (2) who the people are with whom they usually get angry, and (3) about what they get angry. More influential than this theory of affects – an economic approach *avant la lettre*, already based on the opposition of pleasure and un-pleasure, that provides the central neurological foundation of Freud's metapsychology – was Aristotle's definition of compassion: "Compassion is defined as pain about the suffering of somebody caused by an evil, striking a person who doesn't deserve it, namely an evil that can also strike ourselves or one of our relatives" (*Rhetoric* II.1.1378a). This definition of compassion would make its way through centuries of the history of Western thought. The shortest definition is that of Spinoza's *Ethica* (1677) "*Tristia concomitante idea mali*", misery connected to the idea of an evil (Spinoza, 1677/1977, p. 304). In the wake of this ancient theory of affects, compassion was situated on the side of un-pleasure.

Against the horizon of the ancient tradition, for which compassion is one affect out of a catalogue (albeit probably the most prominent), the initiation of sympathy marks a far-reaching caesura; it expands and simultaneously naturalizes one of the affects and turns it into a general property of human nature. From now on it is not just an evil that may also concern us which produces the similarity of a situation that makes us sympathize, but it is a perceived resemblance of all human beings that is interpreted as the foundation of sympathy – and therefore as a characteristic of humankind as such. In this way, the capacity of sympathy was transferred to the other side of values; it was turned into a characteristic of a basically good human nature, a natural virtue as it were. And here imagination already comes into play:

> Our affections depend more upon ourselves, and the internal operations of the mind, than any other impressions; for which reason they arise more naturally from the imagination, and from every lively idea we form of them. This is the nature and cause of sympathy. (Hume, 1738–40/2003, p. 227)

5 Sympathy – Christian Virtues and Pre-modern Ideas of Similarity

While Hume's *Treatise* marks a kind of threshold between the ancient theory of affects and the modern theory of sympathy/empathy, Adam Smith's *Theory of Moral Sentiments* provides an entire theory of sympathy. Although we will never be able to get an immediate impression of the feelings of the other, he argues, sympathy somehow gives access to the other. Smith describes this access quite literally:

> It is the impressions of our own senses only, not those of his, which our imagination copy. By *the imagination we place ourselves in his situation*, we conceive ourselves enduring all the torments, we *enter as it were into his body*, and become *in some measure* the same person with him, and thence

> form some ideas of his sensation, and even feel something which, though weaker in degree, is not altogether unlike them. (Smith, 1790/2006, p. 3, emphasis mine, S. W.)

Smith considers sympathy to be a universal feature of human nature, but not with regard to the passions. His conviction that there exist "some passions of which the expression excite no sort of sympathy" (Smith, 1790/2006, p. 5) – he thinks, for example of anger – is obviously due to the Christian legacy of his theory. Smith is quite explicit about this when he cites the Christian law of love to the neighbour, then transforms it into a law of nature by turning it into a mutual attitude: "As to love our neighbour as we love ourselves is the great law of Christianity, so it is the great precept of nature to love ourselves only as we love our neighbour, or, what comes to the same thing, as our neighbour is capable to loving us" (Smith, 1790/2006, p. 20). This passage highlights how much the concept of sympathy is contaminated with Christian ideas. As regards the history of knowledge, the eighteenth-century idea of sympathy may be regarded as a synthesis of classical affect theory and good and bad virtues, turned into a consideration of human nature. Here, the ancient concept of compassion is superimposed by the Christian heritage of virtues, while simultaneously these virtues get transformed into an innate capacity. This alliance of a general human property with moral virtues has recently returned in a secular and scientific guise, that is, in empathy as the basic trait of altruism or pro-social behaviour.

The modern concept of sympathy entails a remarkable mutual explication of similarity and sympathy. This marks a fascinating reversal of the pre-modern system of similarities grounded in the correspondence of macrocosm and microcosm, as Michel Foucault has so brilliantly described in his reading of Paracelsus in *Les Mots et les Choses* (1966). When he analyses the four forms of similarity within the pre-modern system of understanding nature as being full of meaning, *sympatheia* counts as one of these similarities. The others are: *convenientia*, a sort of neighbourhood of things, *aemulatio*, a sort of resonance independent from visibility, and *analogia*, that in pre-modern thought concerned mainly the human body in relation to nature and the cosmic world. Whereas in this system the human body and soul echo the cosmic nature, one could say that the modern ideas of sympathy and empathy present a reversal in which the respective correspondence is transformed into a more active operation of the individual. The human being is no longer a mere resonance body but s/he actively affects the world with her/his feelings and turns the outer world and the other human into something similar to him/herself, namely a vis-à-vis that resonates her/his own emotional state. Empathy now forms a resonance mechanism by means of the individual's emotions and imagination.

Within this horizon, empathy may be described as an offspring of the *mimetic* faculty of humankind, that is, the faculty to become similar to the outer world. In a small essay "On the Mimetic Faculty" (1933/1999), Walter Benjamin outlines a short cultural history of mimetic attitudes founded in the nature of similarity. He interprets man's gift for seeing similarities as

> nothing but a rudiment of the once powerful compulsion to become similar and to behave mimetically. There is perhaps not a single one of his higher functions in which his mimetic faculty does not play a decisive role./This faculty, however, has a history, both in the phylogenetic and the ontogenetic sense (Benjamin, 1933/1999, p. 720).

In terms of this history, he discusses examples from children's play as well as cultural techniques of the ancient past such as cult, dance, and astrology. In the course of history, both the gifts of producing and of receiving similarities have changed a lot, and man lost a great part of this faculty while transforming it into practises of "nonsensual similarities, nonsensual correspondences" (Benjamin, 1933/1999, p. 722), for example aspects of similarity which appear just momentarily in language.

It was the concept of sympathy that strengthened the notion of imagination within the "as if" relation to others, and it was the concept of *Einfühlung* that explicitly accomplished this reversal in the resonance system between the Self and the world. These ideas somehow profited from the traditional notions but at the same time overcame the connotation of passivity. Within the theory of affects, the trace of passivity stems from a certain constriction of the meaning of *pathos* within the translational afterlife of the ancient term. While in ancient Greek *pathos* means something that happens to me – neither actively nor passively – in the Western tradition *pathos* became increasingly connected to suffering. Translated into Latin as *affect* or *passion*, the latter being a highly ambiguous term interpreted as both suffering [*Leiden*] and excitement [*Leidenschaft*] (see Auerbach, 1941/1967; Weigel, 2004), the conceptual successors of pathos were predominantly ideas of suffering and unpleasure, especially in the discourse on pity/compassion.

In this respect, sympathy and *Einfühlung*, on the one hand, liberated the passions from their link to suffering and compassion. On the other hand, both ideas regained aspects of the echo or resonance between the Self and the other/the objects/the nature that were lost since the Early Modern Age in the course of the constriction of the world to a reality in which subjects are related to their surroundings solely by rational and instrumental activity – or action neurons.

References

Aristotle (350 BCE/2002). *Nicomachean Ethics* (J. Sachs, Trans.). Newburyport, MA: Focus Publishing.

Aristotle (335 BCE/2013). *Poetics* (A. Kenny, Trans., reprint). Oxford: Oxford University Press.

Aristotle (367–22 BCE/2004). *Rhetoric* (R. Roberts, Trans.). Mineola, NY: Dover Publications.

Auerbach, E. (1941/1967). Passio als Leidenschaft [Passio as passion]. In *Gesammelte Aufsätze zur romanischen Philologie* [Collected writings on romanist philology] (pp. 161–75). Bern /Munich: Francke.

Batson, C. D. (1991). *The altruism question*. Hillsdale, NJ: Erlbaum.

Batson, C. D. (2011). *Altruism in humans*. New York: Oxford University Press.

Benjamin, W. (1933/1999). On the Mimetic Faculty. In *Selected Writings* (vol. 2, 1927–34, pp. 720–723, M. Jennings, H. Eiland & G. Smith, Eds.). Cambridge, MA: Harvard University Press.

Decety, J., & Meyer, M. (2008). From emotion resonance to empathic understanding: A social developmental neuroscience account. *Development and psychopathology*, *20*(4), 1053–1080.

Decety, J. & Ickes, W. (Eds.) (2011). *The Social Neuroscience of Empathy*. Cambridge, MA: MIT Press.
Decety, J. & Svetlova, M. (2012). Putting together phylogenetic and ontogenetic perspectives on empathy. *Developmental Cognitive Neuroscience, 2*, 1–24.
Fleck, L. (1935/1979). *The Genesis and Development of a Scientific Fact: An Introduction to the Theory of Thought Style and Thought Collective* (T. J. Trenn & R. K. Merton, Ed.). Chicago: University of Chicago Press.
Foucault, M. (1966). *Les mots et les choses. Une archéologie des sciences humaines* [The order of things: An archaeology of the human sciences]. Paris: Gallimard.
Freud, S. (1896/1925). Zur Ätiologie der Hysterie [Aetiology of hysteria]. In *Gesammelte Schriften* [Collected works] (vol. 1, pp. 404–438, A. Freud et al., Eds.). Leipzig, Vienna, Zürich: Internationaler Psychoanalytischer Verlag.
Gallese, V. (2009). Mirror Neurons, Embodied Simulation, and the Neural Basis of Social Identification. *Psychoanalytic Dialogues, 19*, 519–536.
Gallese, V., Fadiga, L., Fogassi, L., & Rizzolatti, G. (1996). Action recognition in the premotor Cortex. *Brain, 119*, 593–609.
Hamburger, K. (1985). *Das Mitleid* [Sympathy]. Stuttgart: Klett Cotta.
Hein, G., Silani, G., Preuschoff, K., Batson, C. D., & Singer, T. (2010). Neural responses to ingroup and outgroup members' suffering predict individual differences in costly helping. *Neuron*, 68, 149–160.
Hickok, G. (2009). Eight Problems for the Mirror Neuron Theory of Action Understanding in Monkeys and Humans. *Journal of Cognitive Neuroscience, 21*(7), 1229–1243.
Hume, D. (1738–40/2003). *A Treatise of Human Nature*. Mineola, New York: Dover Publications.
Lipps, Th. (1907). Das Wissen von fremden Ichen [The knowledge of other Is]. *Psychologische Untersuchungen, 1*, 694–722.
Müller, E. (2011). Introduction: Interdisciplinary Concepts and their Political Significance. *Contributions to the History of Concepts, 6*(2), 42–52.
Panksepp, J., & Panksepp, J. (2013). Toward a cross-species understanding of empathy. *Trends in Neuroscience, 36*(8). doi:10.1016/j.tins.2013.04.009
Papapetros, S. (2012). *On the Animation of the Inorganic. Art, Architecture, and the Extension of Life*. Chicago: Chicago University Press.
Rifkin, J. (2009). *The Empathic Civilisation: The Race to Global Consciousness in a World in Crisis*. New York: Jeremy P. Tarcher Inc.
Riva, F., Triscoli, Ch., Lamm, C., Carnaghi, A., & Silani, G. (2016). Emotional Egocentricity Bias across Life-Span. *Frontier in Aging Neuroscience, 8*(74). doi:10.3389/fnagi.2016.00074

Rizzolatti, G., Fadiga, L., Gallese, V., & Fogassi, L (1996). Premotor cortex and the recognition of motor actions. *Cognitive Brain Research, 3*, 131–141.

Rizzolatti, G., Fogassi, L., & Gallese, V. (2002). Motor and cognitive functions of the ventral premotor cortex. *Current Opinion in Neurobiology, 12*, 149–154.

Rizzolatti, G., Fogassi, L., & Gallese, V. (2006). Mirrors in the Mind. *Scientific American, 295*(5), 30–37.

Scheler, M. (1923/1954). *The Nature of Sympathy* (P. Heath, Trans.). Hamden, London: Routledge & Kegan Press.

Singer, T. (2012). The past, present and future of social neuroscience: a European Perspective. *Neuroimage, 61*, 437–449.

Singer, T. & Klimecki, O. (2014). Empathy and Compassion. *Current Biology, 24*(18), R875–R878.

Smith, A. (1759/2006). *Theory of Moral Sentiments*. Mineola, New York: Dover Publications.

Snow, C. P. (1959/2001). *The Two Cultures*. London: Cambridge University Press.

Spinoza, B. de (1677/1977). *Ethica Ordine Geometrico Demonstata /Ethik nach der geometrischen Methode dargestellt* [Ethics presented according to the geometric method]. Stuttgart: Philipp Reclam.

Tomasello, M. (1999). *The Cultural Origins of Human Cognition*. Cambridge, MA: Harvard University Press.

Umiltà, M. A., Berchio, C., Sestito, M., Freedberg, D., & Gallese, V. (2012). Abstract Art and Cortical Motor Activation: An EEG Study. *Frontiers in Human Neuroscience*, b:311. doi:10.3389/fnhum.2012.00311

Vischer, F. Th. (1887/1889). Das Symbol [The Symbol]. In F. Th. Vischer (Ed.).. *Altes und Neues. Neue Folge* [Old and new. New series] (pp. 290–342). Stuttgart: Adolf Bonz.

Vischer, R. (1873/1927). Über das optische Formgefühl [On the optical sense of form]. In *Drei Schriften zum ästhetischen Formproblem* [Three contributions to the aesthetic problem of form] (pp. 1–44). Halle: Niemeyer.

Vischer, R. (1873/1994). On the Optical Sense of Form. A Contribution to Aesthetics. In H. F. Mallgrave & E. Ikonomou (Eds.). *Empathy, Form, and Space. Problems in German Aesthetics, 1873–1893* (pp. 89–123). Santa Monica: Getty Center Publications.

Weigel, S. (2004). Pathos – Passion – Gefühl. Schauplätze affekttheoretischer Verhandlungen in Kultur- und Wissenschaftsgeschichte [Pathos – passion – emotion. Sites of negotiations on affect theory in cultural history and history of science]. In S. Weigel. *Literatur als Voraussetzung der Kulturgeschichte.*

Schauplätze von Shakespeare bis Benjamin [Literature as prerequisite of cultural history. Sites from Shakespeare to Benjamin] (pp. 147–72). Munich: Fink.

Weigel, S. (2012). Mitleid /Compassio. Über Rituale. Diskurse und die Kulturgeschichte des Mitgefühls [Pity /compassio. On rituals. Discourses and the cultural history of sympathy]. In C. Nichols & G. Staupe (Eds.). *Die Leidenschaften – Ein Drama in fünf Akten* [The passions. A drama in five acts] (pp. 222–28). Göttingen: Wallstein.

Weigel, S. (2016). Embodiment in Simulation Theory and Cultural Science, with Remarks on the Coding-Problem of Neuroscience. In S. Weigel & G. Schabert (Eds.). *A Neuro-Psychoanalytical Dialogue for Bridging Freud and the Neurosciences* (pp. 47–71). Vienna: Springer.

Part 1

Epistemic Interventions

2

Levels of Empathy – Primary, Extended, and Reiterated Empathy

Thomas Fuchs

About a century after it was first introduced, the notion of empathy has raised a widely ramified debate on how it should be defined, understood, and explained. Coined by the philosopher Robert Vischer (1872), the original German term *Einfühlung* was meant to denote a special kind of aesthetic perception. Theodor Lipps (1906) then transferred it into the field of social cognition where it was translated as "empathy" by the American psychologist Edward Titchener (1909). It is now used to designate our basic capacity to recognize and understand others as minded and expressive creatures. However, the nature of this capacity is still far from being unanimously conceived. One of the main reasons for this dissent may be seen in the Cartesian framework from which the debate took its origin. Up to now, the dominant theories of intersubjectivity have conceived of the mental as an inner realm separated from others by an epistemic gulf that can only be crossed by inference or projection. Since the mind is not visible in the body, we are, according

T. Fuchs (✉)
Psychiatric Department, University of Heidelberg, Heidelberg, Germany
e-mail: thomas.fuchs@med.uni-heidelberg.de

V. Lux, S. Weigel (eds.), *Empathy*, Palgrave Studies in the Theory and History of Psychology, DOI 10.1057/978-1-137-51299-4_2

to this view, in principle hidden from each other. We must infer, imitate, or simulate others' inner states in order to understand them. Hence, both the "theory theory" (TT) and the "simulation theory" (ST) of social cognition are based on a representationalist view: Concepts such as the theory of mind, simulation, or mentalization have in common that they conceive of social understanding and empathy as a projection onto others of inner modellings or representations.

1 Philosophical Premises of Empathy Theories

These Cartesian assumptions have been criticized by phenomenologists since the beginning of the last century. Max Scheler argued that in a face-to-face encounter with another person, we are confronted neither with a mere physical body nor with a hidden psyche, but with the embodied person as an expressive unity [*Ausdruckseinheit*] (Scheler, 1973, p. 256). Similarly, Maurice Merleau-Ponty wrote that "we must abandon the fundamental prejudice according to which the psyche is that which is accessible only to myself and cannot be seen from outside" (Merleau-Ponty, 1951/1964, p. 116). Ludwig Wittgenstein also rightly asked: "Do you look into *yourself* in order to recognize the fury in his face?" (Wittgenstein, 1967, § 220, p. 40). In most everyday situations, we do not use imaginative, introspective simulation routines, or inferences when we interact with another person. Instead, we immediately perceive the other's intentions and emotions in his expressive behaviour and in his meaningful actions as related to the context. Accordingly, *interaction theory* has more recently been proposed as an alternative approach to social cognition, focussing on expressive bodily behaviour, interbodily resonance, intentions as visible in action as well as the shared situational context in order to explain social understanding (De Jaegher & Di Paolo, 2007; Fuchs & De Jaegher, 2009; Gallagher, 2001, 2008; Zahavi, 2001, 2008).

The differences between these divergent theories may also be expressed in terms of different attitudes or *perspectives* that we take on the persons we encounter, namely first-, second-, and third-person perspective:

(1) Following the classical *theory of mind* concept or *theory theory*, other minds can be known by referring to the best suitable hypothesis on the reasons and motives for their behaviour. Thus, we explain and predict another person's actions by relying on an innate or acquired theory of how people generally behave. This kind of inference is made on the basis of observation, meaning from a *third-person* point of view. In principle, interacting with others does not add anything to this access (Perner, 1991).
(2) In contrast, according to *simulation theory*, other minds are known through a *first-person model* that we form of their experience: Understanding others means running an inner simulation of their behaviour, thus creating an "as-if" mental state (as if we were in their place), which then has to be projected back onto the other (Gallese & Goldman, 1998; Goldman, 2006).
(3) Finally, *interaction theory* takes a *second-person* route: It is through embodied or face-to-face encounters with others that we gain our primary experience of their feelings and intentions without recourse to inner theories or simulations. In this context, the second-person perspective means the intersubjective, participant, or co-experiencing perspective, referring to situations of mutual relatedness and the intercorporeal "coupling" of the partners.

The introduction of the second-person perspective changes the whole picture, since it implies that the first- and third-person perspectives are no longer confronted with a mind-body gap in the strict sense. On the one hand, our first-person experience extends to interpersonal situations of co-experiencing affective and intentional states (such as a joint laugh) that may not be split between the partners. On the other hand, when observing another person from a 3rd person point of view, we still perceive her as an animate being, who shows her feelings through expressive behaviour (such as shame) and her intentions through actions (such as reaching for something). The problem of other minds only arises when starting out from a strictly Cartesian first-person perspective and/or from a strictly behaviourist 3rd-person perspective. However, these are both abstractions from the 2nd-person engagement that characterizes our everyday interactions with others.

Accordingly, Gallagher and Zahavi (from a phenomenological point of view) and Trevarthen and Reddy (from a developmental point of view) have argued for the primacy of prereflective intersubjectivity and second-person interactions in social understanding (Reddy, 2008; Reddy & Morris, 2004; Trevarthen, 1979, 1993; see Fuchs, 2013). Similar claims have been advocated by enactivist approaches to intersubjectivity, emphasizing the constitutive role of interactive processes for social cognition (De Jaegher & Di Paolo, 2007; Froese & Fuchs, 2012; Fuchs & De Jaegher, 2009).

However, even if we might agree with such positions, we should still assume that all three perspectives have a particular role to play, at least in certain aspects of intersubjectivity. After all, it seems obvious that humans, at some point in their development, do become able to take another person's perspective and to explicitly transpose themselves into their point of view. This implies using one's own first-person experience as a guide for understanding others by imagining what one would probably feel like in their situation. Herein lies the (limited) justification of simulation theory. Moreover, we may sometimes apply methods of conjecturing or inferring another's mental state (belief, desire, intention) from a third-person perspective, particularly in cases where the person in question is absent or his behaviour seems ambiguous. This may also be regarded as a justification of theory theory. For these reasons, I argue that we should look for an integrative concept of empathy that is able to account both for the basic forms of embodied intersubjectivity and for more sophisticated, explicit forms of understanding others.

In this article, I will first present a non-representational concept of primary empathy, based on an *embodied and enactive* view of intersubjectivity. According to this concept, social understanding is not realized within one individual, but arises in the moment-to-moment interaction of two subjects. This process includes several components such as bodily resonance, affect attunement, the coordination of gestures, facial and vocal expression, and others. In order to support this concept, I will also examine the development of social understanding in early infancy.

Then, I will move to forms of *extended empathy*, in particular those enabled by perspective-taking and other cognitive components. Finally, I will address the phenomenon of *reiterated empathy* in which we experience the empathic reaction of others towards ourselves.

2 Primary Empathy

Primary empathy arises from direct, corporeal contact with another person, that is, from an interactive process in which both partners are immersed, or in Merleau-Ponty's term, from intercorporeality. I will take two approaches to this concept: The first is based on enactivism and dynamic systems theory, which regards social interaction as a *dynamic coupling and coordination* of two embodied agents. The second is based on the phenomenology of the lived body; here I want to focus on a process that I term *mutual incorporation*, which results in what we might call an *extended body*.

2.1 Dynamic Coupling and Coordination

From an enactive point of view, organisms do not passively receive information from their environment, which they then translate into internal representations. Rather, they actively participate in the generation of meaning; they are sense-making beings. Thus, their world is not a pregiven, external realm, represented by the brain, but a relational domain enacted and opened up by the living being's agency and sensorimotor coupling with the environment (Thompson, 2005, 2007). On this basis, social cognition is regarded as the result of a special form of action, namely *social interaction*. The enactive approach looks at the circular dynamic within a dyad of embodied agents instead of linear processes. Analyses of social interactions and conversations show that participants unconsciously coordinate their movements and utterances (Condon, 1979; Grammer, Kruck, &Magnusson, 1998; Issartel, Marin, & Cadopi, 2007; Kendon, 1990). For example, they might turn their gazes on the same object to share attention, exhibit similar postures or facial expressions, synchronize the rhythm and speed of their speech, or unconsciously mimic the other's gestures. Their perception-action loops are coupled and interlaced with each other. Through this connection, social agents engage in *joint or participatory sense-making* (De Jaegher & Di Paolo, 2007). Hence, social understanding emerges from a dynamic, open process of moment-to-moment interactions and the coordination of two embodied subjects.

Since in normal interactions neither participant is completely able to steer the process deliberately, but is drawn into the feedback and feedforward cycles of the interaction, the process itself becomes prevailing over the two interactors. The process gains a "life of its own". The emergence of coordination demarcates the interaction as an identifiable pattern with its own internal structure. This occurs because the interactors are themselves highly plastic systems susceptible to being affected by the specific history of their coordination. "Sustained interactions can be expected to have undergone several instances of loss and regain of coordinating structures, each of them leaving the interactors slightly better able to remain in such interaction or reinitiate it" (De Jaegher & Di Paolo, 2007, p. 496). This interactional experience continually increases the skilfulness of the participants. They acquire what developmental psychologists have called *implicit relational knowing* – I will come back to this later.

2.2 Mutual Incorporation

The comprehensive system that arises through the coupling of two interactors is not a coordination of two mind or brain states, but of two embodied subjects. Through the mutual coupling of their lived bodies – mediated through eye contact, facial expressions, voice, touch, and gesture – they enter into a dyadic bodily state. In every face-to-face encounter, our bodies are affected by the other's expression, and we experience the kinetics and intensity of his emotions through our own bodily kinaesthesia and sensations. Our body schemas and bodily experiences expand and incorporate the perceived body of the other. This extension creates a dynamic interplay that forms the basis of social understanding. I will call it "*mutual incorporation*" (Schmitz 1989, 2011, pp. 29–54; see Froese & Fuchs, 2012; Fuchs & De Jaegher, 2009).

Incorporation is a pervasive characteristic of the lived body that always transcends itself and partly merges with the environment. This is the case, for example, in every skilful handling of an instrument, as when a pianist plays the piano and lets his or her fingers find their way by themselves; or when a blind man probes his environment with a stick and feels the surface at the top of it. In such cases, the instrument is integrated into the body's motor schema like an extension of the body, subjectively felt as "melting" or becoming one with the instrument. However, this kind of incorporation also occurs with other people, even at a distance. An example of this is the experience of fascination. Thus, we may listen to a spellbinder, literally hanging on his lips (as the German expression goes) – and feel drawn towards him. Or, we may watch the *salto mortale* of an aerial acrobat with a mixture of fascination and anxiety. Our lived body extends and connects with the acrobat's swinging movements; we may even feel prompted to co-movements. Now, *mutual incorporation* implies a reciprocal interaction of two agents in which each body schema extends and embodies the other. This may be illustrated by the following diagram (Fig. 2.1) (cf. Froese & Fuchs, 2012):

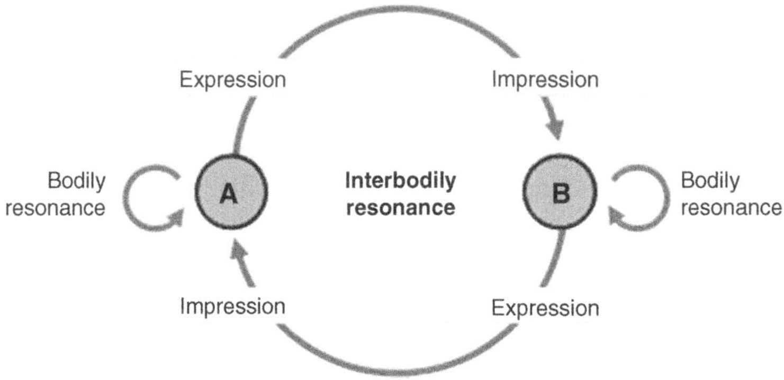

Fig. 2.1 Mutual incorporation

Let us assume that A is a person whose emotion, for example, anger, manifests itself in typical bodily (facial, gestural, interoceptive, adrenergic, circulatory, etc.) changes. His lived body thus functions as a felt "resonance board" for the emotion: A feels the anger *as* the tension in his face, *as* the sharpness of his voice, the arousal in his body, etc. These proprio- and interoceptive bodily feelings may be termed *bodily resonance.* This resonance is an *expression* of coinciding emotions, that means, the anger becomes visible and is perceived as such by A's partner B simultaneously. But what is more, the expression will also produce an *impression*, namely by triggering corresponding or complementary bodily feelings in B. Thus, A's sinister gaze, the sharpness of his voice or expansive bodily movements might induce in B an unpleasant tension or even a jerk, a tendency to withdraw, and so on (similarly, witnessing shame might induce an embarrassed aversion, sadness, a tendency to connect and console, and so forth). Thus, B not only sees the emotion in A's face, gaze, and gesture, but also senses it within his own body, through his own bodily resonance.

However, the mutual resonance procedure does not stay like this, for the impression and bodily reaction caused in B becomes in turn an expression for A. It will immediately affect the latter's bodily reaction, change his expression, however, slightly, and so forth. This creates a circular interplay of expressions and reactions that occurs in split seconds, constantly modifying each partner's bodily state. The process becomes highly autonomous and is not directly controlled by either of the partners. They have become parts of a dynamic sensorimotor and interaffective system that connects their bodies by reciprocal movements and reactions. Each lived body reaches out, as it were, to be complemented by the other; both are coupled to form an extended body through *interbodily resonance or intercorporeality* (Merleau-Ponty, 1960).

No mental representation is necessary for this process. There is no strict separation between the inner and the outer, as if a hidden mental state in A produced certain external signs which B would have to decipher. For A's anger may not be separated from its bodily expression; and similarly, B does not perceive A's body as a mere object, but as a living, animate and expressive body that he is coupled with. One feels the other in one's own body, albeit in a manner of feeling that mostly remains implicit and is not thematized as such. Nor is a simulation required for the process of mutual incorporation. We certainly do not simulate the other person's angry gaze or voice, even less his anger, but rather feel tense, threatened, or even invaded by his expressive bodily behaviour. Bodily sensations, tensions, action tendencies, and so on that arise in the interaction do not serve as a separate simulation of the other person but they feed into mutual perception.

In Michael Polanyi's terms, one could also say that the felt bodily resonance is the *proximal*, while the other's perceived body is the *distal* component of empathic perception, with the proximal component receding from awareness in favour of the distal, or becoming *transparent* for it (Polanyi, 1967). This may be compared to the sense of touch, which is simultaneously a self-feeling of the body (proximal) *and* a feeling of the touched surface (distal); or it may be compared to the subliminal experience of thirst (proximal) that first becomes conspicuous as the perceptual salience of water flowing nearby (distal). The same goes for both partners in an interaction, their bodily resonance does not simulate the other, but *mediates* the perception of the other.

Susan Stuart (2012) has coined a suitable term, *enkinesthesia*, meaning "feeling one's own movements into the other", or empathy through co-movement. In this sense, we can refer to the experience of the other in terms of "embodied" perception, which, through the interaction process, is also "embodied" communication. In Merleau-Ponty's account: "The communication or comprehension of gestures comes about through the reciprocity of my intentions and the gestures of others, of my gestures and the intentions discernible in the conduct of other people. It is as if the other person's intentions inhabited my body and mine his". (Merleau-Ponty, 1945/1962, p. 185)

As we can see, the concept of mutual incorporation leads to the opposite of the representationalist account: Primary empathy is not an inner modelling in a detached observer. Here the other's body extends onto my own, and my own extends onto the other. As regards the affective side of experience, this amounts to *interaffectivity*, which means a continuous interaction and mutual modification of both partners' emotions. This is the phenomenological equivalent to the dynamic coupling of embodied agents as described on the system level.

2.3 The Early Mother-Infant Dialogue as a Mutual Incorporation

The intercorporeal concept is confirmed when we take a look at the development of social perception in early childhood. Soon after birth, the infant is capable to connect with the body of others and to imitate their facial expressions (Meltzoff & Moore, 1977, 1989). Through the mimetic capacity of their bodies, infants are able to transpose the other people's gestures and expressions that they see onto their own proprioception and movement. Perception, proprioception, and action are integrated within a common sensorimotor space. The infant does not need to carry out any process of inner simulation. Its body schema is characterized by a transmodal openness that immediately allows it to incorporate and imitate others. Hence, what primary intersubjectivity starts with is not mindreading, but embodied interaction or intercorporeality. Since bodily imitation evokes corresponding feelings as well, mutual affective resonance gradually develops within the dyad. Six- to eight-week-olds already engage in proto-conversation with their mothers by smiling and vocalizing (Trevarthen, 1979, 1993). Both caregiver and infant exhibit a finely tuned coordination of movements, rhythmic synchrony, and mirroring of expressions, which has often been compared to a couple dancing. They also follow a turn-taking pattern, shifting the roles of agent and recipient in a non-random sequence.

Daniel Stern has emphasized the temporal flow patterns and vitality affects that are shared by both partners (Stern, 1998). Infants perceive affects as the intermodal extract, rhythms and dynamics of melodic, vocal, facial, and gestural utterances. These intermodal characters and contours provide some of the main bridges needed for mutual incorporation and with it primary understanding. Affect attunement and mutual incorporation create *dyadic affective states* (Tronick, 1998), often an intense pleasure or joy. The emerging affect during a joyful play situation between mother and infant may not be divided and distributed among them. It arises from the "between", or from the shared situation in which both are immersed. Thus, affects are not enclosed in an inner mental sphere to be deciphered from the outside, but come into existence, change, and circulate between self and other in intercorporeal dialogue.

Due to the neuroplasticity of the human brain, an infant's history of interactions continuously influences its disposition and skills. The patterns of interaction, even the earliest experiences of being held, comforted and addressed by their caregivers, are imprinted in their implicit memories and result in what Lyons-Ruth et al. (1998) have called *implicit relational knowing*. This prereflective knowledge or skill of how to engage with others includes knowing how to share pleasure, elicit attention, avoid rejection, and re-establish contact. In order to maintain specific types of interactions, infants acquire special interactive schemes ("*schemes of being-with*", Stern, 1998) and corporeal micropractices (Downing 2004) that they need for keeping up the respective interaction. Implicit relational knowledge is a temporally organized, "musical" memory for the rhythm and dynamics that are subliminally present in interactions with others. It implies an intuitive grasp on interactive vitality contours ("crescendo" or "decrescendo", "ritardando" or "accelerando", flowing or explosive dynamics, etc.) together with the emotions that they express. It may also be regarded as *interbodily memory* that shapes the actual relationship as a procedural field, encompassing and connecting both partners. Hence, the earliest experiences become lasting dispositions that manifest themselves tacitly in a child's later actions and habitus, that is, their entire set of learned dispositions.

3 Extended Empathy

This concept of embodied intersubjectivity underlying primary empathy as outlined so far does not exhaust the possibilities of empathic understanding. On the basis of primary empathy, we may also conjecture about the situation of the other and envision how the world might seem from his perspective, for example: *What could have made him so angry, shocked, or upset? Why was he particularly sensitive in the given situation?*

This happens in particular when an irritation, misunderstanding, or other kind of disturbance occurs, and we try to grasp why the other said or did what he did, what he might be thinking or feeling, etc. Through additional information and inference, we can enhance our understanding and in this way often deepen our empathy. But the possibility of putting oneself in another person's shoes goes further than merely conjecturing about why *he* feels the way he does: in fact, I can imagine then how *I* would feel and react if I were in the same situation. At this point, we are certainly employing some form of simulation, which I prefer to call *perspective-taking* or *imaginative transposition.*

This mode of empathy is without doubt quite different from the first one discussed. To begin with, it entails an *explicit, cognitive operation*, namely, the purposeful envisioning of the situation of the other, which often employs information about the person that one could not infer directly from the situation at hand. But moreover, it involves an *imaginative operation*, that means, a transposition into an "as-if" scenario (i.e., as if I were the other) which transcends the bodily level. Instead of the involuntary coupling of mutual incorporation, we deliberately take the other's stance. Thus, it seems necessary to differentiate between a primary, implicit, or bodily empathy and an extended, explicit, or imaginative empathy.

Imagining others' views presupposes a reflective stance or a *meta-perspective* on myself and the other from which I can perform the operation of self-transposition (Fuchs, 2013). This allows me to gain a new perspective on the world, the perspective of the other. The imaginative transposition may imply a spatial "as-if", as when I imagine how a certain object might look from someone else's position: my "here" becomes his "there", and his "there" becomes my "here". One test for this shifting capacity is known as the "turtle task" in which a picture of a turtle is placed between an adult and the child. The child then has to tell how it sees the turtle ("right side up") and how the adult sees it ("upside down"). Whereas younger children give egocentric replies, claiming that the adult sees the turtle as they do, children at the age of four and a half are able to switch to an allocentric perspective and acknowledge the adult's differing view (Masangkay et al., 1974; see also Flavel, 1992, for an overview).

More frequently, however, perspective-taking is applied in order to imagine more complex psychological situations experienced by others. The process often involves taking into account differing views and interpretations of the same situation. The capacity to understand these conflicting views that arise from presuppositions based on disparate experience and knowledge can be tested using "false-belief tasks" such as the "Sally-Anne test".[1] Usually, children become able to correctly solve such tasks when they are four to five years old. With this ability, they extend their capacity to understand another's particular (and often limited) point of view and, thereby, augment their empathy.

It is obvious that theory theory and the simulation theory of social cognition are based on the additional cognitive faculties that a child gradually acquires over the course of social interactions from age two on, in particular through situations of joint attention, cooperative practice, and mutual awareness of the other's intentions (Fuchs, 2013). However, it also becomes clear that these theories erroneously take these indirect cognitive operations to pertain to all kinds of empathic understanding. Both deny that it is possible to experience other minds; both presuppose that minds are fundamentally opaque or invisible. Thus, they fail to acknowledge the level of primary empathy and its implicit and immediate understanding of the other's expressive behaviour as meaningfully related to the context of a situation.

Moreover, simulation theory mistakes bodily resonance (crucial for primary empathy) for a simulation in the "as-if" sense. However, even if I unconsciously mimic another's smile, there is no "as-if" involved, for I do not pretend that my own felt smile is the other's smile or project it onto the other. Indeed, at this level of sensation one cannot speak of an "as-if" modality at all because bodily sensations and movement

[1] False belief tests are typically performed in the following way. After introducing two dolls, Sally and Ann, the experimenter presents a short skit: Sally takes a marble and hides it in her basket. She then leaves the room and goes for a walk. While she is away, Anne takes the marble out of Sally's basket and puts it in her own one. Sally is then reintroduced and the child is asked the key question: "Where will Sally look for her marble?" Children before the age of four will typically point to Ann's basket, because they (wrongly) assume Sally to have the same knowledge as they have themselves (Baron-Cohen, Leslie, & Frith, 1986; Perner, Stummer, Sprung, & Doherty, 2002).

tendencies that are evoked when encountering another person are only implicitly present in one's perception of his expressions and emotions.[2] As already mentioned, the proximal or bodily component (to come back to Polanyi's terms) is *transparent* for the distal or perceived component, namely the emotion of the other; it functions as the preconscious *medium* of interaffectivity and empathic understanding. In contrast, simulation and inference are operations that can only be performed on an explicit level. Simulation theory also incorrectly generalizes the possibility of imaginative transposition or simulation to include all kinds of empathy (as in Goldman, 2006). Granted, one can think of typical examples of simulation: When I hear, for example, that someone has missed his plane, I can imagine myself in the same situation as if I had just gone through the same ordeal and, as a result, feel his disappointment or anger. Yet, this form of imagination only appears on higher, and most likely verbally structured, levels of social cognition; on the basic level of empathy, however, it is not necessary for the direct understanding of another person's anger.

One could ask whether cognitive forms of empathy or perspective-taking may develop or exist independently from embodied empathy. Indeed high-functioning autistic individuals are able to compensate for the lacking capacity of primary intersubjectivity by developing strategies of explicit mentalization and learning to infer from social cues (Fuchs, 2015). Temple Grandin, a woman with autism spectrum disorder, described her problems with interpersonal relations as follows to Oliver Sacks:

> She is now aware of the existence of these social signals. She can infer them, she says, but she herself cannot perceive them, cannot participate in this magical communication directly, or conceive the many-leveled kaleidoscopic states of mind behind it. Knowing this intellectually, she does

[2] This is also the case when bodily resonance includes imitative components, for example, movement impulses that mirror gestures and actions of others – possibly as mediated by the brain's system of mirror neurons. However, these imitative tendencies, too, remain typically unaware, which inhibits the complex process of simulation and reflective projection from taking place at all. For a critique of the trend to shift simulation to *subpersonal,* or more specifically, to neuronal processes, see Gallagher (2007).

> her best to compensate, bringing immense intellectual effort and computational power to bear on matters that others understand with unthinking ease. This is why she often feels excluded, an alien. (Sacks, 1995, p. 272)

This may be rightly called a "theory of mind", a rule- and knowledge-based system of inferring other people's state of mind. It also becomes obvious, however, that such compensatory strategies fail to establish an intuitive understanding of others, normally provided by intercorporeality. There are other kinds of disorders in which the cognitive components of empathy are well developed, but with the primary goal of manipulating, deceiving, and exploiting others. This is the case particularly in the "dark triad" of narcissistic, Machiavellian, and sociopathic individuals (McHoskey, Worzel, & Szyarto, 1998; Paulhus & Williams, 2002), who can be very talented in perspective-taking, while having no sympathy whatsoever for fellow human beings, especially their victims. One could add that even a torturer needs certain components of cognitive empathy, if only to better calibrate his cruelty. This shows that empathy in its full sense means an integration of primary and extended, or of intuitive and more explicit, modes of empathy.

4 Reiterated Empathy

The third and final step of empathy I want to look at involves not just imagining myself in your place but an additional move: I can also empathically perceive you as an other who experiences me as an other to you. In other words, the imaginary transposition in this kind of empathy implies the possibility of seeing myself from your perspective, as you empathically perceive me. This is what Edith Stein (1989) has called "reiterated empathy" [*iterierte Einfühlung*]. At first sight, it corresponds to self-consciousness as seeing oneself with another's eyes or assuming a different perspective on oneself. However, what Stein is referring to demands not only a cognitive operation, but also an empathic self-other relationship, experienced from a second-person, embodied perspective. It is based on primary intercorporeality, and at the same time transforms it onto a higher level. I am experiencing my body in the first person, but it also appears to you in the second-person mode, and in empathically grasping that experience of you, I experience myself as other to you. Thus, through reiterated empathy, the experience of oneself as an other for the other, we gain a non-egocentric and intersubjective view of our own lived body in the public world.

A paradigmatic experience of this kind of reiterated empathy is *shame*. In feeling ashamed, I experience myself as being looked at and devaluated by others; I feel their gazes literally burning my face. In Sartre's account, I become an object-body for others. Let us take the example of an indecent utterance in the presence of others that creates a moment of painful embarrassment. After I commit the faux pas, I feel the others' abashment over my behaviour, which in turn induces or increases my own feeling of shame. Another, rather contrary experience of reiterated empathy is the mutual gaze of affection and love: When I perceive the other's loving gaze, I experience myself as being recognized and esteemed by him or her.

In the end, this may be regarded as the synthesis of primary and secondary empathy: Reiterated empathy integrates intuitive components (being affected by the other's expression, interbodily resonance) and cognitive components (taking the other's perspective). On this third level, empathy combines intercorporeality, interaffectivity and intersubjectivity – being aware of the other *as* other – thereby enabling a truly interpersonal relation, which Buber (1970) called the I-thou relationship.

5 Conclusion

I have outlined a non-representational concept of social understanding and empathy based on embodied interaction in face-to-face encounters. According to this concept, intercorporeality and interaffectivity form the basis of empathy. It emerges from the interactive practices and participatory sense-making of the individuals involved. I have described these processes, first, from an enactive point of view in which empathy figures as a dynamic coordination of embodied agents, then, from a phenomenological point of view as a mutual incorporation or a reciprocal extension of the lived bodies and body schemes of the participants. Empathy in this sense can easily be experienced in intensive encounters with others; but in a subtler way, it plays a role in every social interaction. Mutual incorporation is not just a subjective illusion based on a virtual body model projected onto the other. On the contrary, it corresponds exactly to the coupling and coordination of embodied agents that can be observed on the system level.

In early mother-infant interactions, mutual incorporation begins during the first months in the form of imitation, affect attunement and dyadic states of awareness. Infants do not need to form internal models or representations of others in order to communicate. Social understanding develops as a practical, intercorporeal sense, a musicality for the rhythms, and patterns of early dialogue. In a non-mentalizing way, children become able to see the intentions and emotions in the actions of others, in their postures, gestures, and facial expressions, as related to the context of the situation at hand. This provides primary understanding without recourse to a concept of mental states. Moreover, developmental accounts point out that empathy is also based on intercorporeal memory (Fuchs, 2012) or an implicit relational knowledge of how to interact with others that is acquired in early childhood and conveys a basic sense of social attunement.

In this view, how we understand others and empathize with them is not the result of mental inference or simulation, as mainstream cognitive science would have it. Social understanding is grounded in a prereflective interbodily reciprocity that creates a "mixture of myself and the other" (Merleau-Ponty, 1951/1964, p. 155). On the other hand, mutual incorporation is not the only way of social understanding. Primary embodied empathy may be augmented by cognitive means such as inference on the basis of additional information and explicit imaginary transposition into the other's situation. Combining these additional components with primary empathy will usually enhance our potential to understand others. However, these higher-level cognitive capacities are neither necessary nor sufficient as such to constitute empathy as an interaffective relation to the other. Despite those later developments, embodied intersubjectivity remains the basis for our everyday social understanding.

References

Baron-Cohen, S., Leslie, A. M., & Frith, U. (1986). Mechanical, behavioural and intentional understanding of picture stories in autistic children. *British Journal of Developmental Psychology*, *4*, 113–125.

Buber, M. (1970). *I and Thou* (W. Kaufmann, Trans.). New York: Charles Scribners's Sons.

Condon, W. S. (1979). Neonatal entrainment and enculturation. In: M. Bullowa (Ed.) *Before Speech* (pp. 131–148). Cambridge: Cambridge University Press.

Flavell, J. H. (1992). Perspectives on perspective taking. In H. Beilin & P. B. Pufall (Eds.). *The Jean Piaget symposium series: Vol. 14. Piaget's theory: Prospects and possibilities* (pp. 107–139). Hillsdale, NJ: Erlbaum.

Froese, T., & Fuchs, T. (2012). The extended body: A case study in the neurophenomenology of social interaction. *Phenomenology and the Cognitive Sciences*, *11*, 205–236.

Fuchs, T. (2012). The phenomenology of body memory. In S. Koch, T. Fuchs, & C. Müller (Eds.). *Body memory, Metaphor and Movement* (pp. 9–22). Amsterdam: John Benjamins.

Fuchs, T. (2013). The phenomenology and development of social perspectives. *Phenomenology and the Cognitive Sciences*, *12*, 655–683.

Fuchs, T. (2015). Pathologies of intersubjectivity in autism and schizophrenia. *Journal of Consciousness Studies*, *22*, 191–214.

Fuchs, T., & De Jaegher, H. (2009). Enactive intersubjectivity: Participatory sense-making and mutual incorporation. *Phenomenology and the Cognitive Sciences*, *8*(4), 465–486.

Gallagher, S. (2001). The practice of mind: theory, simulation or primary interaction?. *Journal of Consciousness Studies*, *8*, 83–108.

Gallagher, S. (2007). Simulation trouble. *Social Neuroscience*, *2*, 353–365.

Gallagher, S. (2008). Direct perception in the intersubjective context. *Consciousness and Cognition*, *17*, 535–43.

Gallese, V., & Goldman, A. (1998). Mirror neurons and the simulation theory of mind-reading. *Trends in cognitive sciences*, *2*, 493–501.

Goldman, A. (2006). *Simulating Minds. The Philosophy, Psychology, and Neuroscience of Mindreading*. Oxford: Oxford University Press.

Grammer, K., Kruck, K. B., & Magnusson, M. S. (1998). The courtship dance: Patterns of nonverbal synchronization in opposite-sex encounters. *Journal of Nonverbal Behavior*, *22*, 3–29.

Issartel, J., Marin, L., & Cadopi, M. (2007). Unintended interpersonal coordination: "can we march to the beat of our own drum?". *Neuroscience Letters, 411*, 174–179.

De Jaegher, H., & Di Paolo, E. A. (2007). Participatory sense-making: An enactive approach to social cognition. *Phenomenology and the Cognitive Sciences, 6*(4), 485–507.

Downing, G. (2004). Emotion, body and parent- infant interaction. In: Nadel, J., Muir, D. (Eds.). *Emotional development: Recent research advances* (pp. 429–449). Oxford: Oxford University Press.

Kendon, A. (1990). *Conducting Interaction: Patterns of Behavior in Focused Encounters*. Cambridge: Cambridge University Press.

Lipps, T. (1906). *Ästhetik: Psychologie des Schönen und der Kunst* [Aesthetics: The psychology of beauty and art]. Hamburg, Leipzig: Voss.

Lyons-Ruth, K., Bruschweiler-Stern, N., Harrison, A. M., Morgan, A. C., Nahum, J. P., Sander, L., Stern, D. N., & Tronick, E. Z. (1998). Implicit relational knowing: its role in development and psychoanalytic treatment. *Infant Mental Health Journal, 19*, 282–289.

Masangkay, Z. S., McCluskey, K. A., McIntyre, C. W., Sims-Knight, J., Vaughn, B. E., & Flavell, J. H. (1974). The early development of inferences about the visual percepts of others. *Child Development, 45*, 357–366.

McHoskey, J. W., Worzel, W., & Szyarto, C. (1998). Machiavellianism and psychopathy. *Journal of Personality and Social Psychology, 74*, 192–210.

Meltzoff, A., & Moore, M. K. (1977). Imitation of facial and manual gestures by human neonates. *Science, 198*, 75–78.

Meltzoff, A., & Moore, M. K. (1989). Imitation in newborn infants: exploring the range of gestures imitated and the underlying mechanisms. *Developmental Psychology, 25*, 954–962.

Merleau-Ponty, M. (1945/1962). *Phenomenology of perception* (C. Smith, Trans.) [*Phénomenologie de la perception*. Paris: Éditions Gallimard]. London: Routledge and Kegan Paul.

Merleau-Ponty, M. (1951/1964). The child's relations with others (W. Cobb, Trans.) [Les relations avec autrui chez l'enfant]. In *The primacy of perception* (pp. 96–155), Evanston: Northwestern University Press.

Merleau-Ponty, M. (1960). Le philosophe et son ombre [The philosopher and his shadow]. In: *Signes* [Sings] (pp. 201–28). Paris: Éditions Gallimard.

Paulhus, D. L., & Williams, K.M. (2002). The dark triad of personality. *Journal of Research in Personality, 36*, 556–63.

Perner, J. (1991). *Understanding the Representational Mind.* Cambridge, MA: MIT Press.

Perner, J., Stummer, S., Sprung, M., & Doherty, M. (2002). Theory of mind finds its Piagetian *perspective*: Why alternative naming comes with understanding belief. *Cognitive Development, 17*, 1451–72.

Polanyi, M. (1967). *The tacit dimension.* Garden City, New York: Anchor Books.

Reddy, V. (2008). *How Infants Know Minds.* Cambridge, MA: Harvard University Press.

Reddy, V., & Morris, P. (2004). Participants don't need theories. *Theory and Psychology, 14*, 647–665.

Sacks, O. (1995). *An anthropologist on Mars. Seven paradoxical tales.* New York: Alfred Knopf.

Scheler, M. (1973). *Wesen und Formen der Sympathie* [The nature of sympathy]. Bern: Francke.

Schmitz, H. (1989). Über leibliche Kommunikation [On body-to-body communication]. In *Leib und Gefühl. Materialien zu einer philosophischen Therapeutik* [Living body and feeling. Materials for a philosophical therapeutics] (pp. 175–218). Paderborn: Junfermann.

Schmitz, H. (2011) *Der Leib.* Berlin: De Gruyter.

Stein, E. (1989). *On the problem of empathy* (W. Stein, Trans.). Washington, D.C.: ICS Publications.

Stern, D. N. (1998). *The Interpersonal World of the Infant: A View from Psychoanalysis and Developmental Psychology.* New York: Basic Books.

Stuart, S. A. (2012). Enkinaesthesia: The essential sensuous background for co-agency. In Z. Radman (Ed.). *Knowing without thinking: mind, action, cognition and the phenomenon of the background* (pp. 167–186). Basingstoke: Palgrave Macmillan.

Thompson, E. (2005). Sensorimotor subjectivity and the enactive approach to experience. *Phenomenology and the Cognitive Sciences, 4*, 407–427.

Thompson, E. (2007). *Mind in Life: Biology, Phenomenology, and the Sciences of Mind.* Cambridge, MA: The Belknap Press of Harvard University Press.

Titchener, E. B. (1909). *Lectures on the Experimental Psychology of the Thought-Processes.* New York: Macmillan.

Trevarthen, C. (1979). Communication and cooperation in early infancy: a description of primary intersubjectivity. In M. Bullowa (Ed.). *Before Speech* (pp. 321–347). Cambridge: Cambridge University Press.

Trevarthen, C. (1993). The self born in intersubjectivity. In: U. Neisser (Ed.). *The Perceived Self: Ecological and Interpersonal Sources of Self-Knowledge* (pp. 121–173). Cambridge: Cambridge University Press.

Tronick, E. Z. (1998). Dyadically expanded states of consciousness and the process of therapeutic change. *Infant Mental Health Journal, 19*, 290–299.

Vischer, R. (1872). *Über das optische Formgefühl – ein Beitrag zur Ästhetik* [On the Optical Sense of Form: A Contribution to Aesthetics]. Doctoral dissertation, Eberhard-Karls-Universität Tübingen.

Wittgenstein, L. (1967). *Zettel* [Snippets] (G. E. M. Anscombe & G. H. von Wright, Eds.). Oxford: Blackwell.

Zahavi, D. (2001). Beyond Empathy. Phenomenological approaches to intersubjectivity. *Journal of Consciousness Studies*, 8, 151–167.

Zahavi, D. (2008). Simulation, projection and empathy. *Consciousness and Cognition,* 17, 514–22.

3

Embodied Empathy – Clinical and Developmental Perspectives in Psychoanalysis

Marianne Leuzinger-Bohleber

> [. . . E]mpathy has, since at least the seminal work of David Hume and Adam Smith, been seen as centrally important in at least two respects. First, it has been seen as important in relation to our capacity to gain a grasp of the content of other people's minds, and to predict and explain what they will think, feel, and do. And secondly, it has been seen as important in relation to our capacity to respond to others ethically – enabling us not only to gain a grasp of the other's suffering, but also to respond in an ethically appropriate way [. . .]. (Coplan & Goldie, 2011, p. IX)

As this book shows, empathy has become a central concept for research in many different disciplines from aesthetics, phenomenology, and hermeneutics to psychoanalysis, clinical psychology, developmental, and on to social psychology, care ethics, contemporary cognitive

---

M. Leuzinger-Bohleber (✉)
Sigmund Freud Institute, Frankfurt a.M, Germany
e-mail: m.leuzinger-bohleber@sigmund-freud-institut.de

V. Lux, S. Weigel (eds.), *Empathy*, Palgrave Studies in the Theory and History of Psychology, DOI 10.1057/978-1-137-51299-4_3

neurosciences, and embodied cognitive science. As a psychoanalyst, I aim to contribute to the interdisciplinary discussion in this book by first shortly summarizing some of the discussions of the role of empathy in the clinical psychoanalytical situation. Empathy is no longer understood as a personality trait of the analyst in the sense of a "one-person psychology" but as a phenomenon that takes place in an exchange between analyst and analysand – in a "two-person psychology" (Section 1). Following this summary, I discuss a similar theoretical perspective that characterizes the development of the self, attachment, and the capability to mentalize. The caregiver's empathy in the early interactions with an infant has proven to be the most influential variable for the child's development in numerous empirical studies (Section 2). Finally, I will shortly present some current attempts to further develop the understanding of empathy in psychoanalysis based on insights gained in the interdisciplinary dialogue with embodied cognitive science. I look at the radical changes in the conceptualization of empathy in the clinical psychoanalytical situation after the so-called "embodied revolution" which altered our understanding of empathy, memory, transference-countertransference as well as therapeutic transformations, as Rolf Pfeifer and I have suggested in several papers (Leuzinger-Bohleber & Pfeifer, 2002, 2011, 2013). Our considerations will be illustrated by an extensive clinical example (Section 3).

1 Empathy – A Central Concept in Clinical Psychoanalysis Theoretically Tabooed for a Long Time

The different psychoanalytical schools have all shared the conviction that the experiences, and particularly early experiences as an infant, are kept in the unconscious and that the professional empathy of a psychoanalyst is required to approach the idiosyncratic world of unconscious fantasies and conflicts created in the idiosyncratic life histories of the analysands in psychoanalytic treatments. Sigmund Freud in *The Interpretation of Dreams* (1900) states: "We must always be prepared to drop our conceptual scaffolding if we feel that we are in a position to replace it by something that approximates more closely to the unknown reality" (Freud, 1900/1953, 4, p. 610). Thus, the psychoanalyst's basic attitude when encountering the unknown, the unconscious, has always been one of curiosity, openness, and intuition. It could be characterized as a basic attitude of a clinical researcher [*Forschungshaltung*] (see Leuzinger-Bohleber, 2007, 2010). One tool for the discovery of the unconscious is the empathy of the analyst. In his considerations on "Group Psychology and the Analysis of the Ego" (1921), Freud characterized empathy as "the mechanism by means of which we are able to take up any attitude at all towards another mental life" (Freud, 1921/1955, p. 110).

As Don C. Grant and Edwin Harari (2011) observe, it is surprising that Freud only formulates this definition of empathy in a footnote and does not elaborate this important concept any further. Also in mainstream psychoanalysis, particularly in the three different schools represented in the British Psychoanalytical Society (Kleinians, Freudians, and the Middle Group), empathy has not been discussed in theoretical papers very frequently. Although most psychoanalysts agree on the relevance of empathetic communication including "listening with the third ear" (Theodor Reik), that is, the professional perception of and reflections on unconscious information exchanged between analysand and psychoanalyst, the term "empathy" seems to have remained a taboo in psychoanalytical literature for a long time. One of the reasons might have been that many psychoanalysts feared "empathy" could be used in an idealistic and idealized way, thereby harmonizing the existential and often destructive dimension of unconscious wishes, conflicts, and fantasies, and their enactments in the psychoanalytical situation.[1]

Psychoanalysts have thus preferred to talk about, for example, transference and countertransference, projection and projective identifications, "rêverie," or holding and containing, in order to characterize unconscious communication in the psychoanalytical situation, which

[1] Stefano Bolognini also sees this danger and describes empathy in contrast to such an idealistic understanding (Bolognini, 2007, p. 869).

means they preferred to use genuine psychoanalytical terms instead of the non-psychoanalytic term "empathy" (see Bion, 1962; Heimann, 1950; Klein, 1959/1977). Wilfred Bion avoids the term "empathy" although he describes in detail the findings of empirical infant and attachment research, in which the mother's empathy [*Feinfühligkeit*] proved to be the most influential factor in the early mother-child interaction (see Section 2). Instead, he talks of "maternal rêverie" and defines this central capability as "that state of mind [. . .] capable of reception of the infant's projective identifications" (Bion, 1962, p. 36) similarly to Freud's original statement quoted above (see also Grant & Harari, 2011, p. 5ff.). The analyst – in an analogous position to the emotionally attuned primary object – in his "rêverie" tries to offer a "container" for his analysand's unconscious communication, into which the analysand can project his unbearable fantasies, affects, and impulses. Given the analyst's professional skills (his "capability for rêverie"), the analyst will finally be able to capture these projections and attempt to understand and verbalize them, for example, in metaphors or interpretations. Peter Fonagy and Mary Target (2003) describe these professional skills as a capability to mentalize (see Section 2).

Donald Wood Winnicott (1971) agreed with Melanie Klein's formulations regarding the pre-Oedipal development, particularly her notion that the child's play represents projections of internal object relations. Primitive internal objects are split into "good" and "bad" objects or "benign" and "persecutory" objects in Winnicott's terms. More intensively than Klein, Winnicott emphasizes the role of early experiences with the caregiver. The "maternal preoccupation" enables the "good enough mother" to transmit more satisfying than unsatisfying experiences to the child. Thus, hopefully, more adequate than inadequate responses of the caregiver to the child's instinctual need will dominate experiences of "good enough" early object relations, as Winnicott summarizes it (Winnicott, 1971). The good experiences tend to be introjected and become part of the Self/Ego. The bad experiences are projected onto external objects. Winnicott also agreed with Klein's conceptualization of the schizoid-paranoid and depressive positions in which the infant tries to integrate the good and the bad parts of the object and the self. He often speaks of the depressive position as an achievement in development, as a "stage of concern." In contrast to the schizoid-paranoid position, the infant develops concern and guilt about attacks in the phantasy onto the bad object because it realizes that the "bad object" is the "good object" at the same time. Winnicott postulates that the life drive, the eros, urges reparation and restitution toward the object, which is now – at the end of the first year of life – no longer perceived and experienced as a "partial object" but as a "whole object." Grant and Harari summarize the integrative achievements in these reflections of Winnicott's work:

> Winnicott's theories of primary maternal preoccupation and good enough mothering release us from any need to choose between instinctual drives and environmental influences as the hand that guides mental development. His theories point to the interactions between nature and nurture as the crucial factor. This is congruent with modern knowledge of genetics [. . .], which has shown there is an even more intimate interplay between the environment and genes than was previously thought, with many genes needing to be switched on by environmental experiences. (Grant & Harari, 2011, p. 6f.)

Anna Freud (1965) also proclaimed the importance of the interaction between biological/genetic factors, which means the forces of the drives on the one hand and environmental influences on the other hand – what she called the "developmental lines." As many other psychoanalysts, she hardly speaks of "empathy"; even so she describes this psychic capacity of caregivers in great detail, for example, in her famous studies on the influence of early separations on child development during the London bombings (see Freud & Burlingham, 1951).

It was Heinz Kohut (1959) who took up the neglected topic of empathy and made it one of his central theoretical issues. Kohut redefined psychoanalysis as that aspect of inner reality that can be encompassed through introspection and empathy.

> Thus, Kohut has focused here on introspection and vicarious introspection (empathy) as the *definer* of the field of the data of psychoanalysis, as well as its *essential method of observation*. In other words, Kohut extended

> here the psychoanalytic domain over all subjective, inner experience that can be encompassed (or potentially encompassed) via introspection and empathy. It is the field of the patient's directly introspected inner experience and the analyst's empathy (vicariously introspected) method of its study that define psychoanalysis. Previously definitions included specific theories – in the very definition itself. This represented obstacles to progress by tying the field to such specific theoretical constracts as if those were sacrosanct, untouchable, rather than leaving them open to change. One striking example of the impact of the new definition is Kohut's own clinical and theoretical work on narcissistic personality and behavior disorder, where the Oedipus complex does not appear to play a primary pathogenic role. (Ornstein, 2011, p. 441)

Paul H. Ornstein (2011) further summarizes Kohut's achievements explicitly bringing back the central concept of empathy to the psychoanalytic discourse. He starts by drawing the concepts of empathy back to its origins in Greek, namely *empathein* that literally means *indwelling*, best expressed in the German word *Einfühlung*, because it means to enter the inner life of another imaginatively:

> Empathy is the act of *feeling* oneself and *thinking* oneself into the inner life of another, to understand, both emotionally and cognitively what the other thinks and feels. In fact, the philosophical conundrum of how we know of the existence of other minds is resolved, at least for some philosophers and some psychoanalysts. Thus it is possible for us to know that other minds exist, via our capacity for empathy and to comprehend what others think and feel. (Ornstein, 2011, p. 442)

Although there is no doubt that this human capacity is innate and biologically anchored while its development and the way the human personality unfolds depend on the specific milieu provided by the caretakers, the nature of empathy remains controversial:

> The nature of empathy, its origin, and its development are, in contemporary psychoanalysis still – or again – embroiled in controversy – along with how to conceive of its specific functions in the psychoanalytic treatment process. Recent criticism of the centrality of empathy as a

> mode of observation in psychoanalysis have centered on the assertion that empathy belonged to a one-person-psychology, hence passé. I claim that empathy clearly belongs (and has always belonged) to a two-person-psychology – even if that recognition remained unarticulated, and the language in which empathy was generally discussed used the language of a one-person-psychology operationally, without the patient acknowledgement having felt understood, the analyst would not claim that he or she arrived at a valid understanding. (Ornstein, 2011, p. 442ff.)

To summarize, empathy has been a central issue in clinical psychoanalytical work with patients in all the different psychoanalytical schools but, strangely enough, was tabooed as a conceptual term in the psychoanalytical literature for a long time. From a clinical point of view, it is generally agreed that empathy is not exclusively based on observation, although it may complement or intersect with observational data. Rather, it seems to involve other forms of communication, both conscious and unconscious, between analyst and analysand: "Empathy, in my view, is a cognitive-affective form of experiencing that attunes the subject to communications from another person, leading to some intimation of the state of mind or inner experience of that other" (Meissner, 2010, p. 424).

Conceptually different aspects of empathy have been described by specific terms like trial identification and introjection (Freud, 1921/1955, p. 13), generative empathy (Schafer, 1959), coenesthetic communication (Spitz, 1965), vicarious introspection (Kohut, 1959, 1965), emotional knowing (Greenson, 1960), resonant cognition (Kelman, 1987) and even as a form of projective identification (Ogden, 1979; Tansey & Burke, 1985, 1989).[2] Dan H. Buie (1981) describes four subcategories of the analyst's experience of empathy in therapeutic interactions: conceptual empathy, self-experiential empathy, imaginative-imitative empathy, and resonant empathy (see Meissner, 2010, p. 430). William W.

[2] Projective identification is known to psychoanalysis as the earliest expression of an emotional tie with another person (Freud, 1912f./1955, p.105). As such, it allows communications from unconscious to unconscious, without the mediation of words (see also Zanocco, de Marchi, & Pozzi, 2006).

Meissner thus concludes: "The clinical applications of empathy have been exhaustively explored, but little progress has been made regarding the mechanisms and psychic processes that bring it about" (Meissner, 2010, p. 421). Therefore, he develops a new model of empathy in which he includes clinical psychoanalytical, conceptual knowledge as well as new insights of modern neurosciences. He tries to differentiate between the above mentioned mechanisms as projection, projective identification, or countertransference reactions on the one hand and empathy on the other hand. I quote his conclusion extensively as one example of an attempt at theoretical integration.[3]

Meissner's model integrates and differentiates three aspects of empathy in psychoanalysis, first, "the neurological, neurophysiological, neuromuscular, and autonomic mechanisms" that he characterizes as "hard-wired." They operate automatically, non-consciously as an empathic attunement:

> They provide an operational physiological basis for the generation and unconscious communication of affects. They play a fundamental role in affective experience and communication, both in terms of the subtle physical expression of affective states in the one experiencing the emotion and of the perception, reception, registration, and internal processing of one observing the emotional state of another. They are an essential part of any form of empathic attunement and response. (Meissner, 2010, p. 461)

Second, he describes in which way these mechanisms resonate with the introjective organization of both subjects involved in the psychoanalytical setting:

> There is no question of anything *transferred* from experience to the observer, no projection of parts of the self *into* another, no merging, no question of one subject becoming another, no *trial identification*. Rather,

[3] Not all psychoanalysts appreciate such attempts at theoretical integration. They are convinced that the current state of 'pluralism of theories' has many advantages. I myself use the metaphor of a *kaleidoscope*, which enables us to look at the complexities of clinical information from many different theoretical perspectives (see Leuzinger-Bohleber, 2015a; Leuzinger-Bohleber & Bürgin, 2003; see also Bahrke et al., 2013).

> the affective resonance of the analysand's (usually unconscious) self-experience is communicated unconsciously to the analyst in whom it is received and registered. Insofar as the analyst's own introjective configuration features elements of an introjective alignment similar to the patient's, his affective response will tend to be more in tune with the self-experience of the analysand. This basic process would be reinforced by whatever behavioral cues the analysand would generate to communicate this internal stance. (Meissner, 2010, p. 461)

This model of a resonance mechanism of the introjective organization in the participants has consequences for the concept of projection, usually used to describe the relationship between the analysand and the analyst:

> The link between the analysand's projection and the analyst's introjection involves *no transmission or projection of anything into the analyst*, no unmediated or unexplained *unconscious communication;* rather, it is simply a matter of the already existing quality of the introjective organization in the participants. Thus, in an analysand's enactment of a masochistic stance, what the analyst receives can resonate with the masochistic aspects of his own personality organization as centered in his own victim introject, and can result in an empathic response. Thus, the organization of the introjects is pivotal. If, for example, the aggressor-victimizer introject has a more prominent role in the analyst's self-as-object, he would be more likely to respond in those terms. The victimized stance of the analysand, for example, is an open invitation and stimulus to the potential aggressor to become more aggressive and victimizing. The result in the analyst would, of course, take the form of countertransference rather than empathy. (Meissner, 2010, p. 461)

Third, Meissner discusses the question in which way these processes become conscious. Although they function non-consciously on the neurophysiological level, there are ways to register their effects through corporal sensations like blushing, sweating, or heart rate:

> The affect itself can also become conscious and be experienced with any degree of intensity. As long as the affect remains unconscious, its presence can be detected only by autonomic or behavioral concomitants. In the

process of empathic attunement, the affective resonance with the feeling state of another presumably becomes available to conscious awareness and processing only in the latter stages of the progressive development of the response when the neurological processing involved in the inferential process has reached a certain point of elaboration. Before that, whether the expression and reception of emotion involve projective devices or not, the affective component remains unconscious. (Meissner, 2010, p. 461f.)

2 Empathy in the Early Interaction of the Caregiver with the Infant and Its Influence on Early Self-Development, Attachment, and the Capability to Mentalize[4]

2.1 Empirical Infant Research on Self-Development and Affect Regulation

As briefly mentioned earlier, it has been shown that the primary caregiver's empathy is the most influential variable for early self-development, or secure attachment and the development of the mentalization capacity.[5] The findings in these empirically oriented lines of research are seen in light of a "two-person-psychology" or, more specifically, in an intersubjective understanding of early developmental processes, as outlined before. In what follows, I will provide a short summary of the theoretical issues concerned.

[4] The following section is based on my work on early childhood, with emphasis on trauma (Leuzinger-Bohleber, 2009).

[5] In psychology, mentalization is defined as the ability to understand the mental state, of oneself or others, that underlies overt behavior. Mentalization can be seen as a form of imaginative mental activity that lets us perceive and interpret human behavior in terms of intentional mental states (e.g., needs, desires, feelings, beliefs, goals, purposes, and reasons) (see, e.g., Fonagy, Steele, Steele, Moran, & Higgitt, 1991, and Section 2.3 in this chapter).

Self-development and the related successive reorganization of subjective views, both of the self and the other, are at the core of the studies of Daniel Stern, one of the most well-known empirical infant researchers. His theory follows the traditional psychoanalytic approach of describing biological maturation processes on the one hand and the relationship experience (i.e. the social environment) on the other. Having a sense of self makes possible an experience of temporal continuity, that is, of past, present, and future. The self seems to emerge from inner sources but is always also dependent on reassurance by others, who can both support and disturb a sense of self. Stern does not see the self as a static structure, but rather claims a procedural understanding of the self. Self-development begins on the first day of life and is never complete. Stern defines four stages of experiencing the self, each one of them linked to a characteristic type of relatedness with the object. It is important to note that the different stages of the sense of self are acquired at specific ages and show certain preponderance. However, the earlier stages are not overcome in the sense of being outgrown and giving way to later forms of self-experience. Instead, they continue to exist in parallel over the course of one's whole life.

2.1.1 Stage of the Emergent Self (First/Second month)

The basic development toward a "sense of emergent self" can only happen within the experience of interaction, which has already been mentioned with reference to Winnicott as "good-enough-mothering." As also described above, empathy of the primary caregiver is the most important variable in this interaction. Only an empathic primary object will be able to provide an uninterrupted experience of satisfying needs, as well as constant sensorimotor sequences, which are initiated by the infant, too, and which lead to the formation of sensorimotor schemata or basic "embodied memories." A further important feature of the primary objects is their ability to appreciate and experience the infant as an idiosyncratic object, an "other." This parental quality alone allows the infant to perceive its counterpart's curiosity for the very individual, "emerging" features of the self.

2.1.2 Stage of the Core-Self (Second–Ninth Month)

This stage concerns the experience of own self-agency, self-coherency, self-affectivity, and self-history. It is a complex task developing an integrated sense of a body self, that exists as a coherent whole on its own, separate from the other; as well as getting a feeling for one's own actions. Again, relationship experiences play a decisive role. A sense of the core-self evolves from daily routines of caretaking as well as from the recurring help of the primary object in regulating body arousal, intense affects, and impulses. Relational experiences provide the infant with "self-invariants." Stern distinguishes the following four aspects:

(a) The infant experiences "self-agency" by learning to be the creator of its own actions as well as by learning that it is not the creator of other's actions. Increasing abilities to direct and control the body (e.g. my foot moves whenever I want it to) and the predictability of consequences to one's own behavior (e.g. when I smile my mother smiles as well) play a crucial role.
(b) The infant experiences "self-coherence" through perceiving itself as a physical unit with boundaries and as a locus of integrated actions. It is mainly through the perception of coherent time structures that the self, as well as the "other," is perceived as a separate, independent unit (e.g. when one movement is always accompanied by the same noise). Also decisive are the repeated, reliable experiences with different intensities, forms, movements, and locations.
(c) With every structured, specific affect experienced by the infant, he or she notes a characteristic configuration of events, namely of specific body responses, inner sensations of excitement and activity, and emotion-specific qualities of feelings – the infant feels "self-affectivity."
(d) Finally, the infant perceives "self-history," a continuity concerning its past. The infant feels how he/she is changing, while at the same time remaining the same person.

The experiences of agency, coherence, affectivity, and continuity are stored in the episodic memory and are registered as meaningful, interrelated episodes set deep within the memory. They contain both affective as well as sensorimotor elements. These "episodes" become generalized and build the basis for new situations (e.g. how breast-feeding should take place). Nelson & Gruendel (1981) spoke of "generalized event structures" (GERs), which are the essential built units for both cognitive development and autobiographic memory. They mainly refer to actions, while Stern concentrates on the infant's interactional experiences. He speaks of "representations of interactions that have been generalized," the so-called RIGs that determine, according to his theory, the earliest expectations about new relationships, expectations to conditions of the self in absence of "another" (Stern, 1995, p. 143). Stern explains the accumulation of "symbiotic experiences" in a different way than Margaret Mahler, one of the most famous authors in "classical" psychoanalytical developmental theories. Symbiotic experiences of merger are constructed when episodic memories of states of the self are activated while in the presence of the "evoked companion" (see Mahler, Pine, & Bergman, 1978). According to Stern's theory, experiences of merger are the product of an active, creative inner process of the infant. I will come back to this later, in Section 3.

2.1.3 Stage of the Subjective Self, Affect Attunement (Seventh–Ninth Month)

The infant discovers that its subjective experiences can be shared with others and thus develops a capacity for "inter-affectivity." As for the primary caregiver, his/her abilities for "mirroring," "affect matching" as well as "emotional availability" are required to facilitate this development. Stern subsumes these abilities under the term "affect attunements." The mother adjusts herself to the affective mood of the infant (the vitality affects) and for her part expresses these in different sensory channels (e.g. by humming to the exact same rhythm as the rocking of her child). This amodal attunement to the child's affective state is crucially important because it guarantees that it is not the behavior to which the mother attunes. This would be mere imitation. The mother attunes through amodal perception to the quality of the emotion she is sharing with her infant. In this way she creates "interpersonal communication." The two of them become parts of a mediated, shared inner universe.

2.1.4 Stage of the Verbal (Narrative) Self (After the 18th Month)

At the age of approximately 18 months, the child gains a reversibility in the co-ordination of mental and motoric schemata. An "objective self" emerges, and the child is now able to recognize himself when he sees himself "from the outside" in a mirror. At the same time language development starts. Stern impressively describes the ambivalence of this developmental step. On the one hand, the acquisition of language facilitates "unambiguous communication" with the other, something the child is usually very proud of. On the other hand, one often observes a mourning reaction in the children because they lose that amodal, holistic understanding with their primary objects. They perceive themselves as increasingly separate (see in more detail Mahler's descriptions of the process of individuation respective separation).

2.1.5 Stage of the Self-Reflecting Self (in Adolescence)

It is often taken too little into consideration, even among experts, that the capacity for abstract self-reflection only develops due to cognitive development in adolescence. It is not until this age that the individual is able to think about himself or herself in an abstract way and to acquire a meta-perspective toward him/herself and his/her own values and ideals.

2.2 Early Development in Light of Empirical Attachment Research

Attachment theory has built the bridge between psychoanalysis and academic psychology like almost no other psychoanalytic approach.

However, sometimes the psychoanalytic roots of attachment theory are denied by academic developmental psychologists or are described as a split-off approach from psychoanalysis.

John Bowlby elaborates his theory of an infant's biologically innate attachment need, partly in following with his interest in ethnologic research by Konrad Lorenz and Harry Harlow, among others (Bowlby, 1958). The child strives for attachment relationships and then uses them as a home base for his exploration of the world. Crying is also a biologically innate behavior that is supposed to elicit care-taking behavior in the attachment figure. If these needs are not satisfied, there is a high chance of the child developing symptoms such as partial depression, an exaggerated need to be loved, severe feelings of guilt or depression, among others. Also personality traits such as superficiality, lack of motivation, difficulties concentrating, a disposition to deceive, or obsessive stealing are – alongside developmental delays or mental retardation – possible consequences of early experiences of deprivation (see also the well-known studies of René Spitz and the films of James and Joyce Robertson). Therefore, Bowlby sees attachment behavior as a biologically innate survival strategy of the human infant. This "behavioral system" enables the infant to explore the world and establish social relationships. It also provides protection against enemies and security through closeness to the attachment figure. Bowlby thus believes the attachment system to be a more central motivational system than the drives.

The antagonism outlined by Bowlby between attachment and exploratory behavior has high explanatory power. Both motivational systems cannot be activated simultaneously. When a child feels safe it can activate its exploratory system and learn from his environment. At the perception of danger, fear emerges: the attachment system is activated. The child interrupts his exploratory behavior and seeks security in his attachment figure (see Fig. 3.1).

Bowlby's model has been further developed by Bretherton (1985) Crittenden (1990), Main, Kaplan, & Cassidy (1985), Sroufe (1996), among others. The development of a test to measure attachment behavior by Bowlby's colleague Mary Ainsworth marked an important step in this respect. In the so-called "strange situation" (a standardized

Fig. 3.1 Attachment exploration

observation situation), the quality of the attachment of a child to his mother (or father) can be rated. Originally, this test described three attachment types:

I. *Secure attachment ("B"):* These children react very strongly to being separated from their mother or father. They cry, search for their parent, and interrupt their play. When the attachment figure returns, the child quickly calms down. It can be soothed and then re-engage in play.
II. *Insecure-avoidant attachment ("A"):* Children here show very little overt signs of sorrow or sadness when the parent leaves the room. During the separation they keep on playing, apparently undisturbed. They mainly ignore their parents at their return, especially after a second, more stressful separation. They do not actively seek consolation through body contact and can be soothed even better by a stranger than by their parent. Measurement of cortisol in the saliva, however, has shown that during the separation these children have a higher concentration of cortisol, meaning they experience a higher level of stress.
III. *Insecure-ambivalent attachment ("C"):* These children show a very disturbed reaction when the mother or father leaves the room. They cry desperately and are not able to calm down on their own. When a

parent returns, they show remarkably mixed behavior: they cling to their mother or father for a short while only to then reject them vehemently. They cannot be soothed either by a stranger or their parent in order to then return to play.

Through a great number of studies it has been shown that a further, less frequent attachment type exists.

IV. *Insecure-disorganized attachment ("D"):* These children do not show a clear attachment pattern, but instead a range of confused behavior patterns, such as emotional freezing or stereotypical movements when the parents return.

By now a number of studies have been carried out to investigate attachment behavior. In the Baltimore Study by Ainsworth, Bell, and Stayton (1974), 68% of the children were classified as securely attached, 20% as insecure-avoidant, 12% as insecure-ambivalent (Type D did not yet exist). Interesting cultural differences have been found: Type "A" has higher prevalence rates in Western Europe and the USA than, for example, in Japan and Israel, where Type "C" is more prevalent. Marinus van IJzendoorn carried out a meta-analysis comparing many studies from different countries. For non-clinical populations of children he found the following frequency distribution: 55% secure attachment, 23% avoidant, 8% ambivalent and 15% disorganized attachment (van IJzendoorn, Frenkel, Goldberg, & Kronenberg, 1992).

Again, attachment types are considered the consequence of early relationship experiences in the first year of life. The child develops a respective "inner working model" which he has learned to be most successful in the contact with his primary attachment figure. The securely attached child (B) has had, thanks to an *empathic primary attachment figure*, the chance to develop a secure attachment to her (him), in which the whole spectrum of human feelings can be perceived, experienced, and expressed, in the sense of communicating with the other. The insecure-avoidant child (A) in contrast has repeatedly had the experience that the primary object (most frequently the mother) feels most comfortable when the child does not show intense affects and behaves in a controlled, distanced way. The ambivalently attached child (C) has spent its first year with a mother who sometimes reacts in an adequate way, while at other times being rejecting or overprotecting, that is altogether in an inconsistent and therefore unpredictable way. The hypothesis about disoriented/disorganized children (D) is that they cannot develop a stable inner working model at all because their mothers (or other primary objects) suffer from the consequences of an acute trauma (for example, the dramatic loss of a significant other). Being completely absorbed by the trauma psychically, they are hardly able to establish a coherent relationship to their infant.

Attachment researchers also see maternal sensitivity as the most important determinant for the development of attachment types. Grossmann et al. (1989, p. 40) describe the following features of maternal empathy: (a) perception of the infant's behavioral patterns, (b) correct interpretation of its utterances, (c) prompt reaction, (d) appropriateness of reaction. Many studies have confirmed that secure attachment is a protective factor in child development (see Fonagy, 2007; Leuzinger-Bohleber, 2014, among others). This finding is pivotal for all forms of early and earliest prevention of therapy. Maternal empathy is now known to be easily disturbed, even in securely attached mothers. The ability to empathize is diminished or, in extreme cases, lost when a mother experiences distress or tension. This finding is highly relevant when it comes to forms of early preventions (see Emde & Leuzinger-Bohleber, 2014).

2.3 Development of Mentalizing Capacity

Mentalizing is a concept that was first introduced by French psychoanalysts working with psychosomatic patients. They observed a lacking capacity to symbolize mental states in these patients, little freedom in free association, and a distinct way of thinking that is close to bodily sensations and primary-process thinking. Fonagy and his colleagues define mentalization, following the philosophical tradition of Franz Brentano (1874/1973), Daniel Dennett (1978) and others, as a form of pre-conscious imaginative mental activity because human behavior is interpreted in terms of "intentional" mental states. It is imaginative because we have to imagine what others think and feel. Taking into account that we do not really know what is going on in the mind of the other is thus a sign of high level mentalization. The same type of imaginative transfer may be necessary to understand the mental experience of others, especially concerning emotionally charged themes or irrational (potentially unconsciously guided) reactions. Some philosophers have claimed that psychic determinism (the claim that human behavior should be understood as a description of unconscious wishes and ideas alongside conscious states) was Freud's most important contribution (Hopkins, 1992; Wollheim, 1999). In order to understand that the self has a "mind" as has the other, one needs a symbolic representational system of mental states. Although mentalization is probably associated with different cerebral activities, it is usually related to activation in the middle prefrontal cortex – and possibly the paracingular area.

Fonagy and Target discovered that a child's early attachment is indeed related to the primary object's own attachment security (Fonagy, Steele, & Steele, 1991), but it is influenced to an even greater extent by her capacity to understand her relationship to her parents regarding psychic states (Fonagy, Steele, Steele, Moran, & Higgitt, 1991):

> We have tried to map the process by means of which the understanding of the self as a mental agent grows out of interpersonal experience, particularly primary object relationships [. . .]. Mentalizing involves both a self-reflective and an interpersonal component. In combination, these provide the child with a capacity to distinguish inner from outer reality, internal mental and emotional processes from interpersonal events. (Fonagy & Target, 2003, p. 270, own transl.).

The ability to mentalize is not a biologically given capacity, but develops successively in interaction with the most important attachment figures. However, the authors do not understand mentalization as merely a cognitive process:

> [Mentalization] developmentally begins with the 'discovery' of affects through the primary object relationships. Thus, we have focused on the concept of 'affect regulation', which is important in many areas of

> developmental theories and psychopathology [for example, Clarkin & Lenzenweger, 1996]. Affect regulation, the capacity to modulate emotional states, is closely related to mentalization, which plays a fundamental role in the unfolding of a sense of self and agency. In this account, affect regulation is a prelude to mentalization; yet, once mentalization occurs, the nature of affect regulation is transformed: not only does it allow for adjustment of affect states, but more fundamentally it is used to regulate the self. (Fonagy & Target, 2003, p. 271, own transl.)

Thus, these authors as well emphasize the relevance of maternal empathy for a child's mentalization capacity and secure attachment behavior. It is only through exploration of the mental state of the sensitive attachment figure that mentalizing self-organization can develop: "[This] enables the child to find in his image of her mind a picture of himself motivated by beliefs, feelings and intentions" (Fonagy & Target, 2003, p. 276).

Fonagy and Target formulate some theses about these developmental processes:

(1) In early childhood, the reflective function is characterized by two modes of relating internal experiences to the external situation: (a) in a serious frame of mind, the child expects the internal world in himself and others to correspond to external reality, and subjective experience will often be distorted to match information coming from outside ("*psychic equivalence mode*"; see Gopnik & Astington, 1988; Perner, Leekam, & Wimmer, 1987); and (b) while playing, the child knows that internal experience may not reflect external reality (see Bartsch & Wellman, 1989; Dias & Harris, 1990), but then the internal state is thought to have no implications for the outside world ("*pretend mode*").
(2) Normally at around the age of four, the child integrates these modes to arrive at *mentalization,* or the *reflective mode*, in which mental states can be experienced as representations. Inner and outer reality can then be seen as linked, yet differing in important ways, and no longer have to be either equated or dissociated from each other (Baron-Cohen, 1995; Gopnik, 1993).

(3) Mentalization normally comes about through the child's experience of his mental states being reflected on (through play with a parent or sibling, as a further elaboration of complex early mirroring processes in the interaction between mother and child).
(4) "In traumatized children, intense emotion, and associated conflict, may disrupt this integration, so that aspects of the pretend mode of functioning become part of a psychic equivalence manner of experiencing reality" (Fonagy & Target, 2003, p. 274–275).

This last aspect is particularly relevant. The development of mentalization and the reflective function is hampered by maltreatment and other traumata: a child who is scared of his brutal attachment figure rather prefers not to put himself into the mind of the other. Additionally, the child loses resilience, which is closely related to the capacity to understand an interpersonal situation.

According to Fonagy and Target, mentalization and secure attachment are therefore the results of experiencing successful containment in early socialization. Insecure attachment can be understood as the child's identification with the defensive stance of the mother. These mothers are, for example, not capable of mirroring the negative affects and distress of the child because they feel threatened by them. Perceiving negative affects probably elicits memories of unbearable experiences that have to be repressed. Hence, the child can only maintain closeness to the mother by sacrificing his reflective function. On the contrary, entangled mothers either mirror their children's negative affects in an exaggerated way or confuse them with their own experiences, which will feel strange or alarming to the child. In both forms of insecure attachment, the children internalize the state of the attachment figure. The lack of synchronicity between a child's own affective states and a mother's becomes the content of the self-experience.

Even more dramatic are the effects of early traumata on the development or rather non-development of mentalizing. In an impressive work, Peter Fonagy reports interviews and therapies carried out in prison with severely traumatized children and adolescents (Fonagy, 2007). Their acts of violence have significantly been influenced by their lacking ability to mentalize, that is, not being able to empathize with the physical and psychic state of their victims. Fonagy speaks of "violent attachment" or attachment trauma. He points to a number of studies which have shown that mentalization is underdeveloped in most people who have experienced trauma. Those children do not learn the words for emotions (Beeghly & Cicchetti, 1994); and traumatized adults have greater difficulties in recognizing intentions in facial expressions (Fonagy & Target, 2003).

3 "Embodied Empathy"[6]: A Clinical Example and Some Theoretical Reflections

At the Joseph Sandler Research Conference 2013,[7] important debates took place on how the embodiment concept adds another dimension to the understanding of "empathy" as described in empirical developmental research and following the so-called intersubjective turn in contemporary clinical psychoanalysis, described above (Bohleber, 2013; Leuzinger-Bohleber, 2015a; Leuzinger-Bohleber, Emde, & Pfeifer, 2013). This will be illustrated in what follows by a clinical example and some theoretical considerations.

3.1 Case Study of Ms. M

> Before I can properly open the door for Ms. M., she rushes into my office. She grabs my hand taking it between both of hers and holds it tight in a strange, 'sexually stimulating' way. At the same time she comes very close to me, overstepping the normal boundaries of bodily proximity:

[6] Zanocco, de Marchi, & Pocci (2006) also emphasized the relevance of body reactions in empathetic interactions. They spoke of "sensory empathy" and illustrated their ideas with observations on enactment.

[7] Vittorio Gallese, Rolf Pfeifer, Bradley Peterson, Mark Solms, and others elaborated their understanding of "embodiment" at this conference, the proceedings of which have been published in German (Leuzinger-Bohleber, Emde, & Pfeifer, 2013). See also Chapter 7, in this book.

> "Hellöchen,[8] I am so, so happy that I can talk to you. . . . " I immediately become aware of a strong negative countertransference reaction connected with intense tension in my stomach and other averse bodily reactions. I observe some of my own thoughts: "What an overwhelming woman! I don't like this bodily contact. It is too much and not appropriate! Why did I offer her a session? Will I ever get rid of her again?" Then she asks me where she can find the toilet and perturbs me further by leaving the door open. Only when she finally sits down in her chair do I notice that she has a pretty, girlish face with a constant, sociable smile (according to Krause & Benecke, 2001) and a beautiful female body, although she is dressed like a man in simple jeans and a baggy, plain sweater. She is in her mid-forties.
>
> Ms. M. tells me that a general practitioner sent her to me because of a psychosomatic and psychic breakdown. For weeks, she has been suffering from anxiety and could not sleep or eat properly. She suffered from headaches and diffuse heart symptoms. She went to the doctor, convinced that she had a somatic illness, but he did not find anything. "I don't have any idea why I don't function anymore . . . I have always been a tough and perfectly functioning mother and social worker. . . . " When I ask her for the context of her breakdown, she finally mentions that on that extraordinary day her lover of one year, who is married to someone else, told her that he is moving to another city and will not be able to visit her every Friday night anymore. Only later in analysis did we understand that her "falling into a deep, deep hole . . . " was probably triggered by this unexpected experience of losing a (former) love object in combination with facing her 14-year-old daughter's process of adolescent separation and individuation.

My initial "empathy" for the patient, including the negative countertransference feelings, was based on what we call "embodied interaction": complex, unconscious sensorimotor interactions between two subjects (as with my intense bodily reactions and the tension in my stomach). These "embodied interactions" are the basis for a subsequent understanding of Ms. M.'s unconscious communication with the analyst. This

[8] A strange and infantile way to say "hi." The case summary was previously published in German in a modified form (Leuzinger-Bohleber, Henningsen, & Pfeifer, 2008), and will be published in a more extended version again in Leuzinger-Bohleber (in press). Personal details have been changed in order to guarantee confidentiality.

might also be called "embodied empathy" because empathy is not only a cognitive-affective process but also always "embodied."

Already in the very first interaction with Ms. M., in the "initial scene," as Hermann Argelander (1967/1987) characterized it, she "remembered" early traumatizations, but not through any sort of "verbal schemata." Instead, she acted out specific unconscious fantasies through sensorimotor-affective co-ordinations that became observable in her bodily enactments and in my countertransference reactions, although neither of us understood this as such at the time (see Leuzinger-Bohleber & Pfeifer, 2013; Pfeifer & Leuzinger-Bohleber, 1989, 1992). According to embodied cognitive science, memory is not to be conceived of as stored structures but as a function of the whole organism, as a complex, dynamic, recategorizing and interactive process that is always "embodied." It is important to note that sensorimotor, "embodied" co-ordination does not simply mean non-verbal: it implies that there is a *coupling* between the sensory and the motor processes, that is, a mutual influence. Biologically, this coupling is implemented via neural maps embedded in the sensorimotor systems of the organism. In this respect, William J. Clancey (1993) defines memory as the ability to organize neurological processes in such a way that they coordinate and, therefore, categorize sensory and motor processes in a way that is similar to past situations. This conceptualization of memory is central to the discussion of a main controversy within current psychoanalysis on the role of "historical versus narrative truth," particularly in dealing with trauma. Fonagy and Target, in examining the results of recent memory research, have postulated: "Whether there is historical truth and historical reality is not our business as psychoanalysts or psychotherapists" (Fonagy & Target, 1997, p. 216).[9]

---

[9] Fonagy and Target (1997) conclude their excellent overview "Perspectives on the Recovered Memories Debate" with the clarification that unconscious memory is implicit memory: "The psychotherapist or psychoanalyst's pressure on the patient to find the episodic roots of these memory traces is doomed to failure, as episodic experience is stored separately, without the significance for the determination of behavior, expectation, and belief that common-sense psychology attributes to it." They emphasize the fact that psychic change cannot be generated by the episodic roots of implicit memories:

Change will occur through the re-evaluation of mental models, or the understanding of self-other representations implicitly encoded as procedures in the human mind. Change is a change of form more than of content: therapy modifies procedures, ways of thinking, not thoughts. Insight

In my view their thesis has been contradicted by concepts developed through the valuable clinical research with traumatized patients and the empirical findings of several studies, as, for example, the DPV follow-up study (Leuzinger-Bohleber, Rüger, Stuhr, & Beutel, 2002) as well as the ongoing LAC depression study (Leuzinger-Bohleber, Röckerath, & Strauss, 2010). To summarize the conclusions of these studies, elaborated in detail elsewhere (Leuzinger-Bohleber, 2015b; Leuzinger-Bohleber, Henningsen, & Pfeifer, 2008; Leuzinger-Bohleber & Pfeifer, 2002), memory always consists of new and constructive processes in the "here and now" of a current interactional situation (system – environment – interaction) which is indispensable for constituting memories. At the same time, the constitution of memories is not arbitrary. They depend on how a given system-environment interaction is structured and the way the sensorimotor patterns are interpreted and determined by an individual's history. Memories are constructed by analogy to previous situations with similar sensorimotor patterns. Although this physical stimulation is always subject to interpretation, which varies depending on an individual's past, the sensory stimulation itself is still "objective" and not arbitrary. This is a consequence of embodiment. Sensorimotor states are, at least theoretically, measurable physical processes; sensorimotor co-ordination is established by the way the neural maps are integrated in a single organism and is thus also "objective." In this sense, memories result from constructive processes on the one hand but are influenced by the "historical truth" on the other hand, which means that, for example, the processes dealing with a (traumatic)

---

or new ideas, by themselves, cannot sustain change. The internalization of this therapeutic process as an indication for appropriate termination of therapy implies a change in mental models, an alteration of the hierarchical organization of implicit memory procedures. It is not necessarily associated with increased self-awareness as a specific self-conscious activity. Recovered memory therapies are in pursuit of a false goal. There can be only psychic reality behind the recovered memory – whether there is historical truth and historical reality is not our business as psychoanalysts or psychotherapists. (Fonagy & Target, 1997, p. 215f.)

Although I sympathize with the authors' political position and agree that psychoanalysts or psychotherapists should "avoid, wherever possible, becoming entangled in legal procedures concerning childhood sexual abuse" (Fonagy & Target, 1997, p. 209), I do not share all the conclusions from the studies in the field of embodied cognitive science mentioned above.

situation that formed first chronologically constrain the recategorization of the new analogous situation. Consequently, *recategorizations in later interactional situations are related to the original trauma.* Metaphorically, we could postulate that memory is always based on new and idiosyncratic (hermeneutic) narratives that take place in the present interactional situation, but at the same time memory contains traces of the "historical truth." To register, observe, reflect and finally understand this "historical truth" of the "embodied memories" can only take place by "embodied empathy," which means the careful and self-critical analysis of one's own "embodied countertransference" reactions in the assessment interviews as well as in the psychoanalytical sessions.

Embodied memory[10] is particularly interesting for understanding traumatized patients because trauma, due to its extreme quality and consequences, is also inscribed in the body in an extreme way (see Bohleber, 2000). As we know, the symbolization and verbalization of trauma is difficult and sometimes even impossible. Many psychoanalysts use the metaphor "Trauma is inscribed in the body." With the concept of "embodiment," cognitive scientists (Rolf Pfeifer and his group for example) and neuroscientists (e.g., Fuchs, Sattel, & Henningsen, 2010) try to describe the exact same phenomena. While we might observe this phenomenon in all of our patients, those patients that we consider "healthier" are the ones who are more flexible and dynamic with their recategorizations. Traumatic experiences are defined by their extreme quality which means that the functional recategorization and adaptation to new interactional situations is often limited, severely disturbed and sometimes even impossible. The trauma becomes observable in embodied memories and enactments as strange, bizarre and inadequate behavior as with Ms. M. in her first interaction with me. Embodiment opens a door for the analyst's professional empathy. Carefully observing his/her bodily reactions in the transference (his/her countertransference) is part

[10] This specific concept of embodied memory was new ten years ago and has been taken up by many authors in cognitive neuropsychology in the meantime, although its radical dimension has been greatly reduced.

of the process of trying to understand the traumatic background of the analysand, which, as is well known, is so hard to discover and to endure emotionally (see, e.g., Leuzinger-Bohleber, 2015b).

This means that Ms. M. does not enact a stored, unconscious memory of traumatic experiences with her primary object in the transference of a "statically stored, fixed, and verbal" unconscious truth: "I have to grab on quickly and blatantly to my love object demonstrating to her how grateful I am for being in contact with her – otherwise the love object abandons me, which means for me 'falling into a deep, deep hole', a catastrophe. . . . " Instead, *she constructs these memories by co-ordinating current sensorimotor stimulations in the interaction with the analyst, an important "other" upon whom she will be existentially dependent for several years in a way similar to her dependence on her primary object from the original traumatic situation.* In this manner – rushing through my office door, grasping my hand, etc. – Ms. M. "remembers" traumatic experiences of being overwhelmed and psychologically abused by the primary object and, later during adolescence, experiences of being sexually abused. My "embodied empathy" enables me, as I reflect on the current interaction with Ms. M., to finally understand the unconscious, enacted embodied memories of the patient.

Let me briefly summarize the insights that supported the first hypotheses during the five year long, intensive psychoanalysis. Of course, I only could understand these memories during psychoanalysis successively, particularly by analyzing my "embodied countertransference reactions": Before they were for the most part unknown (unconscious) to Ms. M.

3.1.1 "What an Overwhelming Woman!" Overriding the Normal Bodily Distance in a Strange and Kind of Sexually Weird Way, and Leaving the Door of the Toilet Open: Remembering Psychological and Sexual Abuse

Here is a summary of the most important biographical experiences of the analysand:

Shortly before his traumatic experiences during incarceration in Russia and his subsequent death by torture, Ms. M.'s 52-year-old father told her that he left his wife when Ms. M. was ten years old because he could not stand his spouse's bitterness and rigidity anymore. These traits of her mother were often a central issue during psychoanalysis. For a long time she protected her mother from critical observations and guarded her own unconscious knowledge of *how terribly she had suffered due to her mother's lack of empathy and warmth for her as a child and how destructive the chronic psychic abuse had been.* Her mother's miserable childhood as an orphan in WWI, the years during WWII and a dramatic rape in 1945 provide Ms. M. with "explanations" for her "mother's problems and deficiencies." During the third year of treatment, dreams led to the hypothesis that she might have witnessed her mother being raped, a hypothesis which was strengthened when she asked her mother about the incident: When she was three-years old she observed her mother being raped by three Russian soldiers in a very cruel and frightening way. Her mother now told her how traumatizing this event had been for her: "Since this experience I hated and detested my female body and never wanted sexuality again, perhaps one reason for the failure of our marriage," her mother said.

Ms. M. grew into the role of the "perfect daughter," while her brother seemed to withdraw from family life. He failed in school and immigrated to Canada when he was 18. In contrast, Ms. M. became the "the apple of her mother's eye" ["*Augapfel*"] and tried to please her by getting good grades in school, particularly in art and music. Until the age of 16 she slept in the "marriage bed" with her mother and spent her spare time and holidays almost exclusively with her. When she was 15, her uncle abused her sexually in his studio where she took art lessons. She did not resist. Only during psychoanalysis did she realize how harmful these experiences had been for her. She had felt guilty and responsible for the abuse "because I was longing for love and tenderness so much. I was not able to fight for normal boundaries." Afterward, she developed a variety of psychosomatic symptoms: migraines, sleep disturbances, and bulimia. At that time she did not receive any professional help.

Despite her symptoms, she managed to finish school successfully and started attending university, still living with her mother. The 1968 student revolts afforded her at least a minimal (physical) distanciation from her mother. She moved into a shared flat with other female students and had numerous sexual affairs. This behavior might be seen as being of a promiscuous nature. She was exposed several times to cruel and dangerous situations. In psychoanalysis, she understood that these had been enactments in a severe state of dissociation. In this "strange state of mind," she enacted unconscious fantasies connected to the rape of her mother. Psychodynamically, she seemed to "prove" her unconscious truth: "I do not deserve a better fate than my mother." She had seven abortions within 10 years.

Once she finished university, she chose very stressful jobs working with adolescents with drug abuse problems and in juvenile detention centers. She also worked with extremely ill cancer patients and for the past ten years now she has been working with juvenile delinquents from high-risk areas in her city. In treatment, we came to understand that the "flight into an extremely stressful 12-hour work day" was an unconscious attempt to live her own life in her own apartment separate from her mother. It was also a manic defense against severe depression. Although she longed for a family of her own and had numerous love relations, she always had to break them off after a short period of time.

At the age of 35, she adopted a severely handicapped girl, Anna. She moved into the same house as her mother who then took care of the child while Ms. M. was at work during the day. At the age of 38, she unexpectedly became pregnant again. "Of course" she planned another abortion. But after Anna nearly died from an asthma attack, it became clear to Ms. M. how fragile the equilibrium of her life was and how real a breakdown of that equilibrium would be if she lost Anna. Thus, she decided to give birth to the child. Raising her younger, healthy daughter Marion and Anna became the common center of her and her mother's lives. They bought a house together and established an "open door" policy, which meant always keeping all the doors in the house open (e.g., they never closed the door to the bathroom while urinating). Their life together was characterized by harmony on the surface and a shared sense of purpose [*Lebenssinn*]. They even shared Ms. M.'s lover who seemed to be as equally attached to Ms. M. as he was to her mother. They seemed to have found a kind of a stable balance until Marion entered adolescent development and the simultaneous sudden loss of the boyfriend, a "good friend of the whole family." The combination of the two provoked Ms. M.'s severe crisis and psychic breakdown.

3.1.2 "Will I Ever Be Able to Get Rid of Her Again . . . ". Remembering and Denying Traumatic Early Separations?

Other "embodied memories" seemed to be connected to Ms. M.'s early traumatic loss of the primary object. Again, this was only understood after many, many psychoanalytic sessions. Shortly after her birth in 1942, Ms. M.'s mother received news that her husband was missing in action on the Russian front, which was one reason for her psychic breakdown and her incapacity to care for and breast feed her baby. After three months of severe depression, she gave the baby to her mother-in-law, a "hard and staunch National Socialist." Years later, this same mother-in-law would still report proudly that she "educated her granddaughters strictly following Johanna Harer's book," *Die deutsche Mutter und ihr erstes Kind* (The German Mother and Her First Child). To mention just one example, the baby was locked in the basement for two nights where her crying could not be heard: "Afterwards she never cried at night anymore." In general, the young Ms. M. developed into a strikingly well-educated and brave little girl. At the age of one, she was already clean, obedient and "easy to take care of," which were some of the reasons why her psychically instable mother dared to take her back at the end of 1944.

We finally understood in analysis that the loss of her lover was probably due to the unconscious recollection of the early traumas of living with a severely depressive primary object and finally losing her – an experience of despair and panic, "falling into a deep, deep hole." In the initial interview, she also seemed to remember that making contact with an "important Other" whom you depend on can only be done by grabbing on to her, holding her tight and playing the grateful "sunshine child." In my countertransference fantasy of "How can I ever get rid of her," I unconsciously perceived the message that the patient had gone through an early traumatic object loss, an experience that should not be repeated in the therapeutic relationship.

3.2 Conceptual Considerations on "Embodied Empathy," Memory, Trauma and Depression: A Dialogue Between Psychoanalysis and Embodied Cognitive Science

As discussed above, the "objective" biographical information (the mother's depressive illness, early separation in the first weeks of her life, sexual abuse, etc.) proved to be helpful in Ms. M.'s psychoanalytic sessions to finally recognize the traces of these "historical traumata" in her current behavior (e.g., seeing the similarities between her current psychosomatic and emotional reactions and those of a baby interacting with a depressive, helpless mother and then trying to be her "sunshine" in order to revitalize the "dead mother"; see for instance Green, 1999; Stern, 1995). Thus, stable therapeutic change in our patients depends on both approaches: understanding the idiosyncratic ways of unconscious functioning (see Bollas, 1992; Green, 1999; Hinshelwood, 1991; Laub, 2005; Sandler & Sandler, 1997) and recategorizations as well as the attempt to understand the highly individual, biographical (historical) truth as the "specific, undeniable reality of trauma" (see also Bohleber, 2000; 2005; Fischer & Riedesser, 1998; van der Kolk, McFarlane, & Weisaeth, 1996).[11]

[11] To reiterate this central argument, experiences and memories have an objective and a subjective aspect. The *objective* one is given by patterns of sensory stimulation in a particular sensorimotor interaction, which is, in principle, physically measurable. The *subjective* aspect refers to how individual experiences associated with these patterns are determined by an individual's history. The sensory stimulation to which the organism is 'objectively' exposed is not a matter of passively undergoing physical stimulation but it is rather generated as the organism interacts with its environment. The resulting patterns of sensory stimulation are structured as a consequence of this interaction and contain correlations which can be easily interpreted by neural mechanisms. The types of interactions are in turn a result of developmental processes. The experiences of extreme pain and bodily unease and loneliness, all experiences that Ms. M. went through as a baby in her first three months, have a determining influence because the developmental processes strongly depend on the adequacy, richness, and structure of sensory stimulation. This might be one of the reasons for her chronic manic defense: her constant attempts at self-stimulation and her neglecting any signs of exhaustion, tiredness, etc. until the "total breakdown" mentioned above. Thus, the coupling with sensorimotor mechanisms provides the basis from which the developmental processes can be bootstrapped.

Another finding by Suomi (2010) is also highly relevant to psychoanalysts. He was also able to show that undoing the separation trauma in baby monkeys might 'undo' neurobiological and

The following graph illustrates the importance of "unconscious embodied memories" in psychoanalytic treatment and the vital role they play in therapeutic transformations. They may be understood by an analysis of the analogies between the sensorimotor co-ordinations in the current recent past (the psychic state which was triggered after the loss of the lover in Ms. M.), and the past (the loss of the primary object due to her severe depression and afterward by the real separation from her mother). As discussed above, this analysis does not concern the analogy between cognitive structures (as originally postulated, e.g., by Karl Menninger in his famous "Menninger triangle of insight"; see Leuzinger-Bohleber & Pfeifer, 2002) but the analogies in the sensorimotor co-ordinations, the "embodied" reactions occurring in the transference situation, the current and the past (traumatic) interaction with a beloved person as well (analyst, lover, mother). Other insights into similar processes were important in understanding how the embodied memories connected with the traumatic loss of the father, the sexual abuse by the uncle as well as the rape of the mother. All these unconscious embodied memories had unconsciously contributed to producing Ms. M.'s breakdown (Fig. 3.2).

4 Summary

How can "embodied empathy" then be understood? After a discussion on the critical place of empathy (concerning the clinical situation) in the psychoanalytical debate and a systematic consideration of research on the role of empathy of the primary care giver for the development of the self, the attachment, and the capability to mentalize, I tried to illustrate what "embodied empathy" concretely means by a clinical example. Remembering traumatic childhood experiences can only recur in a new interaction with a "meaningful other" (that is to say in the

---

behavioral damage. This is, of course, a revolutionary finding for all forms of early prevention and psychotherapy, even though his results are based on studies involving animals. These interdisciplinary findings are a strong motivating force behind several ongoing studies on early prevention with at-risk families at the Sigmund-Freud-Institute (see www.sigmund-freud-institut.de).

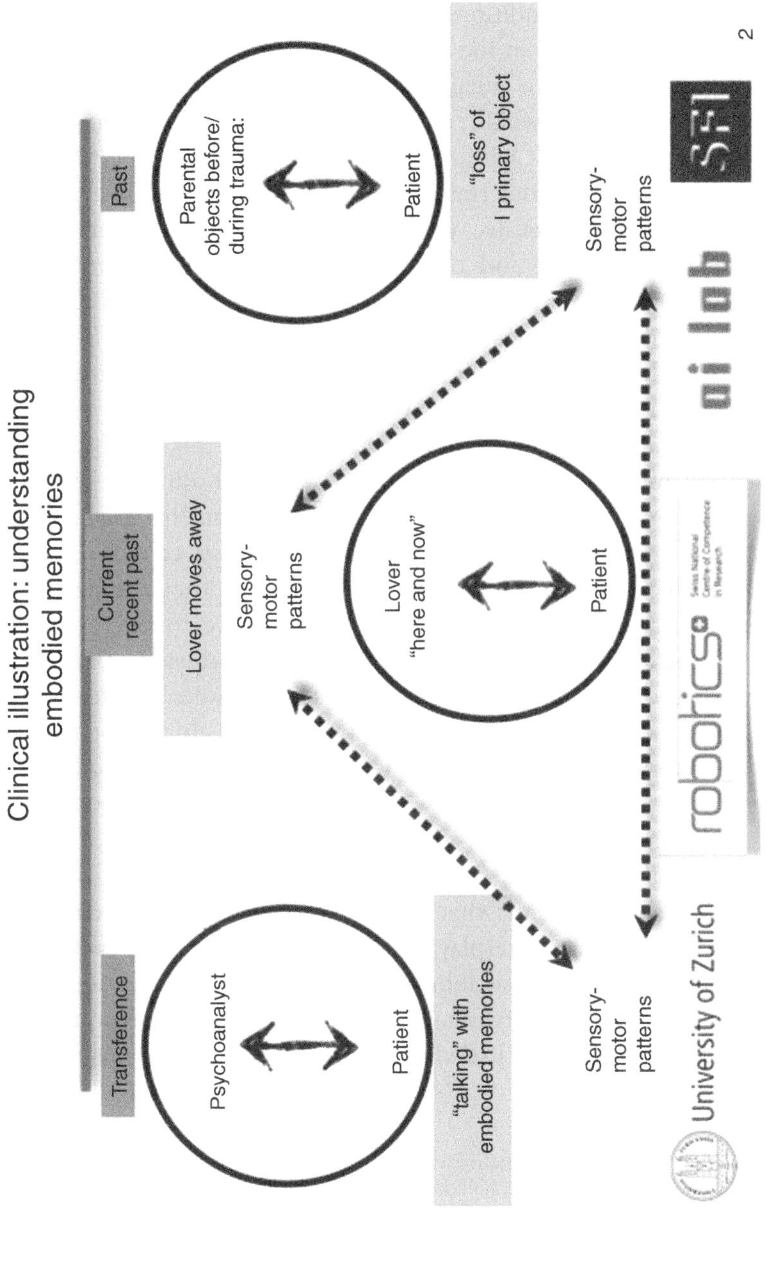

Fig. 3.2 Understanding embodied memories

transference to the analyst). A situative, constructive understanding of interactions is the precondition for remembering. Remembering is also dependent on a dialogue in the inner and outside reality with an object, an interactive process, an integrative, "embodied" experience between two persons. Ms. M. would not have been able to remember her traumata alone by herself lying in bed at home.[12]

The unconscious but determining influence of early trauma can only be studied through intensive work with traumatized patients in the psychoanalytic situation and enables psychoanalysis to communicate these discoveries in an interdisciplinary dialogue with developmental and epigenetic researchers, for example (see Leuzinger-Bohleber, 2015b). On the other hand, it seems that clinical research in psychoanalysis from the last few decades has gained interdisciplinary support from biologically oriented memory research. And this psychoanalytic research postulates more and more radically that only by working through traumatic experiences in early object relations by means of the *transference according to a specific technique of treatment* can we achieve a structural change in our patients. It seems that the findings from neuroscience and embodied cognitive science prove to be "externally coherent" (Strenger, 1991) with psychoanalytic conclusions.

In this respect, the interdisciplinary dialogue between psychoanalysis and neuroscience can be fruitful and innovative. In this chapter, I was not able to touch upon the ambitious epistemological and methodological problems that are, of course, connected to this dialogue, but I discussed them elsewhere (see, e.g., Leuzinger-Bohleber, 2015b; Leuzinger-Bohleber, Emde, & Pfeifer, 2013). It is interesting that the old psychoanalytic dialectic that attempts to understand psychic phenomena in the complex interplay between mind and body, genetics and environment, biology and sociology, is again a central dimension in the contemporary dialogue between psychoanalysis and the neurosciences. Trauma and depression, as I tried to illustrate in the psychoanalysis with

[12] See also results from recent trauma research, for example, Brenneis (1994), Brooks-Brenneis (1997), Kihlstrom (1994), Leuzinger-Bohleber (2010, 2015b), Leuzinger-Bohleber, Henningsen, & Pfeifer (2008), Leuzinger-Bohleber & Pfeifer (2002, 2013); Leuzinger-Bohleber, Röckerath, & Strauss (2010), Person & Klar (1994), van der Kolk, McFarlane, & Weisaeth (1996).

Ms. M., have unconscious, "embodied" determinants as well as societal ones: Ms. M. was one of many traumatized children from the WWII period, whom German psychoanalysts have had in treatment. Understanding the complex and highly individual interactions between all these unconscious determinants in the psychoanalytical situation has proven to be indispensable for overcoming depression and for at least diminishing the influence of early trauma. In my experience, the interdisciplinary dialogue with neuroscientists or embodied cognitive scientists can even aid in discovering and understanding the unconscious worlds of our psychoanalytic patients.

I would like to conclude with a personal remark. Based on my experiences, a productive interdisciplinary dialogue also can be looked at from a psychoanalytical perspective. This can only happen if the participating researchers share a mature, high level of psychic functioning, and if they experience their interdisciplinary partner as an independent "Other," that is, as separate and as an object (and specifically not as a "self-object") in a psychoanalytical sense. In this case, curiosity and a spirit of joint investigation can occur and overcome the desire or fear of being consumed or "eaten up" by the partner and thereby losing one's own self and identity. Only in this case can the "Eros" of interdisciplinary cooperation defeat its counterpart "Thanatos," as Freud taught us in a different context.

Translation: Alice Färber

References

Ainsworth, M.D.S., Bell, S.M., & Stayton, D.J. (1974). Infant-mother attachment and social development: Socialisation as a product of reciprocal responsiveness to signals. In M.P.M. Richards (Ed.). *The integration of a child into a social world* (pp. 99–135). London: Cambridge University Press.

Argelander, H. (1967/1987). *Das Erstinterview in der Psychotherapie* [The initial psychotherapy interview] (3., unveränd. Aufl.). Darmstadt: Wissenschaftliche Buchgesellschaft.

Bahrke, U., Beutel, M., Fiedler, G., Haas, A., Hautzinger, M., Kallenbach, L., Keller, W., Leuzinger-Bohleber, M., Negele, A., Rüger, B., & Schött, M. (2013). Psychoanalytische und kognitiv-verhaltenstherapeutische

Langzeittherapien bei chronischer Depression (LAC) [Psychoanalytic and cognitive-behavioral long-term therapy of chronic depression]. In M. Leuzinger-Bohleber, U. Bahrke & A. Negele (Eds.). *Chronische Depression. Verstehen – Behandeln – Erforschen* [Chronic depression. Comprehend – Treat – Research] (pp. 217–239). Göttingen: Vandenhoeck & Ruprecht.

Baron-Cohen, S. (1995). *Mindblindness. An essay on Autism and Theory of Mind.* Cambridge, MA: MIT Press.

Bartsch, K. & Wellman, H.M. (1989). Young children's attribution of action to beliefs and desires. *Child Development, 60*, 946–964.

Beeghly, M. & Cicchetti, D. (1994). Child maltreatment, attachment, and the self system: Emergence of an internal state lexicon in toddlers at high social risk. *Development and Psychopathology, 6*, 5–30.

Bion, W. R. (1962). *Learning from experience.* New York, NY: Basic Books.

Bohleber, W. (2000). Die Entwicklung der Traumatheorie in der Psychoanalyse [The development of trauma theory in psychoanalysis]. *Psyche – Z Psychoanal, 54*, 797–839.

Bohleber, W. (2005). Zur Psychoanalyse der Depression [Psychoanalysis of depression]. *Psyche – Z Psychoanal, 59*, 781–788.

Bohleber, W. (2013). The concept of intersubjectivity in psychoanalysis: Taking critical stock. *International Journal of Psychoanalysis, 94*, 799–823.

Bollas, C. (1992). *Being a character: Psychoanalysis and self experience.* New York: Hill & Wang.

Bolognini, S. (2007). Probleme der psychoanalytischen Einfühlung. Eine theoretisch-klinische Studie [Problems of psychoanalytic empathy. A theoretical-clinical study]. *Psyche –Z Psychoanal, 61*, 864–888.

Bowlby, J. (1958). The nature of the child's tie to its mother. *International Journal of Psychoanalysis, 39*, 350–373.

Brenneis, B. (1994). Belief and suggestion in the recovery of memories of childhood sexual abuse. *Journal of the American Psychoanalytic Association, 42*, 1027–1053.

Brentano, F. (1874/1973). *Psychology from an empirical standpoint.* London: Routledge and Kegan Paul.

Bretherton, I. (1985). Attachment theory: Retrospect and prospect. In I. Bretherton & F. Waters (Eds.). *Growing points of attachment theory and research* (pp. 3–35). Monographs of the Society for Research in Child Development, 50 (1–2, Serial No. 209).

Brooks-Brenneis, C. (1997). *Recovered memories of trauma: Transferring the present to the past.* New York: International Universities Press.

Buie, D.H. (1981). Empathy: its nature and limitations. *Journal of the American Psychoanalytic Association, 29*, 281–307.

Clancey, W.J. (1993). The biology of consciousness: Comparative review of Israel Rosenfield. *The Strange, Familiar; and Forgotten: An Anatomy of Consciousness* and Gerald M. Edelman, *Bright Air, Brilliant Fire: On the Matter of the Mind. Artificial Intelligence, 60*, 313–356.

Clarkin, J.F. & Lenzenweger, M.F. (Eds.) (1996). *Major Theories of Personality Disorders*. New York: Guilford Press.

Coplan, A. & Goldie, P. (Eds.) (2011). *Philosophical and psychological perspectives*. Oxford: Oxford University Press.

Crittenden, P.M. (1990). Internal representational models of attachment relationships. *Infant Mental Health Journal, 11*, 259–277.

Dennett, D.C. (1978). Beliefs about beliefs, *Behaviour and Brain Sciences, 4*, 568–570.

Dias, M.G. & Harris, P.L. (1990). The influence of the imagination on reasoning by young children. *British Journal of Developmental Psychology, 8*, 305–318.

Emde, R.N. & Leuzinger-Bohleber, M. (Eds.) (2014). *Early Parenting Research and Prevention of Disorder: Psychoanalytic Research at Interdisciplinary Frontiers*. London: Karnac Books.

Fischer, G. & Riedesser, P. (1998). *Lehrbuch der Psychotraumatologie* [Textbook of psychotraumatology]. Munich, Basel: Reinhardt.

Fonagy, P. (2007). Violent Attachment. Unpublished lecture given at the conference *In Gewalt verstrickt – psychoanalytische, pädagogische und philosophische Erkundungen*, Universität Kassel, 9./10.2.2007.

Fonagy, P. & Target, M. (1997). Perspectives on the recovered memories debate. In J. Sandler & P. Fonagy (Eds.). *Recovered memories of abuse: True or false?* (pp. 183–217). London: Karnac Books.

Fonagy, P. & Target, M. (2003). *Psychoanalyse und die Psychopathologie der Entwicklung* [Psychoanalytic theories: Perspective from developmental psychopathology]. Stuttgart: Klett-Cotta.

Fonagy, P., Steele H., & Steele M. (1991). Maternal representations of attachment during pregnancy predict the organization of infant-mother attachment at one year of age. *Child Development, 62*, 891–905.

Fonagy, P., Steele, M., Steele, H., Moran, G.S., & Higgitt, A.C. (1991). The capacity for understanding mental states: The reflective self in parent and child and its significance for security of attachment. *Infant Mental Health Journal, 13*, 200–217.

Freud, A. (1965). *Normality and pathology in childhood.* New York: International Universities Press.
Freud, A. & Burlingham, D. (1951). *Heimatlose Kinder. Zur Anwendung psychoanalytischen Wissens auf die Kindererziehung* [Infants without families. Applying psychoanalytic knowledge to parenting]. Frankfurt/Main: S. Fischer.
Freud, S. (1900/1953). *The interpretation of dreams.* Standard Edition of the Complete Pschological Works of Sigmund *Freud* (Vol. 4, ed. by J. Strachey, in collaboration with A. Feud). London: Hogarth Press.
Freud, S. (1912f./1955). *Totem and Taboo.* Standard Edition of the Complete Pschological Works of Sigmund *Freud* (Vol. 13). London: Hogarth Press.
Freud, S. (1921/1955). Group psychology and the analysis of the ego. In *Standard Edition of the Complete Pschological Works of* Sigmund *Freud* (Vol. 18, pp. 65–144). London: Hogarth Press.
Fuchs, T., Sattel, H.C., & Henningsen, P. (Eds.) (2010). *The embodied self: Dimensions, coherence and disorders.* Stuttgart: Schattauer.
Gopnik, A. (1993). How we know our minds: The illusion of first-person knowledge of intentionality. *Behavioral and Brain Sciences, 16*, 1–14.
Gopnik, A. & Astington, J.W. (1988). Children's Understanding of Representational Change and Its Relation to the Understanding of False Belief and the Appearance-Reality Distinction. *Child Development, 59*(1), 26–37.
Grant, D. & Harari, E. (2011). Empathy in psychoanalytic theory and practice. *Psychoanalytic Inquiry, 31*, 3–16.
Green, A. (1999). The greening of psychoanalysis: André Green in dialogues with Gregorio Kohon. In G. Kohon (Ed.). *The dead mother: The work of André Green* (pp. 10–58). London, New York: Routledge.
Greenson, R. R. (1960). Empathy and its vicissitudes. *International Journal of Psychoanalysis, 41*, 418–424.
Grossmann, K.E., August, P., Fremmer-Brombik, E., Freidl, A., Grossmann, K., Scheuerer-Englisch, H., Spangler, G., Stephan, C., & Suess, G. (1989). Die Bindungstheorie: Modell und entwicklungspsychologische Forschung [Attachment theory: model and research in development psychology]. In H. Keller (Ed.). *Handbuch der Kleinkindforschung* [Compendium of infant studies] (pp. 31–55). Berlin et al.: Springer.
Heimann, P. (1950). On counter-transference. *International Journal of Psychoanalysis, 31*, 80–84.
Hinshelwood, R.D. (1991). *A dictionary of Kleinian thought* (2nd ed.). London: Free Association Books.

Hopkins, J. (1992). Psychoanalysis, interpretation, and science. In J. Hopkins & A. Saville (Eds.). *Psychoanalysis, mind and art: Perspectives on Richard Wolheim* (pp. 3–34). Oxford: Blackwell.

Kelman, H. (1987). On resonant cognition. *International Review of Psychoanalysis, 14*, 111–123.

Kihlstrom, J.F. (1994). Hypnosis, delayed recall and the principles of memory. *International Journal of Clinical and Experimental Hypnosis, 42*, 337–345.

Klein, M. (1959/1977). Our adult world and its roots in infancy. In *Envy and gratitude and other works* (pp. 247–263). New York: Delta.

Kohut, H. (1959). Introspection, empathy, and psychoanalysis: an examination of the relationship between mode of observation and theory. *Journal of the American Psychoanalytic Association, 7*, 459–483.

Kohut, H. (1965). Autonomy and integration. *Journal of the American Psychoanalytic Association, 13*, 851–856.

Krause, R. & Benecke, C. (2001). Fühlen und Affektausdruck. Das affektive Geschehen in der Behandlung von Herrn P. [Feelings and expressions. Affekt in the Treatment of Mr. P.] *Psychotherapie und Sozialwissenschaft, 3*, 52–73.

Laub, D. (2005). 'Traumatic shutdown of narrative and symbolization: A death instinct derivative? *Contemporary Psychoanalysis, 41*, 307–326.

Leuzinger-Bohleber, M. (2007). Forschende Grundhaltung als abgewehrter "common ground" von psychoanalytischen Praktikern und Forschern? [The explorative attitude as repelled "common ground" of psychoanalytic practitioners and researchers]. *Psyche – Z Psychoanal, 61*, 966–994.

Leuzinger-Bohleber, M. (2009). *Frühe Kindheit als Schicksal? Trauma, Embodiment, Soziale Desintegration. Psychoanalytische Perspektiven*[Earl childhood as destiny? Trauma,embodiment, social desintegration. Psychoanalytic perspectives]. Stuttgart: Kohlhammer.

Leuzinger-Bohleber, M. (2010). Depression and trauma – a transgenerational psychoanalytical perspective. Unpublished paper, 1st Asian Conference of the IPA: *Freud and Asia. Evolution and Change: Psychoanalysis in the Asian Context*, Peking, 23.10.2010.

Leuzinger-Bohleber, M. (2014). Social Emotional Risk Factors. *Child Indicators Research, 7*(4), 715–734.

Leuzinger-Bohleber, M. (2015a). *Finding the Body in the Mind – Embodied Memories, Trauma, and Depression.* International Psychoanalytical Association, London: Karnac Books.

Leuzinger-Bohleber, M. (2015b). Working with severely traumatized, chronically depressed analysands. *International Journal of Psychoanalysis, 96*(3), 611–636.

Leuzinger-Bohleber, M. (in press). "Embodied memories" – Enactments – "szenisches Verstehen" – Annäherungen an transgenerative Mechanismen bei der Weitergabe schwerer Traumatisierungen ["Embodied memories" – enactments – "scenic understanding" – Approaching transgenerative mechanisms of trauma transmission]. In M. Leuzinger-Bohleber, S. Arnold, U. Bahrke, T. Fischmann, & S. Hau (Eds.). *Migration, Flucht und Trauma. Die Folgen für die nächste Generation* [Migration, flight, and trauma. Impacts on the next generation]. Göttingen: Vandenhoeck & Ruprecht.

Leuzinger-Bohleber, M. & Bürgin, D. (2003). Pluralism and unity in psychoanalytic research: Some introductory remarks. In M. Leuzinger-Bohleber, A.U. Dreher, & J. Canestri (Eds.). *Pluralism and unity? Methods of research in psychoanalysis. (The international psychoanalysis library)* (pp. 1–25). London: International Psychoanalytical Association.

Leuzinger-Bohleber, M. & Pfeifer, R. (2002). Remembering a depressive primary object? Memory in the dialogue between psychoanalysis and cognitive science. *International Journal of Psychoanalysis, 83*, 3–33.

Leuzinger-Bohleber M. & Pfeifer, R. (2011). Minding the traumatized body – clinical lessons from embodied intelligence. Unpublished paper, Berlin, 12th International Neuropsychoanalysis Congress "Neuropsychoanalysis: Minding the Body", 25.6.2011.

Leuzinger-Bohleber, M. & Pfeifer, R. (2013). Psychoanalyse und Embodied Cognitive Science in Zeiten revolutionären Umdenkens. Erinnern, Übertragung, therapeutische Veränderung und "embodied metaphors" [Psychoanalysis and embodied cognitive science in times of revolutionary reconceptualizations. Remembering, transmission, therapeutic change, "embodied metaphors"]. In M. Leuzinger-Bohleber, R.N. Emde, & R. Pfeifer (Eds.). *Embodiment – ein revolutionäres Konzept? Implikationen für frühe Elternschaft, Frühprävention und Psychotherapie* [Embodiment – a revolutionary concept? Implications for early parenthood, prevention, and psychotherapy] (pp. 39–74). Göttingen: Vandenhoeck & Ruprecht.

Leuzinger-Bohleber, M., Emde, R.N., & Pfeifer, R. (eds) (2013) *Embodiment-ein revolutionäres Konzept? Implikationen für frühe Elternschaft, Frühprävention und Psychotherapie* [Embodiment – a revolutionary concept? Implications for early parenthood, prevention, and psychotherapy]. Göttingen: Vandenhoeck & Ruprecht.

Leuzinger-Bohleber, M., Henningsen, P., & Pfeifer, R. (2008). Die psychoanalytische Konzeptforschung zum Trauma und die Gedächtnisforschung der Embodied Cognitive Science [The psychoanalytic research on the conceptualization of trauma and memory research in embodied cognitive science]. In M. Leuzinger-Bohleber, G. Roth, & A. Buchheim (Eds.). *Psychoanalyse – Neurobiologie – Trauma* [Psychoanalysis – Neurobiology – Trauma] (pp. 157–71). Stuttgart: Schattauer.

Leuzinger-Bohleber, M., Röckerath, K., & Strauss, L.V. (Eds.) (2010). *Depression und Neuroplastizität. Psychoanalytische Klinik und Forschung* [Depression and neuroplasticity. Psychoanalytic clinical practice and research]. Frankfurt/Main: Brandes & Apsel.

Leuzinger-Bohleber, M., Rüger, B., Stuhr, U., & Beutel, M. (2002). *"Forschen und heilen" in der Psychoanalyse. Ergebnisse und Berichte aus Forschung und Praxis* ["Research and healing" in psychoanalysis. Findings and reports from research and praxis]. Stuttgart: Kohlhammer.

Mahler, M.S., Pine, F., & Bergman, A. (1978). *Die psychische Geburt des Menschen. Symbiose und Individuation* [The psychic birth of man. Symbiosis and individuation]. Frankfurt/Main: Fischer.

Main, M., Kaplan, N., & Cassidy, J. (1985). Security in infancy, childhood, and adulthood: A move to the level of representation. *Monographs of the Society for Research in Child Development, 50*(1–2), 66–104.

Meissner, W.W. (2010). Some notes on the epistemology of empathy. *Psychoanalytic Quarterly, 79*, 421–469.

Nelson, K. & Gruendel, J.M. (1981). Generalized event representations: Basic building blocks of cognitive development. In M.E. Lamb & A.L. Brown (Eds.). *Advances in developmental psychology* (Vol.1, pp. 131–158). Hillsdale, NJ: Lawrence Erlbaum Associates.

Ogden, T. H. (1979). On projective identification. *International Journal of Psychoanalysis, 60*, 357–373.

Ornstein, P.H. (2011). The centrality of empathy in psychoanalysis. *Psychoanalytic Inquiry, 31*, 437–447.

Perner, J., Leekam, S.R., & Wimmer, H. (1987). Three-year-olds' difficulty with false belief: The case for a conceptual deficit. *British Journal of Developmental Psychology, 5*(2), 125–137.

Person, E.S. & Klar, H. (1994). Establishing trauma: The difficulty distinguishing between memories and fantasies. *Journal of the American Psychoanalytic Association, 42*, 1055–1081.

Pfeifer, R. & Leuzinger-Bohleber, M. (1989). Motivations- und Emotionsstörungen: ein Cognitive Science Ansatz. Teil I: Theoretische Überlegungen [Motivational deficiency and affective disorders: a cognitive science approach]. *Zeitschrift für Klinische Psychologie, Psychopathologie und Psychotherapie, 37*, 40–73.

Pfeifer, R. & Leuzinger-Bohleber, M. (1992). A dynamic view of emotion with an application to the classification of emotional disorders. In M. Leuzinger-Bohleber, H. Schneider, & R. Pfeifer (Eds.). *"Two butterflies on my head . . . " Psychoanalysis in the interdisciplinary scientific dialogue* (pp. 215–45). New York: Springer.

Sandler, J. & Sandler, A.-M. (1997). A psychoanalytic theory of repression and the unconscious. In J. Sandler & P. Fonagy (Eds.). *Recovered memories of abuse: True or false?* (pp. 173–81). London: Karnac Books.

Schafer, R. (1959). Generative empathy in the treatment situation. *Psychoanalytic Quarterly, 28*, 342–73.

Sroufe, L.A. (1996). *Emotional development: The organization of emotional life in the early years.* New York: Cambridge University Press.

Spitz, R.E. (1965). *The first year of life.* New York: International Universities Press.

Stern, D. (1995). *Die Mutterschaftskonstellation. Eine vergleichende Darstellung verschiedener Formen der Mutter-Kind-Psychotherapie* [The motherhood constellation. A comparative description of forms of mother-child therapy]. Stuttgart: Klett-Cotta.

Strenger, C. (1991). *Between hermeneutics and science: An essay on the epistemology of psychoanalysis.* New York: International Universities Press.

Suomi, S. (2010). Trauma and epigenetics. Unpublished paper given at the 11th Joseph Sandler Research Conference: *Persisting shadows of early and later trauma*, Frankfurt/Main, February 7, 2010.

Tansey, M.H. & Burke, W.F. (1985). Projective identification and the empathic process: interactional communications. *Contemporary Psychoanalysis, 21*, 42–69.

Tansey, M.H. & Burke, W.F. (1989). *Understanding countertransference: From projective identification to empathy.* Hillsdale: Analytic Press.

van der Kolk, B., McFarlane, A.C. & Weisaeth, L. (Eds.) (1996). *Traumatic stress: The effects of overwhelming experience on mind, body, and society.* New York: Guilford Press.

van IJzendoorn, M., Frenkel, O.J., Goldberg, S., & Kroonenberg, S. (1992). The relative effects of maternal and child problems on the quality of

attachment: A meta-analysis of attachment in clinical samples. *Child Development, 63*(4), 840–858.
Winnicott, D.W. (1971). *Playing and reality*. London: Tavistock Publications.
Wollheim, R. (1999). *On the emotions*. New Haven: Yale University Press.
Zanocco, G., de Marchi, A., & Pozzi, F. (2006). Sensory empathy and enactment. *International Journal of Psychoanalysis, 87*, 145–158.

4

Empathy and Other Minds – A Neuropsychoanalytic Perspective and a Clinical Vignette

Mark Solms

My starting point is the well-known philosophical problem of other minds: if one has access only to one's own mind (since the mind is intrinsically subjective) then how does one know the mental state of others? The obvious answer is that one does so by *empathy*, to the extent that one does so at all. This makes empathy important for psychology – the science of the mind – a discipline that aspires to objective knowledge about subjectivity.

The discovery of mirror neurons was a major step forward (Di Pellegrino, Fadiga, Fogassi, Gallese, & Rizzolatti, 1992; Gallese, Fadiga, Fogassi, & Rizzolatti, 1996). Mirror neurons seemed to provide a mechanism by means of which the subject perceives directly the intentional states of others, in a manner not fundamentally different to how we perceive the objective states of things (Fogassi et al., 2005). We are told by the discoverers that the pattern of premotor neuronal activity

---

M. Solms (✉)
Psychology Department, University of Cape Town, Rondebosch, Cape Town, South Africa
e-mail: Mark.Solms@uct.ac.za

V. Lux, S. Weigel (eds.), *Empathy*, Palgrave Studies in the Theory and History of Psychology, DOI 10.1057/978-1-137-51299-4_4

producing the movements of others is simply mirrored in some of our own premotor neurons, and their intentionality is thereby reproduced in us. This mirroring mechanism is called "embodied simulation" (see Chapter 7). There is no reason to doubt that such things happen. But empathy is a lot more complicated than that. Embodied simulation describes only the simplest form of mind reading. We could call it proto-empathy. In this paper, I want to discuss the mechanism of empathy proper and show how radically it differs from embodied simulation. *Empathy proper* is difficult to achieve. For this reason, what I am going to describe is better thought of as a *process* than a mechanism – a process through which the subject gradually comes to know the minds of others, or not, as the case may be.

1 What Is Empathy?

It is well known that the concept of empathy has shifted somewhat over time, between languages and across disciplines. The mechanism in aesthetics by which the viewing subject *projects* its intentional state into inanimate objects (for which the German term *Einfühlung* was initially used) became a mechanism in psychology by which the subject *apperceives* the intentional states of others (for which the English term "empathy" was used, on the model of *Einfühlung*). The distinction between "empathy" (feeling into) and "sympathy" (feeling with) was blurred in this disciplinary transition, mainly due to the fact that psychological objects possess subjective intentionality whereas aesthetic objects, despite appearances, do not; artworks are actually as dead as doornails. This raises the possibility of empathic *error* in psychology: it is possible to misperceive the state of another mind in ways that do not arise with the appreciation of a landscape. Who is to say whether a willow is weeping?[1]

[1] Misperception of the intentionality *of the artist* (as opposed to the artwork) is another matter entirely. Also, artists can represent their intentions poorly.

The change in the directionality of empathy (from aesthetic projection to psychological apperception) was only apparent, though. This is reducible to the problem of error. In both the aesthetic and the psychological cases, the subject attributes its own states to objects; the empathising subject "feels its way into" objects, not the other way round. When the objects in question are other minds, the subject may get the feelings of the object wrong. This is misperception of feeling. But when the objects in question are inanimate artworks, the subject always gets the feelings wrong (artworks do not ever really possess feelings). In this respect, the mechanism of empathy remains the same; it is always projective, albeit constrained by error – but also hopefully able to be corrected.

This rule applies even in the case of embodied simulation – what I am calling *proto-empathy* – which purportedly involves *direct* perception of the intentional state of others. When the pattern of premotor activity in the perceiving subject directly mirrors that of the other, how does the subject know whether the intended movement is its own or not? A recent study by Vittorio Gallese's group answers this question: something must be added to the premotor mirror neuron activity before the subject can perform "me" versus "not me" attributions, namely something like activity in cortical areas upstream from mirror neurons (Ebisch et al., 2012). When this something is missing (as occurs in schizophrenia, for example) the subject misattributes intentionality – the subject cannot determine who willed the movements.

Empathy involves a unitary mechanism: the empathic subject always projects itself (always "feels its way into") the object. The structure and etymology of the word reflect this:

ἐμ/πάθεια
em/pathy
Ein/fühlung
into/feeling

So empathy involves two things –"feeling" and "into" – one of them being affective and the other being spatial. The "feeling", by definition, belongs to the subject. The "into" (the attribution) is where the difficulty lies and is the source of empathic error. The crux of the problem of empathy, therefore, is the *accurate* spatial attribution of affect.

1.1 In the Beginning Was the Affect...

Feelings come first; only after that do we ask where they came from. Answering such questions (about the sources of feelings) is difficult. Two properties of affect need special emphasis here. First, affect is devoid of spatial qualities. We might experience a feeling of fear, for example, as coming from an object, but really the fear is a subjective *response to* the object. Our subjective responses do not actually arise from things outside of ourselves. Affect can only ever arise from within us. But we must also remember that subjective space is figurative. When we say that affect arises "within" us, we position our subjectivity with reference to the objects around us and *in doing so we objectify it.* Subjectivity itself lacks spatial extension—as René Descartes pointed out in his *Meditationes de prima philosophia* (1641/1996, *Meditations on First Philosophy*) where he described subjectivity as *res cogitans* in distinction from *res extensa*, the world of objects. Thus, subjectivity – mental life – lacks substance. This applies especially to the core feature of subjectivity: affect. You can never see, touch, taste, hear or smell an affect. To objectify affect you must bring it into conjunction with other things. And this is what we typically do. Second, affect has peremptory motivational qualities. In this respect, too, it is different from space. Space is neutral. We may feel compelled to approach or withdraw from places (or from objects in space), but this is due to the feelings they evoke, it is not due to the objective features of the places or things themselves. Things that are attractive to one person may be repulsive to another.

These two qualities (immateriality and peremptory motivation) make affect more difficult to think about than objects. Affect is typically discharged, it is *acted* upon (or reacted to) rather than thought about. To think about an affect we have to "tame" it first. Objectifying affect – turning it into external, visualisable, localisable matter that we can think with or about – is the standard way of taming it (see Solms, 2013). This is what cognition does to affect. But the taming of affect takes time, and the outcome is usually unstable.

2 The Structure of Consciousness

Consciousness has two major components: first, we are aware of ourselves and then of a world around us. This distinction between ourselves and the world coincides with the distinction between subject and objects. Objects are registered in the classical sensory modalities: we see, hear, touch and smell things. Space is computed from an integration of these modalities; it maps the location of things in relation to the external surface of one's own body. The subjective equivalent of the objective modalities is affect. Affect registers the internal state of the subject – or the interior of the body, if you want to describe subjectivity objectively. Affect tells us *how we are doing* within a biological scale of values and how we feel, including how we feel about objects. Affect in this rudimentary form broadcasts the state of the subject to itself, in relation to its vital needs (survival and reproductive success). Viewed objectively (anatomically), elemental affect derives from primitive "need detector" mechanisms located in the medial hypothalamus and other structures of the visceral brain (e.g., solitary nucleus, area postrema, parabrachial nucleus, circumventricular organs) which project to the periaqueductal grey (PAG) and the extended reticulothalamic activating system. Still, when we view affect anatomically it is important to remember that we are re-representing it in a visual/spatial format; we are not *reducing* affect to anatomy but rather *correlating* it with anatomy (see Solms, 1997, 2016).

By contrast, space and its objects derive from thalamocortical mechanisms and the sensory receptor organs associated with them. Via these mechanisms we construct, through our lifetimes, a model of the outside world – a *predictive* representation of it (see Friston, 2010). The purpose of doing so is to learn how best to meet our needs there, that is, how best to marry affect with objects. Affective consciousness, which arises mainly from brainstem structures, is extended upwards into thalamocortical structures so that we may know what our feelings are *about* – according to Franz Brentano's concept of "intentionality" as a characteristic of the mental that he defined as "aboutness" [*Beziehung auf einen Inhalt/ein Objekt*] (see Brentano, 1874, p. 124). The structure of consciousness therefore coincides with the structure of empathy; it projects feelings into space. It is important to recognise that the *re-representation* of the affective self as an object (as a body in space) relies heavily on a particular cortical region: the perisylvian cortex of the right cerebral hemisphere. Speaking anatomically, this is *where* the spatial learning process unfolds – the process whereby a subject progressively comes to know the minds of others. When this part of the brain is damaged, as we shall see later, empathy collapses.

It is true that not all affect/object relationships need to be learned. Some emotional responses are "unconditioned" (to use a technical psychological term). These innate affect/object complexes are called "basic emotions" (see Panksepp, 1998). Basic emotions are built-in predictions that are so vital for survival and reproductive success that you cannot afford to learn them via your own experience (Friston, 2010, calls them "priors"). For example, approaching a cliff triggers a degree of fear, always. And the fear tells you what to do, what action is appropriate, namely, in this case: freeze or retreat. If you had to learn what might happen if you continued over the cliff, that would be the last thing you learned; and genes producing such proclivities would (appropriately) not be propagated.

I suspect that embodied simulation relies on such mechanisms. When another mind is gripped by fear and its body moves accordingly, the state of fear is mirrored in the perceiving subject. But such exceptions only prove the rule: most emotional states are far more complicated than reflexes. Moreover, the affective state of others is an ever-changing landscape. You have to feel your way into them in order to read them. This type of mind reading – the everyday type – must be performed *in vivo*; there are no genetic stereotypes for it. And predicting what others are going to do, divining their intentional states, is a very important activity. This type of mind reading is a developmental achievement. When a child says that a glass lying on its side is "tired", that is not good empathy. The child is wrong; the glass is not tired. The child is projecting something he might feel when lying down into an object that cannot feel at all. This is presumably why we value empathy. Not everybody is good at it. What is more, we value empathic capacity morally. Feeling your way into the affective state of others (accurately) is a *good* thing. It is not only good *for* you; it is also good *of* you. Likewise, failing to feel someone's pain is bad. This moral dimension of empathy requires explanation, too.

But why is accurate empathy so difficult? As I have said: the difficulty resides in the non-topological quality of affect. It is not difficult to feel a feeling; what is difficult is to discern *where it comes from*, which in turn reveals what it is about: what events in the world might have caused me to feel this? And what actions might be required to change it? I believe it is the second quality of affect mentioned above, the peremptory quality, that makes it so difficult to localise.

3 The Theory of Narcissism

In the beginning was the affect; this seems to be a reasonable assumption. Everything we know about the phylogeny and ontogeny of consciousness-producing structures points to this conclusion (Merker, 2007; Solms & Panksepp, 2012). The most rudimentary form of affect, generated at the level of the PAG (and associated with its ventral and dorsal columns respectively) is pleasure versus unpleasure. Higher (limbic) varieties of the affect/object complex, too, can be classified in this way; the "basic emotions" are special kinds of pleasure and unpleasure (orgasm, attachment, safety, and so on, are varieties of pleasure; pain, loss, fear, and so on, are varieties of unpleasure). Affect, therefore, comes in two basic forms: as pleasurable or as unpleasurable feeling (Fig 4.1).

All animals seek out pleasure inducing stimuli and avoid unpleasure inducing ones. The same applies to us; we want to be (and to remain) in pleasurable states and we avoid unpleasurable ones. This is the "pleasure principle", which forms the basis of the theory of narcissism (see Freud, 1925/1953–74ff.). It is true that Freud also recognised a "Nirvana principle", which lies beyond the pleasure principle, but I will discuss this later.

Fig. 4.1 Symbolic representation of the primary affective state (where + is pleasure and – is unpleasure)

The theory of narcissism applies the pleasure principle to the formation of the human subject. The subject (the "within") is a place set apart from objects. Since we aspire to be in pleasurable states as opposed to unpleasurable ones, the first conception of "me" (of the place where my subjectivity intends to exist) is where the pleasure is; conversely, the place my subjectivity intends to avoid (the "not me") is where the unpleasure is. In the beginning of ego development, therefore, "me" coincides with pleasure and "not me" with unpleasure (see Fig. 4.2). It seems reasonable to assume that our first intentional states take roughly this form; this is the default mode of subjectivity. Observations of immature minds (e.g., very young children) and of severe psychopathologies (e.g., schizophrenia) point to the same conclusion. In this state called "primary narcissism", the subject maintains a rigid split between pleasurable and unpleasurable feelings by "introjecting" the sources of the former and "projecting" the sources of the latter.[2] In short, the

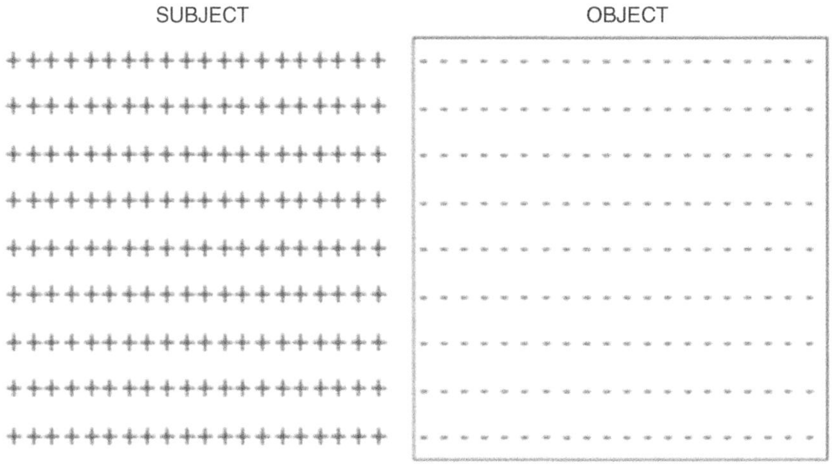

Fig 4.2 Symbolic representation of the state of narcissism, depicting splitting, which is achieved via introjection and projection

[2] This is closely related to the well-established "self-serving bias" of social psychologists (see Forsyth, 2007).

nascent subject voids itself of bad feelings by relegating them to nascent objects. This leads to the not very nice but unavoidable conclusion that "hate, as a relation to objects, is older than love" (Freud, 1915a/1953–74ff., p.136).

Now consider the implications for empathy. When something feels good, we try to locate it within our beloved selves; when something feels bad, we compulsively locate it in objects. We accordingly want to distance ourselves from things imbued with feelings other than our own. This is not a good basis for empathy. Yet this would seem to be our default (automatic) mode of response. That is the reason why I do not think empathy relies on automatic mechanisms. Fortunately, the exigencies of life militate strongly against the viability of narcissism. We living creatures *need* objects if we are to survive and reproduce. We therefore have to allow some bad feelings to be relocated inside us (e.g., "I feel hungry") and some good ones outside (e.g., "she provides relief"). On this basis, we have to accept that *we are not fundamentally different from other objects* and that we possess "objective" (unwanted) attributes of a kind that we would rather assign only to others. This mature state, the basis for "object love", is the opposite of narcissism. The transition from narcissism (self-love) to object love is necessitated by the reality principle (Fig. 4.3).

Having made this transition – in the face of strong emotional resistances – the subject is in a position to attribute feelings more realistically. Now it can begin to answer the question: where does this feeling come from? Such questions, if they are going to be answered accurately, require the subject to *tolerate* objects. It requires a *receptive* attitude towards them. Still, real objects by their very nature are apt to produce unwelcome feelings in us, such as lack, need and desire. In these circumstances, allowing oneself to feel the intentional state of the object *as it actually is* opens us to unwelcome truths. For example, it may be that the object has no intention of rectifying our lack, meeting our need, requiting our desire. Since "hate, as a relation to objects, is older than love", locating pleasure in the other is apt also to arouse envy, just as finding pain there may arouse guilt. To tolerate such affects is to overcome narcissism. With these simple facts, I believe we have explained why empathy is considered good, both practically and morally.

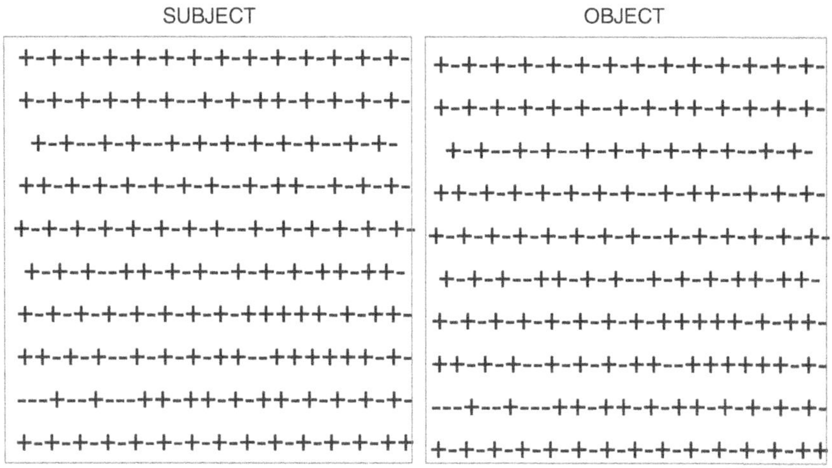

Fig. 4.3 Symbolic representation of realistic object relations

Freud made an interesting observation about how we deal with the vulnerabilities introduced by object love. Since the exigencies of life require us to tolerate separateness – the "otherness" of the things we need and want – and, therefore, to tolerate unwelcome feelings within ourselves, we try to avoid thinking about them. We relegate such things to a part of our minds we pay no attention to. That is, we render them *unconscious*, we "repress" them (Fig. 4.4).

In his famous essay on *The Unconscious*, Freud elaborated:

The assumption of an unconscious is [. . .] a perfectly *legitimate* one, inasmuch as in postulating it we are not departing a single step from our customary and generally accepted mode of thinking. Consciousness makes each of us aware only of his own states of mind; that other people, too, possess a consciousness is an inference which we draw by analogy from their observable utterances and actions, in order to make this behaviour of theirs intelligible to us. (It would no doubt be psychologically more correct to put it this way: that without any special reflection we attribute to everyone else our own constitution and therefore our consciousness as well and that this identification is a *sine qua non* of our understanding [of others]) [. . .] Psychoanalysis demands nothing more than that we should apply this process of inference to

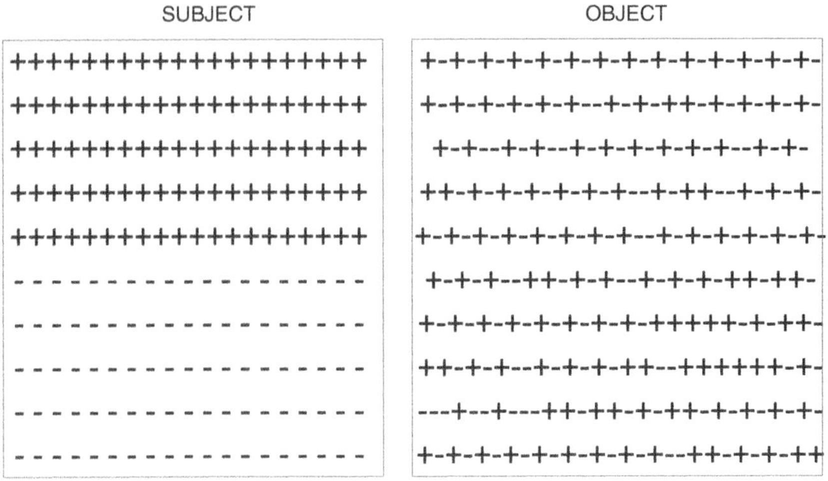

Fig 4.4 Symbolic representation of repression

ourselves too – a proceeding to which, it is true, we are not constitutionally inclined. If we do this, we must say: all the acts and manifestations which I notice in myself and do not know how to link up with the rest of my mental life must be judged as if they belonged to someone else: they are to be explained by a mental life ascribed to this other person. (Freud, 1915b/1953–74ff., p. 169)

This so-called other person, Freud explained, is the unconscious part of our own intentionality. It is the *other within* us. The "fundamental rule" of clinical psychoanalysis asks the patient to adopt the same tolerant and receptive attitude towards this unconscious part of its self that it (hopefully) learned to adopt towards other people. It asks us to "empathise" with unwanted parts of ourselves.

I quoted this passage from Freud to remind us how difficult it is to empathise, and to clarify the nature of the attitude it entails. Every psychoanalyst knows how much mental work is required to (accurately) know the mind of another person. The mechanism of embodied simulation does not begin to do justice to the task. It is also noteworthy in this respect that the analyst seeks to know the patient *by looking inwards*, by allowing her/himself to notice what s/he feels, and then gradually works out what belongs to the analyst and what to the patient. This also involves putting hypotheses to patients and taking in their responses (correcting our errors). Only then can we begin to know what the patient's feelings are *really* about.

4 Clinical Vignette

To put flesh on these theoretical bones, I will conclude with a brief vignette. The patient is a middle-aged woman who, a few days before the interview reported below, suffered a stroke which destroyed a large part of the perisylvian region of her right cerebral hemisphere (Fig 4.5).

This stroke left the patient bedridden, due to dense paralysis of the left side of her body (arm and leg). However, she *flatly denied that she was paralysed*, and asked incessantly to be sent home. This symptom is called "anosognosia" and is quite common after a right hemisphere stroke, that is, after damage to the part of the brain that internalises the rules of space. Patients with right perisylvian damage unlearn those rules. Then they regress to narcissism (see Kaplan-Solms & Solms, 2000). They represent space as they would like it to be, rather than as it is. They forget the most difficult of all spatial rules, namely that one's self is no different from other objects: although I love myself so much more, I am bound by the same indifferent rules. From the point of view of others, it is *me* who is the object and *they* who are the subject.[3] These patients lose the capacity to know the intentional state of others, particularly when it requires them to face unwelcome "objective" facts.

In the vignette that follows, I explained to the patient beforehand that I am interviewing her in front of a camera so that I can demonstrate her case to other doctors. You (the reader) are therefore explicitly included in the conversation as "they".

Me: Can you tell me why you're in hospital?
Patient: [Silent.]

---

[3] One is reminded of the Christian empathic moral: "Love thy neighbor as thyself".

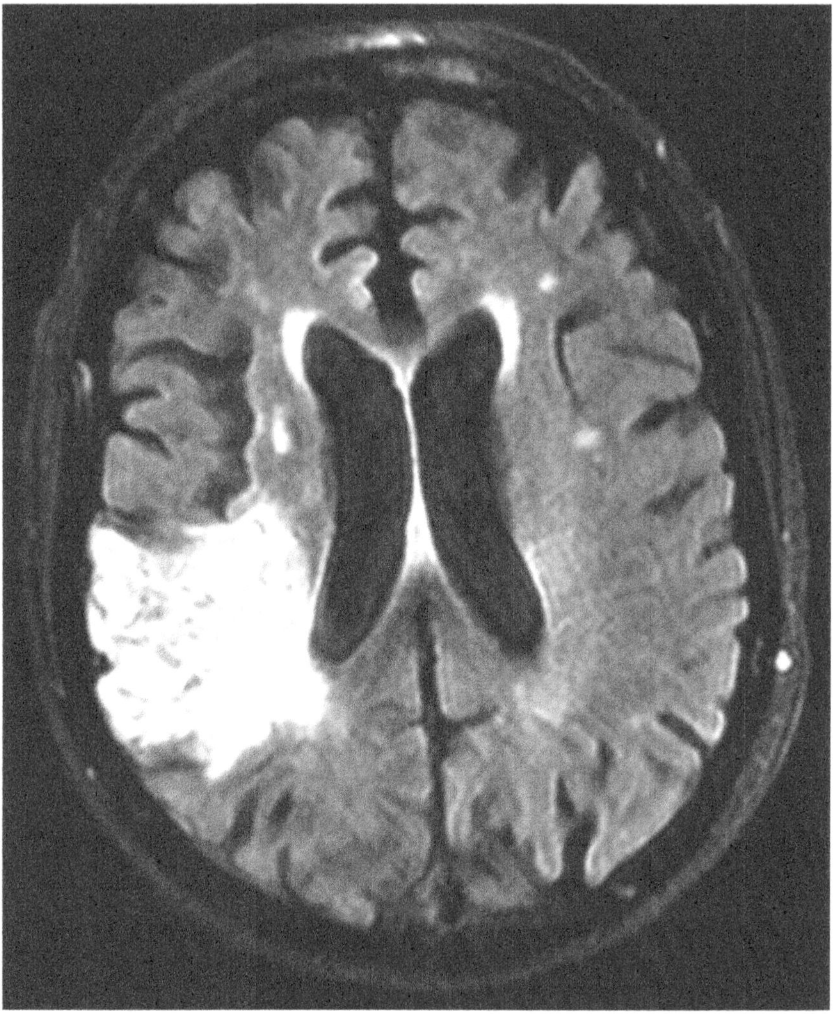

Fig. 4.5 Magnetic resonance image of infarction in the territory of the right middle cerebral artery

Me: Can you tell me why you're here?
Patient: Apparently I had a stroke; that's why I'm here.
Me: That's right. But why did you say "apparently"; do you agree that you've had a stroke?

Patient: Yes, but I don't feel any symptoms. What do you feel? How are you supposed to feel?
Me: Well, one of the most common consequences of a stroke is paralysis; you get loss of movement in an arm or a leg. Are you having those symptoms?
Patient: [Lifts up her paralysed left arm with her intact right arm.] Here, they can see; I'm lifting my arm up.
Me: You're lifting it up so that the doctors can see?
Patient: Yes.
Me: So are you showing them that you *can* move that arm or that you *can't* move that arm?
Patient: I *can* move it.
Me: But you're lifting it by lifting it with this [right] hand. Can you lift it by itself?
Patient: I lift it with my mind.
Me: With your mind?
Patient: [Nods.]
Me: And when you lift it with your mind, do you actually see it and feel it moving?
Patient: Yes.
Me: So if I had to ask you the question – "Is this arm working normally or not"? – what would your answer be?
Patient: No.
Me: No, it's not working normally?
Patient: [Shakes her head.]
Me: Okay; what's the matter with that arm?
Patient: Nothing. There's nothing wrong with it.
Me: There's nothing wrong with it?
Patient: Because I can move it.
Me: There's nothing wrong with it because . . . ?
Patient: Because I can touch it.
Me: There's nothing wrong with it because you can touch it?
Patient: [Nods]
Me: And when you touch it, it feels normal?
Patient: [Nods.]
Me: And when you try to move it by itself does it feel normal?

Patient: [Nods.]
Me: So, as far as you are concerned, there's absolutely nothing wrong with you now?
Patient: [Nods.]
Me: Even though apparently you had a stroke?
Patient: [No response.]
Me: The normal effect of a stroke, which is paralysis, that hasn't happened to you?
Patient: [Shakes her head.]
Me: Okay, can you lift up this hand? [Points to her right hand.]
Patient: [Lifts the hand.]
Me: That's it. Okay, put it down. Can you lift up this hand? [Points to her left hand.]
Patient: [No response.]
Me: Do you see, Mrs —, when you lift up this hand [right], it actually goes up, you see, but when you lift up this hand [left], it stays there. You see, that's what we call paralysis. Do you see?
Patient: [No response.]
Me: That's because of the stroke. That's what has happened as a result of the stroke. So when you say you don't have any symptoms, it's not quite right, because this is a symptom you *do* have as a result of the stroke. Do you see? [Points to the left arm.]
Patient: [No response.]
Me: So now, while you are here in hospital, the physiotherapists are going to work with you and they are going to see what they can do to help you, to regain the movement in that arm. Okay?
Patient: [No response.]
Me: Just so that the doctors [via the camera] understand, can you tell me again now, after we have discussed this: is there anything wrong with you as a result of this stroke?
Patient: [Shakes her head.]
Me: No?
Patient: [Shakes her head.]

Me: Nothing? Are you sure? But what have we just discussed now; what did I just tell you?

Patient: [Points to her left hand.] This side has a symptom.

Me: I said that that side has a symptom; that's right. And did I say what the symptom was?

Patient: Not lifting up this hand. [Lifts up her left arm with her right arm.]

Me: I beg your pardon?

Patient: Because I'm not lifting up this hand by itself.

Me: I said that you can't lift that hand by itself. That's right. Isn't that true?

Patient: [Yawns. Nods.]

Me: So do you agree with me, you can't lift this [left] hand by itself?

Patient: [Nods.]

Me: So do you agree: that is the effect of the stroke?

Patient: [Nods.]

Me: That's very important. That's very good. So may I just ask you again – because the doctors are going to be watching this from the camera, so I just want to be sure that you and I agree, and that they understand that you and I agree – can you tell me again: this stroke, has it caused you any problems, has it caused any harm to any part of your body?

Patient: [Nods.]

Me: It has. And what has that harm been, what has that effect been?

Patient: [No response.]

Me: What symptoms has it caused you, that stroke?

Patient: At home, when I know its bedtime, I get into a bath. But here they don't have that.

Me: At bedtime you can't get into a bath?

Patient: [Nods.]

Me: But why are you telling me that?

Patient: Because I can only sleep when I've had a nice bath.

Me: Oh, so it's affecting your sleep . . .

Patient: Yes.

Me: . . . so you would rather not be here. I understand that; you would rather be at home.

Patient: Yes.

Me: I know you would rather be at home. But remember what I told you: the reason that you're here is because of this paralysis [pointing to her left hand] because of the stroke. That's why you can't be at home right now. But you will be able to get back home; it won't be very long.

Patient: You see, at home you're comfortable.

Me: That's right.

Patient: Everybody knows at a hospital that you are sick.

Me: Yes.

Patient: And they come and talk crap to you every time.

Me: I see. So am I busy talking crap to you?

Patient: No.

Me: But it makes you feel bad for everybody to be coming and talking to you about being sick.

Patient: [Nods.]

Me: You don't want to feel sick.

Patient: Yes.

Me: You don't want to be treated as a sick person.

Patient: [Nods.]

Me: Nobody does. Well, most people don't like to be treated as a sick person.

Patient: [No response.]

Me: The important thing is that, at the moment, even though you don't *feel* sick – that's why you don't feel like a sick person – this arm [left] isn't working at the moment, because of that stroke. And remember, that's the thing we have agreed about; because I think it is very important for us to be able to help with that. Okay?

Patient: [No response.]

Me: So can we discuss it one last time? Can you tell me again: this arm [left] is it working or not working? At the moment; is it working or not working? At the moment; right now. Is this arm working properly or not?

Patient: [Nods.]
Me: Are you saying it is working properly? Are you saying that it's not paralysed?
Patient: [Nods.]
Me: But just a few minutes ago you agreed with me that it is.
Patient: No I didn't.
Me: Is that just because I forced you to?
Patient: No, you didn't force me; how did you force me?
Me: No, I am trying to understand. Why did you agree with me a few minutes ago and now you're not agreeing?
Patient: [Points to her head.] Because you can't read my mind. In my mind's eye you can see that you are lifting your hand. But *you* can't see that.
Me: I understand. That's very important. So in your mind's eye you can see that you're lifting the hand?
Patient: [Nods.]
Me: But what about with your physical eyes? Even though in your mind's eye you *believe* you are lifting it, because you've made the decision that you're going to lift it, and you feel yourself putting that decision into effect – in your mind's eye, therefore, you feel that you are lifting it – but if you look at your hand with your physical eyes, with your actual eyes, can't you see it is actually not lifting?
Patient: [Nods.]
Me: So, as you say, I'm outside of you, I'm not inside of your mind, I'm outside; I look at it with my eyes and I don't see it moving, and that's why I think it is paralysed.
Patient: Yes.
Me: So now which one do you think is right: what our actual eyes see or what our mind's eye sees?
Patient: What your mind's eye sees.
Me: Does your mind's eye see something that is more real than what your actual eyes see?
Patient: [Nods.]
Me: So that's why you believe you're not paralysed?
Patient: [Nods.]

Me: Okay. Alright Mrs —-, I don't want to keep pestering you. Okay, I'll come back and talk to you again another time.
Patient: [Nods.]

The process of learning how space works in relation to our feelings (that is, how it works in contradiction of the pleasure principle) is all too easily reversed. Our (subjective) minds' eye readily sees things that our physical (objective) eyes do not, even without the devastation of a right hemisphere stroke. We easily see only what we want to.

In the last section of this chapter, I illustrated this truism with reference to an extreme example, to render the mechanisms at work as clear as possible. But hopefully we can all recognise the same mechanisms in our beloved selves, albeit in subtler forms. Who among us finds it easy to know the minds of others, and to truly see ourselves objectively? Narrowing the gap between the subjective and objective perspectives on space in relation to feelings is a developmental achievement of capital importance. But a gap will always remain. That is why empathy is difficult.

I would have liked to describe the personality of the patient Mrs — above (for a fuller description of the personality of several such patients, see Kaplan-Solms & Solms, 2000). In short, she, like all anosognosic patients, is grossly deficient in empathy; and this deficit is directly proportional to her loss of learnt spatial cognitive capacity caused by right perisylvian damage (see Besharati et al., 2016). Upon this empirical evidence I rest my case: the crux of the problem of empathy is the accurate spatial attribution of affect.

References

Besharati, S., Forkel, S., Kopelman, M., Solms, M., Jenkinson, P., & Fotopoulou, A. (2016). Mentalizing the body: spatial and social cognition in anosognosia for hemiplegia. *Brain, 139*, 971–985.

Brentano, F. (1874). *Psychologie vom empirischen Standpunkte* [Psychology from an empirical standpoint]. Leipzig: Dunker & Humblot.

Descartes, R. (1641/1996) *Meditations on First Philosophy*. With Selections from the Objections and replies (J. Cottingham, Ed., Transl. from the Latin). Cambridge: Cambridge University Press.

Di Pellegrino, G., Fadiga, L., Fogassi, L., Gallese, V., & Rizzolatti, G (1992). Understanding motor events: a neurophysiological study. *Experimental Brain Research, 91*, 176–180.

Ebisch, S., Salone, A., Ferri, F., De Beradis, D., Romani, G.L., Ferro, F.M., Gallese, V. (2012). Out of touch with reality? Social perception in first-episode schizophrenia. *Social Cognitive & Affective Neuroscience, 8*, 394–403.

Fogassi, L., Ferrari, P.F., Gesierich, B., Rozzi, S., Chersi, F., & Rizzolatti, G. (2005). Parietal lobe: from action organization to intention understanding. *Science, 308*, 662–667.

Forsyth, D. (2007). Self-Serving Bias. In W.A. Darity (Ed.). *International Encyclopedia of the Social Sciences* (2nd ed.). New York: Macmillan.

Freud, S. (1915a/1953–74). Instincts and their vicissitudes. In *Standard Edition of the Complete Psychological Works of Sigmund Freud* (Vol. 14, pp. 117–140, ed. by J. Strachey in collaboration with A. Freud). London: Hogarth Press.

Freud, S. (1915b/1953–74). The Unconscious. In *Standard Edition of the Complete Psychological Works of* Sigmund *Freud* (Vol. 14, pp. 159–204, ed. by J. Strachey in collaboration with A. Freud). London: Hogarth Press.

Freud, S. (1925/1953–74). On Negation. In *Standard Edition of the Complete Psychological Works of Sigmund Freud* (Vol. 19, 235–9, ed. by J. Strachey in collaboration with A. Freud). London: Hogarth Press.

Friston, K. (2010). The free-energy principle: A unified brain theory? *Nature Reviews Neuroscience, 11*, 127–138.

Gallese, V., Fadiga, L., Fogassi, L., & Rizzolatti, G. (1996). Action recognition in the premotor cortex. *Brain, 119*, 593–609.

Kaplan-Solms, K. & Solms, M. (2000). *Clinical Studies in Neuropsychoanalysis: Introduction to a Depth Neuropsychology*. London: Karnac Books.

Merker, B. (2007). Consciousness without cerebral cortex: A challenge for neuroscience and medicine. *Behavioral & Brain Sciences, 30*, 63–134.

Panksepp, J. (1998). *Affective Neuroscience: The Foundations of Animal and Humans Emotions*. Oxford: Oxford University Press.

Solms, M. (1997). What is consciousness? *Journal of the American Psychoanalytic Association, 45*, 681–778.

Solms, M. (2013). The conscious id. *Neuropsychoanalysis, 15*, 5–19.

Solms, M. (2016). Consciousness by surprise: a neuropsychoanalytic approach to the hard problem. In R. Poznanski, J. Tuszynski & T. Feinberg (Eds.). *Biophysics of Consciousness: A Foundational Approach* (pp. 129–148). New York: World Scientific.

Solms, M. & Panksepp, J. (2012). The id knows more than the ego admits. *Brain Sciences, 2*, 147–175.

5

Measuring the Emotional Quality – Empathy and Sympathy in Empirical Psychology

Vanessa Lux

Psychological definitions of empathy struggle to distinguish between empathy and sympathy.[1] The meaning of both English terms significantly overlaps. However, "empathy" somehow became "the word of choice in psychology" (Wispé, 1986, p. 316). Introduced as a translation of the German word *Einfühlung*, the neologism was supposed to be a more technical term and free from the diverse historical connotations associated with sympathy. The distinction seemed to have worked well for quite some time, despite empathy's early association with multiple theoretical "landscapes" (see Chapter 12). But in the 1970s, the focus in psychological empathy research shifted from the mere cognitive dimensions of empathy toward underlying affective dimensions. On the one

[1] For its partial synonymous use in psychology until the mid-1980s, see Wispé (1986, p. 314); for a more recent account of its conceptual diffusion in psychology and philosophy, see Coplan (2011, p. 25).

V. Lux (✉)
Faculty of Psychology, Ruhr University Bochum, Bochum, Germany
e-mail: vanessa.lux@rub.de

V. Lux, S. Weigel (eds.), *Empathy*, Palgrave Studies in the Theory and History of Psychology, DOI 10.1057/978-1-137-51299-4_5

hand, this shift was influenced by conceptual developments within psychoanalytic theory. On the other hand, the civil rights and anti-war movements of the 1960s and 1970s put pro-social behavior on the research agenda. The meaning of empathy changed significantly: from a mental mechanism underlying aesthetic experiences to the emotional precondition of compassion and pro-social behavior. Eventually, the emotion-based concept of empathy differed so much from the original *Einfühlung* that it got retranslated into German as *Empathie*.

In the following, I trace the emotional turn of the empathy concept in psychology and the retranslation of the English term empathy into German as *Empathie*. In addition, I discuss different methods used to measure the emotional quality experienced by individuals during empathy studies as well as the problems these studies face in distinguishing between empathy and sympathy. Finally, I argue that the lack of distinction implicated in the measurements is one of the reasons that empathy has been strongly related to compassion, pro-social behavior, and moral judgment originally associated with sympathy, not empathy.

1 Empathy Is (Not) Sympathy

Around 1900, the question of how to translate the German philosophical and aesthetic concept of *Einfühlung* into English was in the air (see Chapter 12). However, it was Edward B. Titchener's translation as "empathy" in 1909 (Titchener, 1909, p. 21) that would subsequently dominate academic psychology and become a point of reference ever since (see, e.g., Lanzoni, 2012, p. 303; Wispé, 1986, pp. 315–16). Titchener's concept of empathy was strongly related to his approach of experimental introspection. He used empathy as a technical term to describe the process of feeling oneself into an object or situation in aesthetic experiences and other situations. He especially highlighted the kinesthetic dimension of the underlying inner sensations:

> All that I have to remark now is that the various visual images, which I have referred to as possible vehicles of logical meaning, oftentimes share their task with kinesthesis. Not only do I see gravity and modesty and

> pride and courtesy and stateliness, but I feel or act them in the mind's muscles. This is, I suppose, a simple case of empathy, if we may coin that term as a rendering of Einfühlung. (Titchener, 1909, p. 21)

With his translation, Titchener also established a clear distinction between the more commonly used word sympathy and the new term empathy (see Lanzoni, 2012, p. 309; Titchener, 1915, p. 201). Empathy was meant to describe a projection of one's own *feelings into* an object or situation resulting in the feeling of "being moved" by the observed thing or event. In contrast, sympathy for Titchener described the emotional response of *feeling together with* somebody:

> As we read about the forest, we may, as it were, become the explorer; we feel for ourselves the gloom, the silence, the humidity, the oppression, the sense of lurking danger; everything is strange, but it is to us that the strange experience has come. We are told of a shocking accident, and we gasp and shrink and feel nauseated as we imagine it; we are told of some new and delightful fruit, and our mouth waters as if we were about to taste it. This tendency to feel oneself into a situation is called empathy – on the analogy of sympathy, which is feeling together with another; and empathic ideas are psychologically interesting, because they are the converse of perceptions: their core is imaginal, and their context is made up of sensations, the kinesthetic and organic sensations that carry the empathic meaning. (Titchener, 1915, p. 198)

Thus, Titchener saw empathy and sympathy as distinct psychological mechanisms: Empathy involved a complex cognitive-affective process of imagination, and sympathy represented an affective state that grounds instinctive behavioral tendencies in social situations (for the latter, see Titchener, 1915, pp. 298–9). Titchener markedly criticized any conceptual overlap of sympathy with moral judgment.[2] According to him, moral and social sentiments are "a mixed medley of particular responses"

---

[2] For example, Adam Smith emphasizes a strong link between sympathy and moral judgment (see Smith, 1759), while Scheler (1913) criticizes the conceptual confusion due to the multiple connotations of sympathy; see also Chapter 1.

and should not simply refer to "a native sympathy or empathy" (Titchener, 1915, p. 301).

In the following years, the term empathy spread to different fields of psychology, among them social and personality psychology, psychotherapy, and developmental psychology (see Eisenberg & Strayer, 1987, p. 3; Wispé, 1987, p. 17). Although Titchener's translation was widely adopted, his notion of empathy – as imagination and projection of inner sensations into perceived situations or objects – was not. Instead, empathy, like the German *Einfühlung*, was discussed as related to motor mimicry, imitation, and the perspective taking involved in the process of how we get to know the feelings and intentions of others. For example, the social psychologist Gordon W. Allport, known for his theory of personality, discussed empathy as a kind of "kinesthetic inference" that enables us to understand another person's actions and motives (Allport, 1937, p. 532). Referring to his own readings of Theodor Lipps, Edith Stein, and Wolfgang Köhler, Allport explains Lipps' empathy theory as an alternative view of perspective taking, "mid-way" between inference theory and the theory of intuition. "The theory of empathy is a peculiar blend, and must in fact be regarded both as a theory of inference and as a theory of intuition, depending somewhat upon the coloring given it by different authors" (Allport, 1937, p. 533). Similarly to Köhler, who was a strong critic of the focus on aesthetics in the German *Einfühlungstheorie*, Allport emphasizes kinesthetic experiences and motor mimicry. In his monkey studies, Köhler impressively illustrated how mind reading and perspective taking build on motor mimicry and (gestural) communication (Köhler, 1917). In 1925, Köhler was still using the English term "sympathetic" to describe the mimicry phenomenon in his chimpanzees (see Köhler, 1925, Plate IV), while by 1937 Allport was using Titchener's term "empathy" (Allport, 1937, p. 530, 1961, p. 533). This change in terminology can be read as a symptom of the by then widespread use of the term empathy as the translation for *Einfühlung*.

Gardner Murphy also discusses empathy in relation to intersubjectivity, mind reading, and perspective taking. His definition shows how the interrelations with intersubjectivity, mind reading, and perspective taking became more and more a defining feature of empathy, independently from its role in aesthetic experiences and judgment. For Murphy, empathy is: "(1) An attribution to a natural object or work of art of the feelings or attitudes aroused in one by the surroundings (actual or depicted) of that object [. . .] (2) Direct apprehension of the state of mind of another person without [. . .] feeling as that other person does" (Murphy, 1947, p. 985).

Thus, Allport and Murphy both highlight the cognitive dimension of empathy and its role in perspective taking and intersubjective communication, even though they put different degrees of emphasis on motor mimicry. Both interpret empathy within an evolutionary framework and conceptualize it as a general human cognitive capacity that develops during ontogeny and differs among individuals. This cognitive and trait version of empathy more or less dominated the field of academic psychology until the late 1970s. For example, the widely used *Hogan Empathy Scale* (*HES*), developed by Robert Hogan in 1969 to test for inter-individual differences of empathic disposition, focuses exclusively on the cognitive dimensions of empathy. Hogan defines empathy accordingly as "the intellectual or imaginative apprehension of another's condition or state of mind" (Hogan, 1969, p. 307).

This definition of empathy, as an ability to correctly judge the feelings, moods, or motives of others through the cognitive operation of perspective taking, stimulated psychological research. Experiments were conducted studying, for example, empathic error or accuracy, the role of perspective taking in mental development, and the relationship between empathy and moral judgment as well as altruism (Wispé, 1987). In light of the social movements of the late 1960s and early 1970s, altruism in particular was granted high practical interest. The relationship between empathy and pro-social behavior was nevertheless considered to be complex, with empathy being a necessary but not sufficient precondition (e.g., by Hogan, 1969).

Parallel to this expansion of experimental empathy research, empathy became a key concept in the field of psychoanalysis and psychotherapy. Here, the affective dimension of empathy was emphasized. This mirrored an emotional turn in psychological empathy research, and, as a consequence, the clear distinction between empathy and sympathy started to fade.

2 Emotional Turn and Retranslation

Carl Rogers is usually cited as the first person to conceptualize the role of empathy in psychotherapy (see Wispé, 1987, p. 27). In his client-centered therapy, the task of the therapist is to actively feel himself into the other person's feelings and situation. This requires openness and acceptance toward the client, but also awareness of the difference between one's own feelings and the feelings of the client. Accordingly, Rogers defines empathy as the ability

> [t]o perceive the internal frame of reference of another with accuracy and with the emotional components and meanings which pertain thereto as if one were the person, but without ever losing the "as if" condition. Thus, it means to sense the hurt or the pleasure of another as he senses the recognition that it is as if I were hurt or pleased and so forth. (Rogers, 1959, pp. 210–1)

For Rogers, empathic understanding was an important professional skill for therapists to have (Rogers, 1951). It was partly acquired through training and experience and partly based on a person's empathic disposition. For the latter, Rogers' concept of empathy very much resembled the trait based or dispositional concept of empathy discussed in academic psychology at the time. However, with regard to the therapeutic setting, his notion of *feeling into* puts a much stronger emphasis on the affective component of empathy. Furthermore, for Rogers empathy is no longer what the observer *projects* into the situation or an object of art, but what he *perceives* and is able to mirror from the feelings of the client. Imagination and projection (central elements in Titchener's concept of empathy) represent sources of error in Rogers' therapeutic empathy. The feelings of the client as perceived by the therapist were an important resource to help understand the client's situation and to detect unconscious thoughts and wishes expressed within the therapeutic setting.

But Rogers' concept of empathy goes beyond mere emotional resonance and its use by the therapist. In combining empathy with the principles of openness and acceptance toward the client, Rogers' empathic resonance obtains a special connotation of *feeling with* or *sympathy*. The therapist's efforts to feel himself into his client's emotions and situation are not only motivated by the goal of helping the client. The principles of openness and acceptance, rooted in Rogers' affiliation to humanistic psychology, require that the therapist sympathizes with the client at least partially. Thus, in its practical consequences Rogers' conceptualization of empathy as an ability to understand the feelings of the client entails *feeling oneself into* his/her feelings and situation, based on the condition of *feeling with* the client.

Rogers' qualification of empathic understanding as a psychotherapeutic method strongly influenced psychoanalytic theory. Before the 1950s, there was no formalized discussion of empathy among psychoanalysts. Despite his proclaimed admiration for Lipps, Sigmund Freud rarely mentions *Einfühlung* in his writings. In a footnote to *Massenpsychologie und Ich-Analyse*, for example, he characterizes *Einfühlung* as that mechanism which allows us to deliver an opinion on the psychic life of others (Freud, 1921/1993, p. 121 Fn 2).[3] Freud's contemporary and colleague Sándor Ferenczi discussed *Einfühlung* more systematically as a method by which to enter the psychic life of the patient during the therapeutic process (Ferenczi, 1938/1964). Ferenczi sketched the constant oscillation of the therapist within the therapeutic process between *Einfühlung*/empathy, introspection, and judgment (Ferenczi, 1938/1964, p. 391). But empathy's rise to becoming a key concept of psychoanalytic therapy did not start before the late 1950s and early 1960s, when Rogers outlined his approach. By then, *Einfühlung* was being translated as empathy in the writings of Sigmund Freud and Sándor Ferenczi. It was also around this time that empathy got retranslated into German as *Empathie*. A telling example of this terminological change is the use of the term in the German psychoanalytic journal *Psyche*: Although the word *Empathie* appeared in two earlier contributions – a note on the situation of psychoanalysis in the US (Weigert, 1953) and a review of a book published in the US (Hofstätter, 1955) – its systematic

[3] German Original: "als Mechanismus, durch den uns überhaupt eine Stellungnahme zu einem anderen Seelenleben ermöglicht wird" (Freud, 1921/1993, p. 121, fn. 2).

use as the translation of empathy did not come about prior to 1961. For example, in 1959 the journal published a German translation of a lecture in English by Fritz Redlich in which empathy was still translated as *Mitfühlen* and *mitfühlendes Verständnis* ["sympathic understanding"] (Redlich, 1959). In 1961, the first paper appeared that explicitly addressed empathy as a theoretical concept, entitled *Zum Problem der Empathie* ["The Problem of Empathy"] (Greenson, 1961). From then on *Empathie* started to appear as a proper term and became a much debated topic (see, e.g., Heimann, 1969; Kohut, 1966[4]). This retranslation of empathy as, first, *mitfühlendes Verstehen*, and, then, *Empathie* (instead of *Einfühlung)* indicates the conceptual shift in the English term *empathy*, which emphasizes the emotional dimension of empathy – the *feeling* in "feeling into." In addition, a new conceptual overlap with sympathy (feeling with or *Mitfühlen*) can be detected. Both, the emphasis on the emotional dimension of empathy and the conceptual overlap with sympathy facilitated that the concept spread quickly among psychoanalysts. Within different psychoanalytic approaches, empathy was used to theorize the phenomenon of counter-transference between client and therapist and, at the same time, adopted as a theoretical concept within the psychoanalytic theory of mental development (see Chapter 3). Heinz Kohut even put empathy at the center of his psychoanalytic approach to personality disorders within his framework of self-psychology (Kohut, 1971).

In the 1970s, the emphasis on this affective component of empathy in psychotherapy and the figure of emotional resonance took on renewed significance in experimental psychology. Here, the emotional component of empathy was considered crucial in linking empathy to pro-social behavior. Part of this effort included testing on the relationship between empathy and altruism, and thus affective states were induced in experimental settings and measured together with psychophysiological measurements of emotional arousal (see Krebs, 1975). Furthermore, the

[4] In Kohut's paper, the term is introduced first with the translation "seelischen Einfühlungskraft (Empathie)" and then used throughout the following paragraphs without further explanation (Kohut, 1966, p. 578).

content of self-rating questionnaires measuring empathy shifted toward emotional empathy. For example, Albert Mehrabian and Norman Epstein developed the Questionnaire Measure of Emotional Empathy in 1972 (Mehrabian & Epstein, 1972). Following this shift toward emotions, the question of how to differentiate empathy and sympathy was intensely debated. In a widely cited paper, Lauren Wispé points out that "[t]he concepts of sympathy and empathy are frequently confused, and both have been variously and vaguely defined" (Wispé, 1986, p. 318). Wispé ultimately distinguishes between the terms by casting empathy in purely cognitive terms and reserving the emotional dimension exclusively for sympathy:

> Briefly, sympathy refers to the heightened awareness of another's plight as something to be alleviated. Empathy refers to the attempt of one self-aware self to understand the subjective experiences of another self. *Sympathy is a way of relating. Empathy is a way of knowing.* I suggest that these are different psychological processes and that the differences between them should not be obfuscated. (Wispé, 1986, p. 314; emphasis added, V.L.)

But Wispé's proposition for a clear-cut distinction was not adopted by other researchers. Nancy Eisenberg and Janet Strayer, for example, critically characterized his view as framing empathy "in more cognitive terms" (Eisenberg & Strayer, 1987, p. 4). Instead, in their introduction to *Empathy and Its Development*, published in 1987, they define empathy as "sharing the perceived emotion of another – 'feeling with' another [, . . . an] emotional response that stems from another's emotional state or condition and that is congruent with the other's emotional state or situation" (Eisenberg & Strayer, 1987, p. 5). Eisenberg and Strayer substitute the former *feeling into*, which characterized empathy for Titchener and Rogers, with *feeling with*, which for Titchener characterized sympathy and not empathy. In contrast, sympathy according to Eisenberg and Strayer is:

> "feeling for" someone, and refers to feelings of sorrow, or feeling sorry, for another. That is to say, sympathy often involves feelings of concern,

> although the conscious cognitive realization that one is concerned about another's welfare is an outcome, rather than a part, of sympathizing. (Eisenberg & Strayer, 1987, p. 6)

Furthermore, they clearly differentiate empathy from perspective taking: "Often sympathy is the consequence of empathizing, although it may be possible for sympathy (as well as empathy) to result from processes such as cognitive perspective taking" (Eisenberg & Strayer, 1987, p. 6).

In this last quote, the emotional quality has not only become the distinguishing factor between empathy and sympathy, but it also constitutes them in distinction to related cognitive processes such as perspective taking. Thus, Eisenberg and Strayer abandon the cognitive dimension that originally constituted empathy in social and developmental psychology. Their definition documents a remarkable conceptual shift in the concept of empathy in psychology.

More recent attempts to conceptualize empathy re-emphasize the (neuro)cognitive dimension underlying perspective taking and mind reading. They interpret the affective component and emotional quality as part and consequence of the cognitive process (e.g., Decety, 2005, Preston & de Waal, 2002). Accordingly, the emotional qualities of empathy were no longer characterized by feelings of sorrow for the other, feelings which most researchers agree are a characteristic of sympathy and not of empathy. Instead, the distinction is grounded in the degree of similarity or difference between the emotional responses of the observed person and of the observer, thereby re-emphasizing the role of mimicry in empathy but with a focus on emotional components. For example, Jean Decety describes the emotional quality of empathy as a combination of a partially mirrored emotional response of the other and the perceived (or felt) difference that lets a person know that these emotions are a reflection of the other and not one's own (Decety, 2005, p. 150). The resonated emotional response is processed further, and the emotional response as well as the cognitive component of perspective taking prove to be fundamental to empathy:

> Thus, in the view developed here, empathy is not a simple resonance of affect between the self and the other, and it is perspective taking that

creates an explicit representation of the other. This makes empathy as described here a representational capacity. (Decety, 2005, p. 153)

Within this perspective, the cognitive dimension of empathy is understood as the representational format of the affective state and emotional quality. Sympathy, on the other hand, is characterized by the caring aspect, that is, by "feelings of concern about the welfare of others" (Decety, 2010, p. 258). This does not necessarily imply that one has to actually feel the same feelings or emotions: In contrast, "sympathy may stem from the apprehension of another's emotional state, it does not have to be congruent with the affective state of the other" (Decety & Michalska, 2010, p. 886).

Despite such efforts at a clear-cut definition in the research context, the caring aspect is still strongly associated with empathy. This is the case not only in popular discourse but also in the professional discourse of social workers, psychotherapists, and other health professionals. As Shaun Gallagher puts it: "Yet, saying that I empathize with you, seems to suggest more than just understanding your mental state; it seems to mean more than simply perceiving that you are in pain" (Gallagher, 2012, p. 358). The philosopher Amy Coplan even lists "Caring about someone else" as the second most common definition of empathy in her overview of the psychological and philosophical use of the term (Coplan, 2011, p. 4). These unclear boundaries between empathy and sympathy are deeply engrained in psychological measurements.

3 Measuring Emotional Quality

One major problem in measuring someone's emotional state is that emotions are experienced from a first-person perspective. This also applies to the emotional qualities of empathy and sympathy: the emotional resonance of an observed affective state (joy or pain) of another person and the concern for the welfare of another person. In psychological empathy research, we basically find two strategies to measure such emotions: the first uses psychophysiological measurements related to emotional arousal and quality and the second collects self-reports of emotional experiences.

3.1 Psychophysiological Measurements

Dennis Krebs was one of the first scientists to use psychophysiological measurements of emotional arousal systematically in empathy research (Neumann & Westbury, 2011, p. 126). Krebs claims that there is a strong causal relationship between empathy and altruism (Krebs, 1975). In his early experimental studies, he recorded skin conductance, heart rate, and blood pulse volume in participants who observed another person play a roulette game. Some participants were told that the person playing would win money or experience pain (by electro shocks) depending on whether they won or lost rounds of the game. Others were told that the game was merely a cognitive task with no further consequences. Those participants who were told that the person would win something or experience pain during the game showed greater physiological reactions than the control group with the cognitive task instructions. Also, psychophysiological responses were stronger in participants who identified themselves with the observed player. In addition, at a later stage, the participants were offered the opportunity to help the person by taking over the painful punishments. Krebs summarized his results as follows: "The major finding of this study was that subjects who experienced the strongest empathic reactions toward another were most willing to help him, even though it meant jeopardizing their own welfare" (Krebs, 1975, p. 1144).

In the early 1990s, Robert W. Levenson and Anna M. Ruef searched explicitly for a specific "physiological substrate" of empathy. While showing a video tape of a married couple, they measured participants' heart rate, skin conductance level, general somatic activity, pulse transmission time to the finger, and finger pulse amplitude (Levenson & Ruef, 1992, p. 237). In addition, they asked subjects to rate the affect displayed by one partner during the interaction with his spouse. Results showed that "the greater the physiological linkage between subject and the target, the greater the accuracy of the subject's rating of the target's negative affect," while there was "no relation between physiological linkage and the accuracy of subjects rating of positive affect" (Levenson & Ruef, 1992, p. 239). Instead, "[a]ccurate rating by one person of another person's positive emotions was associated with a state of low cardiovascular arousal" (Levenson & Ruef, 1992, pp. 244–5). They interpreted the findings as support for a physiological substrate of empathy which is sensitive to the directions of emotions (Levenson & Ruef, 1992, p. 244).

Although these basic physiological measurements reliably measure emotional arousal and may even reflect some differences between positive and negative emotions in the observed person, they are unspecific as to the emotional quality experienced by the observer. A rising heart rate does not indicate whether the change is due to pain or pleasure experienced while observing another person's losses in a roulette game or a spouse feeling sad. In most cases, we would assume that the emotional arousal corresponds with the emotions displayed by the observed person. But this assumption is based on everyday experience and not on physiological measurements. In experimental settings, therefore, participants were usually asked in post-experiment interviews or via self-rating scales about the feelings they experienced.

Facial muscle movements measured by facial electromyography (EMG), another form of physiological measurements, is more specific when dealing with the quality of emotional arousal: EMG measures the electric signals that occur when muscle fibers contract. It has been observed that facial muscle activity roughly reflects the facial expression of emotions (Darwin, 1872, Dimberg, 1990). For example, Dimberg et al. showed that subjects responded to negative facial expressions, such as angry faces and disgust, with corrugator activity, and to positive facial expressions, such as happiness, smiling, and laughter, with zygomatic activity. Furthermore, subjects could not avoid producing facial reactions that corresponded to the stimuli, thereby indicating that differential facial muscle activity is an automatic response (Dimberg, Thunberg, & Grunedal, 2002). Facial muscle activity is considered a valid measure of the emotional reactions induced by observing the pain or pleasure of another person. In their review of psychophysiological measurements in empathy research, David L. Neumann and H. Rae Westbury summarize that "the facial EMG data" from empathy experiments "are consistent with the notion that facial mimicry is an early automatic response to others' displays of facial emotions" (Neumann & Westbury, 2011, p. 127). The idea that facial and other forms of motor mimicry are part of the psychophysiological functions contributing to *Einfühlung* was already discussed by Lipps in his *Leitfaden der Psychologie* (Lipps, 1903). Lipps proposed that we tend to mimic observed facial expressions and gestures related to emotions and that, by doing so, we experience the emotions incorporated by these expressions and gestures (Lipps, 1903, p. 193). The role of motor mimicry was particularly important in the psychological empathy research that followed Köhler's (1925) and Allport's (1937, 1961) work and the notion of empathy as the foundation of intersubjectivity and personality development. In more recent research, motor mimicry has been strongly related to emotional empathy (see Hatfield, Cacioppo, & Rapson, 1994; Meltzoff & Decety, 2003; Preston & de Waal, 2002).

However, psychophysiological measures are always less specific than the experienced quality of emotions. As Neumann and Westbury conclude: "Psychophysiological responses [. . .] can be elicited by a range of different stimuli and thus have their own interpretational challenges when trying to relate them to specific components of empathy" (Neumann & Westbury, 2011, p. 132). For example, corrugator activity is not specific to facial mimicry and was also reported to be elicited by non-facial visual stimuli or even sounds and words (Larsen, Norris, & Cacioppo, 2003). This would imply that there is a mechanism at work that is less stimuli-specific and more general, as indicated by embodied simulation theory and the concept of mirror neurons (see Gallese, 2005, 2011). This conclusion, however, tends to emphasize a projective and imaginative component of empathy without any indication as to how to differentiate between the emotional quality of empathy and that of sympathy.

3.2 Self-Reports

The most commonly used measurements to record specific emotional qualities are self-reports. In the history of psychological empathy research, we find at least three different types of self-reports: (1)

immediate self-reports during introspection in Titchener's empathy experiments, (2) ex post self-reports in the form of written reports, and (3) data collected through self-report scales constructed according to psychological (classical or probabilistic) test theory.

Susan Lanzoni describes in detail the role of self-reports during introspection in Titchener's empathy experiments (Lanzoni, 2012, and Chapter 12). The self-reports were produced by trained participants recruited from a pool of Titchener's lab members and colleagues. These professors, assistant professors, and doctoral students practiced the immediate description of their inner perceptions and feelings. The reports were given verbally and transcribed by an assistant, often in shorthand. They even developed an experimental language with which they tried to record their inner feelings as neutrally and objectively as possible. Nevertheless, introspection and this method of spontaneous self-reports have been heavily criticized as subjective and unreliable, and they quickly vanished from psychological laboratories with the rise of behaviorism in the 1930s.

The written stories on pity, collected around 1900 by F. H. Saunders and G. Stanley Hall, pose another early form of self-reporting that relates to the broader conceptual history of empathy. On March 28, 1899, Saunders and Hall published a catalogue of questions to be addressed in these stories of observed or experienced pity. The reports ought to be "concrete, definite, and detailed accounts [. . .] of experiences where pity has been particularly and exceptionally acute, with all circumstances, symptoms, after effects, etc." (Saunders & Hall, 1900, p. 534). They asked for stories, poems, and novels as well as for real life incidents that provoked intense feelings of pity. They requested that the reports include not only the case but also how the person felt in addition to any physical symptoms such as tears, sobbing, sadness, fear, changes in pulse or respiration, appetite, digestion, sleep or any other physiological process affected. They further asked whether these feelings were also experienced in regard to animals, flowers, trees, dolls or inanimate objects, music, and pictures (Saunders & Hall, 1900, pp. 534–5).

Here is one example of a story about a crying boy and his father:

> M., 30. Saw a little boy walking home with his hand in his father's, crying bitterly. Something made me think that the boy wanted some trifle the father could not afford. Do not know which I pitied most, for the father's honest face bronzed with exposure and hard work showed how sad he must feel to deny his boy. (Saunders & Hall, 1900, p. 540)

Saunders and Hall identified the faculty of imagination or the "vivid depiction of the inner life of others" as an influential covariant and agent of pity (Saunders & Hall, 1900, p. 575). They interpreted the knowledge about pity garnered from these reports as relevant to aesthetic theory and the evolutionary function of sympathy. They pointedly emphasized the evolutionary advantage of caring for kin as a potential source of the feelings of pity and contextualized their findings within this narrative (Saunders & Hall, 1900, p. 575).

Today, very similar stories are displayed to participants in contemporary empathy experiments. For example, in a multilevel comparison of empathy in schizophrenia, Seung Jae Lee et al. used a picture story of a woman who comforts a little girl grieving the loss of a close relative to test for emotional empathy (Lee et al., 2010). As this example shows, the way (emotional) empathy is stimulated in contemporary empathy research is very similar to the way pity or sympathy were conceptualized around 1900, before the English term empathy was introduced. Nevertheless, this overlap between empathy and sympathy is situated at the level of experimental measurements and remains rather detached from the working definitions of these terms that still tend to distinguish between them.

Conceptual overlap at the level of measurements can also be observed in the third form of self-reports – self-rating questionnaires – used to evaluate dispositional empathy in psychological research starting in the late 1960s. These questionnaires commonly combine items that measure general attitudes and personality traits with items that address situational behavior. The most important questionnaires include Hogan's Empathy Scale (Hogan, 1969), Mehrabian and Epstein's Questionnaire Measure of

Emotional Empathy (QMEE, Mehrabian & Epstein, 1972), and Mark H. Davis's Interpersonal Reactivity Index (IRI; Davis, 1980, 1983).

The IRI is one of the most popular self-rating scales in current empathy research (Stueber, 2014). It consists of 28 questions organized into four distinct subscales: perspective taking, empathic concern, personal distress, and fantasy. The strong conceptual overlap between empathy and sympathy in the IRI is already noticeable in the subscales. For example, the subscale "empathic concern" assesses "'other-oriented' feelings of sympathy and concern for unfortunate others" and the subscale "personal distress" measures "'self-oriented' feelings of personal anxiety and unease in tense interpersonal settings" (Davis, 1983, p. 114). This conceptual overlap is also present at the level of individual items. For example, in the subscale "fantasy", which refers to the respondents' tendencies to transpose themselves imaginatively into the feelings and actions of fictitious characters in books, movies, and plays (Davis, 1983, p. 114), we find the item: "I really *get involved* with the feelings of the characters in a novel" (Davis, 1980, p. 6, emphasis added, V.L.). Due to a potential ambiguity in the meaning of the verb "to get involved", the item might measure either the ability to project feelings into the fictional character, which is conceptually related to aesthetic empathy, or alternately it might measure a sense of feeling with or caring for the character, which is more a feature of sympathy. The emotional aspects of empathy and sympathy overlap even more in the subscales "empathic concern" and "personal distress." Here some of the items explicitly measure how emotionally and morally involved a participant gets with the fictional other in the described situations. The subscale "empathic concern" includes, for instance, the item: "When someone gets hurt in my presence, I feel sad and want to help them" (Davis, 1980, p. 7); and the subscale "personal distress" includes the item: "It bothers me to see poor people on the street" (Davis, 1980, p. 7). In these items, the *feeling with* the fictional other(s) gets morally yoked to *feeling for* the other(s). Thus, at the item level, empathy and sympathy are not clearly distinguished in the IRI, but are instead treated as overlapping concepts and linked phenomena.

The IRI is not a unique case. The relatively new Empathy Quotient (EQ), developed by Simon Baron-Cohen and Sally Wheelwright

(Baron-Cohen & Wheelwright, 2004), also shows conceptual overlap between "feeling into," "feeling with," and "feeling for" at the item level. The EQ was originally constructed to discern social impairment in autism spectrum disorders. The questionnaire consists of 60 items, including "I really enjoy caring for other people"; "I tend to get emotionally involved with a friend's problems"; "It upsets me to see an animal in pain"; and "I get upset if I see people suffering on news programs" (Baron-Cohen & Wheelwright, 2004, p. 174). As Karsten Stueber points out, in his entry "Empathy" in the *Stanford Encyclopedia of Philosophy*, "at least in regard to the affective component of empathy", none of the empathy scales or items currently being used "sufficiently distinguish between affective empathy, sympathy, and personal distress" (Stueber, 2014, n. p.).

The IRI and the EQ are both widely used in psychological empathy research as well as in corresponding neuroimaging studies (for example, Lawrence et al., 2006; Singh et al., 2015). The conceptual overlap between empathy and sympathy as it is inscribed in the psychological measurements confounds any attempt to differentiate the two phenomena in these studies. This is especially relevant to neuroimaging studies that address the question of whether empathy and sympathy rely on the same or distinct neural circuits – a question that also applies to related phenomena such as perspective taking, emotion contagion, pity, and pro-social behavior.

4 Conclusion: The Constitutive Role of Emotions and Self-Reports

In psychological empathy research, the specificity of the emotional quality of empathy and sympathy can only be measured through self-report measurements. But a closer look at the widely used self-rating scales for dispositional empathy shows that sympathy is constructed as a subdimension of empathy and not as a distinct emotional quality. This contradicts the terminological debates that focus on clear-cut definitions between the two. In addition, the overlap within the self-rating scales has consequences for the validity of psychophysiological measures that do not differentiate emotional qualities but are nevertheless correlated with self-rating scales for differential validation (see Neumann & Westbury, 2011). The overlap of the concepts is therefore deeply inscribed in the measurements used in psychological empathy research.

Taking into account the constitutive role that the quality of emotions has for the terminological distinction between empathy and sympathy, the vague and confounding situation with regard to the measurements has further methodological implications. From this perspective, it is not surprising that scientists and scholars continue to confuse the concepts in their publications and experimental practice. Even if specialized research groups are able to develop precise definitions and measurements, they will still have to face the conceptual diffusion that occurs when transferred into other fields, both intra- and interdisciplinary.

One of the main reasons for these measurement problems is that emotional quality is only reliably accessible from a first-person perspective. In her call for a narrow definition of empathy, Coplan defines empathy accordingly as "experiential understanding" – an experiential understanding of the thoughts, intentions, and feelings of another person that clearly differ from our own experiences but are still bound to the biases of our first-person perspective (Coplan, 2011, pp. 17–18). Access to these kinds of experiences from a first-person perspective is only possible via self-reports. But then again, self-reports are always mediated by language. This is not only true for the historical practice of introspection, but also for today's self-rating scales. Moreover, language – including non-verbal symbols and gestures – is the privileged medium through which the differential quality of emotional experiences is shared and made accessible to others. In psychological empathy research, language also functions as a mediator between psychophysiological activity and the felt phenomenological experience. This, however, makes the confounding terminology a key issue in psychological empathy research. Different historical layers of the concepts of sympathy, *Einfühlung*, empathy, and *Empathie* may still be present in popular discourse, which may in turn influence participants in experiments when they are asked to qualify their emotional experiences of empathy or sympathy. For example, the link between dispositional empathy and the ability to sensitively care for others is propagated among social workers and health care professionals. Participants of empathy experiments could use these common definitions as implicit references that would guide their responses.

Thus, the relationship between the ability to put oneself into someone else's shoes (*feeling into*) and the ability to feel sympathy or compassion (*feeling with* or *for*) is part of the conceptual history of empathy and cannot be simply reduced to cause (*empathy*) and effect (*sympathy* and demonstrated *pro-social behavior*). Moreover, this history of conceptual diffusion and overlap is still deeply inscribed in the measurements themselves. Psychological empathy research needs to be aware of this conceptual diffusion. Without this awareness, it is all too easy to confuse the complex phenomena of empathy, aesthetic experiences, sympathy, and pro-social behavior. Also, instead of trying to establish clear-cut distinctions, the complex cultural and conceptual history of empathy could be the starting point to investigate the interrelations between cultural history, language, and the multifaceted first-person experience of empathic feelings.

References

Allport, G. W. (1937). *Personality: A psychological interpretation*. New York: Henry Holt and Company.

Allport, G. W. (1961). *Pattern and growth in personality*. London: Holt, Rinehart and Winston.

Baron-Cohen, S., & Wheelwright, S. (2004). The Empathy Quotient: An Investigation of Adults with Asperger Syndrome or High Functioning Autism, and Normal Sex Differences. *Journal of Autism and Developmental Disorders, 34*(2), 163–175.

Coplan, A. (2011). Understanding Empathy: Its Features and Effects. In A. Coplan & P. Goldie (Eds.). *Empathy. Philosophical and psychological perspectives* (pp. 3–30). Oxford, New York: Oxford University Press.

Darwin, C. (1872). *The Expression of the Emotions in Man and Animals*. London: John Murray.

Davis, M. H. (1980). A Multidimensional Approach to Individual Differences in Empathy. *JSAS Catalog of Selected Documents in Psychology; 10*(85), 1–19.

Davis, M. H. (1983). Measuring individual differences in empathy: Evidence for a multidimensional approach. *Journal of Personality and Social Psychology, 44*(1), 113–126.

Decety, J. (2005). Perspective Taking as the Royal Avenue to Empathy. In B. F. Malle & S. D. Hodges (Eds.). *Other minds. How humans bridge the divide between self and others* (pp. 143–157). New York: Guilford Press.

Decety, J. (2010). The Neurodevelopment of Empathy in Humans. *Developmental Neuroscience, 32*(4), 257–267.

Decety, J., & Michalska, K. J. (2010). Neurodevelopmental changes in the circuits underlying empathy and sympathy from childhood to adulthood. *Developmental Science, 13*(6), 886–899.

Dimberg, U. (1990). Facial Electromyography and Emotional Reactions: For Distinguished Early Career Contribution to Psychophysiology: Award Address, 1988. *Psychophysiology, 27*(5), 481–494.

Dimberg, U., Thunberg, M., & Grunedal, S. (2002). Facial reactions to emotional stimuli: Automatically controlled emotional responses. *Cognition and Emotion, 16*(4), 449–471.

Eisenberg, N., & Strayer, J. (1987). Critical issues in the study of empathy. In N. Eisenberg & J. Strayer (Eds.). *Empathy and its development* (pp. 3–13). Cambridge, MA: Cambridge University Press.

Ferenczi, S. (1938/1964). Die Elastizität der psychoanalytischen Technik [The elasticity of psychoanalytic technique]. In *Bausteine zur Psychoanalyse. Band III: Arbeiten aus den Jahren 1908–1933* [Building blocks of psychoanalysis. Vol. III: Works of the years 1908–1933] (2nd ed., vol. 3, pp. 380–398). Bern, Stuttgart: Verlag Hans Huber.

Freud, S. (1921/1993). Massenpsychologie und Ich-Analyse [Group psychology and the analysis of the ego]. In *Gesammelte Werke: chronologisch geordnet* [Collected works: in chronological order] (5th corr. ed., pp. 71–161). Frankfurt/Main: Fischer [u.a.].

Gallagher, S. (2012). Empathy, Simulation, and Narrative. *Science in Context, 25*(3), 355–381.

Gallese, V. (2005). Embodied simulation: From neurons to phenomenal experience. *Phenomenology and the Cognitive Science, 4*, 23–48.

Gallese, V. (2011). Embodied Simulation Theory: Imagination and Narrative: Commentary on Siri Hustvedt. *Neuropsychoanalysis, 13*(2), 196–200.

Greenson, R. R. (1961). Zum Problem der Empathie [On the problem of empathy]. *PSYCHE, 15*(2), 142–154.

Hatfield, E., Cacioppo, J. T., & Rapson, R. L. (1994). *Emotional contagion.* New York: Cambridge University Press.

Heimann, P. R. (1969). Gedanken zum Erkenntnisprozeß des Psychoanalytikers [Thoughts on the psychoanalyst's process of knowledge production]. *PSYCHE, 23*(1), 2–24.

Hofstätter, P. R. (1955). Psychotherapie und Tiefenpsychologie: Sullivan, H. S., The Interpersonal Theory of Psychiatry (herausgegeben von H. S. Perry und M. L. Gawel) New York (Norton) 1953. 393 Seiten, $ 5.00' [Psychotherapy and depth psychology]. *PSYCHE, 8*(12), 32–34.

Hogan, R. (1969). Development of an empathy scale. *Journal of Consulting and Clinical Psychology, 33*(3), 307–316.

Köhler, W. (1917). Intelligenzprüfungen an Anthropoiden. I [Intelligence tests with anthropoids]. *Abhandlungen der königlich-preussischen Akademie der Wissenschaften,* 1–213.

Köhler, W. (1925). *The mentality of apes.* London: K. Paul, Trench, Trubner & Co.

Kohut, H. (1966). Formen und Umformungen des Narzißmus [Forms and transformations of narcissism. *PSYCHE, 20*(8), 561–587.

Kohut, H. (1971). *The Analysis of the Self: A Systematic Approach to the Psychoanalytic Treatment of Narcissistic Personality Disorders.* New York: International Universities Press.

Krebs, D. (1975). Empathy and Altruism. *Journal of Personality and Social Psychology, 32*(6), 1134–1146.

Lanzoni, S. (2012). Empathy in Translation: Movement and Image in the Psychological Laboratory. *Science in Context, 25*(03), 301–327.

Larsen, J. T., Norris, C. J., & Cacioppo, J. T. (2003). Effects of positive and negative affect on electromyographic activity over zygomaticus major and corrugator supercilii. *Psychophysiology, 40,* 776–785.

Lawrence, E. J., Shaw, P., Giampietro, V. P., Surguladze, S., Brammer, M. J., & David, A. S. (2006). The role of 'shared representations' in social perception and empathy: An fMRI study. *NeuroImage, 29*(4), 1173–1184.

Lee, S. J., Kang, D. H., Kim, C.-W., Gu, B. M., Park, J.-Y., Choi, C.-H., Shin, N. J., Lee, J.-M., & Kwon, J. S. (2010). Multi-level comparison of empathy in schizophrenia: An fMRI study of a cartoon task- *Psychiatry Research: Neuroimaging, 181*(2), 121–129.

Levenson, R. W., & Ruef, A. M. (1992). Empathy: A Physiological Substrate. *Journal of Personality and Social Psychology, 63*(2), 234–246.

Lipps, T. (1903). *Leitfaden der Psychologie* [Guidelines to psychology]. Leipzig: Verlag von Wilhelm Engelmann.

Mehrabian, A., & Epstein, N. (1972). A measure of emotional empathy. *Journal of Personality, 40*(4), 525–543.

Meltzoff, A. N., & Decety, J. (2003). What imitation tells us about social cognition: a rapprochement between developmental psychology and cognitive neuroscience. *Philosophical Transactions of the Royal Society London, 358*, 491–500.

Murphy, G. (1947). *Personality. A biosocial approach to origins and structure.* New York: Harper.

Neumann, D. L., & Westbury, H. R. (2011). The Psychophysiological Measurement of Empathy. In D. J. Scapaletti (Ed.). *Psychology of empathy* (pp. 119–42). New York: Nova Science Publishers.

Preston, S. D., & de Waal, F. B. M. (2002). Empathy: Its ultimate and proximate bases. *Behavioral and Brain Sciences, 25*(1), 1–20; discussion 20–71.

Redlich, F. C. (1959). Die Psychoanalyse und das Wertproblem [Psychoanalysis and the question of value]. *PSYCHE, 13*(9), 481–498.

Rogers, C. (1951). *Client-centered therapy: Its current practice, implications, and theory.* Boston: Houghton Mifflin Co.

Rogers, C. (1959). A theory of therapy, personality and interpersonal relationships, as developed in the client-centered framework. In S. Koch (Ed.). *Psychology: A study of science* (pp. 184–256). New York: McGraw-Hill.

Saunders, F. H., & Hall, G. S. (1900). Pity. *The American Journal of Psychology, 11*(4), 534–591.

Scheler, M (1913). *Zur Phänomenologie und Theorie der Sympathiegefühle und von Liebe und Haß* [Phenomenology and theory of the feeling of sympathy and of love and hate]. Halle: Max Niemeyer.

Singh, S., Modi, S., Goyal, S., Kaur, P., Singh, N., Bhatia, T., Deshpande, S. N., & Khushu, S. (2015). Functional and structural abnormalities associated with empathy in patients with schizophrenia: An fMRI and VBM study. *Journal of Biosciences, 40*(2), 355–364.

Smith, A. (1759). *The Theory of Moral Sentiments.* London: A. Millar.

Stueber, K. (2014). Empathy. In E. N. Zalta (Ed.). *The Stanford Encyclopedia of Philosophy.* Retrieved from http://plato.stanford.edu/archives/win2014/entries/empathy/

Titchener, E. B. (1909). *Lectures on the Experimental Psychology of the Thought-Processes.* New York: The Macmillan Company.

Titchener, E. B. (1915). *A Beginner's Psychology*. New York: The Macmillan Company.

Weigert, E. (1953). Die Entwicklung der psychoanalytischen Ausbildung in U. S.A. (Mitteilung) [The progress of psychoanalytic training in the US]. *PSYCHE, 6*(10), 632–640.

Wispé, L. (1986). The Distinction Between Sympathy and Empathy: To Call Forth a Concept, A Word Is Needed. *Journal of Personality and Social Psychology, 50*(2), 314–321.

Wispé, L. (1987). History of the concept of empathy. In N. Eisenberg & J. Strayer (Eds.). *Empathy and its development* (pp. 17–37). Cambridge, MA: Cambridge University Press.

6

From Absorption to Judgment: Empathy in Aesthetic Response

David Freedberg

Empathy has become one of the growth areas in cognitive neuroscience. For some time, it has also been seen as a clue to the understanding of aesthetic engagement with visual works of art. Vittorio Gallese and I have written at length about the relevance of empathetic responses to paintings, sculptures and even calligraphy (Freedberg & Gallese, 2007a). But our positions (especially mine) have been misunderstood. It has been said that we propose that empathetic engagement is constitutive of art (as in the attempted critique of our position by Roberto Casati and Alessandro Pignocchi (2007), to which we replied in Freedberg & Gallese, 2007b). Far from it.

D. Freedberg (✉)
Department of Art History and Archaeology, Columbia University, New York, USA
Italian Academy for Advanced Studies in America, Columbia University, New York, USA
e-mail: daf5@columbia.edu

V. Lux, S. Weigel (eds.), *Empathy*, Palgrave Studies in the Theory and History of Psychology, DOI 10.1057/978-1-137-51299-4_6

1 The History of Empathy: A Short Introduction

The history of empathy in art history is long, and the ancient precedents are frequently cited. Among the famous works of ancient sculpture described by Pliny the Elder is the statue of a limping man by Pythagoras of Rhegion, which so clearly showed the pain resulting from the ulcer on his leg that even spectators seemed to feel it (Pliny the Elder, 1857, p.19). Viewers today have similar feelings when seeing press photographs of the war-wounded and tortured of our own time. But the lessons of the images that issued from the war in Iraq and other battlefields go back to the earliest photographs showing humans mutilated by war, as, most strikingly, in the case of the American Civil War (on these see Rosenheim, 2013).[1]

Pliny's passage also comes to mind when one considers medieval and later sources that tell of spectators who have to catch their breath or even clasp their thighs as they notice the horrible boil on the leg of Saint Roch in paintings and sculptures of him. Pictures and sculptures of the suffering Christ were supposed to have similar effects, too (see the remarkable compendium of examples in James H. Marrow, 1979). The textual bases for suffering with Christ, for suffering just as he did, were applied to pictures of Him and his martyred saints as well. The well-known and very popular fourteenth-century *Meditations on the Life of Christ* are full of appeals to physically imagine oneself in the place of Christ, particularly as he suffers bodily (just as Saint Ignatius's *Spiritual Exercises* would a couple of centuries later draw on very similar notions of *imitatio* and *compassio*). They contain frequent exhortations – of the kind regularly transmitted by preachers to non-literate as well as literate audiences – to transform the act of looking into corporeal feeling, in order to better understand Christ's suffering: "*Look* at him well then, as

[1] I discussed not only the well-known war photos by Brady and Gardner, but also those by Reed Brockway Bontecou in a lecture entitled *The Great Paradox of Civil War Photography: Art History, Neuroscience and the Real War*, given at the Metropolitan Museum of Art on May 31, 2013, which I hope to publish on another occasion.

he goes along bowed down by the cross and gasping aloud. *Feel* as much compassion for him as you can, placed in such anguish," runs a typical passage, emphasizing the conjunction between looking and feeling as well as how one is supposed to imagine the scene visually (Bonaventura, 1961, p. 331). As He hung on the cross, Christ himself said, "My Father, see how afflicted my mother is. *I* ought to be crucified, not she, but she is with me on the cross" (Bonaventura, 1961, p. 335). "And she was grieved, and looking at the wounds of her son, was weakened by the sorrow of death. Do you see how often she is near death today?" (Bonaventura, 1961, p. 340) The link between looking and feeling, between sight and actual physical sensation, could not be clearer.

Saint Ignatius Loyola's *Spiritual Exercises* required its adepts to imagine Christ's suffering even more vividly *as if* He were before their own eyes, bleeding from his every wound, casting his eyes upward and hopelessly towards his Father. That *as if* is very critical indeed. Those engaged in these *Exercises* were supposed to feel the wounds on his knees as he dragged his heavy cross along the road to Calvary, to feel the nail penetrating Christ's hands and feet, to sense the weight of the body, the blood of his wounds, and the smell of his wounds. They were exhorted to feel not only the physical pain of the Son, but the emotional suffering of his Virgin mother as she sees him hanging so pathetically on the Cross. Through repeating the exercises and imagining the pictures they had seen, they were supposed to feel the heat of the fires of Purgatory as if – *as if* – they were already there. The same, for example, for the boiling oil into which John the Evangelist was plunged during his martyrdom in the many treatises that adapted these Jesuit techniques of vivid imagination and co-suffering.

There is a clear theoretical line from Ignatius Loyola to Robert Vischer and on to Antonio Damasio that draws on more than just imagining oneself in the position of who or what one sees. The claim is that one suffers in some similar way to the sufferer one sees, that one feels the same emotions as one might feel if one were somehow present in the scene represented by the image itself. In *Das Optische Formgefühl* of 1873, Vischer outlined the grounding modern theory of empathy in art, that of *Einfühlung*, or "feeling in," while in *Descartes' Error* of 1995, Damasio already set out the basis for an as-if theory or responses to the movements of others by describing the cortical reorganization that occurs upon the feeling of such movements as one's own. The history of empathy tells us not only about responses to real people and real images, but also to the imagination of such scenes.

On the one hand, then, empathy for pain; on the other, empathy for emotion and – above all – for movement. The implications for painting concerning the relationship between bodily movement and the immediate deduction of the emotions were classically set out for Western art in Leon Battista Alberti's treatise *On Painting* (first published in Latin in 1435):

> The painting will move the soul of the beholder when the figures painted there each clearly shows the movement of his own soul. [. . .] we weep with the weeping, laugh with the laughing, and grieve with the grieving." And then he adds, "These movements of the soul are known from the movements of the body. (Alberti, 1966, p. 41)

1.1 Picturing Compassion: Rogier's "Deposition"

In discussing the relevance of modern theories of empathetic engagement (and, in particular, of contemporary findings about the neural substrate of physical and emotional engagement with visual images), I have long begun with the example of Rogier van der Weyden's great *Deposition* altarpiece from around 1435 which originally came from the Church of Our Lady outside the Walls in Louvain and is now in the Prado in Madrid. What is striking about this particular is the degree to which historical understandings of how the work was supposed to function coincide with recent neural accounts of responses to the movements and emotions of others. Both in the fifteenth century and today, the effects of a work like this are finely predicated on the relationship between movement and the evocation of emotion, as well as on the ways in which beholders' inward, embodied simulation of the depicted movements result in the evocation of the emotions the artist and his patrons intended. It is precisely for this reason, rather than any closeness to a written text, that Rogier's altarpiece continues to be so compelling.

In the fifteenth century, viewers of a work like Rogier's were supposed to feel both what Christ and those present at the scene of the *Deposition* felt. The onlookers' compassion for Christ was felt through their bodies, and their feelings were transmitted through the effects they produced on viewers. Viewers were exhorted to physically feel what Christ felt and to emotionally feel what the witnesses at the scene felt. The bystanders at the scene – the three Maries, Joseph of Arimathea, Nicodemus and so on – were all said to have suffered as Christ did. In Rogier's painting this was exemplified, as Otto von Simson showed many years ago, by the way in which the slump and swoon of Christ's mother, the Virgin, imitates the form of Christ's body descending from the Cross (von Simson, 1953; see also the important material collected in Ringbom, 1984). Her compassion for her son, her *co-suffering*, was – and still is – exemplified and embodied by her repetition of Christ's slump. In almost every previous depiction of this scene, the Virgin is shown standing, not collapsing – let alone in the same way as Christ descended from the Cross. Rogier shows her in this manner not only to exemplify the notion of co-suffering, but also because he knew (consciously or unconsciously) that the Virgin's slump has the ability to evoke a sense of slumping (that is, bodily co-suffering) in his viewers as well. It is as if he knew that the sight of others' movements entailed the embodiment – mostly simulated, occasionally acted out – of the same movements within the viewers themselves.

1.2 Mirror Neurons and Embodied Simulation

The discovery of mirror neurons enabled a much clearer understanding of what Vittorio Gallese appropriately called *embodied simulation* (Gallese, 2005). By this he intended the bodily sense viewers have of imitating the actions of others. It was and remains through this that the evocation of the relevant emotions ensue. Ever since the great revival of the study of the emotions in the 1980s, it has been known that viewing an emotion (for example, fear) activates many of the same cortical and subcortical areas and networks in viewers as would be activated in the figures they see. In the case of fear, the amygdala reacts both in the fearful person and the viewer of that person; the same occurs with feelings of disgust and the activation of anterior insula. It is through such common coding, as Wolfram Prinz so influentially called it (Prinz, 1997), that we have a form of direct access to, and intimate understanding of, the emotions of others. The mirror theorists, like William James before them, provided the link with the movements of the body.

All this applies to works of art as well. Rogier's skill lay as much in his ability to convey the movements and emotions of his protagonists as in his much-vaunted mastery of Early Netherlandish Painting techniques. Few if any surpassed him in terms of his precision of brushwork, depth of color, and command of anatomy, physiognomy, and pathognomy. The ability to convey to a viewer the movements and, consequently, the intentions of others is fundamentally predicated on the existence of mirror neurons that fire in the premotor cortex (and inferior parietal lobule) of the viewers as if they were actually executing the action themselves. It is this process that conveys to the viewer a sense of the movements of the protagonists in a scene and the continued understanding, even now, of the very essence of the painting – namely the evocation of appropriate emotions, *even without the most basic knowledge of the elements of the story*. Of course, such elements may well refine the response and enhance religious experience, but cognitive knowledge of the kind supplied by texts, say, the Bible or the *Meditations on the Life of Christ*, is not necessary for the automatic and precognitive responses that constitute the fundamental conditions for viewers' emotional, bodily, and empathetic engagement with a work like Rogier's altarpiece.

Since the late 1990s, considerable research has been devoted to the extrastriate body area (EBA) in the lower occipito-temporal cortex that fires in response to the sight of other people's bodies (for some groundwork on the EBA, see the early article by Perrett et al. (1985). This was then taken up by a number of writers, especially Peelen (2005) and Peelen and Downing (2005). Beatrice de Gelder and others have shown that it is through the activation of distributed areas involving fusiform areas and the amygdala that viewers grasp what she calls the emotional body language (EBL) of others, either in the flesh or as figures in a representation (de Gelder, 2006). An easy objection to these findings is the claim that such responses only apply to scenes from real life, but they turn out to apply to images and art as well. Body images automatically generate the N170 waveform in the EEG, and it would seem obvious that artistic skill should play a significant role in the efficacy of arousing bodily responses to EBL, though so far little has been made of this possibility. One's sense of another person's bodily travails and of accidents to bodily pose and position, even the inversion of one's own body in the case of viewing figures in works such as Rubens' *The Fall of the Damned* for example has to do with the perception of bodies in motion and thus activates the superior temporal sulcus (STS) as well (de Gelder, 2006). Significantly, although the EBA chiefly responds selectively to static body images, it also projects to the STS, which plays such a critical role in the perception of bodily movements, even in static images.

The discovery of mirror neurons also greatly enhanced our understanding of bodily responses to the pains and travails of others. Mirror circuits are activated not only while observing others' movements, but also in response to the sight of bodily haplessness (as in the case of inversion) and to more serious bodily events and physical insults. In a now well-known article, Gallese and Christiaan Keysers clearly set out how the sight of puncture wounds in the bodies of others generates an automatic sense of bodily infraction in observers (Keysers et al., 2004). This mirroring effect is chiefly registered in the secondary somatosensory cortex, known to produce a frisson when touched or stimulated during epilepsy presurgery exploration and evaluation.[2] It is all too likely that the wounds in pictorial examples – say Christ's hands and feet in Rogier's *Deposition*, Saint Thomas' finger poking into the wound in Christ's side in Caravaggio's *The Incredulity of Saint Thomas*, and the nail smashed through Christ's hand in Grunewald's great *Crucifixion* in Isenheim produce a similar effect (whether weaker or stronger will presumably

[2] The feeling is clear; the precise location of the feeling less so.

have to do with the skill of the artist). Thanks to the research on mirror neurons, we are now in possession of a far more convincing (and concrete) way to account for the kinds of emulational and simulational bodily feelings that arise upon sight of others' movements, of the emotions that such movements entail and express, and of a wide range of insults to the bodies of others. Some of these simulatory forms, like the sense of inwardly simulating the actions of others, are now definable in cortical terms. Others, like the sensation one might have of feeling the physical trials and tortures of others, are less clearly so. Often these responses seem to occur in the relevant body part, but not always. Sometimes they seem to be there but then dissipate, as if localized pain suddenly becomes unlocalizable.

1.3 Empathy: From "feeling-in" to the "as-if" Body Loop

Empathy has many meanings. It usually (but not always) implies the body. Precisely the feeling of the movements that one sees formed the basis of famous theories on empathy or *Einfühlung* in the works of the great nineteenth and early-twentieth century empathy theorists, like Robert Vischer and Theodor Lipps. Aby Warburg's notion of the *Pathosformel* (in which emotion is expressed through the movements of the body) also draws on the relationship between movement, especially that of the body beneath the drapery, and the expression of emotion.

In his invocation of what he called the "as-if body loop," Damasio was one of the earliest to set out a clear neural account of the argument that knowledge of the emotions of others relied upon a simulation of how the perceiver would feel *as if* he or she were in the situation observed. In mirror theory, such responses are often described as being pre-rational and automatic; Damasio's student Ralph Adolphs and others provided direct evidence for the unconscious simulation of emotions (Adolphs, Damasio, Tranel, Cooper, & Damasio, 2000).

2 Empathy as Bodily Engagement with the Movements of Others

In this part, I want to suggest (1) that empathy is fundamentally a matter of bodily engagement; (2) that the use of the term be confined to empathetic engagement with the movements of others, or even with the implied movements of others – and not only be used in reference to their emotional condition or the stories they tell; (3) that even though empathy is not constitutive of art, the form of immersion it entails is often a critical preliminary stage in aesthetic judgment – and always an illustrative one.

My aim in referring to the effects on beholders of works like Rogier's *Deposition*, Caravaggio's *Incredulity*, and Grunewald's *Crucifixion* was to suggest how recent research on the neural substrate of empathetic engagement overlaps with the functions of pictures from the past, and how this research may help us to understand their continuing effectiveness as well. It was not to show that empathy or emotion, or even the successful arousal of an imitative sense of movement, is constitutive of art.

But even what I took to be a relatively uncomplicated claim turned out to be controversial. Some critics flatly maintained that empathy has nothing to do with art and that aesthetic judgment has nothing to do with immersion in or bodily emotional involvement with a work, nor with simulation of movement.[3] The argument, as is commonly known, is that aesthetic judgment is detached, disinterested, and that art is somehow ironic and distanced (as Kant perhaps also wanted to believe) from the kinds of intimate bodily and physical engagements entailed in empathy.[4] Others noted that Alberti's views were written down just a few years before Rogier's painting was installed and claimed that the idea

---

[3] For a vigorous dismissal of what Nelson Goodman called the "tingle-immersion theory," see Goodman (1976, p. 112).

[4] See the more recent and excellent work by Thomas Hilgers that suggests Kant never intended his notion of disinterested judgment to be detached from the body – *pace* Nietzsche in *The Genealogy of Morals*, III, 6 and my own earlier work. See Nietzsche (1887/1996); for Hilgers' work (which I hope will be published soon), see for the moment Hilgers (2010).

that movements involve the readability of the emotions with which they are invested was simply in the air in the 1430s and that the assumptions underlying viewer involvement are entirely historically determined. I was not unaware of the currency of these ideas at the time. The point is that they were in the air for very good reasons indeed (and not just because they were fashionable). In empathy, history and context merge with biology and neurology.

The reasons that such ideas were in the air in the 1430s were basically the same as they always are: they have to do with the inextricable relationship between vision, the body, and movement that lies at the roots of all forms of empathetic engagement with images. This relationship accounts for the appeal of a work such as Rogier van der Weyden's altarpiece, not only in the fifteenth century, but now too. In significant ways, viewers continue to understand this work just as it was intended to be understood at his time. A visit to the Prado suffices to see how visitors flock to it, not because they are devout Christians or because of the undoubted brilliance of the painting's technique (though this is certainly a factor as well), but because they are detained in front of it by a direct emotional involvement facilitated and strengthened by the activation of a sense of the bodily movements that underlie the emotions the artist wishes to convey. This involvement is also facilitated by viewers' instant recognition of the expressions and gestures of the protagonists. These expressions and gestures not only activate mirror responses in the viewer but also activate the same subcortical areas (the amygdala in the case of fear, the anterior insula in the case of disgust) that are activated when viewers feel the same emotions themselves

2.1 *Gesture and the* Pathosformel

The original mirror research emphasized that mirror neurons only fire in response to goal-directed actions, but it has now been shown that mirror circuits may be activated by the sight of intransitive, non-goal directed actions as well (Graziano, Taylor, & Moore, 2002; Rizzolatti, Scandolara, Matelli, & Gentilucci, 1981).[5] Here it is perhaps worth noting that many actions that may not be regarded as goal-directed are often just that, as in the case of the gesture of wiping the eyes with the front or the back of the hand or crossing the arms in front of the chest (a clear and intuitive effort at self-protection against real or perceived danger) likewise the action of warding off by means of an upraised hand and contracted wrist, as with Adam's gesture against the sword-bearing angel in Michelangelo's *Expulsion from Paradise* on the ceiling of the Sistine Chapel. These are gestures that occur across history and cultures, almost always with the same intent. One of the most frequent outward gestures of grief is throwing the arms up in the air, as can be seen in countless lamentations over the dead body of Christ. It finds expression in ancient and modern art. It is used so often to express extreme grief that it raises the question of a possible correlation between the particular gesture and the expression of that emotion.

But this possibility is skewed by the similarity of this pathos-formula to the throwing upwards of the arms not in grief but in joy or triumph, as so often occurs in the case of victorious players in sport events after they have scored a goal or won a match. It may well be, however, that the ability of these gestures to convey joy and triumph has to do with both contextual circumstances (for example cheering spectators, smiles on faces) and with the fact that they are combined with a leap into the air, a detachment from the earth-boundedness of our usual terrestrial existence. Or perhaps it may be that the difference between what such apparently similar gestures convey depends on even smaller physical modulations of their component movements than those we might consciously notice. The latter possibility remains to be examined.

2.2 "Life Enhancement"

Whatever the case, we can nevertheless surmise that such gestures work their effects by arousing in viewers' bodies a form of muscular emulation

[5] On the subject of the enhanced motor potentials evoked upon observing the raised hand and extended wrist gesture (as in Michelangelo's Adam warding off the Angel in the Expulsion from Paradise mentioned in this paragraph), see Battaglia, Lisanby, & Freedberg (2011). For a recent behavioral study of the automatic imitation of "goal-less" actions, see Chiavarino, Bugiani, Grandi, & Colle (2013).

of what they see outside themselves. Indeed, it is precisely this that Bernard Berenson describes in *The Florentine Painters of the Renaissance* when he refers to the life-enhancing qualities of the works of Michelangelo, Pollaiuolo, and others. The idea was that the viewing of works such as the *ignudi* on the Sistine ceiling, or Pollaiuolo's bronze *Wrestlers*, gives viewers a sense of muscular potential, imparting a feeling of physical emulation within their bones, so to speak, that exceeds their actual physical capacity (Berenson, 1896, section VIII, 1960, p. 77). This phenomenon is what Berenson intended (to some extent following his old teacher William James) by what still may seem like the purely sentimental notion of life-enhancement through looking at the muscular movements of others – in art or sports. Far from being sentimental – though perhaps expressed (as so often with descriptions of empathy and empathetic feels) in sentimental and banal language – it is precisely such responses that offer more concrete hopes for therapy via looking than have been recognized as of yet. They pave the way for a more complete understanding of the foundations of aesthetic judgment.[6]

Warburg's concept of the *Pathosformel* had less to do with the purely historical notion of the handing down of apparently formulaic expressions of emotion than with the notion that the outward movements of the body and the flow of draperies that cover them reveal inner emotions. This was a modern revival of a more ancient idea. As he wrote in his dissertation, the turbulence of the bodies depicted in works by Botticelli, and even more so in other works by quattrocento artists like Francesco di Giorgio, was directly translated into some form of inner turbulence within the viewer.[7] For him, these were elements of a gestural language that he referred to as "engrams of passionate experience [that] survive as a heritage stored in the memory."[8] Warburg never specified the biological mechanisms involved, though he seems to have presumed

[6] Warburg grappled with this issue from the very beginning. The *Vorbemerkung* to his dissertation on Botticelli's *Birth of Venus and Spring* concludes "Nebenbei sei bemerkt, dass dieser Nachweis für die psychologische Aesthetik deshalb bemerkenswerth ist, weil man hier in den Kreisen der schaffenden Künstler den Sinn für den ästhetischen Akt der 'Einfühlung' in seinem Werden als stilbildende Macht beobachten kann". (Warburg, 2010, pp. 39–40; Engl. transl. in Warburg, 1999, p. 89).

there were some at work. The pathos-formula becomes formulaic not just because it is embedded in a long historical tradition, but because it is rooted in the neural links between movement, the body, and the effective expression of emotion. These links, annoyingly for many contemporary pundits, may well be predicated on precognitive factors that have nothing to do with the pressures of context and experience though they may, often inevitably, act on them.

Everyone now recalls Warburg's dictum that the most difficult problem of all in art is that of capturing still images of life in motion.[9] At the same time, it is important to remember another strain in Warburg's thought. Despite his affinity with Winckelmann's theories on the relationship between calm staticity and beauty, he was at least as much influenced by Nietzsche's views of the close link between movement and sensation and the latter's intense, sometimes sarcastic, disapproval of Kantian notions of disinterest in aesthetic judgment (Nietzsche, 1887/1996, III, section 6). It was precisely in the same period that Nietzsche would write about how we can "*produce the feelings in ourselves by imitating with our own body the expression of his eyes, his voice, his walk, his bearing*" and acknowledge that this could happen by imitating "*their reflection in words, pictures, and music*" too (Nietzsche, 1881/1997, p. 142).[10] But the generation of like emotion through willed imitation, while clearly a related topic, must remain a subject for another occasion.

---

[7] See the valuable edition of the text and notes in Warburg, 2010. For an extremely useful contribution to the understanding of the origins of Warburg's use of the term *Pathosformel*, see Wedepohl (2012). For more on this, see my remarks in Freedberg (2013).

[8] "Daß diese Engramme leidenschaftlicher Erfahrung als gedächtnisbewahrtes Erbgut überleben und vorbildlich den Umriss bestimmen, den die Künstlerhand schafft" (*Mnemosyne Einleitung*, B 10/VI 929, in Warburg, 2012, p. 631, own transl.). See also Gombrich and Saxl (1986, p. 245).

[9] "Das schwierigste Problem für die bildende Kunst, lenkt das Festhalten der Bilder des bewegten Lebens" (Warburg 2012, p. 107). See also the contribution to this subject by Philippe-Alain Michaud (1998).

2.3 Vision, Movement, and Emotion

The connection between movement and emotion was always present in Warburg's writings, just as in the work of William James. In the *Principles of Psychology* from 1890, James famously set out his own arguments for the ways in which movement is not simply associated with, but actually precedes, emotion (especially what he calls "the coarser emotions"; James, 1890, p. 449). Even before James, however, there was a rich tradition in France of writing about the relationship between vision and movement, which Jonathan Crary (1999) concisely outlines in his book on attention. This more or less explicit group of theories about the connection between motor and aesthetic response, is of considerable importance for the history of the relationship between movement, emotion, and empathy. In all of them, perception of a mental or visual representation is taken to culminate in movement, irrespective of whether such a movement is outer or inner, voluntary or automatic. They are based on the notion that human responses can bypass conscious thought. Sensation is not to be thought of as part of a sequence of mental events resulting in knowledge, cognition, or even perception, but as producing movement. Such ideas formed the basis of "dynamogeny,"[11] a notion taken up by a succession of both scientific and more popular writers.

Jean-Martin Charcot himself wrote of the "dynamogenic influence of the visual on the motor center" (Charcot, 1991, p. 310). In his *Sensation et Mouvement* from 1887, Charcot's assistant Charles Féré set out a theory of "psychomotor induction" (Féré, 1900, p. 87) that influenced the painter Seurat in his views of color not just in terms of optical response, but of the evocation of automatic bodily responses, too (see the strong criticism in Henri Bergson, 1910). Similar ideas also occurred in

---

[10] The passage continues, "Then a similar feeling arises in us in consequence of an ancient association between movement and sensation . . . ". (Nietzsche, 1881/1997, p. 142).

[11] The term seems to have been coined by the neurologist Charles-Edouard Brown Séquard (1871–1894). For its origins, see Crary (1999, pp. 165–9). Crary also notes the relationship between the term "dynamogeny" and the concepts of motor excitation and facilitation (Crary, 1999, p. 165, note 31).

the once-influential work of Eugène Véron in the mid-1870s, and, of course, in both James' and Nietzsche's works in the 1880s, especially in the latter's views on what he called "the ancient association between movement and sensation" (Nietzsche, 1881/1997, p. 142). In all these ways, the curious sounding doctrine of dynamogeny contributed to the late nineteenth-century development of the notion of the life-enhancing feelings that could be engendered by viewing works of art. And so this improbable circle was closed, at least in art historical terms, by James's former student, Berenson. By the end of the decade, Warburg himself was referring to the notion of "dynamograms" to describe the persistence in memory of the elements of gestural language conveying emotion, without, perhaps significantly, going as far in the therapeutic or body-changing mode as so many of his contemporaries did.[12]

French ideas about how the visual is transformed into the motoric culminated in the phenomenology of Merleau-Ponty. It is perhaps not surprising that some of the most important recent work on the embodied and emotional dimensions of seen movement, parallel and even a bit prior to the mirror theorists, is to be found in the research on motor cognition by Marc Jeannerod and his pupil Jean Decety.[13] But first let us turn to a recent writer with a very different view.

2.4 Emotion and Cognition

In her monumental work on the emotions entitled *Upheavals of Thought*, Martha Nussbaum insisted on what she called a neo-stoic theory of the emotions (Nussbaum, 2001). If she had attended to

[12] Several examples in Gombrich and Saxl (1986, pp. 248–50). Gombrich cites the *Allgemeine Ideen*, and the notebooks for 1927–1928, p. 20 ("Das antikische Dynamogramm wird in maximaler Spannung aber unpolarisiert in Bezug auf die passive oder aktive Energetik des nachfühlenden, nachsprechenden (erinnernden) überliefert. Erst der Kontakt mit der Zeit bewirkt die Polarisation. Diese kann zur radikalen Umkehr (Inversion) des echten antiken Sinnes führen") and p. 67 ("die Polarization der Dynamogramme durch die Antikische Mneme"); Koos, Pichler, Rappl, and Swoboda (1994). The source for the first of these passages is given as 1.6.1929.

[13] See my discussion of their work further below. For a general view of Jeannerod's theory of motor cognition and its relationship with what neuroscientists call imagery (what humanists would call the imagination of images), see Jeannerod (2006).

the lessons provided by visual works of art (such as Rogier van der Weyden's altarpiece) on the notion of *compassio* and the literal co-suffering on which it depends, and if she had acknowledged the unconscious and spontaneous dimensions of emotional responses to what one sees, then she might have drawn entirely different conclusions. In Nussbaum's view, emotions are entirely cognitive. They are upheavals of *thought* specifically. They are strictly the product of appraisal. Before the neuroscientific revival of studying emotion, one might indeed have continued to think so. It might have seemed the only way to deal with what was thought to be the unruly, unclassifiable, and disordered state of the emotions themselves.[14]

Cognitive neuroscience changed all of this. With the work of neuroscientists like Damasio and Adolphs on the role of emotions in decision-making and evaluation and of Joseph LeDoux on fear responses, the emotions were restored to the body. What this entailed, of course, was that emotions might not be entirely intellectual. Especially from the mid-1980s on, much research has shown what is not cognitive about emotions and empathy. It became possible to argue for ways of conceptualizing emotions and the movements that underlie them as automatic, unconscious and pre-rational, rather than products of cognitive appraisal.

Nussbaum devoted an entire chapter to *compassio* as a strictly cognitive and evaluative emotion. If she had instead reflected on the fact that *compassio* means to *suffer with*, quite literally, and if she had acknowledged the neural accounts of how the sight of a wound often produces a clear and precognitive somatosensory reaction, she might have come to a similar conclusion. But she would nevertheless have rejected out of hand Gallese and his mentor Giacomo Rizzolatti's account of how the embodied simulation of responses to the actions and feelings of others precedes reflection, and, in my view, also evaluation and appraisal. "In our brain," they state,

[14] The whole study of emotion was long neglected precisely because of this attitude (I remember discussing this in 1980 with Amélie Rorty, whose anthology *Explaining Emotions* (Rorty, 1980) played a major role in the renewed philosophical interest in the topic).

> there are neural mechanisms (mirror mechanisms) that allow us to directly understand the meaning of the actions and emotions of others by internally replicating ("simulating") them without any explicit reflective mediation. Conceptual reasoning is not necessary for this understanding. As human beings we are able to reason about others and to use this capacity to understand other people's minds at the conceptual declarative level. The fundamental mechanism that allows us a direct experiential grasp of the mind of others is not conceptual reasoning but direct simulation of events through the mirror mechanism. (Gallese, Keysers, & Rizzolatti, 2004, p. 396)

The possibility that gestures and emotions might be understood through embodied simulation suggests a form of translation not necessarily constrained by cultural bounds. You understand the emotions such movements entail because you have a body, not because you know the story. It is the achievement of a good painter or sculptor to have the measure of this, consciously or unconsciously. Artists convey the emotions they wish through their knowledge of the body's capacity for movement, under whatever circumstances, and through their ability to transmit and evoke exactly the same sense of movement in the viewer. It is for this reason that empathy should be considered not so much as an all-purpose account of a sense of understanding the emotions of others, but as an account of bodily engagement with their seen movements.

Whether or not one agrees about the role of mirror neurons in aesthetic response, to continue to insist on a purely neo-stoic, intellectual, and evaluative view of the emotions would be to ignore the now abundant evidence for the degree of automaticity and direct precognitive involvement entailed in emotional responses and what we now broadly call empathy.

2.5 Empathy as the Felt Simulation of Observed Movement

But why restrict the concept of empathy to the movements of the body or to the feeling of direct imitation of another person's movements? Not only because this specification provides a better sense of the frequent automaticity of responses to images, but because it also allows us a pragmatic refinement of the use of what has now become rather too loose a term. I argue for the constitutive role of movement in empathy both for the sake of analytic clarity and to distinguish the concept of empathy more clearly from other forms of deep emotional engagement with others.

Damasio's "as-if" body-loop theory described a neural circuit subtending the movement of one's own limbs that produces a reaction as if the body were engaged in the same movements as those of the bodies one observes (and not necessarily corresponding to the current reality of the observing body). Both his views and those of the mirror theorists outline brain circuits that are activated when viewers feel themselves seemingly perform actions they see, but do not actually carry them out. At about the same time that Damasio was working on these problems, the Parma mirror neuron team not only suggested a plausible theory of bodily engagement with images; they also gave a vivid account of why such engagements were pre-rational. In short, the renewed association of the emotions with the body gave a new impulse to empathy theory, in which empathy became less cognitive, so to speak, than before.[15]

In all the examples I have cited so far, observation is central. Against this it will no doubt be argued that empathy can issue from verbal as much as from visual description, but I want to suggest that the feeling-in that arises from vision implicates the body more directly than the kind of imagination that is aroused by words alone, whether read or heard. The feeling-in that results from seeing an object is instructive even for the imagination roused by verbal description and for the form of inner vision that neuroscientists, confusingly for art historians, simply call *imagery* – in other words, the imagination of a scene, particularly, in the case of imagined movement.

David Milner and Andrew Goodale compellingly argued that vision evolved for movement and action, rather than for perception

[15] To say this, however, is not to claim that bodily movements that precede emotion are necessarily precognitive, though they may in many instances be automatic. Automatic responses can just as well be the result of training as the result of precognitive mechanisms.

(Goodale & Milner, 1995, 2nd ed., 2008). As we now know from many areas of research, identification of an object may well be preceded by a motor response predicated on the location and orientation of the stimulus in relation to the body of the viewer, a process that occurs in the first instance in the parietal lobe. The transformation of vision into movement always implicates the body, or the simulation of movements implied by the body or even of traces left by manual actions. The model of empathy proposed here is thus not just predicated on the automatic transformation of vision into movement, not only on the body in the picture, but also on the implied body, the body, and movement behind the trace in the work. This is what lies behind much of Merleau-Ponty's *Phenomenology of Perception* and his work, for example, on Cézanne.

No one who looks at a painting by Jackson Pollock, such as his *Number 1, 1949*, or *Number 7, 1950*, for example (there are, of course, many other possible examples), can fail to have a sense of being swept up in the movement of the thrown paint. Even if one insists on the pure abstraction of the scene, or has never seen the famous films by Hans Namuth of Pollock in action, one still feels compelled to move in the general direction of the perceived motion of the work. One may not actually move, but one still has the feeling of doing so, even of somehow being compelled to move. Sophisticates may deny all of this, or counter that if it is so, it has little to do with the aesthetic constitution of the work.

But the evidence for motor responses continues to mount, in research on both the behavioral and the neuronal level. Recent research by Maria Alessandra Umiltà, Gallese and myself has demonstrated the elicitation of corticomotor responses to the sight of brushstrokes in works by Franz Kline and to cuts in the canvases of Lucio Fontana (Freedberg & Gallese, 2007a; Freedberg, 2011; Umiltà, Berchio, Sestito, Freedberg, & Gallese, 2012). Though these may be non-conscious responses, they may also be related to a vaguely conscious sense of inner movement, seeming to recapitulate the actions that are felt to have produced the brushstrokes and cuts of the artist. It is the further transformation of such forms of motor engagement that bring us closer to the roots of aesthetic judgment. This does not, of course, get us any closer to the constitution of art. It does not take us further into what happens beyond empathetic engagement with what we see (or hear). Nevertheless, I will argue for the importance of this early form of engagement with a visual work as constituting a critical step in the passage from sight to aesthetic judgment.

2.6 Motor Responses in Empathy

More or less at the same time as the Parma team under Rizzolatti published the first results of their discovery of mirror neurons, Decety and Jeannerod were working on the relationship between vision, movement and imitative motor cortex activity. It is not surprising that Decety in particular, along with his later colleague Philip Jackson,[16] should have made a fundamental contribution to the study of empathy.

They started unpromisingly – or at least their basic article from 2004 entitled "The Functional Architecture of Empathy" started unpromisingly. They began by observing that at the phenomenological level "empathy denotes a sense of similarity between the feelings one experiences and those expressed by others" (Decety & Jackson, 2004, p. 71). But this observation was certainly insufficient. It should be possible to distinguish between mere similarity of feeling (between oneself and another) and the kind of bodily and motor identification that the words "empathy" and *Einfühlung* intend. It is not just a matter of similarity, nor just of feeling or emotion. Instead of beginning with the notion of shared representation, Decety and his colleagues might have done well to proceed directly to the question of perception and action coupling in order to further clarify the link between sensory and motor activity in empathetic responses to others. It is true that they called on James J. Gibson's now hackneyed view of affordances to account for the direct link between perception and action. Affordances are properties of objects or events in the surroundings that respond to the needs

[16] Jackson came from Andrew Meltzoff's team at Washington University in Saint Louis that did fundamental and abundant work on neonate imitation of expression in the late 1970s (Meltzoff, 1988; Meltzoff & Moore, 1977, 1983).

of the perceiver. They are physical, psychological and ecological. But Decety et al. were paradoxically inexplicit – at least in this early yet fundamental article – about the ways in which empathetic involvement with others is predicated above all on motor involvement. Decety was presumably as aware of this as anyone. In fact, he and Jackson were clearly familiar with the work by Günther Knoblich and Rüdiger Flach that adopted Prinz's common coding theory. The core assumptions of this theory claim that actions are coded in terms of perceivable effects and that the perception of an action activates action representations to the degree that the perceived and represented actions are similar (Knoblich & Prinz, 2001). It is in this respect that sensory and motor representations are shared between individuals.

I take these positions two steps further. First, I extend these claims not only to the relations between individuals and depictions of individuals but also to depictions that *imply* the actions of individuals. Second, I propose that empathy is not just a matter of shared representations or common coding, but is only to be understood in terms of felt engagement with the movements of others.

Together with colleagues like Julie Grèzes, Decety emphasized that the neural circuit involved in action-execution overlaps with the circuit activated when actions are observed (for a review of the empirical experimental evidence, see Jeannerod, 2001). As is now well-known, this circuit involves the premotor cortex, the parietal inferior lobule, the supplementary motor area and the cerebellum (Decety & Grèzes, 1999; 2001; 2002). Significantly, Decety also did substantial experimental work showing that imagining one's own actions (Decety et al., 1994; Hari et al., 1998), imagining another's actions (Decety & Grèzes, 1999) and imitating the actions performed by a model[17] all activate the same areas of the premotor cortex and posterior parietal lobe in the observer as in the observed (Decety, 1996; Decety & Grèzes, 1999). Both the Lyons and the mirror groups acknowledged that these shared motor representation mechanisms provided an important foundation for intersubjectivity. What they left out initially – though it was hinted at by Damasio and then others – was that these mechanisms might also provide an important foundation for the intersubjective understanding of what art historians call visual imagery – that is, material visual images, not just imagined images ("imagery" in neuroscientific parlance). Decety notes that this form of intersubjectivity is necessary but not sufficient for emotional understanding (Decety & Jackson, 2004, p. 77). The question still remains as to precisely how one gets from action to emotion.

2.7 From Action to Emotion

In the works of ancient and Renaissance writers, this connection was almost taken for granted. One of the earliest statements on the relationship between artistic representations of emotion and the feelings they arouse in the spectator was made by Socrates. The observation, recorded in Xenophon's *Memorabilia*, lies at the basis of doctrines such as that of the *affetti*. After asking Cleiton the sculptor whether the accurate representation of the different parts of the body as they are affected by the pose – the flesh wrinkled or tense, the limbs compressed or outstretched, the muscles taut or loose – makes them look more real and convincing, Socrates goes on to inquire: "Does not the exact imitation of the feelings that affect bodies in action also produce a sense of satisfaction in the spectator?" "O yes," replies the sculptor. "Then must not the threatening look in the eyes of fighters be accurately represented, and the triumphant expression on the face of conquerors be imitated?" "Most certainly." Socrates concludes that "it follows then that the sculptor must represent in his figures the activities of the soul" (Xenophon, *Memorabilia*, III, 10).[18]

Both here and in Alberti's famous dictum about how the movements of the body reflect the movements of the soul, we find the habitual conflation of the two meanings of the idea of movement: one physical, the other metaphysical; one corporeal, the other emotional. But the latter two are not mutually exclusive. In such passages, action is coupled with emotion as closely as it is with perception.

[17] Originally suggested by Meltzoff and Moore's famous neonate experiments of 1977, as in the articles already noted, but especially Meltzoff and Moore (1977). For adult subjects, see Decety et al. (1997, 2002) and Iacoboni et al. (1999).

The phenomenon of emotional contagion is often described in terms of its physical manifestations, such as the automatic mimicking and synchronizing of the expressions, postures, vocalizations and movements of others, which are then taken as outward signs of the tendency for associated emotions to converge with each other (Hatfield, Cacioppo, & Rapson, 1994; see also the useful literary and art historical examples in Schaub, Suthor, and Fischer-Lichte (2005). This is not, of course, what we generally intend by empathy, though what is fundamentally at stake in both phenomena is, as I have suggested, the matter of automaticity, not cognitive appraisal. The latter may indeed play a critical role in emotional responses,[19] but the question we confront here is *how* we most immediately perceive the affective state of another person. We perceive it, for the most part, through the actions that express their emotion, their expressions (after all another form of action), or even through their implied actions. We do not perceive emotions in the first instance through the prefrontal modulation of subcortical responses. We may *process* them and become more clearly conscious of them via such routes, but the more problematic issue is to define what happens first. It should perhaps be noted here that even in the absence of bodily functionality or in cases of bodily deficits, empathy involves the neural substrate of sensorimotor responses.

3 Empathy, Compassion, and Sympathy

But what about empathy without a body? What about compassion in the modern psychological sense? Someone tells you her sad story, perhaps on a plane or train. You are a captive audience; you listen to her. She may even interest you for one reason or another; you may find her sympathetic, as one colloquially says, and so you listen. She tells you the

[18] This translation from E. C. Marchant, London-New York: 1923. Not surprisingly the passage is quoted on the very first page of Jennifer Montagu (1994).

[19] For basic surveys of the neural substrates of emotional appraisal in terms of prefrontal modulation of lower level responses, see Ochsner, Bunge, Gross, and Gabrieli (2002) and Ochsner and Gross (2005).

sad story of her life, her vicissitudes, her loss of jobs; maybe she recounts the successive deaths of her nearest and dearest. You feel sorry for her; you understand her pain. You understand her simply because you have suffered similarly yourself; you have lost parents or children; you have suffered the same pains she has. This is not empathy. This is not a matter of spontaneously feeling the pain of others, except in an entirely metaphorical sense. This is rooted in your past. It is based on anecdotes that involve appraisal, but not on automatic responses of the body. It is a form of compassion based on comparison – comparison between what has happened to you and what has happened to another. You may think that you can understand what it is like to be in her shoes because you have been in them yourself. But until your body is involved, the feelings of compassion remain one stage away from empathy, closer to sympathy than anything else. This may be a question of terminology, but unless we take heed of the distinction between "sympathy" and "empathy," both terms become anodyne.

It is not just the computation of sympathy. It is not a matter of hearing a story. When you feel sorry for someone who tells you about misfortunes that have befallen them, about bereavement or loss upon loss, your involvement depends on your experience, your personal history, your own context. You are more sympathetic when you have suffered similarly. It is indeed a cognitive and richly semantic experience.

Here I want to distinguish this general use of "empathy" from the more palpable and restricted form that has to do with the body. In this reading, empathy is a form of engagement with the other that is, at least at first, unconscious and summoned forth by a motor response. It takes the form of a shared motor representation with the viewed other. It is not just a shared emotional representation, though motoric and emotional representations, as we have already noted, are not always easily separable.

3.1 Benjamin's View

Sophisticates are hostile to empathy; historical materialists shudder at the thought. In one of his scathing attacks on the vulgar use of empathy, Walter Benjamin wrote that "the true method of making things present is: to represent them in our space (not to represent ourselves in their space)." And he continued "The same with the aspect of great things from the past – the cathedral of Chartres, the Temple of Paestum: to receive them into our space (not to feel empathy with their builders or their priests)" (Benjamin, 1999, p. 845). Exactly. The notion of empathy with builders or priests is still-born. What would one know about their lives, except perhaps by way of their production? Even if we knew *something*, that would be a form of sympathy for them. We still could not see them, only their works. And this would entail an entirely different form of empathy – a representation in ourselves of the movements of the body involved in the labor of *producing* the work. This is the only workable notion of empathy. Though it may seem literalist to some, it actually *opens* the way to history, not to its denial.

Benjamin wants anecdote as antidote, because he thinks the kind of false empathy of which he speaks is totalizing. He charges its exponents with failing to take into account the fact that "the 'modernity' that concerns men with respect to the bodily is as varied in its meaning as the different aspects of one and the same kaleidoscope." But the only way to achieve that variation of meaning is to acknowledge the possibility of the modification of bodily involvement through sight, not to deny it. "Empathy," Benjamin says, "this is what newspaper reading terminates in" (Benjamin, 1999, p. 846). We might say "Empathy: this is what looking at press photographs terminates in," but we would have to add: "What does this imply for the images we think of as art?" And we would have to conclude "Empathy: this is what looking at great – and perhaps lesser – works of art begins with." The deep question is what happens afterwards. To deny the importance of unmediated responses as a step in the analysis of all serious responses to works of art is to stop wondering at the stars.[20]

3.2 Empathy and Art

Though not constitutive of art or of aesthetic judgment, empathy clearly forms an important element in our engagement with works of art. How do we get from empathetic engagement to art? Let us turn to another factor in this process.

The detachment of empathy from art already began in the work of Theodor Lipps, who is often cited, but still misunderstood. He has usually been taken – as I, too, once did – as a proponent of the constitutive role of empathy in the visual arts, but this is not entirely accurate. A closer reading reveals just the opposite. While he may have commented on the way a Romanesque column arouses some sense of equivalent torsion in the viewer's body, he nevertheless makes clear that *Einfühlung* is precisely *not* aesthetic, especially in his still all too neglected essay on the relation between empathy, inner imitation and the experience of one's own bodily self (Lipps, 1903).[21] The position I set out here is neither that empathy is constitutive of aesthetic experience or aesthetic judgment nor a reiteration of what Lipps claims. It lies somewhere between the two, not in a compromising or timorous manner, as is so often the case with in-between positions, but strongly and decidedly so.

Lipps' work also leads to Wilhelm Worringer, for whom empathy and abstraction famously became the two poles of artistic experience. For Worringer, both naturalistic works, especially the sculptures and paintings of ancient Greece and Rome and the Renaissance, and abstract ones induce a form of alienation from the self that is critical for absorption into the artwork and that, therefore, leaves the self behind, as paradoxical as it may seem. The difference between the two forms is that while the naturalism of the first group entails the absorption of the self into the other, the other is actually a kind of stylized abstraction away from nature. One way or the other you lose yourself in the artwork, either through empathy or through abstraction. This is not a view that has won much support over the years. In any case, as I have already suggested, there are ways in which *Einfühlung* can extend to abstraction as well. And although this may be a mistaken view, it does raise the matter of what role awareness of the self plays (or loss of the self) in the brain's operations when it judges art.

---

[20] Learned examples of such denial are provided by Willibald Sauerländer (1989) and the many predecessors he cites.

[21] I am grateful to Thomas Metzinger for reminding me of Lipps' views on the precise role of these elements in the relationship between empathy and aesthetics.

3.3 The Feeling of Emulation: The Example of the Capponi Chapel

To look into the Capponi Chapel in Santa Felicita in Florence is to have an immediate physical sense of the figure's actions in Pontormo's scene of *The Deposition from the Cross*. Viewers often have a sense of physically emulating the gestures of those figures, even if they do not actually do so. Not only do they comment on the great staring eyes (always a major attractor in a picture, as in life), they have the feeling, almost within themselves, of the torsion of the huge figure of the woman turning toward the virgin on the right and of the weight of Christ's body as supported by John the Evangelist on the left and the young boy holding him from beneath on the right. Among the different gestures they may seem to emulate, perhaps the most striking are the Virgin's upraised right arm that seems to extend across the entire picture with her hand silhouetted against the sky, the despairing outstretched arms of the woman in green behind her, and, to a lesser extent, the hand stretched across the breast of the tender veiled figure at the very top of the work.

The exceptional colors in this picture play an important role in drawing attention and probably (for this has not yet been studied) in reinforcing the sense of the relevant emotions within it. But what is so notable is the immediate feeling one has of emulating or being about to emulate the gestures. Almost as soon as one looks at the gestures of these figures, almost as soon as one has the sense that one is about to raise one's hands, or drop them, or press one or the other to one's own chest, one notices something else – the strangeness of one or the other hands that form the apex of these gestures, from the curiously tapered fingers and forearms of the Virgin and the woman above to the awkwardness of the gesture and the hand of the woman in green in the upper right, all contrasting so strikingly with the more powerful and seemingly more carefully depicted hands of the other characters in the scene. Who knows whether these weak and flaccid hands were intended to indicate the helplessness of their actions?

In the very moment that we perceive those hands, or possibly some other factor in the picture such as its colors, the automatic simulation of movement halts, and the moment of looking is transformed into one of contemplation. This takes the body of the viewing self out of the picture, even if momentarily, and makes it a third-party judging self. When we see the *way* the picture is depicted, we become aware of ourselves as judging, assessing selves, as well, perhaps, of the fact that even our simulatory or imitative sense of their actions is an effect of the picture. At that moment we consider the other dimensions of this picture as well: formal, emotional, and compositional. And it is at this precise juncture that the self is drawn out of its absorption in the represented other in order to be made to realize that it is a judging self. Absorption in the figures turns into an assessment of them *as represented* there. It is also at this point that one is likely to stop oneself from acting out (that is, literally mimicking) the gesture that one observes in a representation.

I have set out in a rather literal manner the course of reactions viewers may have to a painting like this. In doing so, I do not wish to suggest that it is the same for everyone, but rather to propose that some such sequence of processes (from absorption to inhibition, self-aware detachment, contemplation and reflection) is likely to occur, and that these processes are most clearly understandable, possibly entirely explicable, in neural terms. Empathy paves the way for the forms of inhibition necessary for contemplation and reflection. It will be noticed, I hope, that I do not describe inhibition in the way that Freud might have done as essential to his notion of culture; I speak of it in motoric terms.

All this may seem to recall the centrality of inhibition in the old notion of dynamogeny. Critical to it was "a view of the checking of motor responses" that regarded inhibition as "an integrative force preventing the dissolution of higher organized mental functions" by constraining lower level and more instinctual processes (Crary, 1999, p. 165). This view has had a long and suggestive history. It originated with the French psychologist Théodule-Armand Ribot, but can also be found in the work of foundational British neurologist Hughlings Jackson. In *The Will to Power,* Nietzsche maintained that automatic muscular responses can suspend inhibition in the course of pleasurable responses to art and "the enhancement of the feeling of life" (Nietzsche, 1967, sec. 802, 1886/1989). More than once Aby Warburg spoke of "dynamograms" and the need to keep them under control. This reflection may also seem to prefigure Freud and have overtones of his view on the relationship between repression and culture; but Freud, as so often, is fleshed out by neuroscience.

Earlier I distinguished empathy from ordinary compassion. Empathy is not just a matter of taking perspective, or of imagining the plight of others but rather a state of being in the situation of others; it is often unconscious. It comes before the prefrontal appraisal of emotion; it is precognitive. But by themselves these claims would be too easy and insufficient. They would not tell us why empathy is not constitutive of art, or how the cognitive interacts with the precognitive, or clarify the relationship between bottom-up and top-down responses in empathy. These are all questions that require expansion.

Let us return to the example of responses to Pontormo in Santa Felicita. While his figures may arouse a variety of forms of empathetic engagement, it is not this that constitutes its quality as a work of art. What is critical is the inhibition of empathetic engagement in such a way that one's sense of self is reclaimed from its immersion in the other. The inhibition of this particular form of engagement enables self-awareness. It is as if viewers become aware that upon sight of the work they have automatically given themselves up and put themselves in the place of those figures – or rather that they must get themselves out of the position in which they suddenly find themselves assimilated to someone there. As Walter Benjamin argued in his rejection of vulgar notions of *Einfühlung*, the point is not to represent ourselves in their space, but to represent them in ours. You have to get yourself out of there; but first you have to give yourself up and put yourself there.

4 Frontal Circuits Involved in Judgment

How are these forms of self-awareness and withdrawal of the self from what is observed represented in the brain? The situation of listening to or watching other people's stories requires a person to more or less consciously adopt the subjective point of view of the other. Actually imagining oneself in the place of a man strapped in a machine generating painful heat – the famous Stotland experiment – is a more intense experience than just watching or trying to imagine how the target is feeling (as opposed to thinking about how *you* are feeling) (Stotland, 1969). But this vivid imagining of oneself in the place of the other needs to be kept in check, or toned down at least, otherwise it jeopardizes judgment. A complex inhibitory process is thus necessary to regulate the self-perspective in order to then allow for the evaluation of the other perspective. As Decety and Jackson note, the prepotent self-perspective, driven by the automatic link between perception and action, is the default mode, and its regulation allows a necessary degree of cognitive and affective flexibility (Decety & Jackson, 2004, p. 87).

Such a view is compatible with the role of the prefrontal cortex in top-down control of behavior (Miller & Cohen, 2001). Key structures in the circuitry underlying emotion regulation are relevant in empathy. The orbitofrontal, ventromedial and dorsolateral cortices have all been reported to be implicated in empathy and its modulation. In particular, the ventromedial prefrontal cortex (VMPFC) plays a special role in emotion regulation with its reciprocal connections between brain regions involved in emotional processing (amygdala), memory (hippocampus) and executive functions (Davidson, Putnam, & Larson, 2000). Interestingly, Damasio's somatic marker hypothesis envisaged the VMPFC as key to the adaptation of bodily states ("somatic markers") associated with emotions in the course of decision-making. This once more brings the body into the realm of the top-down moderation of emotion as a result of cognitive input that bears on decision-making, contemplation and judgment.

While lesions to the VMPFC often result in empathy deficits, they significantly affect self-reflection and its connections with memory (Kelley et al., 2002). The frontopolar cortex (which includes VMPFC) is involved in the process of evaluating self-generated responses and is recruited when a task requires monitoring and manipulation of information that has been internally represented. It regulates and inhibits motor processing and emotional inputs, and patients with lesions in this area consequently show a degree of lacking inhibition. This twofold function of the VMPFC is thus entirely consistent with the general view set out here about the relationship between empathy and inhibition in judgment. Moreover, the frontopolar cortex, medial prefrontal cortex, and posterior cingulate are systematically involved when participants adopt the perspective of another individual as opposed to a self-perspective. In addition to its projections to the posterior cingulate cortex, the frontopolar cortex is also linked to the anterior cingulate as well, which, as is well known, plays a critical role in conflict monitoring and emotional regulation.[22] In all these ways, the transition from empathy to judgment (and the passage from imitative motor activity to cognitive modulation and appraisal of emotional response) becomes still clearer.

Recent work on the entire default mode network (DMN), which includes the group of cortical midline structures just mentioned (VMPFC, medial prefrontal cortex, especially dorso-medial prefrontal cortex (DMPFC), and posterior cingulate), has shown that it is essential for self-reflection and self-referential thought (Gusnard, Akbudak, Shulman, & Raichle, 2001; Gusnard & Raichle, 2001; Moran, Kelly, & Heatherton, 2013; Raichle et al., 2001). The DMN includes the hippocampal formation and is active when external perceptual tasks fall away (or where none such exists) (Greicius & Menon, 2004). "During such moments, participants change their focus of external attention and engage in spontaneous cognitive processes including remembering the past and imagining the future" (Andrews-Hanna, Reidler, Huang, & Buckner, 2010, p. 322). It is critical for internal trains of thought (Smallwood, Brown, Baird, & Schooler, 2012; Smallwood et al., 2013). Edward Vessel and others have recently demonstrated that it seems to be especially engaged during the evaluation and appreciation of works

[22] Perceiving and assessing the level of pain experienced by a person in photographs (hands and feet in situations likely to cause pain) is associated with significant changes in activity in the ACC, anterior insula, cerebellum and, to a lesser extent, the thalamus. Activity in the ACC is "strongly correlated with observers' ratings of the others pain suggesting that activity of this region is modulated according to subjects' reactivity to the pain of others" (Jackson, Meltzoff, & Decety, 2005, p. 771).

of art (Vessel, Starr, & Rubin, 2012). Especially relevant is the claim that "MPFC may serve as a processing 'hub' binding together information from all sensory modalities with internally generated information" (Moran et al., 2013, p. 391).

On these grounds alone one might hypothesize that the DMN is activated in the course of the extraction of self-awareness from the empathetic state, that is, at that moment of awareness that one is not that person there, but oneself. The process of evaluating the stimulus in terms of one's own experience and context would begin only then. The DMN would then play a significant role in the processes of contemplation and judgment, in which what might once have been called the imaginative mind seeks to make sense, in its own terms, of an awareness that that other body is indeed someone else's, that the viewer has not been absorbed into it, but is able judge it by other criteria supplied to the self. In light of all this, it is not surprising that the DMN should have been shown to be activated during intense aesthetic experience (Vessel et al., 2012).[23]

Let us briefly return to the question of stories. Decety and Chaminade did an experiment about sympathy for sad stories, in which trained actors told their tales with congruent or incongruent motor expressions of emotion (Decety & Chaminade, 2003). Watching sad stories versus neutral ones resulted in increased activity in the emotional processing structures, including the amygdala and parieto-frontal areas, especially the right ones (critical for awareness of others). The mismatch between the narrative content of the stories and the motor expression of emotion elicited a strong hemodynamic increase in the VMPFC and superior frontal gyrus. Both areas help monitor conflict between expected and actual outcomes, just as the anterior cingulate cortex (ACC) is involved in monitoring emotional conflict. The VMPFC's involvement in processing emotions that arise from conflict is precisely what makes it so crucial to making judgments and aesthetic judgments in particular. Vessel's recent work on the DMN makes its role clear in the aesthetic pleasure that arises from evaluation, while research on the interaction between the dorso-lateral prefrontal cortex (DLPFC) and the VMPFC has shown how the DLPFC serves to censor or dampen the VMPFC's processing of emotion on the basis of knowledge and expertise (see Kirk

& Freedberg, 2015). For further references to relevant research on the modulating influence of DLPFC, see Kirk, Harvey, and Montague (2011) and Kirk and Freedberg (forthcoming).

Decety and Jackson (2004) rightly argue that the inhibitory component of frontopolar activity is necessary to regulate and tone down the self-perspective in order to evaluate the other-perspective in empathy. Here too, the posterior cingulate plays a role. But it is possible to take a slightly different point of view when it comes to art. The issue here is not so much the insertion of the self into the other or bringing the other to the self, but to have a sense that one remains oneself even in one's involvement with the work. This is the essential dialectic at the heart of aesthetic judgment. No one has ever claimed that aesthetic judgment is a matter of immersion; but immersion or absorption of some form or another is what precedes and is subject to inhibition, contemplation and assessment. In these processes, the VMPFC certainly plays a role and so does censoring by the DLPFC, which has been shown to come into play in cases of those trained in art who resist favors and interest.[24] But the real issue is deeper down, something that does not leave much space for Kant. It is the issue of how automatic motor responses are inhibited at the basal ganglia level and how this inhibition has to do not only with the necessary restraints that lie at the core of all movement, but also with the monitoring and regulation of immediate emotional responses that occur at the level of the anterior cingulate. Hence the importance of projections from DLPFC to basal ganglia and vice versa.

These inhibitory movements are bound up with GABAergic uptake and dopamine release at striatal level. This results in some of the pleasure and nucleus accumbens (NAcc) activation involved both in sensory responses and in the satisfactions that ensue from self-aware aesthetic judgment. That prefrontal interactions, particularly between the VMPFC and the DLPFC, are indispensable here too is clear; but the

[23] Other areas of the brain (in particular, the inferior parietal lobule and the hippocampal formation) are also generally regarded as parts of the DMN, but discussion of their role in the relationship between detachment, contemplation and judgment can wait for another occasion (see Buckner, Andrews-Hanna, & Schacter, 2008; Andrews-Hanna et al., 2010; Smallwood et al., 2013).

body remains as a critical factor in aesthetic judgment in the course of its monitoring and regulation at ACC and basal ganglia levels as well. It is for this reason that, although not constitutive of art, empathy is an essential preliminary and motivating element for the forms of contemplation that lead to judgment and its multiple satisfactions.

What is finally at stake is the inhibition of empathetic forms of engagement. This involves forward processing by the VMPFC, regulation and censorship of emotional processing by the DLPFC, and inhibition in the basal ganglia and feedforward loops (both to cingulate and prefrontal cortices). So while empathetic engagement is a critical element in one's engagement with artworks, it is not constitutive of it. It is precisely the constraints on this engagement that are – and these are arguably cognitive, regulatory and productive of self-awareness.

5 Summary

What I have sought to emphasize in this article are the vicissitudes and potentials of a form of perception and understanding that is prior to cognition. My aim has been to foreground the ways in which sight leads to identification *with* rather than identification *of* the body of the other – empathy in its pure corporeal sense. Sight provides more direct access to the bodies and movements of others than has ever been imagined. It has always been regarded with suspicion precisely because of this access. The long prioritization of imagination over more direct sensual responses in the West and the East is both a consequence and a manifestation of the fear of evoking the body in the very processes of sight itself. Only by understanding – and then accepting – the possibilities inherent in the bottom-up processes of sight can we begin to grasp how we relate to what we see, rather than to what we imagine on the basis of the books we read

[24] See earlier Kirk et al. (2011). For a further analysis of the aesthetic implications, see Kirk and Freedberg (2015) and Kirk and Freedberg (forthcoming). Significantly, patients with DLPFC lesions seem to have "deficits in empathetic ability related to cognitive flexibility" as opposed to those with right VMPC regions where empathetic deficits are profound and relate to affective recognition and emotional and body states (as highlighted in the present discussion). See, for example, Shamay-Tsoory, Tomer, Berger, and Aharon-Peretz (2003).

or the stories we hear, of the concerts we attend or even the redolent aromas we smell – whatever their emotional and visual correlates may be.

Empathy is above all a visual phenomenon, however much we may wish to think of it as an imaginative state. It is true that empathy (or what may seem like empathy) occasionally arises from the imagination, but it does not primarily do so. One might say that it is by imaginative empathy that death touches us; one might think of the Holocaust as an example – and rightly so: it often moves us more by its narratives than by its representation in visual form, for death cannot be represented. At best it is representation truncated. It is the stories that move us to the core, the waste of life, ability, and talent – the numbers. But death precludes empathy. For death, there can be no feeling-in. Empathy needs the living body. It cannot be thought of without it. If you say you have empathy for the psychological condition of the other, you are deluding yourself and will disappoint the other, not necessarily in terms of strength or vitality of feeling, but in terms of feeling-in and feeling the same. It is easy enough to delude oneself into thinking that one's sympathy is empathetic. Empathy, in such cases, is spurious, a form of feeling-in in name only. Empathy remains fundamentally a physical condition. It entails feeling with the body; it is neither sympathy for the narratives of others, nor even the assertion of sympathetic or allegedly empathetic feeling. The basis of empathy, like the empathetic basis of aesthetics, is always precognitive. The two conditions, of course, are not unrelated because we see that picture as if the body it shows *or implies* were our own.

References

Adolphs, R., Damasio, H., Tranel, D., Cooper, G., & Damasio, A. R. (2000). A Role for Somatosensory Cortices in the Visual Recognition of Emotion as Revealed by Three-Dimensional Lesion Mapping. *Journal of Neuroscience, 20*(7), 2683–2690.

Alberti, L. B. (1966). *On Painting* (rev. ed.). New Haven: Yale University Press.

Andrews-Hanna, J. R., Reidler, J. S., Huang, C., & Buckner, R. L. (2010). Evidence for the Default Network's Role in Spontaneous Cognition. *Journal of Neurophysiology, 104*(1), 322–335.

Battaglia, F., Lisanby, S., & Freedberg, D. (2011). Corticomotor Excitability During Observation and Imagination of a Work of Art. *Frontiers in Human Neuroscience*, *5*(79), 1–6.

Benjamin, W. (1999). *The Arcades Project* (H. Eiland & K. McLaughlin, Trans., based on the German edition by R. Tiedemann). Cambridge: Belknap Press of Harvard University Press.

Berenson, B. (1896). *The Florentine Painters of the Renaissance*. New York: G. P. Putnam's Sons.

Berenson, B. (1960). *The Italian Painters of the Renaissance*. London: Fontana.

Bergson, H. (1910). *Time and Free Will. An Essay on the Immediate Data of Consciousness* (F. L. Pogson, Trans.). Retrieved from http://www.columbia.edu/cgi-bin/cul/resolve?clio7879851

Bonaventura (1961). *Meditations on the Life of Christ: an Illustrated Manuscript of the Fourteenth Century* (I. Ragusa & R. Green, Trans. & Ed.). Princeton Monographs in Art and Archaeology, no. 35. Princeton: Princeton University Press.

Buckner, R. L., Andrews-Hanna, J. R., & Schacter, D. L. (2008). The Brain's Default Network: Anatomy, Function, and Relevance to Disease. *Annals of the New York Academy of Sciences*, *1124*, 1–38.

Casati, R., & Pignocchi, A. (2007). Mirror and canonical neurons are not constitutive for aesthetic response. *Trends in Cognitive Science*, *11*(10), 410.

Charcot, J. M. (1991). *Clinical Lectures on the Diseases of the Nervous System* (R. Harris, Ed.). London, New York: Routledge.

Chiavarino, C., Bugiani, S., Grandi, E., & Colle, L. (2013). Is Automatic Imitation Based on Goal Coding or Movement Coding? A Comparison of Goal-Directed and Goal-Less Actions. *Experimental psychology*, *60*(3), 213–225.

Crary, J. (1999). *Suspensions of Perception: Attention, Spectacle, and Modern Culture*. Cambridge: MIT Press.

Davidson, R. J., Putnam, K. M., & Larson, C. L. (2000). Dysfunction in the Neural Circuitry of Emotion Regulation – a Possible Prelude to Violence. *Science*, *289*(5479), 591–594.

Decety, J. (1996). Do Imagined and Executed Actions Share the Same Neural Substrate? *Brain Research. Cognitive Brain Research*, *3*(2), 87–93.

Decety, J., & Chaminade, T. (2003). Neural Correlates of Feeling Sympathy. *Neuropsychologia*, *41*(2), 127–138.

Decety, J., & Grèzes, J. (1999). Neural Mechanisms Subserving the Perception of Human Actions. *Trends in Cognitive Science*, *3*(5), 172–178.

Decety, J., & Grèzes, J. (2001). Functional Anatomy of Execution, Mental Simulation, Observation, and Verb Generation of Actions: A Meta-Analysis. *Human Brain Mapping, 12*(1), 1–19.

Decety, J., & Grèzes, J. (2002). Does Visual Perception of Object Afford Action? Evidence from a Neuroimaging Study. *Neuropsychologia, 40*(2), 212–222.

Decety, J., & Jackson, P. L. (2004). The Functional Architecture of Human Empathy. *Behavioral Cognitive Neuroscience Review, 3*(2), 71–100.

Decety, J., Chaminade, T., Grèzes, J., & Meltzoff, A. N. (2002). A Pet Exploration of the Neural Mechanisms Involved in Reciprocal Imitation. *Neuroimage, 15*(1), 265–272.

Decety, J., Perani, D., Jeannerod, M., Bettinardi, V., Tadary, B., Woods, R., Mazziotta, J. C., & Fazio, F. (1994). Mapping Motor Representations with Positron Emission Tomography. *Nature, 371*(6498), 600–602.

Decety, J., Grèzes, J., Costes, N., Perani, D., Jeannerod, M., Procyk, E., Grassi, F., & Fazio, F. (1997). Brain Activity During Observation of Actions. Influence of Action Content and Subject's Strategy. *Brain, 120*(10), 1763–1777.

Féré, Ch. (1900). *Sensation Et Mouvement, Études Expérimentales De Psycho-Mécanique* [Sensation and movement. Experimental studies of psycho-mechanics] (rev. 2nd ed.). Paris: Alcan.

Freedberg, D. (2011). Movement, Embodiment, Emotion. In T. Dufrenne & A.-C. Taylor (Eds.). *Cannibalismes Disciplinaires. Quand L'histoire De L'art E L'anthropologie Se Rencontrent* [Disciplinary canibalism. When history of art and anthropology meet] (pp. 37–61). Paris: INHA/Musée du Quai Branly.

Freedberg, D. (2013). Dürer's Limbs'. In S. Buck & S. Porras (Eds.). *The Young Dürer* (pp. 37–46). London: Courtauld Institute of Art.

Freedberg, D., & Gallese, V. (2007a). Motion, Emotion and Empathy in Aesthetic Experience. *Trends in Cognitive Science, 11*(5), 197–203.

Freedberg, D., & Gallese, V. (2007b). Mirror and Canonical Neurons Are Crucial Elements in esthetic Response. *Trends in Cognitive Science, 11*(7), 411.

Gallese, V. (2005). Embodied Simulation: From Neurons to Phenomenal Experience. *Phenomenology and the Cognitive Sciences, 4*, 23–48.

Gallese, V., Keysers, C., & Rizzolatti, G. (2004). A Unifying View of the Basis of Social Cognition. *Trends in Cognitive Science, 8*(9). 396–403.

de Gelder, B. (2006). Towards the Neurobiology of Emotional Body Language. *Nature Reviews Neuroscience, 7*(3), 242–249.

Gombrich, E. H., & Saxl, F. (1986). *Aby Warburg: An Intellectual Biography* (2nd ed.). Chicago: University of Chicago Press.

Goodale, M. A., & Milner, A. D. (1995). *The Visual Brain in Action*. Oxford and New York: Oxford University Press.

Goodale, M. A., & Milner, A. D. (2008). The Visual Systems Re-Viewed. *Neuropsychologia, 46*(3), 774–785.

Goodman, N. (1976). *Languages of Art: An Approach to a Theory of Symbols* (2nd ed.). Indianapolis: Hackett.

Graziano, M. S., Taylor, C. S., & Moore, T. (2002). Probing Cortical Function with Electrical Stimulation. *Nature Neuroscience, 5*(10), 921.

Greicius, M. D., & Menon, V. (2004). Default-Mode Activity During a Passive Sensory Task: Uncoupled from Deactivation but Impacting Activation. *Journal of Cognitive Neuroscience, 16*(9), 1484–1492.

Gusnard, D. A., Akbudak, E., Shulman, G. L., & Raichle, M. E. (2001). Medial Prefrontal Cortex and Self-Referential Mental Activity: Relation to a Default Mode of Brain Function. *Proceedings of the National Academy of Science USA, 98*(7), 4259–4264.

Gusnard, D. A., & Raichle, M. E. (2001). Searching for a Baseline: Functional Imaging and the Resting Human Brain. *National Review of Neuroscience, 2*(10), 685–694.

Hari, R., Forss, N., Avikainen, S., Kirveskari, E., Salenius, S., & Rizzolatti, G. (1998). Activation of Human Primary Motor Cortex During Action Observation: A Neuromagnetic Study. *Proceedings Of The National Academy Of Sciences Of The United States Of America, 95*(25), 15061–15065.

Hatfield, E., Cacioppo, J. T., & Rapson, R. L. (1994). *Emotional Contagion*. Cambridge: Cambridge University Press.

Hilgers, T. (2010). *On Aesthetic Disinterestedness*. Ph.D. dissertation, University of Pennsylvania.

Iacoboni, M., Woods, R. P., Brass, M., Bekkering, H., Mazziotta, J. C., & Rizzolatti, G. (1999). Cortical Mechanisms of Human Imitation. *Science, 286*(5449), 2526–2528.

Jackson, P. L., Meltzoff, A. N., & Decety, J. (2005). How Do We Perceive the Pain of Others? A Window into the Neural Processes Involved in Empathy. *Neuroimage, 24*(3), 771–779.

James, W. (1890). *The Principles of Psychology*. New York: H. Holt.

Jeannerod, M. (2001). Neural Simulation of Action: A Unifying Mechanism for Motor Cognition. *Neuroimage, 14*(1)(pt. 2), 103–109.

Jeannerod, M. (2006). *Motor Cognition: What Actions Tell the Self.* Oxford Psychology Series. Oxford and New York: Oxford University Press.
Kelley, W. M., Macrae, C. N., Wyland, C. L., Caglar, S., Inati, S. & Heatherton, T. F. (2002). Finding the Self? An Event-Related FMRI Study. *Journal of Cognitive Neuroscience, 14*(5), 785–794.
Keysers, C., Wicker, B., Gazzola, V., Anton, J. L., Fogassi, L., & Gallese, V. (2004). A Touching Sight: Sii/Pv Activation During the Observation and Experience of Touch. *Neuron, 42*(2), 335–346.
Kirk, U., & Freedberg, D. (2015). Contextual Bias and Insulation against Bias during Aesthetic Rating: The Roles of Ventromedial and Dorsolateral Prefrontal Cortex. In J. P. Huston, M. Nadal, F. Mora, L. Agnati & C. J. Cela-Condé (Eds.). *Art, Aesthetics and the Brain* (pp. 158–173). Oxford: Oxford University Press.
Kirk, U. & Freedberg, D. (forthcoming). Cognitive Framing Modulates Emotional Experience through the DLPFC-VLPFC Network: an fMRI Study.
Kirk, U., Harvey, A., & Montague, P. R. (2011). Domain Expertise Insulates against Judgment Bias by Monetary Favors through a Modulation of Ventromedial Prefrontal Cortex. *Proceedings of the National Academy of Science USA, 108*(25), 10332–10336.
Knoblich, G., & Prinz, W. (2001). Recognition of Self-Generated Actions from Kinematic Displays of Drawing. *Journal of Experimental Psychology. Human Perception and Performance, 27*(2), 456–465.
Koos, M., Pichler, W., Rappl, W., & Swoboda, G. (Eds.) (1994). *Begleitmaterial zurAusstellung 'Aby M. Warburg, Mnemosyne'* [Accompanying material for the exhibition *'Aby M. Warburg, Mnemosyne'*]. Hamburg: Dölling und Galitz.
Lipps, T. (1903). Einfühlung, Innere Nachahmung und Organenempfindungen [Empathy, inner imitation, and organic sensations]. *Archiv für die gesamte Psychologie, 1*(2–3), 185–204.
Marrow, J. H. (1979). *Passion Iconography in Northern European Art of the Late Middle Ages and Early Renaissance: A Study of the Transformation of Sacred Metaphor into Descriptive Narrative.* Ars Neerlandica, Kortrijk: Van Ghemmert.
Meltzoff, A. N. (1988). Infant Imitation and Memory: Nine-Month-Olds in Immediate and Deferred Tests. *Child Development, 59*(1), 217–225.
Meltzoff, A. N., & Moore, M. K. (1977). Imitation of Facial and Manual Gestures by Human Neonates. *Science, 198*, 75–78.

Meltzoff, A. N., & Moore, M. K. (1983). Newborn Infants Imitate Adult Facial Gestures. *Child Development, 54*(3), 702–709.
Michaud, P.-A. (1998). *Aby Warburg Et L'image En Mouvement* [Aby Warburg and the moving image]. Vues, Paris: Macula.
Miller, E. K., & Cohen, J. D. (2001). An Integrative Theory of Prefrontal Cortex Function. *Annual Review Neuroscience, 24*, 167–202.
Montagu, J. (1994). *The Expression of the Passions. The Origin and Influence of Charles Le Brun's Conférence Sur L'expresson Générale Et Particulière*. New Haven, London: Yale University Press.
Moran, J. M., Kelley, W. M., & Heatherton, T. F. (2013). What Can the Organization of the Brain's Default Mode Network Tell Us About Self-Knowledge? *Frontiers in Human Neuroscience, 7*, 391.
Nietzsche, F. W. (1881/1997). *Daybreak* (M. Clark & B. Leiter, Ed., R. J. Hollingdale, Trans.). Cambridge: University of Cambridge Press.
Nietzsche, F. W. (1886/1989). *Beyond Good and Evil: Prelude to a Philosophy of the Future* (W. A. Kaufmann, Trans.). New York: Vintage Books.
Nietzsche, F. W. (1887/1996). *On the Genealogy of Morals* (D. Smith, Trans.). Oxford, New York: Oxford University Press.
Nietzsche, F. W. (1967). *The Will to Power* (W. A. Kaufmann, Trans.). New York: Random House.
Nussbaum, M. C. (2001). *Upheavals of Thought: The Intelligence of Emotions*. Cambridge, New York: Cambridge University Press.
Ochsner, K. N., Bunge, S. A., Gross, J. J., & Gabrieli, J. D. (2002). Rethinking Feelings: An FMRI Study of the Cognitive Regulation of Emotion. *Journal of Cognitive Neuroscience, 14*(8), 1215–1229.
Ochsner, K. N., & Gross, J. J. (2005). The Cognitive Control of Emotion. *Trends in Cognitive Science, 9*(5), 242–249.
Peelen, M. V. (2005). Selectivity for the Human Body in the Fusiform Gyrus. *Journal of Neurophysiology, 93*(1), 603–608.
Peelen, M. V., & Downing, J. J. (2005). Is the Extrastriate Body Area Involved in Motor Actions? *Nature Neuroscience, 8*(2), 125.
Perrett, D. I., Smith, P. A., Mistlin, A. J., Chitty, A. J., Head, A. S., Potter, D. D., Broennimann, R., Milner, A. D., & Jeeves, M. A. (1985). Visual Analysis of Body Movements by Neurones in the Temporal Cortex of the Macaque Monkey: A Preliminary Report. *Behavioural Brain Research, 16*(2–3), 153–170.
Pliny the Elder (1857). *Historia naturalis* [Natural history], XXXIV (J. Bostock & H. T. Riley, Trans.). London: Henry G. Bohn.

Prinz, W. (1997). Perception and Action Planning. *European Journal of Cognitive Psychology, 9*, 129–154.
Raichle, M. E., MacLeod, A. M., Snyder, A. Z., Powers, W. J., Gusnard, D. A., & Shulman, G. L. (2001). A Default Mode of Brain Function. *Proceedings of the National Academy of Science USA, 98*(2), 676–682.
Ringbom, S. (1984). *Icon to Narrative: The Rise of the Dramatic Close-up in Fifteenth-Century Devotional Painting* (2nd ed.). Doornspijk: Davaco.
Rizzolatti, G., Scandolara, C., Matelli, M., & Gentilucci, M. (1981). Afferent Properties of Periarcuate Neurons in Macaque Monkeys. Ii. Visual Responses. *Behavioural Brain Research, 2*(2), 147–163.
Rorty, A. (1980). *Explaining Emotions. Topics in Philosophy*. Berkeley: University of California Press.
Rosenheim, J. (2013). *Photography and the American Civil War*. Metropolitan Museum of Art series. New York: The Metropolitan Museum of Art.
Sauerländer, W. (1989). Überlegungen zu dem Thema Lavater und die Kunstgeschichte [Considerations on Lavater and the history of art]. *Idea. Jahrbuch der Hamburger Kunsthalle, 8*, 15–30.
Schaub, M., Suthor, N., & Fischer-Lichte, E. (2005). *Ansteckung: Zur Körperlichkeit eines ästhetischen Prinzips* [Contagion. On the bodily character of an aesthetic principle]. Paderborn: Wilhelm Fink.
Shamay-Tsoory, S. G., Tomer, R., Berger, B. D., & Aharon-Peretz, J. (2003). Characterization of Empathy Deficits following Prefrontal Brain Damage: the Role of the Right Ventromedial Prefrontal Cortex. *Journal of Cognitive Neuroscience, 15*(3), 324–337.
Von Simson, O. G. (1953). Compassio and Co-Redemptio in Rogier Van Der Weyden's Descent from the Cross. *The Art Bulletin, 35*(1), 9–16.
Smallwood, J., Brown, K., Baird, B., & Schooler, J. W. (2012). Cooperation between the Default Mode Network and the Frontal-Parietal Network in the Production of an Internal Train of Thought. *Brain Research, 1428*, 60–70.
Smallwood, J., Tipper, C., Brown, K., Baird, B., Engen, H., Michaels, J. R., Grafton, S., & Schooler, J. W. (2013). Escaping the Here and Now: Evidence for a Role of the Default Mode Network in Perceptually Decoupled Thought. *Neuroimage, 69*, 120–125.
Stotland, E. (1969). Exploratory Investigations of Empathy. In L. Berkowitz (Ed.). *Advances in Experimental Social Psychology* (pp. 271–314). New York: Academic Press.

Umiltà, M. A., Berchio, C., Sestito, M., Freedberg, D., & Gallese, V. (2012). Abstract Art and Cortical Motor Activation: an EEG study. *Frontiers in Human Neuroscience, 6*, 311.

Vessel, E. A., Starr, G. G., & Rubin, N. (2012). The Brain on Art: Intense Aesthetic Experience Activates the Default Mode Network. *Frontiers in Human Neuroscience, 6*, 66.

Warburg, A. (1999). *The Renewal of Pagan Antiquity: Contributions to the Cultural History of the European Renaissance.* Texts & Documents. Los Angeles: Getty Research Institute for the History of Art and the Humanities.

Warburg, A. (2010). *Werke in einem Band* [Works in one volume] (P. Ladwig, M. Treml, & S. Weigel, Eds.). Frankfurt/Main: Suhrkamp.

Wedepohl, C. (2012). Von der 'Pathosformel' zum 'Gebärdensprachatlas'. Dürers Tod des Orpheus und Warburgs Arbeit an einer ausdruckstheoretisch begründeten Kulturgeschichte. [From the 'pathos-formula' to the 'atlas of sign language'. Dürer's Death of the Orpheus and Warburg's work on an expression based theory of cultural history]. In M. A. Hurttig (Ed.). *Die entfesselte Antike. Aby Warburg und die Geburt der Pathosformel* [The unleashed antiquity. Aby Warburg and the birth of the pathos-formula] (pp. 33–50). Cologne: Wallraf-Richartz Museum and Fondation Courboud/Buchhandlung Walther König.

7

The Empathic Body in Experimental Aesthetics – Embodied Simulation and Art

Vittorio Gallese

The human body plays a fundamental, although often neglected, role in human cognitive life. Body physiognomy not only provides knowledge about the nature of the body, but also about the role the body plays in affecting our cognitive judgments. To sanction behaviors, decisions, and institutions as "right," "high," or "elevated" means to translate the configuration of our body and its spatial relationships into a set of moral values. In the course of evolution, the symmetry axis of our upright body developed a division of labor between the right and left

Some of the ideas and proposals presented in this chapter were previously addressed in recent papers (Gallese, 2012, 2014a, 2014b, 2014c; Gallese & Di Dio, 2012; Gallese & Gattara, 2015).

V. Gallese (✉)
Department of Medicine and Surgery, Unit of Neuroscience, University of Parma, Parma PR, Italy
Institute of Philosophy, School of Advanced Study, University of London, London, UK
e-mail: vittorio.gallese@unipr.it

V. Lux, S. Weigel (eds.), *Empathy*, Palgrave Studies in the Theory and History of Psychology, DOI 10.1057/978-1-137-51299-4_7

halves, in terms of hand preference, emotional expression, and faculty of language. Such division of labor finds corresponding lateralized specializations of brain function related to those domains. This shows how body, brain, experience, and expression constitute a multifaceted and diversified unit. The symbolic translation of the body into gestures and expressions or into material outcomes betrays the intrinsic and double theatrical nature of our body. The body literally stages subjectivity by means of a series of postures, feelings, expressions, and behaviors. At the same time, the body projects itself in the world and makes it its own stage where corporeality is actor and beholder; its expressive content is subjectively experienced and recognized in others.

One should start from this constitutive relationship between body and symbolic expression when addressing the issues of artistic creativity and of its reception from a natural or more precisely neurobiological perspective. The present chapter suggests why and how cognitive neuroscience should investigate our relationship with art and aesthetics, framing this empirical approach as "experimental aesthetics." Experimental aesthetics is discussed in relation with current neuroscientific approaches to art and aesthetics, usually referred to as "neuroaesthetics." By exploiting the neurocognitive approach, viewed as a sort of "cognitive archeology," we can empirically investigate the neurophysiological brain mechanisms that make our interactions with the world possible, detect possible functional antecedents of our cognitive skills and measure the sociocultural influence exerted by human cultural evolution onto the very same cognitive skills. In so doing we can deconstruct some of the concepts we normally use when referring to intersubjectivity or to aesthetics and art, as well as when referring to the experiences we have of them.

1 Art and the Brain

Before introducing mirror mechanisms and embodied simulation and relating them to our appreciation of (artistic) images, two clarifications are in order about the explananda and the methodology required to investigate them.

Art, together with language, is among the most distinctive traits of the human species. What do we mean exactly when we speak of art, though? The *concept of art* is problematic; what we call art today is the outcome of a complex and multilayered sociocultural construction process, developed along thousands of years. Can we define the paintings realized during the Paleolithic age inside the caves of Chauvet, Lascaux, and Altamira as artworks in the same way as we would Michelangelo's frescos or Picasso's paintings? Can we call those people artists who ventured deep into mountains' bellies, covering caves' inner walls with their hand prints, and wonderful images of tigers, lions, deer, and bison? As argued by Larry Shiner in his *The Invention of Art: A Cultural History* (2001), the notion of "fine arts" was developed during the Enlightenment era. As many other contemporary concepts, the European idea of "fine arts" was considered universal and related to ideals and practices that originated in Greece and Rome during the classical era, rediscovered during the Renaissance. Shiner also points out that the Italian word "arte" comes from the Latin *ars* and the Greek *techne*; both words refer to every human practical activity, like making pottery or shoes, taming horses, or writing poems. In ancient thought the opposite of human's art was not craftsmanship but nature. Today art is "whatever humans call art" (Formaggio, 1981, p. 11). In spite of our main interest in elucidating typical human artistic forms (like visual arts, cinema, architecture, and fiction narrative) from a neuroscientific perspective, this new understanding of art is reason enough to talk about symbolic creations and expressions rather than focus our discussion on the concept of art itself, which is more prone to the molding impact of time and history.

Let's now focus on what we mean by *neuroscientific perspective.* A possible way to go would maintain that art, as any other expression of human intelligence, is explained by the activity of our brain. Such a statement is, on the one hand, tautologically true because it is a fact and an undisputable truth that there cannot be any mental life without the brain. On the other hand, it is a half-truth – this latter argument is far more controversial than the former – because the brain fully expresses its own functionality to the extent that it is inextricably linked to an acting and experiencing body, situated in a specific physical world, which, in turn, adheres to specific physical laws, and is inhabited by other individuals. This is the reason why a neuroscientific approach to the symbolic expression characterizing our species cannot limit itself to correlate the concepts we employ to describe symbolic expression with the brain areas activated by the use of the same concepts. Unfortunately, this is still a dominant method of neuroaesthetics, according to which the scientific investigation of art often translates into the search for a 1:1 mapping between the concepts of beauty, sublime, symmetry, wonder, and the like, and distinct locations in the brain. Because of the brain-body system's situated relationships with the world, we must study how symbolic expression might have originated, developed and been experienced.

Cognitive neuroscience is a multifarious methodological approach. It comprises the recording of single neurons (most of the time in animals, far more rarely in human patients), brain imaging techniques like functional magnetic resonance imaging (fMRI), magnetoencephalography (MEG), high-density electroencephalography (EEG), transcranial magnetic stimulation (TMS), electromyography (EMG), and the neuropsychological study of neurological patients. All of these approaches can be used in very different ways, by asking the brain very different questions, for example, by investigating the relationship between action, perception, and cognition. Depending on the very formulation different questions hence obtain answers that will potentially be also very different. The neuroscientific study of art exemplifies this logic of any kind of empirical research pretty well.

2 Neuroaesthetics Versus Experimental Aesthetics

In the last decade neuroscientific research displayed a growing interest towards art and aesthetics. The neuroscientist Semir Zeki was a pioneer in this field. It is to him we primarily owe the opening of the new field of research defined as "neuroaesthetics" (Zeki, 1999). Following Zeki, neuroscientists started addressing different problems: some of them used art to better understand brain function, employing paintings or movie stills as mere stimuli to investigate the neurobiological foundations of non-art-specific cognitive functions. Others (Zeki among them) employed fMRI to study the concepts "beauty" and "aesthetic pleasure" and, more generally, to study the neural mechanisms responsible for the visual perceptual analysis of several formal characteristics of artworks.

Many scholars in the humanities expressed reservations, if not annoyance, towards neuroaesthetics, which they considered as a useless undue interference or, at best, an approach of little heuristic value. These conclusions, aside from being wrong, are premature. They are partly generated by poor knowledge of the brain, of the neuroscientific approach, and of its potential and limitations, not to mention the prevalent penchant of corporative defense of one's own discipline. However, these negative reactions, to be honest, are also generated by the excessive neurodeterminism sometimes displayed by cognitive neuroscience when approaching art and by the poor answers concerning the specific characteristics of art its approach often produces. If one reduces "art" exclusively to measurable factors, without taking into account historical perspectives, the risk of a poor heuristic outcome might be very high.

The crucial point when using art in neuroscientific research is not to study the brain, but to study the brain-body system in order to understand what makes us human, since aesthetic work is characteristic for human beings. To make use of this characteristic capacity as an epistemological profit, namely to use art practices in experimental research is the reason why I call this approach "experimental aesthetics": the scientific investigation of the brain–body's physiological correlates of the aesthetic experience of particular outcomes of human symbolic expression, in other words what we now call "artworks." Differently from neuroaesthetics, which predominantly focuses on canonic notions like beauty and aesthetic pleasure, experimental aesthetics as I define it here, is more concerned with the investigation of the neurobiological and bodily conditions enabling the aesthetic experience of artworks.

The notion "aesthetics" is used here mainly in its bodily meaning, according to its etymology from *aisthesis*; it refers to the sensorimotor and affective features of our experience when we perceive these objects. These components of aesthetic experience are one instantiation of the multimodal perception of the world made possible by our body. With experimental aesthetics, the experience of artworks can be deconstructed into its bodily grounding elements. Obviously, this only covers one aspect of aesthetic experience, namely, the one dealing with experiences likely to happen before any explicit aesthetic judgment is formulated.

3 Vision, Motor Cognition, and Embodied Simulation

Observing the world is complex, more complex than merely activating the visual brain. Cognitive neuroscience has demonstrated that vision is multimodal, as it encompasses the activation of motor, somatosensory, and emotion-related brain networks. Motor neurons control action but also respond to visual, tactile, and auditory stimuli, provided they are body-related. The same motor circuits controlling our motor behavior also map the space around us, the objects at hand in that very same space and the actions of others, thus defining and shaping their representational content in motor terms, that is, in the very same format specifying how to move in space the very same body part (for a review, see Gallese, 2000; Rizzolatti, Fogassi, & Gallese, 2002). The space surrounding our body (peripersonal space), whose limits are the limits of our outstretched arm, is defined by the motor potentialities of our body. Premotor neurons controlling the movements of the upper arm also respond to tactile stimuli applied to it, to visual stimuli within the arm's peripersonal space, and to auditory stimuli also originating from the same peripersonal space (Fogassi et al., 1996; Rizzolatti, Fadiga, Fogassi, & Gallese, 1997). Manipulable objects when observed are classified by the motor brain as potential targets of the interactions we might entertain with them. Premotor and parietal "canonical neurons" control the grasping and manipulation of objects and also respond to their mere observation (Murata et al., 1997; Raos, Umiltà, Fogassi, & Gallese, 2006). Finally, mirror neurons – motor neurons activated during the execution of an action and its observation performed by someone else – map the action of others on the observers' motor representation of the same action (Di Pellegrino, Fadiga, Fogassi, Gallese, & Rizzolatti, 1992; Gallese, Fadiga, Fogassi, & Rizzolatti, 1996; Rizzolatti, Fadiga, Gallese,

& Fogassi, 1996; Rizzolatti, Fogassi, & Gallese, 2001). More than 20 years of research have demonstrated the existence of a mechanism also in the human brain – at first discovered in macaque monkeys – that directly maps action perception and execution, called the "Mirror Mechanism" (MM) (for review, see Ammaniti & Gallese, 2014; Gallese, 2014a; Gallese, Keysers, & Rizzolatti, 2004). In humans as well, the motor brain is multimodal. Thus, it does not matter whether we see someone cracking peanuts or just hear the noise produced by the action. Different sensory accounts (both visual and auditory) of the same motor behavior activate the very motor neurons normally causing it. The brain circuits with evidence of the MM, connecting frontal and posterior parietal multimodal motor neurons most likely analogous to macaques' mirror neurons, map a given motor content like "reach out", "grasp," or "break" not only when controlling its performance, but also when visually and/or aurally perceiving it performed by someone else, when imitating it, or when imagining performing it while perfectly still.

These results radically change our understanding of the role of bodily actions and the cortical motor system. The cortical motor system is not just a mere muscle controller. It is an integral part of our cognitive system (Gallese, Rochat, Cossu, & Sinigaglia, 2009) because its neurofunctional architecture not only structures action execution but also action perception, imitation, and imagination by means of neural connections to motor effectors and/or other sensory cortical areas. When the action is executed or imitated, the cortico-spinal pathway is activated, leading to the excitation of muscles and the ensuing movements. When the action is observed or imagined, its actual execution is inhibited. The cortical motor network is activated, though not in all of its components and not with the same intensity, hence action is not produced, but only simulated.

The prolonged activation of the neural representation of motor content in the absence of movement likely defines the experiential backbone of the actions we perceive or imagine perceiving. This allows a direct apprehension of the relational quality linking space, objects, and others' actions to our body. The primordial quality that turns space, objects, and behavior into intentional objects resides in their constitution as the objects of the motor intentionality expressed by our body's motor potential (Gallese, 2000, 2003; Gallese, 2014a; Gallese & Sinigaglia, 2010).

Other mirror mechanisms are involved in our capacity to directly apprehend the emotions and sensations of others because of a shared representational bodily format. When perceiving others expressing disgust, or experiencing touch or pain, the same brain areas are activated as when we subjectively experience the same emotion or sensation. We do not fully experience their qualitative content, which remains opaque to us, but its simulation instantiated by the mirror mechanism enables us to experience others as experiencing emotions or sensations that we know from the inside, as it were.

4 Embodied Simulation and the Empathic Body

The discovery of mirror neurons gives us a new empirically founded notion of intersubjectivity first and foremost conceived as *intercorporeality* – the mutual resonance of intentionally meaningful sensorimotor behaviors. Our understanding of others as intentional agents does not depend exclusively on propositional competence, but also on the relational nature of action. In many situations, we can directly understand the meaning of other people's basic actions thanks to the motor equivalence between what others do and what we can do. Intercorporeality thus becomes the main source of basic knowledge we have of others. Motor simulation instantiated by neurons endowed with "mirror properties" is probably the neural correlate of this human faculty, describable in functional terms as "embodied simulation" (see Gallese, 2005, 2014a; Gallese & Sinigaglia, 2011). The multiple MMs present in our brain, thanks to the "intentional attunement" they generate, allow us to recognize others as other selves, allowing basic forms of intersubjective communication and mutual implicit understanding (Gallese, 2014a). Embodied simulation provides a unified theoretical framework for all of these phenomena. It proposes that our social interactions become meaningful by means of reusing our own mental states or processes in functionally attributing them to others. In this context, simulation is conceived of as a non-conscious, pre-reflective functional mechanism of the brain-body system, whose function is to model objects, agents, and events. This mechanism can be triggered during our interactions with others, and is plastically modulated by contextual and cognitive factors as well as ones related to personal identity.

Embodied simulation is also triggered during the experience of spatiality around our body and during the contemplation of objects. The functional architecture of embodied simulation seems to constitute a basic characteristic of our brain, making possible our rich and diversified experiences of space, objects, and other individuals; it is also the basis for our capacity to empathize. Altogether these results suggest that empathy, or at the very least many of its bodily qualities, might be underpinned by embodied simulation mechanisms. According to my proposal, empathy is the outcome of the natural tendency to experience our interpersonal relations first and foremost at the implicit level of intercorporeality. It is perhaps worth emphasizing that embodied simulation not only connects us to others. It connects us to *our* world, a world populated by natural objects, man-made objects with or without symbolic meaning, and other individuals, a world in which most of the time we feel at home. The sense we attribute to our lived experience of the world is grounded on the relational quality of our bodily action potentialities, that are laden with affects and enabled by the way they are mapped in our brains.

5 Empathy, Embodied Simulation, and Aesthetic Experience

The idea that the body might play an important role in the aesthetic experience of visual artworks is rather old. In modern times the notion of empathy (*Einfühlung*) was originally introduced in aesthetics by the German philosopher Robert Vischer in 1873, thus well before its use in psychology. Vischer qualified *Einfühlung*, literally "feeling-in", as the physical response generated by the observation of forms within paintings. Particular visual forms arouse particular responsive feelings, depending on the conformity of forms to the design and function of the muscles in the body, from those in the eyes to our limbs and to our bodily posture as a whole. Vischer clearly distinguished a passive notion of vision – seeing [*sehen*] – from an active one – looking at [*schauen*]. According to Vischer, *looking* best characterizes our aesthetic experience when perceiving images in general and artworks, in particular. Aesthetic experience implies an empathic involvement that encompasses a series of bodily reactions of the beholder. In his book *Über das optische Formgefühl* [*On the Optical Sense of Form*] (1873), Vischer writes:

> We can often observe in ourselves the curious fact that a visual stimulus is experienced not so much with our eyes as with a different sense in another part of our body [. . .]. The whole body is involved; the entire physical being [*Leibmensch*] is moved. [. . .] Thus each emphatic sensation ultimately leads to a strengthening or a weakening of the general vital sensation [*allgemeine Vitalempfindung*]. (Vischer, 1873/1994, pp. 98–99)

Vischer posits that symbolic forms could acquire their meaning foremost due to their intrinsic anthropomorphic content. Through the nonconscious projection of her/his body, the beholder establishes an intimate relation with the artwork.

Developing Vischer's ideas, August Wölfflin during the early stages of his career proposed in 1886 that observation of specific architectural forms engage the beholder's bodily responses (see Wölfflin, 1886/1999). Shortly afterwards, Theodor Lipps discussed the relationship between space and geometry on the one hand and aesthetic enjoyment on the other (see Lipps, 1897, 1903). The work of Vischer influenced two other German scholars whose contributions are highly relevant for my proposal: Adolf von Hildebrand and Aby Warburg. The German sculptor Hildebrand published a book in 1893 entitled *Das Problem der Form in der bildenden Kunst* [*The Problem of Form in Figurative Art*]. In this book, Hildebrand proposed that our perception of the spatial characters of images is the result of a constructive sensory-motor process. Space, according to Hildebrand, does not constitute an a priori of experience, as suggested by Immanuel Kant, but its product. Artistic images are effectual, that is, are the outcome of both the artist's creative production and the effects images produce on beholders. The aesthetic value of artworks resides, according to Hildebrand, in their potential to establish a link between the intentional creative acts of the artist and their reconstruction by the beholder. In such a way artistic creation and fruition are directly related. To understand an artistic image, for Hildebrand, means to implicitly grasp its creative process. A very modern aspect of Hildebrand's proposal concerns the relevance he assigns to the motor nature of experience. Through movement the available elements in space can be connected. Movements also allow objects to be carved out of their background and perceived as such. It also enables representations and meaning to be formed and articulated. Ultimately, Hildebrand suggests that sensible experience is possible and images acquire their meaning solely based on their relationship to the acting body (see Hildebrand, 1893/2012).

Hildebrand exerted a strong influence on the art historian Aby Warburg. From 1888 to 1889, Warburg studied in Florence at the *Kunsthistorische Institut*, founded by the art historian August Schmarsow. As emphasized by Georges Didi-Huberman, Schmarsow was determined to open art history to contributions from anthropology, physiology, and psychology and emphasized the role of body gestures in visual art, arguing that bodily empathy greatly contributes to the appreciation of visual arts (Didi-Huberman, 2002). As Andrea Pinotti writes, Schmarsow,

> art historian and theoretician, centered his reflections, which exploited both the results of the theories of empathy and the analyses of the formal character of art works, on the idea of the transcendental function of corporeality as a constellation of material a-priori, that is, on the idea of bodily organization as the condition of possibility of sensory experience. (Pinotti, 2001, p. 91)

Warburg clearly learned this lesson as he conceived art history as a tool to shed light on the psychology of human expressive power. His famous notion of "pathos formula" [*Pathosformel*] implies that a variety of bodily postures, gestures and actions can be constantly detected throughout art history, from the classical art of Antiquity to the Renaissance, since they embody in exemplary fashion the aesthetic act of empathy as one of the main creative sources of artistic style. According to Warburg, a theory of artistic style must be conceived of as a "pragmatic science of expression" [*pragmatische Ausdruckskunde*]. Warburg, when writing on the classic marble group known as the *Laocoön*, identified transition as a fundamental element in turning a static image into movement charged with pathos (see Warburg, 1932/1999). Years later, the Russian director Sergej Ejzenstejn, when commenting on the same *Laocoön* sculpture in 1935, writes that the lived expression of human suffering portrayed in this masterpiece of classic art is accomplished by means of the illusion of movement via a particular montage that in one single image condenses different aspects of expressive bodily movements that could not possibly be visible at the same time (Ejzenstejn, 1935/1985).

Later, the philosopher Maurice Merleau-Ponty further highlighted the relationship between embodiment and aesthetic experience by suggesting the relevance of the felt bodily imitation of what is seen in the artwork in art appreciation (Merleau-Ponty, 1962, 1968). Consistent with the role of *Einfühlung*, Merleau-Ponty also emphasizes the importance of the artist's implied actions for the aesthetic experience of the beholder, with reference to the paintings of Paul Cézanne and his famous claim that we cannot possibly imagine how a mind could paint (Merleau-Ponty, 1968).

These scholars believed that the feeling of physical involvement with a painting, sculpture or architectural form provokes a sense of imitating the motion or action seen or implied in the work, which, in turn, enhances our emotional responses to it. Thus, physical involvement constitutes a fundamental ingredient in our aesthetic experience of artworks. Such insights explained already by several scholars a long time ago can today be proved by means of experimental work. The next section discusses recent empirical evidence confirming bodily empathy as an important component of the perceptual experience of artworks, demonstrating its underlying neural mechanisms.

6 Embodied Simulation and Experimental Aesthetics

Embodied simulation can be relevant to aesthetic experience in at least two ways: first, because of the bodily feelings triggered by artworks we relate to, by means of the mirror mechanisms they evoke. In such a way, embodied simulation generates the peculiar *seeing as* that characterizes our aesthetic experience of images we look at. Second, the potential intimate relationship between the symbol-making gesture and its reception by beholders enables its experience by means of simulation in virtue of the motor representation that produces the image (Freedberg & Gallese, 2007; see also Gallese, 2012, 2014a, 2014b, 2014c; Gallese & Di Dio, 2012; Gallese & Gattara, 2015; Gallese & Guerra, 2015). When I look at a graphic sign, I unconsciously simulate the gesture that has produced it.

Our scientific investigation of experimental aesthetics applied to visual arts began with this second aspect. In three distinct experiments, we investigated the link between the expressive gesture of the hand and the images those gestures produced using high density electroencephalography (EEG). We recorded beholders' brain responses to graphic signs like letters, ideograms, and scribbles or to abstract artworks by Lucio Fontana and Franz Kline. The results of the first study showed that observing a letter of the Roman alphabet, a Chinese ideogram or a meaningless scribble, all written by hand, activates the hand motor representation of beholders (Heiman, Umiltà, & Gallese, 2013). In two other studies, we demonstrated that a similar motor simulation of hand gestures is evoked when beholding a cut on canvas by Lucio Fontana (Umiltà, Berchio, Sestito, Freedberg, & Gallese, 2012), or the dynamic brushstrokes on canvas by Franz Kline (Sbriscia-Fioretti, Berchio, Freedberg, Gallese, & Umiltà, 2013). The visible traces of the creative gesture activate in the observer the specific motor areas controlling the execution of the same gesture. Beholders' eyes catch not only information about the shape, direction, and texture of the cuts or strokes, but by means of embodied simulation they breach into the actual motor expression of the artist when creating the artwork. The sensory-motor component of image perception together with the jointly evoked emotional reaction allow beholders to feel the artwork in an embodied manner.

A possible criticism of this model might point out the supposed passivity of its account of aesthetic experience, where beholders are relegated to a deterministic empathic receptivity, hence losing sight of the peculiar individual quality of aesthetic experience, largely determined by one's individual taste, background, memories, education, and expertise.

A second objection frequently raised against empathic-mimetic accounts of aesthetic experience consists of opposing the ambiguity and under-determinacy of art's symbolic content against the supposedly mechanistic quality of empathic responses, therefore falling short of capturing the potential intrinsic ambiguity and polysemic quality of artworks. It is possible to refute such criticism by arguing that there is ample proof that mirror mechanisms and embodied simulation are dynamically modulated and affected by contingent and idiosyncratic factors. Several studies show that one's previous experiences, memories, and expertise strongly determine the intensity of mirror mechanism activation and the ensuing perceptual contents (for recent reviews, see Ammaniti & Gallese, 2014; Gallese, 2014a; Gallese & Guerra, 2015).

I posit that embodied simulation in virtue of its diachronic plasticity and modulation might also be the vehicle of the projective qualities of our aesthetic experience, where our personal and social identity, the context, our mood, and disposition, literally shape the way we relate to a given perceptual object. Embodied simulation, if conceived of as the dynamic instantiation of our implicit memories, can relate perceptual object and beholder with a specific, unique, and historically determined quality. This projective quality of embodied simulation forms the basis for a strong counterargument against the above objections.

7 Conclusions

The results of our empirical research show that the symbolic processes characterizing our species, in spite of their progressive abstraction and externalization from the body, keep their bodily ties intact. Symbolic expression is tied to the body not only because the body is the symbol-making instrument, but also because it is the main medium enabling symbolic experience. Today, we are able to look at the aesthetic-symbolic dimension of human existence not only from a semiotic-hermeneutic perspective, but starting from the dimension of bodily presence. According to Hans Ulrich Gumbrecht, aesthetic experience involves two components: one deals with meaning and the other one with presence.

The notion of presence entails the bodily involvement of image beholders through a synesthetic, multimodal relationship with the artistic/cultural artifact, whose perception is qualified by Gumbrecht as "haptic vision". According to him every culture can be analyzed and studied from the double perspective of meaning and presence because both can be found to varying degrees in every cultural object. When presence predominates, objects acquire their sense in virtue of their intrinsic sensorimotor inherence that they have for perceivers, and not through interpretation (Gumbrecht, 2004).

The added value that experimental aesthetics can bring to the debate in aesthetics consists in revitalizing the scientific study of artistic styles, focusing on their biological bodily roots. Furthermore, by investigating aesthetic experience from an empiric neurobiological point of view, the outcomes of human symbolic expression can be viewed and analyzed in ways less conditioned by concepts of art influenced by the contemporary western cultural and aesthetic canon. The quality of our aesthetic experience of artworks is clearly influenced and modulated by our cultural, ethnic, and personal identity. Experimental aesthetics can indeed investigate the specific role played by all these influences, for example by studying participants with different ethnic origins, age, and professional skills and expertise. What I mean is that we should stop arguing that culture is beyond the grasp of science, as the latter can only deal with nature. Opposing culture to nature is nonsense, as epigenetics clearly shows that DNA, the material constituent of our genes, does not code in a rigid and deterministic way the synthesis of proteins, but is deeply influenced by our relationship with the world. The physical, but also material, historical, social, and cultural environment in which we live, the type of human relations characterizing our life, in essence our *Umwelt*, influences the way genes work. DNA does not change, but its expression does and these changes are passed on to descendants. Given these elements, experimental aesthetics can foster a "bio-cultural" turning point within the human sciences (Cometa, 2017). Such turning point must question the rigid and obsolete separation between nature and culture.

The approach to aesthetics I am proposing can relieve us from the forced choice between the totalizing relativism of social constructivism, which does not leave any room to the constitutive role of the body in cognition, and the deterministic scientism of some quarters of evolutionary psychology, which aims at explaining art exclusively in terms of adaptation and modularity.

Today cognitive neuroscience can shed new light from its own particular perspective and methodology on the aesthetic capacities and practices of human beings and their basic creative inclination. This new research will help us understanding how and why symbolic expression and art are among the most fundamental expressions of our human nature.

References

Ammaniti, M., & Gallese, V. (2014). *The Birth of Intersubjectivity. Psychodynamics, Neurobiology and the Self.* New York: W. W. Norton & Company.

Cometa M. (2017). *Perché le storie ci aiutano a vivere. La letteratura necessaria.* Milano: Raffaello Cortina Editore.

Didi-Huberman, G. (2002). *L'Image Survivante* [Surviving image]. Paris: Les Éditions de Minuit.

Di Pellegrino, G., Fadiga, L., Fogassi, L., Gallese, V., & Rizzolatti, G. (1992). Understanding Motor Events: A Neurophysiological Study. *Experimental Brain Research, 91*, 176–180.

Ejzenstejn, S. (1935/1985). *Teoria Generale del Montaggio.* Venice: Marsilio.

Fogassi, L., Gallese, V., Fadiga, L., Luppino, G., Matelli, M., & Rizzolatti, G. (1996). Coding of Peripersonal space in Inferior Premotor Cortex (area F4). *Journal of Neurophysiology, 76*, 141–157.

Formaggio, D. (1981). *Arte*[Art]. Milan: Mondadori.

Freedberg, D. & Gallese, V. (2007). Motion, Emotion and Empathy in Esthetic Experience. *Trends in Cognitive Sciences, 11*, 197–203.

Gallese, V. (2000). The Inner Sense of Action: Agency and Motor Representations. *Journal of Consciousness Studies, 7*, 23–40.

Gallese, V. (2003). The Manifold Nature of Interpersonal Relations: The Quest for a Common Mechanism. *Philosophical Transactions of the Royal Society London, 358*, 517–528.

Gallese, V. (2005). Embodied Simulation: From Neurons to Phenomenal Experience. *Phenomenology and the Cognitive Sciences, 4*, 23–48.

Gallese, V. (2012). Aby Warburg e il dialogo tra estetica, biologia e fisiologia [Aby Warburg and the dialogue between aesthetics, biology, and philosophy]. *Ph, 2*, 48–62.

Gallese, V. (2014a). Bodily Selves in Relation: Embodied Simulation as Second-Person Perspective on Intersubjectivity. *Philosophical Transactions of the Royal Society B: Biological Sciences, 369*, 20130177, published 28 April 2014.

Gallese, V. (2014b). The Hand and the Architect: Gesture and Creative Expression. In *Unplugged* (pp. 14–17). Projects of L22 and DGW Italy. Milan: L22.

Gallese, V. (2014c). Arte, Corpo, Cervello: Per un'Estetica Sperimentale. *Micromega, 2*, 49–67.

Gallese, V. & Di Dio, C. (2012). Neuroesthetics: The Body in Esthetic Experience. In V. S. Ramachandran (Ed.). *The Encyclopedia of Human Behavior* (vol. 2, pp. 687–693). London: Elsevier Academic Press.

Gallese, V. & Gattara, A. (2015). Embodied Simulation, Aesthetics and Architecture: An Experimental Aesthetic Approach. In S. Robinson & J. Pallasmaa (Eds.). *Mind in Architecture: Neuroscience, Embodiment and the Future of Design* (pp. 161–179). Boston, MA: MIT Press.

Gallese, V, & Guerra, M. (2015). *Lo Schermo Empatico. Cinema e Neuroscienze.* Milan: Raffaello Cortina Editore.

Gallese, V. & Sinigaglia, C. (2011). What Is So Special with Embodied Simulation. *Trends in Cognitive Sciences, 15*(11), 512–519.

Gallese V., Sinigaglia C. (2010). The Bodily Self as Power for Action. *Neuropsychologia*, 48, 746–755.

Gallese, V., Keysers, C., & Rizzolatti, G. (2004). A Unifying View of the Basis of Social Cognition. *Trends in Cognitive Science, 8*, 396–403.

Gallese, V., Fadiga, L., Fogassi, L., & Rizzolatti, G. (1996). Action Recognition in the Premotor Cortex. *Brain, 119*, 593–609.

Gallese, V., Rochat, M., Cossu, G., & Sinigaglia, C. (2009). Motor Cognition and Its Role in the Phylogeny and Ontogeny of Intentional Understanding. *Developmental Psychology, 45*, 103–113.

Gumbrecht, H. U. (2004). *Production of Presence: What Meaning Cannot Convey*. Stanford, CA: Stanford University Press.

Heimann, K., Umiltà, M. A., & Gallese, V. (2013). How the Motor-Cortex Distinguishes Among Letters, Unknown Symbols and Scribbles: A High Density EEG Study. *Neuropsychologia, 51*, 2833–40, doi: 10.1016/j.neuropsychologia.2013.07.014

Hildebrand, A. v. (1893/2012). *The Problem of Form in Painting and Sculpture* (R. M. Ogden, Ed.). New York: Ulan Press.

Lipps, Th. (1897). *Raumästhetik und geometrisch- optische Täuschungen* [Aesthetics of space and geometrical optical illusions]. Leipzig: J. A. Barth.

Lipps, Th. (1903). *Ästhetik: Psychologie des Schönen und der Kunst* [Aesthetics: The psychology of beauty and art]. Hamburg /Leipzig: Leopold Voss.

Merleau-Ponty, M. (1962). *Phenomenology of Perception* (C. Smith, Trans.). London: Routledge.

Merleau-Ponty, M. (1968). *The Visible and the Invisible* (A. Lingis, Trans.). Evanston: Northwestern University Press.

Murata, A., Fadiga, L., Fogassi, L., Gallese, V., Raos V., & Rizzolatti, G. (1997). Object Representation in the Ventral Premotor Cortex (Area F5) of the Monkey. *Journal of Neurophysiology, 78*, 2226–2230.

Pinotti, A. (2001). *Memorie del neutro. Morfologia dell'immagine in Aby Warburg*. Milan: Mimesis.

Raos, V., Umiltà, M. A., Fogassi, L., & Gallese, V. (2006). Functional Properties of Grasping-Related Neurons in the Ventral Premotor Area F5 of the Macaque Monkey. *Journal of Neurophysiology, 95*, 709–729.

Rizzolatti, G., Fogassi, L., & Gallese, V. (2001). Neurophysiological Mechanisms Underlying the Understanding and Imitation of Action. *Nature Reviews Neuroscience, 2*, 661–670.

Rizzolatti, G., Fogassi, L., & Gallese, V. (2002). Motor and Cognitive Functions of the Ventral Premotor Cortex. *Current Opinion in Neurobiology, 12*, 149–154.

Rizzolatti, G., Fadiga, L., Gallese, V., & Fogassi, L. (1996). Premotor Cortex and the Recognition of Motor Actions. *Cognitive Brain Research, 3*, 131–141.

Rizzolatti, G., Fadiga, L., Fogassi, L., & Gallese, V. (1997). The Space around Us. *Science, 277*, 190–191.

Sbriscia-Fioretti, B., Berchio, C., Freedberg, D., Gallese, V., & Umiltà, M. A. (2013). ERP Modulation during Observation of Abstract Paintings by Franz Kline. *PloS ONE, 8*(10), e75241. doi:10.1371/journal.pone.0075241

Shiner, L. (2001). *The Invention of Art: A Cultural History*. Chicago: Chicago University Press.

Umiltà, M. A., Berchio, C., Sestito, M., Freedberg, D., & Gallese, V. (2012). Abstract Art and Cortical Motor Activation: An EEG Study. *Frontiers in Human Neuroscience*, *6*, 311.

Vischer, R. (1873). *Über das optische Formgefühl: ein Beiträg zur Ästhetik* [On the optical sense of form: A contribution to aesthetics]. Leipzig: Credner.

Vischer, R. (1873/1994). On the Optical Sense of Form. A Contribution to Aesthetics. In H. F. Malgrave (Ed.). *Empathy, Form, and Space. Problems in German Aesthetics, 1873–1893* (pp. 89–123). Santa Monica: Getty Center Publications.

Warburg, A. (1932/1999). *The Renewal of Pagan Antiquity* [orig. *Die Erneuerung der Heidnischen Antike*] (D. Britt, Trans.). Los Angeles: The Getty Research Institute.

Wölfflin, H. (1886/1999). *Prolegomena zu einer Psychologie der Architektur* [Prolegomena to a psychology of architecture]. Berlin: Gebrüder Mann.

Zeki, S. (1999). Art and the Brain. *Journal of Consciousness Studies*, *6*(6–7), 76–96.

Part 2

Debated History

8

Empathy, Imagination, and Dramaturgy – A Means of Society in Eighteenth-Century Theory

Helmut J. Schneider

This chapter pertains to a context first established in the mid-eighteenth century between the social concept of "empathy" (or rather "sympathy", the common term used at the time) and aesthetics, in particular dramaturgy.[1] It is a well-established historical fact that over the course of that century literature and the arts gained what we have become accustomed to calling aesthetic autonomy, meaning the independence of the artifact and its fictional world, ideally, from all external strictures imposed by the state, the church, society at large, as well as from the prescriptions of traditional rhetoric and aesthetic norms. Art was conceived as a sphere of its own, following solely its internal laws, alongside other likewise autonomous spheres such as religion, politics, and the economy. The separation of the different spheres, which characterized modern rationality for Max Weber and the functional differentiation of modern society

[1] The chapter is based on my work on theater in eighteenth century (see Schneider, 2008).

H.J. Schneider (✉)
Department of German Literature, University of Bonn, Bonn, Germany
e-mail: h.j.schneider@uni-bonn.de

V. Lux, S. Weigel (eds.), *Empathy*, Palgrave Studies in the Theory and History of Psychology, DOI 10.1057/978-1-137-51299-4_8

for Niklas Luhmann, still very much shapes our present perspective, despite the many misgivings we may have regarding the status of an "independent realm" of the fine arts.

It was the truly ingenious approach of Enlightenment thinking to realign art and set it free from its traditional social constraints. This was a society conceived not as a set of hierarchical strata (in Luhmannian terms) but as a functional system of mobile individuals operating in a variety of different spheres and sub-spheres. Art was to play a pivotal role in (re-) integrating the autonomous modern individual (the "subject") into new communal bonds, thus gaining a new social function for itself. Enlightenment social theory elaborated ceaselessly on the compatibility of the opposing principles of "self-love" (self-preservation, *Selbsterhaltung*) and "love of others"; both were considered essential psychological prerequisites for society, the first contributing to its progress through the improvement of the individual and the second strengthening solidarity among its members. The harmony of the two principles (under the dominance of the latter) was the central concern of the so-called Scottish school of social thought. This philosophical school, which exerted an enormous influence on the intellectual life on the Continent, particularly in Germany, included Francis Hutcheson, David Hume, Edmund Burke, and Adam Smith. For all of them, the principal basis of society was not, as it had been for their chief historical opponent, Thomas Hobbes, egotism and fear reined in by the rational installation of absolutist rule, but solidarity and mutual respect deeply engrained in a natural "moral sense". This sense was linked to a similarly intense, inborn sense of beauty, as it had been extolled in the earlier work of the Earl of Shaftesbury. To cultivate the appreciation of natural beauty, of literature and the arts, then, meant to foster social cohesion on an egalitarian level.

Adam Smith is of particular relevance for the historical argument I wish to outline in the following. Still famous for his (alleged) advocacy of egotistical self-interest as the driving force of a free market economy, Smith also propounded, although this is less remembered, the principle of "sympathy" as the binding element without which no society and no market economy can subsist. The two seemingly opposing principles are interdependent; the fact that they were set forth in two different (lengthy) books – the early *Theory of Moral Sentiments* (1759) and the later *Wealth of Nations* (1776) – contributed to their separation into two strands of reception: while the first work became influential in aesthetics, especially in Germany, the second remained largely restricted to economics and social theory.

Adam Smith's treatise on the "moral sentiments" speaks to the mutual implication of the psychological and social concepts of "sympathy" (corresponding to our term "empathy")[2] and the aesthetic dimension, brought about by the function of the *imagination*. The faculty of the imagination, crucial for the emergence of the concept of aesthetic autonomy, was also, according to Smith's moral theory, at work in the practice of the individual's empathizing with another person, which meant placing oneself into the situation and feelings of one's fellow being. More specifically, the constitutive fictional element inherent in "sympathy" possessed a *theatrical* characteristic that aligned it with the relation between spectator and actor in the dramatic performance. Although Smith rarely addresses the institution of the theater proper, his description of the sympathetic relation between two individuals in terms of the theater performance opens it up into a public space, for the theater is the one genre of literature (and arguably the arts in general) that implies a social dimension in the most obvious way. It is the place where a large number of people voluntarily gather together in order to share the common experience of immersing themselves into an imaginary world, leaving their habitual station in life behind and, by doing this *together*, arguably anticipate a new, utopian form of community.

This was at least a dominant concept in the eighteenth-century dramaturgy, which drew prominently on the social concepts of empathy and sympathy, *Einfühlung* and *Mitleid*.[3] In the following, I will first outline Smith's theory of sympathy, with an emphasis on its theatrical

---

[2] 'Sympathy' is the more common term, often also in French and English, 'empathy' is an English translation of the German *Einfühlung* from around 1900.

[3] I leave here unconsidered the different, not at all insignificant semantic ring of the German terms; in particular, *Mitleid* evokes a stronger notion of 'suffering' since in German there is not a separate word for 'suffering' proper, whereas in English and French the Latin root *passio* distinguishes 'compassion' from 'to suffer' or 'souffrir') (see Hamburger, 1985).

components, before proceeding to demonstrate its affinity to Denis Diderot's and Gotthold Ephraim Lessing's theories of theater practice. The following section shall explain how this practice was meant to promote the experience of a new community in the theater audience, which can be understood as a kind of an *imaginary collective*. The aesthetic realm was meant to gain an *immediate* social impact and culminate in an Enlightenment utopia that can also be seen in a critical light. In the last section, I will take Käte Hamburger's incisive critique of the common notion of *Mitleid* in the Enlightenment and the humanist (also Christian) tradition as a point of reference in such a critique.

1 Social Theory – Adam Smith's Concept of Sympathy

Essential for the general definition of "social sympathy" were the sense of sight and the faculty of the imagination, understood as internal representation. Sight and imagination work together in bringing about the sympathetic act: at the sight of another person's situation and expression, in particular one of suffering and torment, sympathy mediates that person's inner state of feeling to us through the imagination, which then evokes similar feelings known to us by our own experience; in Smith's words, "an analogous emotion, which springs up, at the thought of his [the sufferer's] situation, in the breast of every attentive spectator" (Smith, 1759–2009, p. 15). Generally speaking, then, sympathy allows humans to share the feelings of fellow humans without being actually hit by the cause of those feelings. Smith's recurring formula for this process is "entering the other person's body". Sympathy removes us from our own body and places us into another's; it provides *imaginary access* – the only possible access – to the interior life of other humans by way of analogy with our own sensations and feelings.

> By the imagination we place ourselves in his [the suffering person's] situation, we conceive ourselves enduring all the same torments, *we enter as it were into his body*, and become in some measure the same person with

> him, and thence form some idea of his sensations, and even feel something which, though weaker in degree, is not altogether unlike them. (Smith, 1759–2009, p. 13–14, my emphasis, H.S.)

In this fashion, sympathy functions as a kind of social "medium", in the literal sense of a *mediation between individuals*. This is essentially a non-reflective medium; one characterized by spontaneity, by a quasi-instinctual automatism ("mechanism", Smith writes), paradoxically, a medium of immediacy. It is precisely this characteristic that qualified sympathy for its function as a pre-rational, pre-institutional, and pre-traditional social glue.

Historically, the urgency to identify this glue appears as a reaction to the momentous transformation of the old European society, that is, the dissolution of the traditional order of the *ancien régime* and the concomitant threat of disorder and potential chaos. Written almost at the same time as Smith's *Theory of Moral Sentiments* (1759), Jean-Jacques Rousseau's *Discourse on Inequality* (1755) identified the emotion of pity, *pitié* or *compassion*, as the key social sentiment of "natural man", *l'homme de la nature*, which in his view was being corrupted by the existing society; and, as we shall see, Lessing and Diderot developed their dramaturgical thoughts around the same concept. (Rousseau, intellectual companion of Diderot, was also instantly translated by Moses Mendelssohn, Lessing's partner in the dramaturgical letter exchange; although Lessing at this crucial time of the first inception of his theory of tragic *Mitleid* could not have known Smith, he had already translated an important text by David Hume, Smith's philosophical teacher.)

The path from Smith and Rousseau to Diderot and Lessing, seen as a path from social theory to the aesthetics of the theater, is already outlined by Smith's work. Although Smith is not directly concerned with the latter, his description of the relation between the sympathizing subject and the person in pain in terms of a theatrical constellation entails a *model for a new society* implicitly based on the idea of a *new theater*. This structure can be described from two sides: the viewer's, or *spectator's*, and the suffering individual's, whom Smith, somewhat surprisingly, perceives as *actor*. These are the two agents who, according to Smith's analysis, must cooperate in order to bring about the sympathetic transaction. When Smith first reflects on the readiness of the spectator to engage in sympathy's imaginary transposition, he introduces, in a seeming contradiction to the emotion's alleged quasi-instinctual character and the importance of visual immediacy, an *intellectual* component. The sheer impact of an unmotivated or unexplained passion or pain, Smith asserts, will obstruct sympathy and make the spectator turn the other way. We need to *know* the context and genesis of the particular situation in which the suffering person finds him/herself, or be able to explain it to ourselves; we have to *accommodate* the sight of suffering to our comprehension. Knowing, which often means knowing more than the person involved, heightens our willingness (or even makes us willing in the first place) to enter into the sufferer's condition, whereas the sudden and contingent sight of decontextualized suffering will only strike us blind. Contextualizing (explaining, making plausible, inventing, and here we may also say *fictionalizing* or *narrativizing*) pain redeems it from its isolation in a single body and makes it accessible for other individuals. Put differently, pain thus understood (or rather *shaped*, that is, fictionally represented) opens the self-enclosure of individuals and leads them beyond the physical boundaries of the body into the social dimension.

The dramaturgical element of the sympathetic constellation becomes even more apparent when we look at the side of the suffering person. Smith suggests that this person has to tone down the outward expression of his/her pain and adjust it to meet the spectator's willingness to sympathize instead of arousing, in the extreme case, "disgust". Just as the latter needs to know, or represent to himself, the cause or background of the pain, the "person concerned" needs to "reduce the violence of the passions to that pitch of moderation, in which the impartial spectator can entirely enter into them" (Smith, 1759/2009, p. 33). That is to say, the sufferer must become his/her own spectator before qualifying as a suitable recipient of sympathy. The flagrant examples of passions a spectator cannot enter into are the gross physical ones like hunger, sexuality, and violence, but they also include extreme anger and hatred, unless – to repeat the former point – they are put into a psychologically or otherwise plausible context.

The "pitch of moderation" stipulated as the dramaturgical prerequisite for the sympathetic act involves an unmistakable suggestion of social normativism (or even "normalism"). Particularly revealing in this respect is Smith's example of a strong resentment where, according to him, the spectator's empathy is likely to be limited by the concern for the potential victim of the revenge (Chapter 3 of Part One, Section II: "Of the Unsocial Passions", pp. 42–48). Thus, the function of sympathy as *social medium* carries the further specific meaning of *mediating* and *mitigating* the one-sidedness and implicitly violence of particular feelings, transforming them into socially compatible qualities. "[T]he pitch", Smith avers, "which the spectator can go along with, must lie, it is evident, in a certain mediocrity" (Smith, 1759/2009, p. 34). In formulations like this, the underlying Enlightenment idea (and ideal) of an egalitarian middle class society becomes manifest. This should not, however, obfuscate the crucial philosophical point of Smith's argument: sympathy holds a privileged social place among the "moral sentiments" because it enacts a movement from the *physical plane* to a more general and, *potentially, universal level* ("common to all men"). The imaginary transfer of "self" into "other" serves as the foundational act for the build-up of the abstract system of modern society precisely because it unites interpersonal (even face-to-face) immediacy with an open process of *intellectualization or spiritualization*; Smith's German followers will call this *Vergeistigung*.

2 Dramaturgy – Diderot and Lessing

In turning from Smith to Lessing and Diderot, we also turn from the implied dramaturgy of social theory to the implied social import of dramaturgy. The dramaturgical element involved in Adam Smith's notion of sympathy finds its symmetrical correspondence in the social function of Gotthold Ephraim Lessing's dramaturgical concept of *Mitleid*. Apparent is the *egalitarian emphasis* that connects the founding fathers of the new "bourgeois" drama with Smith and his fellow (Scottish) theoreticians of sympathy. For Lessing, the theater represents a "school of compassion", in which the spectators exercise their faculty to empathize and prepare themselves for their role as *Mitmensch*, for "the most compassionate [sympathetic] human is the best human" [*der mitleidigste Mensch ist der beste Mensch*], as the famous quote runs – that is, the human best prepared for conversing with his or her fellow human beings on equal footing (Lessing, 1756/1973a, p. 163).[4] The same act of (partial) identification implied by *Mitleid* presupposes protagonists who are "one with us and our station" [*mit uns von gleichem Schrot und Korne*], a "middle character" [*mittlerer Charakter*] (Lessing, 1767–69/1973b, pp. 580–581) – almost a literal echo of Smith's "mediocrity". Furthermore, Lessing imposes the same ban on any extremism of passion or pain on the side of the dramatist and actor – notably in tragedy – and advocates the same ideal of moderation on the stage as his predecessor had done for social interaction. Bringing the theatrical (or rather, to avoid a misunderstanding of the term, theater) character of Smith's theory of sympathy into full view, Lessing, too, insists on the actor's (and the playwright's) need to tone down extreme violence, avoid abrupt shocks and unmotivated turns and maintain a psychologically and pragmatically plausible continuity of action conducive to the spectator's sympathetic identification.

It is a well-established fact of literary history that this dramaturgical stance carried a polemical edge against the prevailing aristocratic court theater of the time with its perceived "theatrical" exaggeration, stately pomp, and rhetorical ostentatiousness. But seen from the vantage point of Adam Smith and the contemporary social theory of sympathy, the emphasis on "egalitarian mediocrity", if we may stick to this term, is more than a socio-historically motivated change in aesthetic and moral norms (for example, simplicity and naturalness versus artificial stylishness, bourgeois authenticity versus aristocratic pretension, etc.). As with Smith, it is a question of what holds (modern) society together, namely a matter of sympathy as social *medium*, only now the focus is on *Mitleid* as experienced in the *aesthetic* space of the *theater proper*, and then carried forward into the real social world. The theater becomes the

[4] In Lessing's letter exchange on the *Trauerspiel* with his Berlin friends, the Enlightenment thinkers Friedrich Nicolai and Moses Mendelssohn, he already developed in the mid-fifties his seminal theory of dramaturgical *Mitleid*, to be published in extended form only later, in 1768/69, in the *Hamburgische Dramaturgie* (Lessing, 1767–69/1973b).

privileged place for the practice of this social emotion. This focus on the theater institution accounts for a more thorough analysis of *Mitleid*, as it is now understood not just as a transaction between two persons with the potential of generalization but as a *collective event*, something that happens here and now and transforms a number of isolated individuals into a community with a specific character – an imaginary collective.

The precondition for this transformation is an even more generalizing, or "spiritual" [*geistig*], notion of sympathy or *Mitleid* than we witness with Smith. For Lessing, *Mitleid* is not just one outstanding emotion among others, but it is a super-emotion, so to speak, that comprises all other emotions – the emotion of emotions or with a term taken from another conceptual register, a *transcendental emotion*, whose function is to negotiate and integrate the (potentially chaotic) manifold of the partial, often egotistical, emotions and passions into one harmonious whole. This quality of non-specificity (a non-quality, properly speaking) makes it the privileged vehicle of universalization. Already in his earliest account of *Mitleid* (formulated in the already cited correspondence with his friends Mendelssohn and Nicolai in the mid-fifties, well before Smith's *Theory of Moral Sentiments*), Lessing insists on its categorical difference from any particular passion or emotion that may be represented on stage. *Mitleid* is not at all a derivative, which would by necessity be a weaker copy of an original emotion (be it real or fictionally represented), as it was by and large in Smith's concept (as is apparent in his choice of words "weaker in degree" from the quote cited before); it is an emotion in its own right originating in the soul of the spectator. This emotion is all-inclusive. Lessing illustrates the relation between the external (or fictionally represented) affect – whatever it may be specifically – and the affect of pity with an analogy to two strings, the first of which is "plucked" [*gezupft*] while the second, without being plucked, joins in the vibration [*mitbeben*]. As a sound box or sounding board, *Mitleid* takes up all particular emotions and factual instances from which they spring, but at the same time "abstracts" (literally "draws away") from their concrete specificity leaving only the sympathetic feeling as such (there is a paradox here between *Mitleid* as an authentic emotion originating in the soul and as an echo chamber).[5] In this sense, and more pronounced than with Smith, *Mitleid* establishes an autonomous sphere of universality that everybody can enter into; sympathy or compassion as "co-vibration", *Mitleid* as *Mitbeben* elevates the partial, the corporeal and sensual to a spiritual plane, where – and this leads us back to the theater – all spectators gather at the same time in the same place and are exposed to the same spectacle. Here they can all unite, regardless of their particular station in life.

The goal of the theater performance for Lessing (and Diderot), then, is not just to make each member of the audience *individually* a better (that is, sympathetic, *mitleidig*) human being and citizen, but to make all of them experience a *better community* together: a community shaped by the principle of solidarity, *Mitmenschlichkeit*, aware of itself as it is realized already in the here and now of the theatre. The goal is to unite the spectators, metaphorically speaking, in a "vibrating body" [*Schwingungskörper*], in which the particular qualities of the individuals are absorbed within a higher totality. The nature of this imaginary collective still needs to be explored more extensively. What is the exact relation between the individual acts of sympathetic spectatorship on the one hand and this spiritual transformation of the audience as a whole on the other?

3 The Theater of the "Fourth Wall" and the Constitution of an Ideal Collective

It is evident that the basis for the imaginary collective cannot be the identification with any specific character or action on stage but rather the communal act of empathetic transfer as such into the scenic representation. In the process of being drawn into this representation, the

[5] See especially Lessing to Mendelssohn, February 2, 1756 (Lessing, 1756/1973a, pp. 203–204. The simile with the strings foreshadows what modern theorists have called the 'resonance theory' of empathy (see Landweer, 2007).

spectators ideally leave behind, or rise above, their particular determinations, whatever they are – social, genealogical, gender, ethnic, religious, etc. – in order to merge with their fellow spectators across all boundaries into what Lessing on one occasion succinctly calls "the communal feeling of sympathizing spirits" [*das gemeinschaftliche Gefühl sympathisierender Geister*] (Lessing, 1778/1979, p. 481).[6] The appeal of any particular content or the theme of a fictional representation (such as the intimate life of the family) must be considered secondary to the primary act of subjective *Einfühlung* and its communal sharing. Essential was the overriding experience of coming together in the awareness of a common humanity.

In order to understand this process more fully, we need to turn from the theoretical discussion to another plane, the media aspect. In the mid-eighteenth century, at the same time when those theories were formulated, a new concept of the theater and theatrical performance emerged that came to be known under the formula of the "fourth wall" (coined by Denis Diderot, in his seminal essay *De la poésie dramatique*, 1758). Its distinctive trait was the strict separation of stage and audience. Whereas previous forms of theater, whether of popular, religious, or court provenance, had always relied on some kind of physical interaction between actors and spectators, any such direct interaction was now banned. The actors were to play as if there were no audience, "play as if the curtain were not drawn", Diderot writes (Diderot, 1758/1988a, p. 231).

Correspondingly, the spectators were to disregard their own, together with the actors' (as actors), physical presence and become absorbed in the world of the scenic illusion. In other words, actors and audience were to suppress the consciousness of what they were doing – namely, acting and watching. The imaginary fourth wall, on the one hand, enclosed the actors within the fictional world they represented, using their "real" bodies as a medium for their respective roles, and, on the other hand, encouraged the spectators to negate their own physical presence as they

[6] This formulation is from the *Freimäurergespräche* with respect to the Freemasonry organization in Lessing's idealized interpretation. It indicates that "the feeling of sympathy" can also be thought of independently of the theater.

became increasingly immersed in the fictional world represented on stage. (Real) disembodiment corresponded to (fictional) re-embodiment.

Even from this perfunctory sketch, we can recognize the two sides of the global process from which we first started out: the autonomy of art (here, the theater performance) and the isolated, individual (modern) spectators on the other side, that of the audience, who are then bound together in a different kind of community. The fourth wall cuts through the physical reality of the here and now of the theater space and event in order to create another reality, an imaginary beyond. While in the "old" theater spectators and actors shared a common space of representation (usually also manifest in an architectural continuity between audience and stage), the imagined fourth wall interrupted that continuity and shook the spectators out of their spatial groundedness into the elusive dimension of the fictional representation. By this process, they gained an incorporeal, or spiritual, existence. It is almost like an allegory of the transition from the old European order of a stratified society and its corresponding order of space and time to the mobility and fluidity of the new order of functional differentiation.

Yet it is more than an allegory. The theater of the fourth wall can be seen as an *arena* where this transition took place and was gone through; it provided a model place to *experience an abstract collective*, which was distinct from earlier notions of collectives based in immediate physical contact and spatial contiguity (for this aspect, see the seminal study by Koschorke, 1999). Ultimately, it gave such modern notions as "the nation", "the republic", and "humankind", a palpable concreteness. Diderot even compared the spectators' experience to that of an earthquake ("as if they felt the earth trembling underneath them") (Diderot, 1758/1988a, p. 198).[7] After all, this theater of the fourth wall remained a *theater*, a place where people physically gather in order to watch a representation by live actors. When at the start of the performance the lights in the auditorium

[7] "Les esprits seront troublés tels que ceux qui, dans les tremblements d'une partie de globe, voient les murs de leurs maisons vaciller et sentent la terre se dérober sous leur pieds" (Diderot, 1758/1988a, p. 198).

were extinguished and the eyes and ears of the otherwise immobilized and muted spectators became exclusively (forcibly, one is tempted to say) fixed on the lit stage in front of them, they were cut off from their existential ties and, by the *collective nature* of this act of aesthetic empathy, re-assembled into a spiritual community. In contrast, older theater formations – in particular the court stage – had relied on the continuity between the world on stage and the social world in the auditorium, each mirroring the other.

To sum up, the theater of the fourth wall provided a space for *experiencing directly and communally the transition from the "old" to the "new" notion of community.* Its ultimate horizon is the utopian vision of a universal transparency of souls. Diderot, for example, sees a touchstone for an individual's moral integrity in the ability to have his emotions heightened by those of others in the theater: "The man whose emotions are not heightened by the great number of those who share in them, must possess some hidden vice; there is in his character something [. . .] of a recluse which I do not like" (Diderot, 1758/1988b, p. 127). Twenty years later, Louis-Sébastien Mercier, a follower of Jean-Jacques Rousseau, invokes the power of the theater to give society's alienated members the experience "that, despite our public life, which seems to legitimize general fractiousness, we can nevertheless be united" (Mercier, 1773/1999, p. 1235, transl. here and in the following mine, H.S.).[8] Mercier calls for the enlargement of the auditorium and the tearing down of its dividing walls and boxes in order to encourage an "infinite flowing together of people" who will join in the general emotion [*Rührung*] of "unanimously shed tears", tears of sympathy that carry the audience "beyond all the narrow purposes of self-love (*amour-propre*) and personal interest" (Mercier, 1773/1999, p. 1337); the future "national drama", he proclaims, will "connect the people with each other through the conquering emotion of pity and mutual sharing" (Mercier, 1773/1999, p. 1141).

[8] "Lorsque tout semble solliciter à l'égoisme, enhardir la cupidité, chérissons les seuls moyens qui peuvent nous persuader que nos compatriotes ne nous sont pas étrangers, que nous pouvons être unis en dépit des mœurs publiques, qui semblent autoriser la scission générale" (Mercier, 1773/1999, p. 1235).

This finally points back to Adam Smith's sympathy, and it also anticipates phenomena of collective enthusiasm in the prerevolutionary and revolutionary era. A prominent example in the German tradition is Friedrich Schiller's address of 1784 *Die Schaubühne als eine moralische Anstalt betrachtet* ["On the Theater as a Moral Institution"], a fervent evocation of the theater event as a truly mystic moment in which all barriers of the conventional world of artifice [*künstliche Welt*] collapse and the spectators unite in perfect transparence: the apotheosis of the theater audience as the epiphany of the idea of humanity, humanity looking itself in the eye.

> And then, finally – what a triumph for you, Nature [. . .] – when humans from all regions and classes, having thrown off all shackles of artifice and fashion, having been torn away from all throes of fate, becoming brothers through *one* all-weaving sympathy, being absorbed into *one* kind, forget themselves and the world and come near their celestial origin. Each one of them enjoys the raptures of all, which fall back on him stronger and more beautiful from a hundred eyes, and there is now in his chest room for only one feeling – it is this: to be a *human*. (Schiller, 1784/1993, p. 831, emph. in the original; transl. mine, H.S.)[9]

4 Modern Critique of Aesthetic Compassion (Käte Hamburger)

Needless to say, this Enlightenment cosmopolitan enthusiasm is not ours today, even though Schiller's similarly euphoric *Ode an die Freude* ("Ode to Joy") – with the line, among others, "all men become

[9] "Und dann endlich – welch ein Triumph für dich, Natur [. . .] – wenn Menschen aus allen Zonen und Ständen, abgeworfen jede Fessel der Künstelei und der Mode, herausgerissen aus jedem Drange des Schicksals, durch *eine* allwebende Sympathie verbrüdert, in *ein* Geschlecht wieder aufgelöst, ihrer selbst und der Welt vergessen und ihrem himmlischen Ursprung sich nähern. Jeder einzelne genießt die Entzückungen aller, die verstärkt und verschönert aus hundert Augen auf ihn zurückfallen, und seine Brust gibt jetzt nur *einer* Empfindung Raum – es ist diese: ein *Mensch* zu sein" (Schiller, 1784/1993, p. 831).

brethren" [*alle Menschen werden Brüder*] – set to the music of Beethoven's Ninth Symphony, has become the official European anthem. In a book first published more than three decades ago, which recently has received increased attention (see, e.g., Gülcher & von der Lühe, 2007), the literary theoretician and historian Käte Hamburger produced an incisive critique of the concept of *Mitleid* in this humanist tradition. The traditional concept *Mitleid* as an "emotional-moral practice" [*gefühlsmoralische Verhaltensweise*], Hamburger claims, is characterized by a vague confusion of feeling and ethics, which tends to ignore what she calls the "structure of distance" [*Distanzstruktur des Mitleids*] inherent in every compassionate emotion and act (Hamburger, 1985, p. 10). There is always a constitutive element of reflection involved in the emotion of *Mitleid.* Hamburger illustrates the actuality of this rational and self-reflexive element with the absence of the *Mitleid* affect in close, intimate relationships; to have "pity" for a lover would be offensive more than anything else, and with regard to close relatives and friends, we rather share their suffering in active feelings of "sorrow and concern", which may stir us to practical relief. In contrast, the vague "feeling-with", or "co-vibration" to use Lessing's term, of *Mitleid* does not touch us as deeply as the phrase of placing oneself into the suffering person's situation would have it, it may even hinder us from acting out of moral principles.

For Hamburger, Lessing's theory of dramaturgical *Mitleid* represents a decisive historical moment in the illegitimate blending of ethics and feeling. While Rousseau, and in his wake Arthur Schopenhauer, provided the philosophical basis for an anthropological and metaphysical understanding (that is, misunderstanding) of compassion, Lessing infused the notion with an aesthetic element. By claiming *Mitleid* as the supreme moral virtue – "the most compassionate human is the best human" – Lessing, like others before and after him, confused an emotional category with an ethical value; but beyond that, by elevating the theater, in particular tragedy, to the status of a "school for *Mitleid*", he also confused the realm of fiction with that of reality. Lessing, Hamburger writes, ignored the "ontological place of *Mitleid*" (Hamburger, 1985, p. 71), which is solely in the realm of interhuman relations. *Mitleid* that is directed at a stage hero, a hero of tragedy, belongs to a wholly different order than the social;

"fictional persons can not be fellow human beings" [*Nebenmenschen, Mitmenschen*] (Hamburger, 1985, p. 73), and we can only demonstrate active empathy, or *Teilnahme*, to real humans.

But if Hamburger vehemently defends *Mitleid* as "a category of reality" against any such perceived aesthetic (dramaturgical) takeover, this does not accord it an intrinsic ethical value. She states that *Mitleid* is a neutral emotion, which may instigate moral behavior but can also be harmful (like in the case of the "compassionate" judge who neglects the formal standard of justice). *Mitleid* is a volatile affect, dependent on changing situations and psychological dispositions. Therefore, there is no "compassionate character" as there is a "just" or "brave" one. Hamburger refers to Ludwig Wittgenstein's formula for *Mitleid* in his *Philosophische Untersuchungen* (1953) as the "conviction that another human is suffering" (Wittgenstein, 1953/1977, p. 155, §287) as a sort of minimal definition which links the rational element with respect for the other's otherness, hence conforming with her own premise of the "structure of distance" (Hamburger 1985, p. 98). However, *Mitleid* possesses a distinctive quality that positively sets it apart from "justice", the strict moral guide in interhuman relations. While justice must abstract from all particular circumstances and characteristics for the sake of universal norms, *Mitleid* takes our fellow humans' individuality fully into account. In this, it can – and indeed often does – support moral action, but it certainly does not supersede moral norms.

In her critical approach to the history of the *Mitleid* concept, Hamburger still holds on to the core of the Enlightenment idea of a common humanity. She refers to David Hume's supposition of a universal human nature as the apparent basis for Wittgenstein's "conviction of another person's suffering" and her own concept of understanding another person in his or her otherness. In fact, this simple and basic premise, she writes, is sufficient to make all speculations about a further "foundation" of *Mitleid* in whatever specific "feeling" [*Gefühlsgrundlage*] superfluous. Hume is, for Hamburger, the only philosopher in the long history of *Mitleid* theory who was able to conceive of "sympathy" in terms of a plain "understanding" of the feeling and suffering of another person in his or her emphatic otherness; an understanding, to repeat the crucial point in her words, which "already as such implies the distance that in my consciousness separates the other *as* the other from me" (Hamburger, 1985, p. 114). Hume, in other words, did justice to *Mitleid*'s "structure of distance" by recognizing the fellow human individual as someone with whom we share a common humanity but do not fuse into an emotional union of suffering.

In this context, Hamburger mentions (but I think severely underestimates) the importance of the imagination for the sympathetic act.[10] Significantly, she deals less with Hume's Scottish compatriot and student Adam Smith, for whom the imagination played an even larger role. As we saw at the beginning, the imagination (as internal representation) enhances the sympathetic transaction through its immediacy. It is by bringing the suffering of another person before one's own inner eye (even when actually within our physical eyesight), that our sympathy is aroused and potentially intensified to "care and concern". It is the arts and, in particular, the theater that activate and "train" (see Lessing's "school of compassion") this faculty, which may then – ideally, to be sure – make an impact in the real world.

Even more important to this complex debate, as we have also seen, is the community-building aspect of sympathy by means of the imagination. Just as any sympathetic act in face-to-face situations already involves the imagination, by which we reach beyond our physical boundaries to the "other", this same activity is capable of being carried beyond the physical borders of immediacy. To be honest, the shortcomings, even dangers of such far-reaching imaginative acts of sympathy are obvious, especially in today's media-generated world. The eighteenth-century theater audience still had its physical basis in a spatial-temporal presence. Can we link contemporary virtual "sympathetic communities" or "communities of empathy" to this older formation? For one thing, the risk of superficiality, complacency, and non-committalism was by no means foreign to the Enlightenment concept; however, it has increased through today's visual media. And it is here that Hamburger's basic reservation against the "gefühlsmoralische Verhaltensweise" of *Mitleid* carries its full weight (although she is not

[10] Although Hamburger states that Hume based sympathy "totally" on the imagination, for her this only proves *Mitleid*'s reflexivity – an unnecessarily complicated argument.

concerned with the media aspect at all). But on the other hand, our common humanity is not only, as Hamburger states in accordance with Enlightenment thought (Hume), the implicit basis for our understanding of another person's suffering. It can, and should, be lifted to the level of a self-conscious experience, as the eighteenth-century theoreticians and dramaturgists envisioned it. Such experience does not necessarily remain on the level of a vague or cheap "good feeling". It may, for instance, strengthen the sense for social and political equality. Alexis de Tocqueville suggested as much, when, in a passage from his book *De la démocratie en Amérique* (1835/40, *Democracy in America*) he considered the close association between empathy and democracy. Half a century after Schiller and with diction still reminiscent of the theater poet's enthusiasm, the social theoretician invokes the same Enlightenment association of sympathy with the imagination in a universalist perspective, as it was so forcefully established by Adam Smith. In a nation where everybody has the same rank, Tocqueville writes, everybody can enter into the feelings of everybody else, and this mutual understanding strengthens the cohesion of society:

> There is no wretchedness into which he cannot readily enter, and a secret instinct reveals to him its extent. It signifies not that strangers or foes are the sufferers; imagination puts him in their place; something like a personal feeling is mixed with his pity and makes himself suffer while the body of his fellow creature is in torture. – In democratic ages men rarely sacrifice themselves for one another, but they display general compassion for the members of the human race. (Tocqueville, 1835/1951, II, p. 165)

References

Diderot, D. (1758/1988a). De la poésie dramatique [On dramatic poetry]. In *Oeuvres esthétiques* [Works on aesthetics] (pp. 189–287). Paris: Garnier.

Diderot, D. (1758/1988b). Entretiens sur le fils naturel [Conversations on the natural son]. In *Oeuvres esthétiques* [Works on aesthetics] (pp. 69–175). Paris: Garnier.

Gülcher, N. & von der Lühe, I. (Eds.) (2007). *Ethik und Ästhetik des Mitleids* [Ethics and aesthetics of sympathy]. Freiburg im Breisgau: Rombach.

Hamburger, K. (1985). *Das Mitleid* [Sympathy (pp. 47–66)]. Stuttgart: Klett-Cotta.

Koschorke, A. (1999). *Körperströme und Schriftverkehr. Mediologie des 18. Jahrhunderts* [Body streams and correspondence. Mediology of the 18th century]. Munich: Fink.

Landweer, H. (2007). Resonanz oder Kognition? Zwei Modelle des Mitgefühls. Zu Käte Hamburgers Analyse der Distanzstruktur des Mitleids. [Resonance or cognition? Two models of sympathy. On Käte Hamburger's analysis of the structure of distance of sympathy]. In N. Gülcher & I. von der Lühe (Eds.). *Ethik und Ästhetik des Mitleids* [Ethics and aesthetics of sympathy] (pp. 47–66). Freiburg im Breisgau: Rombach.

Lessing, G. E. (1756/1973a). Briefwechsel über das Trauerspiel [Letters on tragedy]. In *Werke* [Works] (vol. 4, pp. 153–227, H. G. Göpfert, Ed.). Munich: Hanser.

Lessing, G. E. (1767–69/1973b). Hamburgische Dramaturgie [Hamburg dramaturgy]. In *Werke* [Works] (vol. 4, pp. 229–720, H. G. Göpfert, Ed.). Munich: Hanser.

Lessing, G. E. (1778/1979). Ernst und Falk. Gespräche für Freimäurer [Ernst and Falk Conversations for the Freemasons]. In *Werke* [Works] (vol. 8, pp. 451–488, H. G. Göpfert, Ed.). Munich: Hanser.

Mercier, L.-S. (1773/1999). Du théâtre [On theater]. In *Mon bonnet de nuit suivi de Du théâtre et de Textes critiques* [My nightcap, followed by On theater, and critical readings] (pp. 1127–1478, J.-C. Bonnet, Ed.). Paris: Mercure de France.

Schiller, F. (1784/1993). Die Schaubühne als eine moralische Anstalt betrachtet [The theatre considered as moral institution]. In *Werke* [Works] (G. Fricke & H. G. Göpfert, Eds., vol. 5, pp. 818–831), Munich: Hanser.

Schneider, H. J. (2008). Humanity's Imaginary Body: The Concepts of Empathy and Sympathy and the New Theater Experience in the 18th Century. *Deutsche Vierteljahresschrift für Literaturwissenschaft und Geistesgeschichte, 82*, 382–399.

Smith, A. (1759/2009). *The Theory of Moral Sentiments* (R. P. Hanley, Ed.). New York: Penguin Books.

Tocqueville, A. d. (1835/1951). *Democracy in America* (P. Bradley, Ed., vol. I/II). New York: Alfred A. Knopf.

Wittgenstein, L. (1953/1977). *Philosophische Untersuchungen* [Philosophical investigations]. Frankfurt/Main: Suhrkamp.

9

Einfühlung – A Key Concept of Psychological Aesthetics

Christian G. Allesch

1 Historical Background

Robert Vischer's doctoral thesis *Über das optische Formgefühl – Ein Beitrag zur Ästhetik* ["On the Optical Sense of Form. A Contribution to Aesthetics"] of 1873 (Vischer, 1873/1927a; English transl.: Vischer, 1873/1994) may be regarded as the starting point of the introduction of *Einfühlung* as a theoretical concept in aesthetics. However, the crucial role of empathic processes in the context of aesthetic experience is much older than Vischer's theoretical reflections, as other contributions in this volume rightly note. Such concerns can be found 100 years before the publication of Vischer's thesis in the writings of Johann Gottfried Herder and Giambattista Vico (see Chapter 10: Pinotti, in this volume) or in the writings of Adam Smith whose concept of "sympathy" represents a pivotal element in his *Theory of Moral Sentiments*

C.G. Allesch (✉)
Department of Psychology, University of Salzburg, Salzburg, Austria
e-mail: christian.allesch@sbg.ac.at

V. Lux, S. Weigel (eds.), *Empathy*, Palgrave Studies in the Theory and History of Psychology, DOI 10.1057/978-1-137-51299-4_9

(see Chapter 1: Weigel, in this volume). I would like to supplement these examples with a quote from Edmund Burke, who describes in his essay *A Philosophical Enquiry into the Origin of Our Ideas of the Sublime and Beautiful*, published in 1756/57, the function of "sympathy" in generating aesthetic sentiments: "It is by this principle [that is, sympathy] chiefly that poetry, painting, and other affecting arts, transfuse their passions from one breast to another, and are often capable of grafting a delight on wretchedness, misery, and death itself". (Burke, 1756/1852, p. 589) This is very similar to Adam Smith's characterisation in *The Theory of Moral Sentiments* from 1759:

> It is by the imagination only that we can form any conception of what are his [that is, our brother's] sensations [. . .] It is the impression of our own senses only, not those of his, which our imaginations copy. (Smith, 1759/1966, pp. 3–4)

In this context, Smith uses an example that was often quoted in later writings on psychological aesthetics, namely the excitement aroused by the perception of a dancer on a rope, which can be explained by a sort of emotional identification and, moreover, motor imitation generated by "sympathy": "The mob, when they are gazing at a dancer on a slack rope, naturally writhe and twist and balance their own bodies, as they see him do". (Smith, 1759/1966, p. 4) This corresponds precisely with the concept of "inner imitation" and "organic sensation" as described in the theories of Vischer and Lipps 120 years later.

A simple question arises, if we take into consideration that these statements were all formulated around the same time in 1750, the year that Alexander Baumgarten (1714–1767) published his *Aesthetica*, commonly regarded as the inaugural work of aesthetics as an academic discipline. That question is: Why did it take 120 years to discover "empathy" as a key concept of aesthetic theory? In my opinion, this delay is due to a paradigmatic shift in the objective of aesthetics that took place immediately after its founding in the second half of the eighteenth century. Alexander Baumgarten's *Aesthetica* defines aesthetics as *gnoseologia inferior* – a science of the lower faculties of experience – (Baumgarten, 1750/2007, § 1, p. 10) thus distinguishing it from logic or *gnoseologia superior*, the science of the higher faculties of experience (Baumgarten, 1735/1983, § CXVI, p. 84ss.). This distinction follows the Aristotelian tradition. It is important to point out that Baumgarten saw the new discipline as the study of sensual perception in all its conceivable forms, not just restricted to art and beauty as an ideal.

This perspective changed, however, just one generation later. In 1771 and 1774, Johann Georg Sulzer (1720–1779) published the two parts of his influential two-volume encyclopaedia, *Allgemeine Theorie der schönen Künste* ["A General Theory of the Fine Arts"]. Sulzer defines aesthetics as "the philosophy of the fine arts or the science which derives its general theory as well as its rules of the fine arts from the nature of taste". He does not distinguish between the faculties of rational experience and those of sensory experience as Baumgarten (and Aristotelians before him) did, but postulates two "independent faculties" of man: reason and moral sentiment [*das sittliche Gefühl*]. According to Sulzer, it is "the main purpose of the fine arts to arouse a vivid feeling for the beautiful and the good, and a strong aversion to the ugly and the bad" (Sulzer, 1773/74, p. vi–vii).[1] Consequently, it was the duty of aesthetics, on the one hand, "to support the artist in the invention, arrangement, and performance of his work" and, on the other hand, "to guide the amateur in his assessment and, by the same token, to make him more capable of reaping all the benefits of the enjoyment of the works of art at which they are aimed" (Sulzer, 1773/74, p. 28).[2] The main purpose of aesthetics was therefore to teach people to enjoy works of art in the right manner and to decide, through rational judgement, which was the right kind of art.

This conception of aesthetics, prevalent in teaching and academic writing in Germany up until the second half of the nineteenth century, had, as I believe, some fatal consequences:

[1] "...ein lebhaftes Gefühl für das Schöne und Gute, und eine starke Abneigung gegen das Häßliche und Böse zu erweken". Unless otherwise noted, all translations in this chapter from the German original into English are mine, C. G. A.

[2] "...den Liebhaber in seiner Beurtheilung leiten und zugleich fähiger machen, allen Nutzen, auf den die Werke der Kunst abzielen, aus ihrem Genuß zu ziehen".

(1) Most works on aesthetics published in the nineteenth and twentieth centuries (written mainly by philosophers and art historians) focused on questions, such as: What is art and what characterises a work of art? What is beauty and how can we define the objective qualities of beauty? By contrast, the questions that seem the most interesting from the perspective of psychological aesthetics – how do aesthetic experience and aesthetic judgment come about and how might we conceive the process of aesthetic experience within the framework of aesthetic theory – appeared to be of minor interest to authors of aesthetic theory during the late eighteenth century and the first half of the nineteenth. Most theorists from that time (see, e.g. Eberhard, 1783; Ficker, 1830; Hegel, 1835–38/1979; Krause, 1837; Solger, 1829/1980) thought of aesthetics as a *philosophy* of art and beauty. In their views, the question as to how aesthetic experience comes about in individual perception was not a topic for aesthetics as a philosophical discipline but should be left to psychology or even physiology. This distinction is mainly due to the dominance of idealism in this period of German philosophy, which focused on the concept of an "ideal" beauty that had to be completely separated from any emotional side effects that might accompany beauty and detract from it. Still, there was a rising interest in the physiological processes behind mental activity, which, based on new methods of measurement and experimentation, led to remarkable findings in the field of physiology. This science increasingly attracted empirically oriented researchers in psychology. This is, in my opinion, the main reason that the appearance of "empathy" in aesthetics was so closely connected with the emergence of the psychological approach in aesthetics during the second half of the nineteenth century.

(2) Another consequence was that aesthetics at the end of the eighteenth century became a normative discipline with a clearly conservative bent. It reflected the values and prejudices of the cultural context rather than any objective idea of beauty. The authors of aesthetic theory felt authorised to subjugate both aesthetic production and the ways in which art was presented to the public, namely to the taste and moral sentiment of the leading class of academics and other educated people, the so-called *Bildungsbürgertum*. This normative

conception of aesthetics impeded any interest in empirical questions and inquiry. This was also the main reason that psychological or empirical approaches to aesthetics – as suggested in particular by Gustav Th. Fechner (1801–1887) in the second half of the nineteenth century – had to fight for decades to be accepted within the realm of aesthetics. In 1876, Fechner published his *Vorschule der Aesthetik* ["Pre-school of Aesthetics"], in which he sought to establish an empirical "aesthetics from below" in opposition to the metaphysical concepts of German Idealism (Fechner, 1876/1925). Although Fechner affirmed that it was not his intention to *replace* metaphysical reflexions about the essence of beauty by a merely empirical or "statistical" approach, his efforts were widely met with disapproval by the scientific community of aestheticians. But psychologists' growing interest in aesthetic questions continued to boost scientific research in this field and reached a pinnacle at the beginning of the twentieth century. In this context, the theory of aesthetic empathy emerged as a basic construct for explaining processes of aesthetic experience.

2 The Emergence of the Term *Einfühlung*

Since Robert Vischer's theory is addressed in several contributions of this volume, I can be brief in this point. The central idea is that affective, "physiognomic", or motoric impulses may be involved to different degrees in the process of empathy. When in a poem or in everyday language, we come across the phrase "a tree raises its branches towards the sky", Vischer argues, this phrase is not just a verbal paraphrasing but represents exactly what we *feel* when we see a tree. Vischer describes *Einfühlung* as a process of "formal symbolisation" [*Formsymbolisierung*], which is an essential aspect of every act of visual perception but also plays a particular and important role in aesthetic experience, together with an association of ideas and acts of illusion (R. Vischer, 1873/1927a, pp. 26–27). In his later work, Friedrich Theodor Vischer (1807–1887), Robert Vischer's father and a much more influential author of aesthetics than his son, adopted the term *Einfühlung* (later translated as "empathy"), which his son coined. His vast, methodical work on aesthetics (1846–57/1975) comprises six heavy volumes, the first of which he published exactly one year before his son Robert was born. In these tombs, we find several passages where F. Th. Vischer explicitly uses the term. This might be cited as an indication that he, too, regarded empathic processes as pivotal components of aesthetic experience. For example, he suggests that the aesthetic pleasure that comes from contemplating natural objects is not a result of intellectual processing that developmentally follows perception. Instead, that pleasure is generated in the act of perception itself, which "projects" [*hineinschaut*] aesthetic qualities into the perceived object (F. Th. Vischer, 1846–57/1975, vol. II, § 382). These are casual remarks rather than a systematic elaboration of the concept. But they indicate that we might take the systematic development of the theory as the product of father-son teamwork rather than the singular invention of Robert.

R. Vischer's thesis was favourably reviewed by Johannes Volkelt (1848–1930),[3] who would go on to develop very similar ideas in the following decade and later become one of the most influential theorists in the psychological aesthetics movement. Vehement disapproval came from the school of aesthetic formalism, mainly represented by the Viennese philosopher Robert Zimmermann (1824–1898) and – in the field of music aesthetics – Eduard Hanslick (1825–1904), who in *Vom Musikalisch-Schönen* ["Of Music and Beauty"] (1854) regarded every kind of emotional reaction to aesthetic objects as contradictory to a "pure" aesthetic understanding of art and beauty (Hanslick, 1854/1981, p. 1ff.). In a reply to a negative review of his theory by Zimmermann (1873), R. Vischer clearly formulates the point that distinguishes his approach to human perception from aesthetic formalism but also from psychological theories of perception in the tradition of Johann Friedrich Herbart's associationism and Fechner's psychophysics: "[T]he aesthetically motivated individual does not "merely" perceive. He does not just

[3] In Die Literatur, Wochenschrift für das nationale Geistesleben der Gegenwart, Leipzig; Nr. 25/1874.

see with his eyes and take notice with his brain, but he regards feelingly, with his entire personality and using imagination" (Vischer, 1874/1927b, p. 46). In a later lecture *Über ästhetische Naturbetrachtung* ["On Aesthetically Observing Nature"] (Vischer, 1890/1927c), Vischer once more emphasised his position that vision not only includes a sensory but also a motor function. Sight does not merely produce neural impulses which are computed into complex informational structures in the brain, but sight "understands" the structure of visual objects already in the process of "scanning" [*Abtasten*]: The contemplating eye "layers the hills" and "extends the plains" [*schichtet die Hügel und dehnt die Ebene aus*]; it reconstructs the forces expressed by the motion of objects through "reproductive empathy" [*reproduktive Einfühlung*] and conceives of them as aesthetically stimulating content of experience (R. Vischer, 1890/1927c, p. 62f.).

Although Robert Vischer ought to be regarded as the originator of the aesthetic theory of *Einfühlung*, he was not its most influential representative. This is mainly due to the fact that he was primarily interested in art history and not in theorising aesthetics. The most prominent and influential proponent of the theory of *Einfühlung* in aesthetics was undoubtedly Theodor Lipps (1851–1914), just five years younger than Robert Vischer. In 1891, he published an article on *Ästhetische Faktoren der Raumanschauung* ["Aesthetic Factors of the Notion of Space"]. It was a contribution to the "*Festschrift*" celebrating the 70th birthday of Hermann von Helmholtz and expanded on topics initiated by Robert Vischer (Lipps, 1891). Five years later, Lipps announced the publication of a comprehensive "aesthetic-mechanical theory of optical-geometrical illusions". The announcement appeared in the *Zeitschrift für Psychologie und Physiologie der Sinnesorgane*, a highly renowned psychological journal at the time. The theory was finally published in 1897 under the title *Raumästhetik und optisch-geometrische Täuschungen* ["Spatial Aesthetics and Optical-Geometrical Illusions"]. But the announcement from 1896 already included some basic principles of Lipps' theory of *Einfühlung* ("empathy"), for example, "aesthetic fantasy", whose function was "to endow all things with *our* life". Lipps was convinced that "the aesthetic impact of all geometric figures" was due to this process (Lipps, 1896, p. 40). In his

1897 book, he illustrates his theory by referring to the well-known "Müller-Lyer" illusion (Müller-Lyer, 1889): The horizontal line in the first figure, with the outwards directed ends, is perceived as longer, because the entire structure stretches our empathic feeling outwards, while in the second figure our empathic feeling is narrowed by the inwardly directed structure on the ends (Lipps, 1897, p. 91). That means optical illusions are not deceptive perceptions but defective judgements caused by the fact that we do not just "perceive" a visual structure but, by the same token, "feel" the inherent tendencies represented by the perceived structure (Lipps, 1897, p. 66) (Fig. 9.1).

Although Lipps' explanation from the point of view of modern cognitive theory is not tenable, we still might note an important change in the overall goal of empathy theory: Whereas Robert Vischer conceptualised *Einfühlung* as a principle for understanding aesthetic experiences in the narrower sense of traditional aesthetics, as a theory of art and beauty, Lipps interpreted *Einfühlung* as a basic mechanism of perception in general, thus tracing the meaning of "aesthetics" back to the original Aristotelian concept of αίσθησις [*aesthesis*], as "sensory perception".

In 1900, Lipps published another article entitled *Aesthetische Einfühlung* ["Aesthetical Empathy"], which offered reflections on the concrete implementation of the concept *Einfühlung* in a theory of aesthetics in the traditional sense. Lipps defines *ästhetische Einfühlung* here as the actual cause of aesthetic pleasure [*ästhetische Lust*] or the pleasantness of spatial features. "Aesthetic pleasure", according to Lipps, is in fact "the pleasantness of my ego, insofar it is felt into the object", or "the pleasantness of the object, but not

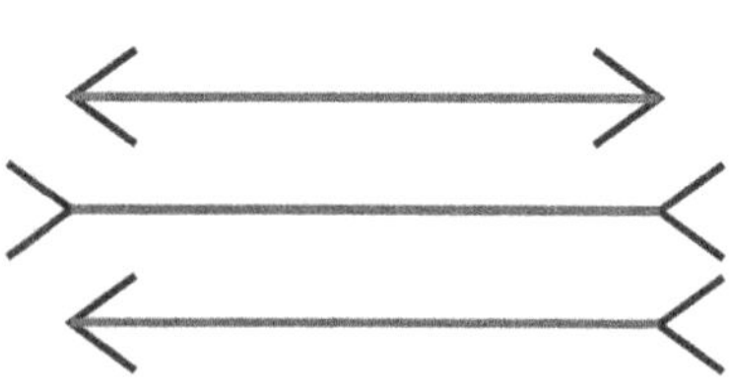

Fig. 9.1 Müller-Lyer Illusion

of the object itself but of the object insofar as I feel myself into it" (Lipps, 1900, p. 416).[4]

Theodor Lipps' theory of empathy paradigmatically stands for the "turn to the subject", which would come to characterise the development of psychological aesthetics around 1900 and its opposition to traditional philosophical aesthetics. In contrast to the idealistic aesthetics of beauty, the psychological approach "from below", as represented by G. Th. Fechner, follows an inductive method: from subjective feelings and judgements to general laws of aesthetic experience. Lipps' approach, in contrast, presumes that it is not the formal structure of the aesthetic object that "produces" aesthetic experience, but the sensitive individual as the agent of aesthetic experience. Lipps clearly emphasises this point in an essay on *Einfühlung, innere Nachahmung und Organempfindungen* ["Empathy, Inner Imitation, and Organ Sensations"] published in 1901, in the first issue of the new journal *Archiv für Psychologie*:

> However certain it is that the sensory appearance of a beautiful thing is the *object* of aesthetic pleasure, it is as certain that it is not its *cause*. It is me or my ego that is the cause of aesthetic pleasure; namely exactly the same ego which I am aware as pleased or delighted "in view of" or "confronted with" the object. (Lipps, 1901, p. 185f.)

Thus, the central hypothesis of Lipps' theory of *Einfühlung* suggests that aesthetic experience is always self-perception: being aware of one's own delightful feelings in the presence of the aesthetic object. In addition, the title of Lipps' 1901 essay contains two other key terms that are characteristic of empathy theory, namely "inner imitation" and "sensations of the organs". The proponents of the theory of *Einfühlung* did not entirely agree on these points. Whereas Vischer and other partisans of this theory emphasised the role of "inner imitation" and bodily sensations, Lipps, on the contrary, stressed the projection of

---

[4] "Die ästhetische Lust hat also ihren G r u n d in der Einfühlung. Sie ist Lust an dem Ich, sofern es in das Object hineingefühlt ist. Oder, was dasselbe sagt: Sie ist Lust an dem Object, aber nicht an dem Object als solchem, sondern sofern ich mich in dasselbe hineingefühlt habe."

inner activity – the feelings and yearnings of the ego or self over muscular sensations – into the perceived object (see Chapter 10: Pinotti, in this volume). Thus, by the 1890s, the concept of *Einfühlung* comprised a bundle of theoretical concepts directed at explaining perception in general and aesthetic experience in particular. As a theory, it was characterised most by its different and divergent opinions about the role of association, imitation, motor movements, and the influence of organic sensations and mental factors.

3 The Heyday of the Theory of *Einfühlung*

Despite the differences in the details, the theory of *Einfühlung* was already dominating theoretical discussions on aesthetics during the last decade of the nineteenth century and had gained numerous followers in German psychological and philosophical circles. By the turn of the twentieth century and in the wake of Lipps' *Grundlegung der Ästhetik* ["The Founding of Aesthetics"] (1903), in which the theory of *Einfühlung* played a pivotal role, discussion of empathy and its correlates extended beyond the German-speaking world to French and Anglo-American psychologists. Back in Germany, one of the most influential supporters of the theory of *Einfühlung* and, more generally, psychological aesthetics was Johannes Volkelt (1848–1930). In his post-doctoral thesis on the concept of the symbol in contemporary aesthetics [*Der Symbolbegriff in der neueren Ästhetik*], published in 1876, he develops similar ideas to those of Lipps, although he originally used the term *Beseelung* ("ensoulment") to characterise this process (Volkelt, 1876). But in his voluminous *System der Ästhetik* from 1905 (Volkelt, 1905–14), he finally switches to the term *Einfühlung*, since, as he writes, it had been widely adopted by contemporary mainstream aesthetic discussions. In fact, the extensive description of empathic processes in aesthetic perception and the numerous examples that Volkelt presents in his *System of Aesthetics* prove him to be the most important theorist of *Einfühlung* of his time, perhaps even more than Lipps himself during his lifetime and most certainly after Lipps' early death in 1914.

Like Lipps, Volkelt conceived of *Einfühlung* as a basic faculty of human perception. He described it as "a process that is widespread in human mental life and by no means restricted to aesthetic behavior" (Volkelt, 1920, p. 43). He only dissented from Lipps with regard to the question whether *Einfühlung* was the unique central mechanism responsible for aesthetic experience or just one among other principles of perception that explain the particularities of aesthetic phenomena. He repeatedly warns of "a need for simplification in philosophical sciences", which ended up prompting some scholars to explain the phenomena based on a single principle.

Another supporter of *Einfühlungstheorie* was Karl Groos (1861–1946), who published an important book in 1902, *Der ästhetische Genuss* ["On Aesthetic Pleasure"], in which he argues for a psychological and empirical approach in aesthetics and suggests some methodological principles for its further development (Groos, 1902). Stefan Witasek (1870–1915), who taught philosophy and psychology in Graz, was also a dedicated practitioner of the psychological approach in aesthetics, though he remained a rather critical supporter. In his *Grundzüge der allgemeinen Ästhetik* ["Essentials of General Aesthetics"], he explicitly adopts Lipps' theory of *Einfühlung* but criticises some of the particular details (Witasek, 1904). While Witasek regarded *Einfühlung* as a process of imagination resulting in a kind of aesthetic judgement, Lipps insisted in regarding empathic feeling as "real experience" and attacked Witasek for supposedly being an opponent of his theory.

With respect to the international dissemination of the theory of *Einfühlung*, one needs only mention a single person. Violet Paget (1856–1935) was mainly responsible for the popularisation of the theory in English speaking countries. An essayist, art historian, and aesthetician, she published over a dozen volumes of essays on art, music, travel, and fiction under the pseudonym Vernon Lee. Born in France to expatriate English parents, she spent the greater part of her life in Italy. By 1897, she had already published an essay on "Beauty and Ugliness", in which she presents ideas that come very close to those of *Einfühlungstheorie* (Lee & Anstruther-Thomson, 1897). But at the time, she had not yet encountered the theoretical writings of the German discourse. Paget's book was based on informal experiments and observations of her own reactions to works of art, which she conducted with her life partner Clementina ("Kit") Anstruther-Thomson, a painter. Based on the findings of the British psychologist Grant Allen and James Sully and on William James' and Carl Lange's physiological theory of emotion, she focused primarily on physiological factors in aesthetic perception and recorded changes to her and Clementina's respiration, balance, emotion, and body movements in response to aesthetic stimuli. Over the years, she became increasingly fascinated by the theoretical writings of Theodor Lipps and Karl Groos. In 1911, she visited Oswald Külpe's institute at the University of Bonn. This research trip, a detailed correspondence with Theodor Lipps, and her scientific collaboration with Karl Groos convinced her that "their way was the future way of studies in aesthetics" (Lee & Anstruther-Thomson, 1912, p. viii). Nevertheless, she still preferred practicing psychological aesthetics in art galleries rather than in laboratories (see Lanzoni, 2009). In her view, both psychological and motor responses to a work of art contribute to aesthetic reception. Thus, her understanding of "empathy" may be regarded as a synthesis between Lipps' theory and the physiological theory of emotion developed by James and Lange. Lipps out right refused this synthesis because he could not accept the central role Lee attributed to motor reactions and the "sensation of the organs" in aesthetic experience. Similar to James and Lange, Lee regarded this "inner imitation" with its correlating organic responses as more than just reactions to mental processing. For her, it signified the participation [*Mitvollzug*] of bodily aspects of perception itself. Hence, inner imitation can be understood as an evolved psychic mechanism to perceive beauty and harmony (Lee & Anstruther-Thomson, 1912, pp. 88ff.; see also Lee, 1910). Although Lipps never would have agreed with Lee's interpretation of his theory, she still became an engaged proponent of his theory and of the "German" way of analysing aesthetic processes. Her writings were regularly cited by English-speaking aestheticians of the early twentieth century. She also cooperated with Edward Titchener, who – according to Lee – coined the term "empathy" as a translation of the German *Einfühlung* (see Chapter 12: Lanzoni, in this volume). Some of Lee's ideas but also the general idea of "aesthetic empathy" have been disseminated by Titchener in the USA.

In Germany, an influential but critical supporter of Lipps' ideas was Max Dessoir (1867–1947). He played an important role in the institutionalisation of aesthetics as the founder of the *Zeitschrift für Ästhetik und allgemeine Kunstwissenschaft* ["*Journal of Aesthetics and of the General Science of Art*"] in 1906 and as the organiser of the first "International Congress of Aesthetics and the General Science of Art", which took place that same year in Berlin. The event brought together hundreds of scientists from different European countries, and the theory of empathy was one of the central topics at the congress. Like many others Dessoir supported Lipps' general ideas but contested their universalising claims for explaining aesthetic phenomena: not every aesthetic delight consisted in a "cheerful feeling of sympathy" [*im beglückenden Sympathiegefühl*], Dessoir argued (Dessoir, 1906, p. 87). The aesthetic impact of a simple ornament, for example, does not need an explanation by a process of *Beseelung* coming from ourselves. Another important argument of Dessoir's was that language, due to a lack of "neutral" concepts to describe such processes, uses anthropomorphic concepts and terms from everyday language in order to characterise what happens in mind. Dessoir rightly suspected that the metaphors used by aesthetic theory are "not an unadulterated reproduction of a real process but their linguistic tools" (Dessoir, 1906, p. 88).[5] Without a critical analysis of its conceptual tools, the theory of empathy would run the risk of "ending in a stereotyped verbalization" [*schablonenhafte Versprachlichung*].

4 The Rise and Fall of the Theory of *Einfühlung*

The development of a psychological approach to aesthetic phenomena forms a crucial paradigm shift from the nineteenth to the twentieth century which is inextricably linked to the invention of *Einfühlung* into the debate. Although a broad majority of aesthetic theorists accepted

[5] "...nicht der unverfälschte Abdruck eines wahrhaften Vorgangs, sondern ihr sprachliches Rüstzeug".

empathy as a basic principle of aesthetic experience, there was little consensus regarding the details, for example, the role of the "sensations of the organs" or the role of empathic phenomena in aesthetic judgements. The longer the dispute lasted, the more critical the objections. In 1920, three years after Lipps' death, Johannes Volkelt felt compelled to defend the empathy concept in a rather lengthy essay, *Das ästhetische Bewusstsein* ["Aesthetic Consciousness"], since he noticed that the theory of empathy "was forced into a defensive position by a significant and constantly growing opposition" (Volkelt, 1920, p. 2). This opposition was a coalition that included representatives of the new phenomenological movement, supporters of neo-Kantian theory of values, and others involved in art theory. The phenomenologists wanted a clear distinction between description and explanation. The neo-Kantians traditionally opposed any claims to a psychological foundation of aesthetics. And the art theorists were part of a new *pura visibilità* movement that stood for a genuinely artistic explanation of art and rejected both philosophical and psychological interpretations. Although Volkelt presented a lot of arguments in defence of empathy's importance and offered crucial revisions to his theory, his 1920 essay still reads more like an obituary than a future-oriented project plan.

While at the first Congress of Aesthetics and General Science of Art the empathy concept still played a central role, it was only marginally discussed at subsequent congresses. In 1932, Rudolf Odebrecht (1883–1945), in his *Ästhetik der Gegenwart* ["Aesthetics in Our Times"], considers the debate on empathy closed: Although it dominated psychological aesthetics during the first decade of the twentieth century, it had undergone "a continuous dialectical reconstruction" and, finally, "had disappeared into thin air for all the conceptual restrictions and reservations" (Odebrecht, 1932, p. 37). Nicolai Hartmann (1882–1950), another important aesthetician, argued in 1945, that the concept of empathy had indeed been "an immensely productive concept in aesthetics" but had lost its productivity due to a conceptualisation that was far too sophisticated (Hartmann, 1945/1966, p. 254). Hartmann was convinced that a concept like *Einfühlung* was indispensable for an analysis of musical experience and also for an understanding of how architecture or ornaments are perceived. According to him, the phenomenon of "empathy" implies a *Formgefühl* (the "sense of form"), a certain constructive faculty of the imagination that surpasses the mere idea of a "projection" of inner states into an external reality. Holger Höge, in his book *Emotionale Grundlagen ästhetischen Urteilens* ["*On the Emotional Foundations of Aesthetic Judgement*"] points to numerous examples of recent work in social and clinical psychology that implement the concept of empathy (Höge, 1984, p. 53ss.). He is, however, sceptical as to its applicability in aesthetics because, as he states, "the interaction between the emotional content of pictures and emotional states of the recipients could not be confirmed in the way empathy theory predicted" (Höge, 1984, p. 401). In contrast, Hans and Shulamith Kreitler report reliable evidence for Lipps' approach, although they call for a revision and differentiation of his theoretical claims. Their book *Psychology of the Arts* (1972) is regarded as a significant contribution to psychological aesthetics in the second half of twentieth century.

In even more recent theoretical discussions in psychological aesthetics, the concept of "empathy" plays only a marginal role. The model of aesthetic experience proposed by Helmut Leder and his colleagues (Leder, Belke, Oeberst, & Augustin, 2004), for example, seems representative for the way in which modelling aesthetic experience has been pursued until recently in the humanities. Their model asserts that aesthetic appreciation and judgments are generated by information processing mechanisms in five consecutive stages: (1) perception, (2) explicit classification, (3) implicit classification, (4) cognitive mastering, and (5) evaluation. The order of these stages is not unilinear, instead it forms a "relative hierarchy of processing stages, with processing potentially falling back onto previous stages" (Leder et al., 2004, p. 493). The first stages represent perceptual analysis tools based primarily on psychobiological mechanisms and processes of pattern recognition that follow regularities as described in particular by Gestalt psychology. The other stages involve a certain kind of culturally learned expertise. Aesthetic pleasure, according to this theory, can largely be explained by a processes of reinforcement induced by the "cognitive mastering" of the aesthetic object through aesthetic judgment. I think that this model is very plausible but it lacks to take those processes into consideration that the empathy concept tries to explain. Since the latter are probably part of the primary process of perception at the first stage, they cannot be grasped by a fundamentally different model based on the assumption that emotional appraisal is dependent on subsequent stages of cognitive evaluation. With regard to the epistemological approach, the crucial difference between the recent cognitive or neuro-cognitive models and traditional (introspective) models like the theory of *Einfühlung* can be seen – to my mind – in the central role of temporality in "information processing" as part of recent cognitive models: While Lipps and his followers were limited to assumptions of simultaneity or non-simultaneity, modern technology allows scientists to record temporal sequences of brain activity on a scale of milliseconds. However, despite the amazing progress in mind mapping technology, many questions about the relationship between subjective experiences and their biological correlates remain unsolved. This is the reason why there is still a need for describing empathic processes on a phenomenological level, even though there have been many credible attempts at establishing causal models of aesthetic experience.

Over the course of the twentieth century, attempts to use the concept of empathy (or similar concepts) to describe mental processes were particularly prevalent in the phenomenological tradition. The French phenomenologist Eugène Minkowski (1885–1972), for example, in *Le temps vécu* (Minkowski, 1933/2005), refers to the concept of "sympathie" (sympathy) in conceptualising the relation of human beings to their actual life space (ibid., vol. 1, p. 273). The German psychiatrist Hubertus Tellenbach (1914–1994), in *Geschmack und Atmosphäre* ["Taste and Atmosphere"] speaks about a "fusion of the subject with the world presenting itself in fragrance and flavour" (Tellenbach, 1968, p. 24). Wilhelm Revers (1918–1987), in his book *Das Musikerlebnis* ["The Experience of Music"] also refers to *Einfühlung* to characterise the human perception of music and characterises the experience of the sounding and resounding world (as described by German terms like *Tönen, Widerhall,* or *Resonanz*) as a "sympathetic primary phenomenon" [*sympathetisches Urphänomen*] (Revers, 1971, p. 123s.).

At the beginning of the twentieth century, Wilhelm Worringer (1881–1965), an art historian, proposed an interesting extension of the theory of *Einfühlung*. He suggested in his book *Abstraction and Empathy* of 1908 that *Einfühlung* is not an isolated process but one in a pair of alternative ways to encounter an aesthetic object. The other is *Abstraktion*, which, for him, means a tendency to dissociate oneself emotionally from an object. Worringer argues that "this modern aesthetics, which proceeds from the concept of empathy, is inapplicable to wide tracts of art history". Thus, we have to presume a second type of aesthetics "which proceeds not from man's urge to empathy, but from his urge to abstraction" (Worringer, 1908/1997, p. 4). This second urge, as exemplified by Egyptian, Byzantine, primitive, or modern expressionist art, articulates a totally different way of encountering the outside world: it is a reaction to the frightening and worrying aspects of reality. The duality of aesthetic reactions, according to Worringer, can explain the variability of styles in art history: In historical periods of anxiety and uncertainty, humans seek to abstract objects from their frail and uncertain appearance and transform them into absolute, transcendental forms. As Worringer puts it:

> Just as the urge to empathy as a pre-assumption of aesthetic experience finds its gratification in the beauty of the organic, so the urge to abstraction finds its beauty in the life-denying inorganic, in the crystalline or, in general terms, in the abstract law and necessity. (Worringer, 1908/1997, p. 4)

A very similar conceptualisation can be found in Ernst E. Boesch's (1916–2014) more recent approach, which he develops in *Das Magische und das Schöne* ["The Magic and the Beautiful"] of 1983. Although he was not familiar with Worringer's essay at the time, he came up with an astonishingly analogous theoretical construction: Magic and aesthetics, Boesch argues, are two contrasting ways of confronting reality. While magic aims to keep a distance from the strange and threatening experiences of the world outside, aesthetics strives to bridge the gulf between the internal and external world through assimilation and empathy. In this approach, the role of empathy in constituting the experience of beauty is the same as in Worringer's theory. The main difference lies in the – relevant – fact that Boesch relates the distancing and abstracting attitude to a magical worldview and not to abstraction in art, as Worringer does. While the magical attitude towards objects expresses a distancing function, the empathic disposition stresses being in harmony with the world. While the aesthetic attitude tends "to expand the validity of the inner images" and "to transform counter-world into I-world", the magical action "would not be content with mere symbolic results: it aims at factual mastery, at influencing or determining the course of events" (Boesch, 1991, p. 230). "By empathy we learn how to be in harmony with the world, confrontation lets us experience our vulnerability". And "mastering" our subject-object relations requires "being able to empathise as well as to master confrontation: a relation to objects that is, at the same time, in a versatile way empathic as well as cunning and compelling" (Boesch, 1983, p. 25).[6]

The theory of *Einfühlung* in that concrete form as it was developed as a theoretical key concept in the early days of psychological aesthetics, might be seen as out dated on several accounts. But the concept of empathy is still alive in certain approaches to recent aesthetics and of cultural psychology, for instance, in Ernst E. Boesch's "Symbolic Action Theory". Thus, writing obituaries might be premature. In dealing with the reality of aesthetic experience, we are confronted with processes that we may appropriately describe as empathic, at least on a phenomenological level. This should at the least make us cautious about developing theoretical models that overemphasise the rational-cognitive aspects of aesthetic experience. In so far as "aesthetic experience" includes more than judgements of preference or pleasantness, the objective of psychological aesthetics cannot be reduced to a theory of aesthetic judgement (and its emotional equivalents) or to simply "information processing". In order to avoid such constraints, phenomenological analyses may lead to the rediscovery of aesthetic experience's variety and stimulate the search for a comprehensive methodological approach.

[6] "... ein Umgehen mit Objekten, das zugleich beweglich einfühlend wie auch überlistend und zwingend ist".

References

Baumgarten, A. G. (1735/1983). *Meditationes philosophicae de nonnullis ad poema pertinentibus* [Reflections on poetry] (H. Paetzold, Ed.). Hamburg: Meiner.

Baumgarten, A. G. (1750/2007). *Aesthetica /Ästhetik. Lateinisch-deutsch* (2 vols., D. Mirbach, Ed.). Hamburg: Meiner.

Boesch, E. E. (1983). *Das Magische und das Schöne* [The Magic and the Beautiful], Stuttgart: frommann-holzboog.

Boesch, E. E. (1991). *Symbolic Action Theory and Cultural Psychology*. Berlin: Springer.

Burke, E. (1756/1852). A Philosophical Enquiry into the Origin of our Ideas of the Sublime and Beautiful. In *The Works and Correspondences* (vol. 2, pp. 555–682). London: Rivington.

Dessoir, M. (1906). *Ästhetik und allgemeine Kunstwissenschaft in den Grundzügen dargestellt* [Aesthetics and the general science of art]. Stuttgart: Enke.

Eberhard, J. A. (1783). *Theorie der schönen Wissenschaften* [Theory of the fine arts and sciences]. Halle: Waisenhausbuchhandlung.

Fechner, G. T. (1876/1925). *Vorschule der Aesthetik* [Propaedeutics to aesthetics]. Hildesheim: Olms.

Ficker, F. (1830). *Aesthetik oder Lehre vom Schönen und der Kunst* [Aesthetics or the theory of the beautiful and the arts]. Vienna: Heubner.

Groos, K. (1902). *Der aesthetische Genuss* [On aesthetic pleasure]. Gießen: Ricker.

Hanslick, E. (1854/1981). *Vom Musikalisch-Schönen. Ein Beitrag zur Revision der Ästhetik der Tonkunst* [Of Music and Beauty. Contribution to a revision of the aesthetics of musical art]. Darmstadt: Wissenschaftliche Buchgemeinschaft.

Hartmann, N. (1945/1966). *Ästhetik* [Aesthetics]. Berlin: de Gruyter.

Hegel, G. W. F. (1835–38/1979). *Vorlesungen über die Ästhetik* [Lectures on aesthetics] (E. Moldenhauer & K. M. Michel, Eds.). Frankfurt/Main: Suhrkamp.

Höge, H. (1984). *Emotionale Grundlagen des ästhetischen Urteilens* [On the emotional foundations of aesthetic judgement]. Frankfurt/Main: Lang.

Krause, K. C. F. (1837). *Abriß der Aesthetik oder der Philosophie des Schönen und der schönen Kunst* [Outline of aesthetics or the philosophy of the beautiful and the fine arts] (J. Leutbecher, Ed.). Göttingen: Dieterich.

Kreitler, H., & Kreitler, S. (1972). *Psychology of the Arts*. Durham, NC: Duke University Press.

Lanzoni, S. (2009). Practicing Psychology in the Art Gallery: Vernon Lee's Aesthetics of Empathy. *Journal of the History of the Behavioral Sciences, 45*, 330–354.

Leder, H., Belke, B., Oeberst, A., & Augustin, D. (2004). A model of Aesthetic Appreciation and Aesthetic Judgement. *British Journal of Psychology, 95*, 489–508.

Lee, V. (1910). Weiteres über Einfühlung und ästhetisches Miterleben [Further remarks on empathy and aesthetic co-experiences]. *Zeitschrift für Ästhetik und allgemeine Kunstwissenschaft, 5*, 145–161.

Lee, V. & Anstruther-Thomson, C. (1897). Beauty and Ugliness. *Contemporary Review, 72*, 544–569, 669–688.

Lee, V. & Anstruther-Thomson, C. (1912). *Beauty and Ugliness*. London: Lane.

Lipps, T. (1891). *Ästhetische Faktoren der Raumanschauung* [Aesthetic factors of the notion of space]. Hamburg: Voss.

Lipps, T. (1896). Die geometrisch-optischen Täuschungen (Vorläufige Mitteilung) [The geometrical- optical illusions (preliminary report)]. *Zeitschrift für Psychologie und Physiologie der Sinnesorgane, 12*, 39–59.

Lipps, T. (1897). *Raumästhetik und geometrisch-optische Täuschungen* [Spatial aesthetics and optical-geometrical illusions']. Leipzig: Barth.

Lipps, T. (1900). Aesthetische Einfühlung [Aesthetical empathy]. *Zeitschrift für Psychologie und Physiologie der Sinnesorgane, 22*, 415–450.

Lipps, T. (1901). Einfühlung, innere Nachahmung und Organempfindungen Organempfindungen [Empathy, inner imitation, and organ sensations]. *Archiv für Psychologie, 1*, 185–204.

Lipps, T. (1903). Grundlegung der Aesthetik [The foundation of aesthetics]. In *Psychologie des Schönen und der Kunst* [Psychology of the beautiful and the arts](vol. 1). Hamburg: Voss.

Minkowski, E. (1933/2005). *Le temps vécu. Études phénoménologiques et psychopathologiques* [Lived time. Phenomenological and psychopathological studies]. Paris: PUF Quadrige.

Müller-Lyer, F. C. (1889). Optische Urteilstäuschungen [Optical illusion]. *Archiv für Physiologie*, Suppl. vol., 263–270.

Odebrecht, R. (1932). *Ästhetik der Gegenwart* [Aesthetics in our times]. Berlin: Junker & Dünnhaupt.

Revers, W. J. (1971). *Das Musikerlebnis* [The experience of music]. Düsseldorf: Econ.

Smith, A. (1759/1966). *Theory of Moral Sentiments*. London: Coss.
Solger, K. W. F. (1829/1980). *Vorlesungen über Ästhetik* [Lectures on aesthetics]. Darmstadt: Wissenschaftliche Buchgesellschaft.
Sulzer, J. G. (1773/74). *Allgemeine Theorie der schönen Künste* [A general theory of the fine arts]. Leipzig: Weidemann.
Tellenbach, H. (1968) *Geschmack und Atmosphäre* [Taste and atmosphere]. Salzburg: O. Müller.
Vischer, F. T. (1846–57/1975) *Ästhetik oder Wissenschaft vom Schönen* [Aesthetics or the science of beauty] (6 parts in 3 vols., R. Vischer, Ed.). Hildesheim: Olms.
Vischer, R. (1873/1927a). Über das optische Formgefühl [On the optical sense of form]. In *Drei Schriften zum ästhetischen Formproblem* [Three contributions to the aesthetic problem of form] (pp. 1–44). Halle: Niemeyer.
Vischer, R. (1873/1994). On the Optical Sense of Form. A Contribution to Aesthetics. In H. F. Malgrave & E. Ikonomou (Eds.). *Empathy, Form, and Space. Problems in German Aesthetics, 1873–1893* (pp. 89–123). Santa Monica: Getty Center Publications.
Vischer, R. (1874/1927b). Der ästhetische Akt und die reine Form [The aesthetic act and pure form]. In *Drei Schriften zum ästhetischen Formproblem* [Three contributions to the aesthetic problem of form] (pp. 45–54). Halle: Niemeyer.
Vischer, R. (1890/1927c). 'Über ästhetische Naturbetrachtung. Ein Vortrag' [On aesthetically observing nature. A lecture]. In *Drei Schriften zum ästhetischen Formproblem* [Three contributions to the aesthetic problem of form] (pp. 55–76). Halle: Niemeyer.
Volkelt, J. (1876). *Der Symbol-Begriff in der neuesten Aesthetik* [The concept of the symbol in contemporary aesthetics]. Jena: Dufft.
Volkelt, J. (1905–14). *System der Ästhetik* [System of Aesthetics] (3 vols.). Munich: Beck.
Volkelt, J. (1920) *Das ästhetische Bewusstsein. Prinzipienfragen der Ästhetik* [Aesthetic consciousness. Questions of principle in aesthetics]. Munich: Beck.
Witasek, S. (1904). *Grundzüge der allgemeinen Ästhetik* [Essentials of general aesthetics]. Leipzig: Barth.
Worringer, W. (1908/1997). *Abstraction and empathy: A contribution to the psychology of style*. Chicago: Elephant Paperbacks.
Zimmermann, R. (1873). Ueber R. Vischer's Optisches Formgefühl [On R. Vischer's Optical Sense of form]. *Philosophische Monatshefte*, *8*(2), 89–92.

10

A Question of Character: Analogy and the Empathic Life of Things

Andrea Pinotti

1 The Wind Whistles, the Storm Rages – Analogy in Philosophy

In the conclusion of the complex section 59 of his "Third Critique" (1790) – which discusses beauty as the symbol of morality and, more generally, the relationship between intuition, understanding and reason as connected to the schematic and symbolic *hypotyposis*, Immanuel Kant reflects on the frequent recourse to analogy [*Analogie*] in the domain of common sense:

> We frequently apply to beautiful objects of nature or of art names that seem to rely upon the basis of moral judgement. We call buildings or trees majestic and stately, or plains laughing and joyful; even colours are called

A. Pinotti (✉)
Department of Philosophy, Università degli Studi di Milano, Milano, Italy
e-mail: andrea.pinotti@unimi.it

V. Lux, S. Weigel (eds.), *Empathy*, Palgrave Studies in the Theory and History of Psychology, DOI 10.1057/978-1-137-51299-4_10

> innocent, modest, soft, because they excite sensations containing something analogous to the consciousness of the state of mind [*Gemütszustandes Analogisches*] produced by moral judgements. (Kant, 2007, p. 181)

The underlying paradigm is the one of proportion: "*x* is to *y* as *z* is to *w*". If we refer to the chromatic example, we might say that a certain white and a certain green are to the chromatic spectrum *as* an expression of innocence and modesty are to the spectrum of moral temper (it is the correspondence of the "sensory-moral effect of colour [*Sinnlich-sittliche Wirkung der Farbe*]" investigated by Johann Wolfgang Goethe in his *Farbenlehre* in 1810 (Goethe, 1988, pp. 278–97). Such a transition [*Übergang*] is made possible by a pontifical function connecting spheres of meaning that would otherwise be separated: a symbolic hypotyposis or indirect presentation that operates through analogy. This function, as exemplified in section 59, brings together [*sym-ballein*] two elements that show "no likeness [*keine Ähnlichkeit*]", like a despotic state and a hand-mill. At the same time, it outlines something analogous, common and shared in the face of their patent heterogeneousness: a likeness not directly between the two elements at hand, but rather between the rules [*Regeln*] governing our reflection upon both. The rules therefore allow for their juxtaposition and enable the representation of the former through the image of the latter.

Even if such an issue, albeit very interesting and not very much explored, cannot be analysed here ("This is not the place to dwell upon it"), Kant does not neglect to call attention to the fact that

> in language we have many such indirect presentations modelled upon an analogy enabling the expression in question to contain, not the proper schema for the concept, but merely a symbol for reflection. Thus, the words ground (support, basis), to depend (to be held up from above), to flow from (instead of to follow), substance (as Locke puts it: the support of accidents), and numberless others, are not schematic, but rather symbolic hypotyposis, and express concepts without employing a direct intuition for the purpose, but only drawing upon an analogy with one. (Kant, 2007, p. 180)

In the first half of the eighteenth century, Giambattista Vico, a philosopher more willing than Kant to consider linguistic questions, had preferred to call this pontifical power of language "metaphoric", rather than "symbolic", as it is termed in the "Third Critique". From the perspective of his philosophy of history in *La Scienza Nuova*, which is motivated by a deep conviction that poetic figurativeness, and not prosaic literality, constitutes the original and authentic form of language, Vico depicts the first human beings as having a "robust sense and vigorous imagination" (section 375, Vico, 1948, p. 104). They are able to be inspired by immediate bodily analogies in order to give a name to things:

> It is noteworthy that in all languages the greater part of the expressions relating to inanimate things are formed by metaphor [*trasporti*] from the human body and its parts and from the human senses and passions. Thus, head for top or beginning; eyes for the looped heads of screws and for windows letting light into houses; mouth for any opening; lip for the rim of a vase or of anything else; the tooth of a plow, a rake, a saw, a comb; beard for rootlets; the mouth of a river; a neck of land; [...] Heaven or the sea smiles; the wind whistles; the waves murmur; a body groans under a great weight. (section 405, Vico, 1948, p. 116)

The "corporeal imagination" (section 376) of the first men permits their body to make up an entire world, to transform themselves into the things, and such a transformation, such a metamorphosis, is precisely metaphor [*metapherein*], the *transference*, the transport moving from the body to the world. The bodily structure therefore becomes the aesthetic condition of possibility necessary to comprehend the meaningful nature of the world: sense (in the sense of sensibility) enables the apprehension of sense (in the sense of meaning). It is significant that Vico, like Kant after him (although in his own peculiar way), employs the term "rule" in order to characterize the procedure of metabolization of the world within the body: "Man in his ignorance makes himself the rule [*regola*] of the universe". (section 405, Vico, 1948, p. 116) Making oneself the rule does not decay once the process of rationalization and intellectualization is achieved; on the contrary, it survives in the figures of speech and idiomatic expressions of ordinary language, even to the present day.

Hence, ordinary language constantly operates through a *transference* – a *symballein* (Kant), a *metapherein* (Vico) – that is able to seize the identical in the diverse, the homogeneous in the heterogeneous, and illuminates similarities not in substance or properties, but rather in relationships, thanks to which it is possible not only for human beings to laugh, but also for the field (Kant) or the sky (Vico). Seizing upon similarities of relationships is a prerogative of analogical reflection.

Nevertheless, the history of ideas teaches us that the origins of such a reflection are to be found in the doctrine of numbers instead of in the theory of language. The fundamentally proportional structure of the analogical relationship [*ana logon*] was already well known to ancient Greek mathematicians. Archytas of Tarentum (Huffman, 2005, pp. 162–3) distinguishes between: an *arithmetic* analogy (that is, an analogy of differences; for example, "10 is to 6 as 6 is to 2", because in both relationships the difference is 4); a *geometric* analogy (that is, an analogy of relations; for example, "8 is to 4 as 4 is to 2", where 2 is their common divisor); and a *harmonic* analogy (e.g., "6 is to 4 as 4 is to 3", where "$6=4+{}^{1/3}\,6$" like "$4=3+{}^{1/3}\,3$"). In Plato and Aristotle, although the original proportional character outlined in the sphere of the numerical relations is maintained, the analogic argumentation is also widely employed beyond the strictly mathematical field. In his *Timaeus* (31c-32a), Plato compares the connection instituted by analogy among numbers to the link instituted by the supreme god among the elements of the cosmos:

> The best bond is the one that most effectively unifies itself and the things it is joining, and nothing does this better than correspondence [*analogia*]. For whenever among three numbers (or, for that matter, three solids or three powers) one is a mean, such that as the first in the series stands to the mean, so the mean stands to the final number of the series (or, conversely, as the final number stands to the mean, so the mean stands to the first), then the mean can also be treated as first or last (or, alternatively, the first and last terms can be treated as means), and so all of them will of necessity turn out to be identical; and since they are all identical, they are all one. (Plato, 2008, p. 20)

In his *Nicomachean Ethics* (1131a 30–32), while discussing distributive justice, Aristotle interprets the just as "a certain proportion" [*analogon*], and explicitly states that analogy is "an equality of ratios" (*analogia isotes esti logon*, Aristotle, 2011, p. 96). In addition to the ethical domain, the poetic sphere too is directly affected by analogy, for the analogical mode is a character of metaphoricity. If, in general, "metaphor is the application [*epiphorà*] of a word belonging to something else", then a transfer can happen in four ways, as described in his *Poetics* 21: "Either from the genus to a species, or from the species to the genus, or from the species to a species, or according to analogy" [*kata to analogon*] (Aristotle, 2002, p. 51, 1457b 7–9). In this last case, the proportional-numerical nature of the analogic metaphorization is confirmed: "By analogy, I mean when the second is to the first as the fourth to the third. For instead of the second one will say the fourth, or instead of the fourth the second. And sometimes they add instead of what it says what is related to it" (Aristotle, 2002, pp. 51–2, 1457b 17–21).

Aristotle clarifies this relationship by means of a simple example that refers to two divinities and their respective attributes. Dionysus is to the cup as Ares is to the shield. Within the operation of an analogic metaphorization, one might consequently say that the cup is Dionysus' shield, or that the shield is Ares' cup. As Aristotle states in his *Rhetoric* (1411a), of the four metaphoric modes *kat'analogian* is the one that is "most admired, as when Pericles said that the young manhood killed in the war vanished from the city as though someone took the spring from the year" (Aristotle, 2007, p. 219).

2 Animation of the Inanimate

Now (recalling Kant's section 59 from which we started), what are the conditions of possibility required to speak of majestic buildings and trees, or of laughing and joyful plains, or of innocent and modest colours? What faculty regulates the construction of the symbolic bridge that allows this transfer from one domain to the other, from the animate to the inanimate world, from the sphere of feelings and moods to the realm of minerals and plants? What function permits the transposition, that Kant calls transition [*Übergang*], Vico, calls transports [*trasporti*], and Aristotle an application [*epiphorà*] to operate?

Without dwelling on the question, section 59 suggests *en passant* that it might be a matter of taste that allows for the passage between two heterogeneous spheres such as the realms of natural or artificial things and the realms of moods and feelings: "Taste makes, as it were [*gleichsam*], the transition [*Übergang*] from the charm of sense to habitual moral interest possible without too violent a leap" (Kant, 2007, pp. 181–2). If we understand taste as the *sensus communis aestheticus* and the "faculty of judging that makes our feeling in a given representation *universally communicable* without the mediation of a concept", as Kant argues in section 40 (Kant, 2007, p. 125), it follows that it would regulate how that communication is formed. This transfer occurs very frequently in ordinary language and involves referring to objects as if they were subjects and to things as if they were human beings. Moreover, if we consider that analogization, as we have seen, is a kind of symbolic presentation or hypotyposis, "the faculty of presentation being the imagination" (section 17, Kant, 2007, p. 63), we should therefore integrate the role of taste with the function of the *Einbildungskraft*.

Vico also dealt with the imaginative faculty, declaring that the first men, "without power of ratiocination, were all robust sense and vigorous imagination" (section 375, Vico, 1948, p. 104): because of such imagination those creatures ("beasts") acted like children, "whom we see take inanimate things in their hands and play with them and talk to them as though they were living persons" (section 377, Vico, 1948, p. 105). The "sublime task" of poetic language, as Benedetto Croce underlines in his monograph on Vico, is "the task of giving life to inanimate objects" (Croce, 1913, p. 66).[1] Father not only of aesthetics, but also of anthropology, Vico inaugurated a reflection on the functions of primitive thought that would subsequently be explored in more detail by

[1] In the same passage Croce actually disagrees with Vico. According to him, such a task "belongs properly not to poetry but to myth. Mythology, embodying its concepts in images, which are always individual things, at last animates them like living beings" (Croce, 1913, p. 66).

anthropologists, from James Frazer's "sympathetic magic" in the third chapter of his *Golden Bough* (1906–15/1951) to Lucien Lévy-Bruhl's "*participation mystique*" in *Les fonctions mentales dans les sociétés inférieures* of 1910 (engl. *How Natives Think*, Lévy-Bruhl, 1985, part 1, chapter 2). Contact, contamination, transference, sympathy, action at a distance – these are operations that articulate the primitive belief in the animation of the inanimate. But how are we meant to understand the "of" in the expression "animation of the inanimate" – as a subjective genitive or as an objective genitive? That is to say, is the inanimate in itself actually animate (subjective genitive), or is the primitive man who animates it (objective genitive) endowing it with the emotional life it is deprived of, since it lacks a soul? Vico immediately discards the first option, at least as an epistemological possibility. Modern men can no longer hope to really grasp authentic primitive experience, they cannot feel like those beasts felt: It is

> beyond our power to enter into the vast imagination of those first men, whose minds were not in the least abstract, refined, or spiritualized, because they were entirely immersed in the senses, buffeted by the passions, buried in the body. [. . .] We can scarcely understand, still less imagine, how those first men thought. (section 378, Vico, 1948, p. 106)

Modernity, by then intellectualized and engaged in the scientific investigation of the causes, by then already "detached from the senses" and assigned to abstract thinking, has ceased to be able to immediately feel nature as a living and animate being and can only imperfectly approximate that originary experience in the form of the "as-if" – representing it as a fiction and a belief (see section 376). Vico's lucid thesis seems here to anticipate the "disenchantment" [*Entzauberung*] of the world, a notion formulated two centuries later by Max Weber in his famous 1919 lecture *Wissenschaft als Beruf* (engl. *Science as Vocation*, Weber, 2004, p. 13, 30). At the same time, Vico offers a radical critique *ante litteram* of much anthropology of the primitive mind.

Now, what about the animation of the inanimate in the sense of the objective genitive? The inanimate is animated by a human being who infuses life and feelings into it. This is the path of so-called *Einfühlung* ("empathy"), that concept that was initially conceived during the late, proto-romantic eighteenth century and was then further developed during the nineteenth century by authors like Friedrich Theodor Vischer, Robert Vischer, and Johannes Volkelt. At the beginning of the twentieth century, it became a key concept in understanding human experience as a whole thanks to its major systematizer, Theodor Lipps.

In spite of Vico's admonitions, early romanticism strived to conceive Nature as an animate cosmos in which man is harmonically immersed by means of a universal co-feeling. In Wilhelm Heinrich Wackenroder's *Herzensergießungen eines kunstliebenden Klosterbruders* [*Outpourings of an Art-Loving Friar*], written with Ludwig Tieck in 1797, Wackenroder speaks of a capacity to feel one's way into all unfamiliar beings [*in alle fremden Wesen hineinzufühlen*] (Wackenroder & Tieck, 1971, p. 110). And in Novalis' *Die Lehrlinge von Saïs* (1798, engl. *The Novices of Saïs*) we read, "No one will fathom nature [. . .] who does not with an inborn creative joy, a rich and fervent kinship with all things, mingle with all of nature's creatures through the medium of feeling, who does not feel his way into [*sich hineinfühlt*] them". (Novalis, 2005, p. 109)

The *Einfühlung* theorists of the late nineteenth and early twentieth centuries considered these authors as ancestors in their genealogic tree. Nevertheless, such a quest for origins might produce in a retrospective chimera; since it is rather Georg W. F. Hegel's doctrine of nature, which pitilessly buries the notion of an animate cosmos (see Perpeet, 1966). Precisely because nature is now simply an ensemble of mere things, the subject can instil into it his/her own sentimental contents. In the diary of his trip through the Bernese Alps (1796), the 26-year-old Hegel expresses his callous and unsympathetic disregard for nature in elegantly enough terms: "The sight of these eternally dead masses gave me nothing but the monotonous and at length boring notion: *that is how it is* [*es ist so*]" (Hegel, 1966, p. 309).

In that respect, Johann Gottfried Herder appears as a true threshold figure who aids us in grasping the problematic and conflictual coexistence of "the animation of the inanimate" in the double sense of the subjective and objective genitive. Under the title of the subjective kind of genitive, his brief 1778 treatise *Vom Erkennen und Empfinden der menschlichen Seele* [engl. *On the Cognition and Sensation of the Human Soul*] invites us to apprehend the symphony of the whole cosmos and its creatures as life feeling life: "In the degree of the depth of our self-feeling [*Selbstgefühl*] lies also the degree of our other-feeling for others [*Mitgefühl*], for it is only ourselves that we can, so to speak, feel into others [*hinein fühlen*]". (Herder, 2002a, p. 214) Nevertheless, in that very same year, in the theory of sculpture offered in his work on *Plastik* [*Sculpture*], the notion of sympathetic feeling is inflected in the direction of the objective genitive:

> I do not know if I dare to term *static* and *dynamic* that which streams from the human body into the body of art: it lives in every *curve* and *hollow*, in every mark of *pliancy* and *firmness*, as if *weighed* upon a balance, and it possesses the power virtually to *transpose* [*versetzen*] our soul into the same sympathetic *situation*. The rise and fall of the breast and the knee, the way the body rests quietly, revealing the soul-all this passes silently and incomprehensibly over into us: we find ourselves, so to speak, embodied in the nature before us, or the nature in question is enlivened by our own soul. (Herder, 2002b, p. 81)

The notion of transposition or transfer [*Versetzung*] will inspire a powerful paradigm for the subsequent discourse on *Einfühlung*. To the question, "How can the *symballein* and *metapherein* between animate and inanimate realms be realized?", they will answer in Herder's wake: by means of a transfusion of sentimental contents that move from a subject who is full of affects into the empty object, thereby animating it – Aristotle's *epiphorà*, Vico's *trasporto*, and Kant's *Übergang*.

3 Communicating Vessels

This paradigm is based on the hydraulic model of communicating vessels. According to a certain understanding of fluid mechanics, the subject acts as a vessel filled with feelings, which is then connected to the object, an empty receptacle. A levelling process between the two containers occurs until they are balanced. The process happens unconsciously, so that the subject believes affects are arising from the object itself, while actually he/she is only retrieving the affects with which he/she previously imbued it.

This simple scheme exerted a powerful attraction, and practically all theorists fell into its trap. Just to mention two figures very different from each other – different because the first articulates "empathy" in the sense of a bodily feeling (Vischer), whereas the second prefers a strong spiritualistic approach (Lipps) – we find that Robert Vischer in his famous dissertation *Über das Optische Formgefühl* (1872, "On the Optical Sense of Form") explicitly speaks of *Einfühlung* as a process in which the body "unconsciously projects [*versetzt*] its own bodily form – and with this also the soul – into the form of the object" (Vischer, 1994, p. 92). Theodor Lipps similarly states in his *Ästhetik* (1907), "Empathy occurs in many ways and fills the aesthetic objects with manifold contents. But these contents always derive from the same source, that is, from my own self-activation" (Lipps, 1907, p. 355; translation mine, A. P.).[2] Even Wilhelm Worringer, although programmatically engaged in limiting Lipps' overpowering notion of *Einfühlung* by means of the counter-notion of *Abstraktion*, ends in *Abstraktion und Einfühlung* (1907) by tracking both the empathic and the abstract impulse back to an originary "need for self-alienation [*Selbstentäußerung*]" (Worringer, 1997, p. 23), literally an ecstasy, a sort of standing outside oneself in order to get into the object.

It is therefore particularly relevant that very early, and before the transformation of the notion of *Einfühlung* into a psychological and aesthetic *koinè*, Paul Stern suggests in the first chapter of his book *Einfühlung und Association* (1897) a pun with the terms *Einfühlung* and *Einfüllung* ("filling"), emphasizing the hydraulic reduction commonly used to describe the animation of the object (see Stern, 1897, p. 6).

[2] "Die Einfühlung vollzieht sich in mannigfacher Gestalt und erfüllt die ästhetischen Objekte mit mannigfachem Inhalt. Immer aber ist dieser Inhalt derselben Quelle, nämlich meiner eigenen Selbstbetätigung entnommen" (Lipps, 1907, p. 355).

Nevertheless, it soon became clear that the hydraulic model was making water all round. Taken to its extreme, it was inspired by a psychological subjectivism that appeared as radical as it was caricatural: the very same landscape – just to give one example of *Stimmungseinfühlung* ("empathy of mood") – appears to me joyful or melancholic depending on how I feel, either joyful or melancholic, at a given time and place; the very same ornamental line – this being an instance of *Tätigkeitseinfühlung* ("empathy of activity") – appears to me nervous or tranquil in its *ductus* because now I feel either nervous or tranquil. In the context of the disenchantment theory, once the world is emptied of sense and feeling, the empathetic experience would be reduced to a grotesque labour of mourning, warped into a function of compensation and (impossible) re-enchantment.

The fundamental presupposition that the external world is an ensemble of mere things was vividly illustrated by Hegel with his "eternally dead masses". Lipps also comments: "What I find in the outer world is mere and factual existence" (Lipps, 1907, p. 357; transl. here and in all following instances mine, A. P.).[3] Because of their simple existence (Hegel's bored "*es ist so*"), things turn out to be essentially inexpressive, and any possibility of expression must be traced back to the subject's expressivity, which has been empathetically transferred onto the object. Expression would then coincide with empathy to the extent that only human beings are able to express a mood, a state of mind or of soul (see Lipps, 1906, pp. 102–3). Having no mind and no soul, the object can only express itself if a certain individual expresses him/herself in it. The subject must empathize with it by means of projecting his/her own sentimental contents.

This projective theory of expression that reduces expressivity to an exclusively human expression has attracted numerous opponents, especially phenomenologists and Gestalt theorists. Both claim that expressivity belongs to the world as well as to human beings, and perception is able to grasp it just as it grasps forms, sounds, and colours. In overt opposition to the *Einfühlung* theory, Max Scheler's *Wesen und Formen*

[3] "Was ich in der Außenwelt finde, ist nur einfach tatsächliches Dasein" (Lipps, 1907, p. 357).

der Sympathie (1923, engl. *The Nature of Sympathy*) discusses originary expressiveness from a phenomenological perspective:

> We certainly believe ourselves to be directly acquainted with another person's joy in his laughter, with his sorrow and pain in his tears, with his shame in his blushing, with his entreaty in his outstretched hands, with his love in his look of affection, with his rage in the gnashing of his teeth, with his threats in the clenching of his fist, and with the tenor of his thoughts in the sound of his words. (Scheler, 1954, p. 260)

My point is that this expressiveness acknowledged by Scheler within the domain of the human body should be recognized within the inorganic world as well. As Martin Heidegger puts it in his essay *Der Ursprung des Kunstwerks* (1935–6, "The Origin of the Work of Art"), "In immediate perception, we never really perceive a throng of sensations, e.g. tones and noises. Rather, we hear the storm whistling in the chimney, the three-motored plane, the Mercedes which is immediately different from the Adler. Much closer to us than any sensation are the things themselves". (Heidegger, 2001, p. 8)

According to the Gestalt theorists, expression is the *primum* apprehended by the subject in that which is outside him/her: not only in another human being, but also in a non-human entity. The correlation object–subject in perception constitutes experience itself. But what the subject perceives in the object is not something that is projected from the subject onto the object. The expressive phenomenon is a veritable *Urphänomen* ("originary phenomenon"), in which a merely sensible element is by no means present at first and then endowed with psychic meaning. On the contrary, what occurs is an immediate grasp of unitary totality. Perceptual facts, Wolfgang Köhler says in *Gestalt Psychology* (1947), "are far from being neutral facts". Any factuality is imbued with expressiveness and dynamic character: "Few people can hear the rumbling crescendo of distant thunder as a neutral sensory fact; it sounds to most of us 'menacing'". (Köhler, 1992, p. 244)

Ernst Cassirer has both Köhler and Scheler in mind when, in the third volume of his *Philosophie der symbolischen Formen* (1929, *Philosophy of Symbolic Forms*), and particularly in the part devoted to "The Expressive

Function and the World of Expression", he stands against the doctrine of empathic projection, stigmatizing it as a psychological "fata morgana" that produces a false picture of our relationship with the physical world, surreptitiously considered in itself inexpressive:

> Phenomenological analysis must here reverse the order and direction of inquiry. Instead of asking by what processes of logical inference or of aesthetic projection the psyche *becomes* psyche, it must follow perception back to the point where it is not a perception of things but it is purely expressive, and where, accordingly, it is inside and outside in one. (Cassirer, 1970, pp. 83–4)

Thus, both people (Scheler) and things (Heidegger, Köhler, Cassirer) are in front of us as fully and autonomously expressive phenomena, and not as empty vessels waiting to be filled.

Rudolf Arnheim picked up on these ideas and made them fruitful for the domain of aesthetics and art theory. His seminal essay *The Gestalt Theory of Expression* (1949) acknowledges Lipps' merit for having described structural analogies among heterogeneous elements (such as the physical forces of the object and the psychic dynamics of the observer), anticipating Gestalt psychology. But Arnheim's approach aims at building a generalized theory of expression, in which human expressiveness is only one particular case:

> Expression does not only exist when there is a mind "behind" it, a puppeteer that pulls the strings. Expression is not limited to living organisms, which possess consciousness. A flame, a tumbling leaf, the wailing of a siren, a willow tree, a steep rock, a Louis XV chair, the cracks in a wall, the warmth of a glazed teapot, a hedgehog's thorny back, the colours of a sunset, a flowing fountain, lightning and thunder, the jerky movements of a bent piece of wire: they all convey expression through the various senses. (Arnheim, 1966, p. 64)[4]

[4] A further development of this argumentation is to be found in chapter X ("Expression") of Arnheim, 1974/2004, pp. 444–62.

This is why the comparison between an object and a human state of mind is a secondary process. It is not because it looks like a sad person that the weeping willow appears sad; it is rather the form, the direction and the character of its branches that express a passive hanging. Only subsequently can we draw a parallel between the tree and the structurally similar psychophysical pattern of human sadness.

The subjective sentimental projection, supported by the idea that objects are inert bodies only secondarily invested with physiognomic qualities thanks to the anthropomorphic and animistic intervention of man, results in the "pathetic fallacy" that John Ruskin had already condemned in 1856.[5]

4 Characterology

Given this radical criticism, is the *Einfühlung* theory to be considered definitively confuted? The answer would unquestionably be yes, if this theory were completely identical with the doctrine of subjective projection based on the hydraulic model described above. There are nevertheless good reasons to doubt such a perfect equivalence. In the first place, the exponents of *Einfühlung* did not rigidly adhere to the projective paradigm. In fact, their approaches to it oscillate significantly. Let's go back to the two authors mentioned earlier as representative of the *Einfühlung* theory. According to Robert Vischer, as we have seen, empathy involves a transfusion from the subject and filling of the object. And yet he says, "The compressed or upward striving, the bent or broken impression of an object *fills us* with a corresponding mental feeling of oppression, depression, or aspiration, a submissive or shattered state of mind". Moreover, "The restful colour blue produced by the longer waves *fills us* with a mild yearning; with its shorter waves, red has the effect of an exuberant, glowing vitality". (Vischer, 1994, p. 104, 108, italics mine, A. P.). Thus, in the empathetic relationship with the non-human world the subject is at the same time the filler and the filled.

[5] See Ruskin 2010, pp. 201–20 (section "Of the pathetic fallacy").

Similarly, in his *Leitfaden der Psychologie* (1903, "Guideline of Psychology") the projectivist Lipps finds himself forced to face the demands spontaneously created by the object as dynamics that belong to the object in its own right: "The line requires from me that I pass through it while contemplating it" (not all lines can be empathized in a frantic way; at least, not the lines that are not frantic). And again: "I experience the 'mood' as deriving from, connected with, founded in the colour or the acoustic structure" (Lipps, 1903, p. 188, 190).[6]

A linguistic marker helps us focus on the issue at stake here: when I see a body moving in one direction, "then I empathize into it [*in ihn*] or I feel in it [*in ihm*] the tendency to proceed in that direction".[7] The difference between "into" as a preposition of movement with the accusative case [*in ihn*] and "in" as a preposition of place with the dative case [*in ihm*] denotes a shift from a subjective projection into the object [*in ihn*] to the acknowledgment of a property that belongs to the object itself and is to be found in it [*in ihm*]. Lipps immediately reasserts that "what the terms tendency, force, and activity mean, is something that without a doubt I can experience and feel only in myself, and from myself I transpose them into the objects" (Lipps, 1907, p. 357).[8] Even with these clarifications in mind, the oscillation of *Einfühlung* still remains, which poses problems for the hydraulic model.

Lipps' pupils in Munich would inherit these problems and approach them from a phenomenological perspective inspired by Edmund Husserl's *Logische Untersuchungen* published in 1901–02 (2001).[9] Their aim was to resolve the tension between subjectivistic-psychologistic projectivism and the acknowledgment of rights claimed by the object. Let us consider

[6] "Die Linie etwa fordert mich auf, sie betrachtend zu durchlaufen"; "die 'Stimmung' als aus der Farbe oder dem Tongefüge stammend, daran gebunden, darin gegründet" (Lipps, 1903, p. 188, 190).

[7] "Dann fühle ich in ihn das Streben ein, oder fühle 'in ihm' das Streben, in dieser Richtung weiter zu gehen" (Lipps, 1907, 357).

[8] "Nichts ist gewisser als daß ich dasjenige, was die Worte Streben, Kraft, Tätigkeit usw. sagen, nur in mir selbst erleben oder fühlen, also nur von mir aus in die Objekte verlegen kann" (Lipps, 1907, p. 357).

[9] For a general overview of the Munich phenomenological circle, influenced both by Lipps and by Husserl, see: Kuhn, Avé-Lallemant, & Gladiator, 1975; Smid, 1982.

Moritz Geiger who in 1911 published two very interesting essays, one offering a very useful and detailed map of the numerous inflections of empathy theories (see Geiger, 1911a), the other – on which we will focus here – analysing a specific type of empathy, the empathy of moods [*Stimmungseinfühlung*] in colours and landscapes. Geiger starts by establishing a simple and fundamental difference: the expressions "I feel merry in front of this landscape" and "This landscape is merry" convey two different meanings. With the former expression I am speaking of my personal sentimental condition; with the latter I am referring to a structural property of the object. Subsequently, we need to clarify the conditions of possibility that allow us to employ the same adjective, "merry", in both cases. To this end, Geiger reports the results of an interesting psychological experiment about the experience of "merry colours". None of the test subjects recorded his/her own personal merriness, but rather an objective property of the colour, a kind of halo, aura or "sentimental character" [*Gefühlscharakter*] that, in spite of the fact that it is not on the same level as the merriness expressed by a human face (that is, by a true mood), can nevertheless be counted among other chromatic qualities such as intensity and brightness: merriness is something perceived as belonging to the object and not the subjects' lived-experiences [*Erlebnisse*]. However, if it is true that a colour with a merry character has nothing to do directly with my state of mind and my feelings, it can still condition me and make me merry. In turn, my feeling can radiate beyond my own emotional sphere and colour the object with a "sentimental tone" [*Gefühlston*] that makes it look different to me. If the sentimental character immediately belongs to the object and is intertwined with its structure, the tone is, on the contrary, superimposed onto it as an external halo. Nonetheless, a "qualitative identity" must be acknowledged here: character and tone are "essentially similar" [*wesensverwandt*] – going back to our example, a merry colour has an objective character that is qualitatively identical to the character displayed by an object when I find myself in a merry mood while observing it. That is why ordinary language employs the same term for both cases. These two factors relate to each other in an "interplay" [*Wechselspiel*]: different characters condition our sentimental life, which subsequently influences the objects that carry those characters:

"A gloomy landscape will therefore make me gloomy, and by extension a gloomy mood will make the landscape appear gloomy to me. There is an eternal back and forth between my mood and the character of the landscape" (Geiger, 1911b, pp. 20–21).[10]

What role does *Einfühlung* play in all this? The empathizing attitude allows us to apprehend the correspondence in essential similarity [*Wesensverwandtschaft*] between the character of the object and the sentimental tone. Such an attitude is addressed neither to the objective and critical ascertainment of the objectual character (otherwise performed by the theoretical attitude), nor to a focus on one's own state of mind (performed by the sentimentalistic attitude), but rather to the mood that is grasped both as my mood and the object's mood: "The ego co-lives the mood of the object" (Geiger, 1911b, p. 39).[11] In a condition of constant interaction, the empathic experience opens up a horizon of character comparisons in which the primary factor resides in a third realm (neither subjective nor objective, or subjective as well as objective) of the qualities expressed by adjectivation, and their embodiment in objective or subjective moments becomes something secondary:

> The domain of characters bridges dispare sensory fields. It establishes similarities, where the constituent elements of sensation do not show any similarities. All sensory fields exhibit such characters: when it comes to smell and taste, a connoisseur of wines, a cigar lover, a gourmet, all have a whole range of characters at their disposal. In the area of touch, as well, expressions such as "smooth" and "rough" are far more than mere descriptions of sense complexes – they also designate certain characters. (Geiger, 1911b, pp. 21–2)[12]

[10] "So wird eine düstere Landschaft mich düster machen, und wiederum diese düstere Stimmung mir die Landschaft grau erscheinen lassen. Zwischen meiner Stimmung und dem Charakter der Landschaft ist ein ewiges Hin und Her" (Geiger, 1911b, pp. 20–1).

[11] "Das Ich lebt die Stimmung des Gegenstandes mit" (Geiger, 1911b, p. 39).

[12] "Das Gebiet der Charaktere schlägt so eine Brücke zwischen den disparaten Sinnesgebieten. Es stellt Ähnlichkeiten her, wo die konstituierenden Merkmale der Empfindung keine solchen Ähnlichkeiten aufweisen. Denn alle Empfindungsgebiete zeigen solche Charaktere: beim Geruch und Geschmack wird der Weinkenner, der Zigarrenliebhaber, der Feinschmecker eine ganze Skala von Charakteren aufstellen, und im Bereich des Tastsinns sind z. B. die Ausdrücke Glatt und Rauh weit mehr als bloße Bezeichnung von Empfindungskomplexen – sie bezeichnen außerdem bestimmte Charaktere" (Geiger, 1911b, pp. 21–2).

Thus, it is the analogically structured realm of characters that permits the passage – Aristotle's *epiphorà*, Vico's *trasporto*, and Kant's *Übergang* – from one sphere of meaning to the other, without prejudice to their heterogeneity.

Geiger reminds us that Alexander Pfänder inaugurated a descriptive and phenomenological psychology founded on "spatial and material analogies" [*räumliche und stoffliche Analogien*], which allowed him to speak of a love that "looks up" and "looks down", of the "'colour', 'brightness', 'transparency', 'brilliance', 'toughness' etc. of human souls" (Geiger, 1933, p. 10).[13] It is not a question of mere similes, as some have objected: if I define a man as "coriaceous",

> It is only a transposition of the *designation*. Nonetheless, in order to make such a transposition possible, there must be a commonality between the leather and the man being described as "coriaceous", a commonality in their phenomenal *appearance*, in their matter or in their efficacy. (Geiger, 1933, p. 10)[14]

A realm of "coriaceousness" must therefore exist as a general phenomenal quality, which does not belong to a Platonic hyperuranium, but rather to a qualitative eidetic domain that "realizes itself" (Geiger, 1933, p. 11)[15] both in leather as a material and in human temperament.

Alexander Pfänder developed these ideas in an explicitly characterological perspective in *Grundprobleme der Charakterologie*, a programmatic essay published in the first volume of the *Jahrbuch der Charakterologie* (1924, "*Yearbook of Characterology*") edited by Emil Utitz.[16] In that text,

[13] "'Hinaufblickenden' und 'hinabblickenden' Liebe"; "'Farbe', 'Helligkeit', 'Durchsichtigkeit', 'Glanz', 'Zähigkeit' usw. der menschlichen Seelen" (Geiger, 1933, p. 10).

[14] "So ist es nur eine Übertragung der *Bezeichnung*. Damit jedoch eine solche Übertragung möglich sei, muß in dem Leder und in den Menschen, die als 'ledern' bezeichnet werden, eine Gemeinsamkeit der phänomenalen *Erscheinung*, der Sache oder der Wirksamkeit liegen" (Geiger, 1933, p. 10).

[15] "sich realisiert" (Geiger, 1933, p. 11).

[16] Utitz not only edited the "Jahrbuch", he also published a characterological treatise (1925).

Pfänder offers a typological description of the "material natures" [*Stoffnaturen*] proper to the human soul and classifiable

> according to heaviness or lightness, hardness or softness, coarseness or fineness of grain, denseness or looseness, flexibility or friability, and dryness or smoothness; according to colour, brightness, transparency, brilliance, and nature of the sound; and according to sweetness or bitterness, in sum according to the property of the *taste* of human souls. (Pfänder, 1924, p. 325)[17]

Pfänder claims that it is a question of figurative [*bildliche*] expressions, in which one can still grasp some essential elements as regards the character of an individual. If characterology were to be considered – as it usually is – as a general theory of character, "as the proper and essential nature of the whole human soul" (Pfänder, 1924, p. 295),[18] then we should of course raise the question again about the possibility of constructing a bridge between human character (the only one to be considered a veritable character) and the characterial dimension of things; and we would again end up slipping into the projective, hydraulic model. The direction taken by Pfänder in the 1930s was quite different, as proven by his 1936 manuscripts, which were intended to be the preliminary texts for a new characterological work.[19] He proposes a general characterological theory, including a description of the characters of materials, plants, and animals, in which the human character would be no more than a chapter. In this wider sense and according to its etymology (from *charassein*, "to impress"), character should be understood as "the permanent imprint, the

[17] "Nach der Schwere oder Leichtigkeit, der Härte oder Weichheit, der Grobkörnigkeit oder Feinkörnigkeit, nach der Dichtigkeit oder Lockerheit, nach der Biegsamkeit oder Mürbheit, nach der Trockenheit oder Sanftigkeit, nach der Farbe, Helligkeit, Durchsichtigkeit, Glanz, nach der Eigenart des Klangs, nach der Süße oder Herbheit, kurz der Eigenart des *Geschmacks* der menschlichen Seelen" (Pfänder, 1924, p. 325).

[18] "als die eigentümliche Wesensart der ganzen menschlichen Seele" (Pfänder, 1924, p. 295). In the same sense, see Bertin (1951) and Utitz (1925).

[19] Materials kept under the title *Charakterologie* in Pfänder-Nachlaß at the Staatsbibliothek in Munich (C IV 14 and 15). See Avé-Lallemant and Avé-Lallemant (1982, p. 205, 223–5).

peculiarity of an object, that takes place in its unique forms of manifestation and in its effects".[20]

During this same period, Ludwig Klages, another pupil of Theodor Lipps, was thinking of a similar way to develop a general theory of characters, although his approach appears quite problematic. His *Vorschule der Charakterkunde* (1937, "*Propedeutic of Characterology*") actually starts by distinguishing the qualities of characters from the qualities of things, in order to exclude the latter and focus exclusively on the former. Nevertheless, in the chapter devoted to material, structure, and quality of character while critically analysing the metaphor of the *tabula rasa*, Klages admits "that the character of one person resembles a wax tablet, of a second person a wooden tablet, of a third one a stone tablet and so on. The 'traces' of the influences of the environment will appear extremely different according to force, form and duration" (Klages, 1937, p. 15).[21] A phenomenology of the properties of various materials (or even of different wood species, as proposed by Pfänder, 1924, p. 325) can offer a very rich and complex palette of adjectives to be used for the metaphorical description – in the strong sense of *metapherein* [*epiphorà, trasporto, Übergang*] specified above – of human characters.

Lipps' school therefore seems to outline what we might call a system of characterological analogy[22] which allows empathy theories to avoid the trap of the hydraulic model. According to this conceptualization, empathy, as the institution of an analogic relationship, is not an arbitrary transfusion performed by the subject, but an experience that brings to light characterological affinities between the world of things and the human world, connections that exist more or less latently, that are discovered by means of perception, but that are not unilaterally

[20] "Charakter = das bleibende Gepräge, die Eigentümlichkeit eines Gegenstandes, die in den einzelnen Äußerungsformen und Wirkungen des Gegenstandes hervortritt" (Pfänder's notes C IV 14/41 and C IV 14/35, as quoted in Avé-Lallemant and Avé-Lallemant (1982, p. 224, fn 5).

[21] "daß der Charakter des einen dann etwa einer Wachstafel gliche, des zweiten einer Holztafel, des dritten einer Steintafel usw., da denn die 'Spuren' der Umgebungseinflüsse nach Stärke, Gestalt und Dauerhaftigkeit äußerst verschieden ausfallen werden!" (Klages, 1937, p. 15)

[22] For the crucial role played by the notion of analogy in Lipps' school see Smid (1983).

produced by the perceiver. As a critical reader of Lipps, Arnheim himself follows the same path. He argues, somewhat akin to Vico's position, that modern civilization is ineluctably destined to draw distinctions between the animate and inanimate, the human and non-human as well as the physical and mental:

> In terms of expressive qualities, the character of a given person may resemble that of a particular tree more closely than that of another person. The state of affairs in a human society may be similar to the tension in the skies just before the outbreak of a thunderstorm. Poets use such analogies, and so do other unspoiled people. (Arnheim, 1974/2004, p. 453)

Thus, poets and "unspoiled people" are characterologists and analogists, but so too are far less unspoiled people, like advertising and marketing people. Take, for example, the so-called brand extension strategy, which extends a brand name and identity to different product categories with very little (or even nothing) in common with the original product realized by that brand– from cars to chocolate, from cigarettes to clothing, from a music record label to air transportation (see Aaker, 1991; Aaker & Joachimsthaler, 2002; Fabris & Minestroni, 2004; Michel, 2000; Sherrington, 2003). How can this extendibility be possible without the identification of a characterological (we might also say physiognomic[23] or atmospherological[24]) constellation that permits the metaphorical transition between radically heterogeneous domains?

In *Art and Visual Perception,* Arnheim reminds us of a passage in the *Farbenlehre* ("Colour Theory") where Goethe expressed his dissatisfaction about the insufficient work done on the notion of character:

> It is our conviction that the quest for adjectives to express diversities of character has by no means exhausted the possibilities. For instance, one may attempt to use metaphorically the differences pointed up in the physical theory of cohesion; there would be strong, firm, dense, elastic,

[23] On the connection between characterology and physiognomics see Gurisatti (2006, pp. 133–55).

[24] On the *brand images* as atmospheres see Griffero (2010, p. 85).

> flexible, agile, rigid, tough, fluid, and who knows what other characters. (Goethe, 1810/1948, p. 576; as transl. in Arnheim, 2004, p. 452)[25]

Once again we see the idea of a material analogizing at work here. After 200 years, we can perhaps say that some steps in the direction of a general characterology have been made. If this was possible, it was thanks to a critical theory of empathy and its emancipation from the hydraulic projective model.

References

Aaker, D. A. (1991). *Managing Brand Equity: Capitalizing on the Value of a Brand Name*. New York: The Free Press; Toronto: Maxwell Macmillan.

Aaker, D. A. & Joachimsthaler, E. (2002). *Brand Leadership*. London: Simon & Schuster.

Aristotle (2002). *On Poetics* (S. Benardete & M. Davis, Trans.). South Bend, Indiana: St. Augustine's Press.

Aristotle (2007). *On Rhetoric. A Theory of Civic Discourse* (G. A. Kennedy, Trans.). New York, Oxford: Oxford University Press.

Aristotle (2011). *Nicomachean Ethics* (R. C. Bartlett & S. D. Collins, Trans.). Chicago, London: The University of Chicago Press.

Arnheim, R. (1966). The Gestalt Theory of Expression. In *Toward a Psychology of Art. Collected Essays* (pp. 51–73). Berkeley, Los Angeles: University of California Press.

Arnheim, R. (1974/2004). *Art and Visual Perception. A Psychology of the Creative Eye* (first ed. 1954). Berkeley, Los Angeles: University of California Press.

Avé-Lallemant, U. & Avé-Lallemant, E. (1982). Alexander Pfänders Grundriß der Charakterologie [Alexander Pfänder's outline of characterology]. In H. Spiegelberg & E. Avé-Lallemant (Eds.). *Pfänder-Studien* [Pfänder studies] (pp. 203–226). The Hague: Nijhoff.

[25] "Man hat, nach unserer Überzeugung, noch lange nicht genug Beiworte aufgesucht, um die Verschiedenheit der Charaktere auszudrücken. Zum Versuch wollen wir die Unterschiede, die bei der physischen Lehre von der Kohärenz stattfinden, gleichnisweise gebrauchen; und so gäbe es starke, feste, dichte, elastische, biegsame, geschmeidige, dehnbare, starre, zähe, flüssige und wer weiß was sonst noch für Charaktere" (Goethe, 1810/1948, p. 576).

Bertin, G. M. (1951). *La caratterologia* [Characterology]. Milan: Fratelli Bocca.
Cassirer, E. (1970). *The Philosophy of Symbolic Forms. Vol. 3: The Phenomenology of Knowledge* (R. Manheim & Ch. W. Hendel, Trans.). New Haven, London: Yale University Press.
Croce, B. (1913). *The Philosophy of Giambattista Vico*. R. G. Collingwood, Trans.). London: Latimer.
Fabris, G., & Minestroni, L. (2004). *Valore e valori della marca*. Milan: Franco Angeli.
Frazer, J. G. (1906–15/1951). *The Golden Bough: A Study in Magic and Religion* (first ed. 1890, 3rd ed. in 12 vols). London: Macmillan.
Geiger, M. (1911a). Über das Wesen und die Bedeutung der Einfühlung [On the nature and meaning of empathy]. In F. Schumann (Ed.). *Bericht über den vierten Kongreß für experimentelle Psychologie in Innsbruck vom 19. bis 22. April 1910* [Report on the 4th congress of experimental psychology in Innsbruck] (pp. 29–73). Leipzig: Barth.
Geiger, M. (1911b). Zum Problem der Stimmungseinfühlung [On the problem of empathy of mood]. *Zeitschrift für Ästhetik und allgemeine Kunstwissenschaft, 6*, 1–42.
Geiger, M. (1933). Alexander Pfänders methodische Stellung [Alexander Pfänder's methodical position]. In E. Heller & F. Löw (Eds.). *Neue Münchener Philosophische Abhandlungen. Alexander Pfänder zu seinem sechzigsten Geburtstag gewidmet von Freunden und Schülern* [New Munich philosophical essays. Dedicated to Alexander Pfänder for his 60th birthday] (pp. 1–16). Leipzig: Barth.
Goethe, J. W. (1988). *Scientific Studies* (D. Miller, Ed. & Trans.). New York: Suhrkamp.
Goethe, J. W. (1810/1948). Materialien zur Geschichte der Farbenlehre [Materials on the history of the theory of colors]. In *Gedenkausgabe der Werke, Briefe und Gespräche* [Commemorative edition of the works, letters, and conversations] (vol. 16, pp. 245–718). Zurich: Artemis.
Huffman, C. A. (2005). *Archytas of Tarentum. Pythagorean, Philosopher and Mathematician King*. Cambridge: Cambridge University Press.
Griffero, T. (2010). *Atmosferologia* [Atmospherology]. Rome-Bari: Laterza.
Gurisatti, G. (2006). *Dizionario fisiognomico. Il volto, le forme, l'espressione* [Physiognomic dictionary. Visage, forms, expression]. Macerata: Quodlibet.
Hegel, G. W. F. (1966). *Reinterpretation, Texts, and Commentary* (W. Kaufmann, Ed.). London: Weidenfeld and Nicolson.

Heidegger, M. (2001). The Origin of the Work of Art. In J. Young & K. Haynes (Eds.). *Off the Beaten Track* (pp. 1–56). Cambridge: Cambridge University Press.
Herder, J. G. (2002a). On the Cognition and Sensation of the Human Soul. In *Philosophical Writings* (pp. 187–244, M. N. Forster, Ed.). Cambridge: Cambridge University Press.
Herder, J. G. (2002b). *Sculpture: Some Observations on Shape and Form from Pygmalion's Creative Dream* (J. Gaiger, Ed.). Chicago, London: The University of Chicago Press.
Husserl, E. (2001). *Logical Investigations* (J. N. Findlay, Trans., 2 vols). London, New York: Routledge.
Kant, I. (2007). *Critique of Judgment* (J. C. Meredith, Trans, revised by N. Walker). New York, Oxford: Oxford University Press.
Klages, L. (1937). *Vorschule der Charakterkunde* [Propaedeutic of characterology] (2nd ed.). Leipzig: Barth.
Köhler, W. (1992). *Gestalt Psychology. An Introduction to New Concepts in Modern Psychology*. New York: Liveright.
Kuhn, H., Avé-Lallemant, E., & Gladiator, R. (Eds.) (1975). *Die Münchener Phänomenologie* [Munich phenomenology]. The Hague: Nijhoff.
Lévy-Bruhl, L. (1985). *How Natives Think* (L. A. Clare, Trans.). Princeton: Princeton University Press.
Lipps, Th. (1903). *Leitfaden der Psychologie* [Guidelines to psychology]. Leipzig: Engelmann.
Lipps, Th. (1906). Einfühlung und ästhetischer Genuß [Empathy and aesthetic pleasure]. *Die Zukunft, 54*, 100–114.
Lipps, Th. (1907). Ästhetik [Aesthetics]. In W. Dilthey (Ed.). *Systematische Philosophie* [Systematic philosophy] (pp. 349–88). Berlin, Leipzig: Teubner.
Michel, G. (2000). *La stratégie d'extension de marque* [The market extension strategy]. Paris: Vuibert.
Novalis (2005). *The Novices of Saïs. And Other Fragments* (R. Manheim, Trans.). Brooklyn: Archipelago.
Perpeet, W. (1966). Historisches und Systematisches zur Einfühlungsästhetik [Historical and systematic remarks on *Einfühlung* aesthetics]. *Zeitschrift für Ästhetik und allgemeine Kunstwissenschaft, 11*(2), 193–216.
Pfänder, A. (1924). Grundprobleme der Charakterologie [Foundational problems of characterology]. *Jahrbuch der Charakterologie 1*, 289–335.
Plato (2008). *Timaeus and Critias* (R. Waterfield, Trans.). Oxford: Oxford University Press.

Ruskin, J. (2010). Modern Painters. In E.T. Cook & A. Wedderburn (Eds.). *The Works of John Ruskin* (vol. 5). Cambridge: Cambridge University Press.

Scheler, M. (1954). *The Nature of Sympathy*. (P. Heath, Trans.). London: Routledge.

Sherrington M. (2003). *Added Value. The Alchemy of Brand-Led Growth*. New York: Palgrave Macmillan.

Smid, R. N. (1982). Münchener Phänomenologie. Zur Frühgeschichte des Begriffs [Munich phenomenology. On the early conceptual history]. In H. Spiegelberg & E. Avé-Lallemant (Eds.). *Pfänder-Studien* [Pfänder studies] (pp. 109–53). The Hague: Nijhoff.

Smid, R. N. (1983). Ähnlichkeit als Thema der Münchener Lipps-Schule [Semblance as topic of the Lipps' School in Munich]. *Zeitschrift für philosophische Forschung, 37*, 606–616.

Stern, P. (1897). *Einfühlung und Association in der neueren Aesthetik* [*Einfühlung* and association in the new aesthetics]. Hamburg, Leipzig: L. Voss.

Utitz, E. (1925). *Charakterologie* [Characterology]. Charlottenburg: Pan Verlag.

Vico, G. (1948). *The New Science* (first ed. 1725, transl. from the 3rd ed. 1744, T. G. Bergin & M. H. Fisch, Trans.). Ithaca, NY: Cornell University Press.

Vischer, R. (1994). On the Optical Sense of Form: A Contribution to Aesthetics. In H. F. Mallgrave & E. Ikonomou (Eds.). *Empathy, Form, and Space: Problems in German Aesthetics 1873–1893* (pp. 89–123). Santa Monica, CA: The Getty Center Publications.

Wackenroder, W. H., & Tieck, L. (1971). Outpourings of an Art-Loving Friar. In *Wilhelm Heinrich Wackenroder's Confessions and Fantasies* (M. H. Schubert, Trans.). University Park: Pennsylvania State Press.

Weber, M. (2004). Science as a Vocation. In *The Vocation Lectures* (pp. 1–31, R. Livingstone, Trans.). Indianapolis, Cambridge: Hackett Publishing Company.

Worringer, W. (1997). *Abstraction and Empathy: A Contribution to the Psychology of Style* (M. Bullock, Trans.). Chicago: Ivan R. Dee.

11

The Roots of Intersubjectivity – Empathy and Phenomenology according to Edith Stein

Patrizia Manganaro

1 Empathy as Living-Experience [*Erlebnis*] – Inter- and Intrasubjectivity

The aim of this chapter is to explain how intersubjectivity constitutes the root of personal identity. Within the philosophical framework of phenomenology, intersubjectivity provides the *phenomenological grammar* of the social relationship that is the outcome of empathic *Erlebnis* analysis. This way of approaching the experience was first introduced and elaborated by Edmund Husserl in 1905 and then further developed by his student Edith Stein. Their considerations proceed from the phenomenological foundation of the idea of *personal otherness* as an essential part of

P. Manganaro (✉)
Department of Philosophy, Lateran University, Vatican City, Italy
e-mail: patriziamanganaro@yahoo.it

V. Lux, S. Weigel (eds.), *Empathy*, Palgrave Studies in the Theory and History of Psychology, DOI 10.1057/978-1-137-51299-4_11

the nature of the human being: namely the *living body*, regarded as psycho-physical dimension; the *Self*, considered as the nucleus of personal identity, called *via individuationis* (see Stein, 1922/1970; 1932–33/2004); and the *lógos,* interpreted as intentional life in the dynamic activity of consciousness.

Edith Stein's work on empathy is one of the earliest phenomenological inquiries into intersubjectivity and (inter)action between living bodies. Stein addressed the question: What is the meaning of this particular "feeling into" and "feeling from within" the other, which is the crucial characteristic of empathy, given that empathy does not take place in an originary or primordial way [*originär*] as the perception of the outer world does? This distinction is the point of departure in her dissertation *Zum Problem der Einfühlung* (1917, engl. "On the Problem of Empathy"):

> Thus, empathy does not have the character of outer perception, though it does have something in common with outer perception: in both cases, the object itself is present here and now. We have come to recognize outer perception as an act given primordially. But, though empathy is not outer perception, this is not to say that it does not have this 'primordiality' [*Originarität*] [. . .]. We must further differentiate the meaning of primordiality. All our own present experiences are primordial. What could be more primordial than experience itself? But not all experiences are primordially given or primordial in their content. Memory, expectation and fantasy do not have their object bodily present before them. They only represent it [. . .]. (Stein, 1917/1989, p. 7)

The peculiarity of empathy as living-experience [*Erlebnis*][1] is based on the conviction that the world-space of *common actions* is enabled by the subject-body [*Leib*].[2] It considers the primordial experience to start from the foreign "I" and empathy as a *sui generis* living-experience. The

[1] Since both German words *Erfahrung* and *Erlebnis* are translated as "experience" I use the translation "living-experience" for *Erlebnis* to emphasize the vital aspect of this kind of experience.

[2] There exist two words for "body" in German: *Körper* and *Leib*, the latter meaning the felt or animated body whereas the first denotes the body seen from outside.

philosophical questions behind empathy concerns the *intentional* and *performative* modes of living, not in solipsistic terms but as, an intersubjective question about phenomenological consciousness (Manganaro, 2012b).

Different disciplines use the term "empathy", and in ordinary language it is often misused. Over the years and in different realms, it has taken on various modes (Manganaro, 2014, p. 33). Edmund Husserl and Edith Stein thought that without *Einfühlung* a subject has not achieved completion. As a consequence of this remarkable statement, the question occurs how "feeling into" an experience is possible, although its origin does *not* reside *in* us. This tension between *in* and *out,* as well as *inside* and *outside* or *internal* and *external* corresponds to the dynamic between *intrasubjective* and *intersubjective* perspectives that is typical of the human being – as Andrea Pinotti puts it, empathy is both "*principium dividuationis* and *individuationis*" (Pinotti, 2011, p. 26).

Analysing intersubjectivity means asking questions that address its complex circularity: How does the other present himself or herself to our consciousness? And what does it mean to recognize living-experience external to ourselves? The phenomenon of empathy responds to both questions perfectly insofar as human beings are endued with a special dynamism, which encompasses *belonging* as well as *strangeness*: This means that I understand the other as being similar to myself, with a nucleus of personal identity similar to mine that, however, transcends the sphere of what belongs to me. It is a "you" that calls himself "I": it is an *alter-ego* in the literal sense. Given that the "you" is constructed analogous to the "I", the alter-ego similar to myself, the question as to the philosophical meaning of this *analogy* has to be addressed (Manganaro, 2001).

From a phenomenological point of view, the analysis of what is one's "own" (personal identity, *ego*) and of what is "more properly mine" (individuality, *self*) cannot be separated from the analysis of the "foreign I" (*fremdes Ich*, meaning personal alterity, *alter-ego*), and of what is "common and shared" (intersubjectivity, *we*). This analysis requires thinking of intentionality, intercorporeality, intersubjectivity, and performative competence as strongly linked. They all must be examined as moments that *are present simultaneously* within the constellation where two subjects encounter in a living experience. When we use the personal pronouns, "I", "Self", "You", and "We" and the relationship between them, this implies a complexity that is at the core of the *phenomenological epistemology.*

2 Empathy and Phenomenology: Husserl and Stein on Intersubjectivity

Much has been said about Edith Stein's intellectual debt towards her teacher, Edmund Husserl. And in fact the founder of phenomenology worked on the empathical *Erlebnis* already from 1905 on, if not yet in a systematic way (see Husserl, 1923–35/1973). His works *Ideen zu einer reinen Phänomenologie und phänomenologischen Philosophie* (1913/1952, *Ideas Pertaining to a Pure Phenomenology and Phenomenological Philosophy,* 1913/1989), *Erste Philosophie* (1923–24./2007), and *Cartesianische Meditationen,* the famous series of lectures held at the University of Sorbonne in Paris (1929/1950), specify the main points in his research on empathy. Indeed, the problem of empathy is an integral part of phenomenological investigations, and Husserl recognized its importance. He addresses it as it pertains to the ample sphere of intersubjectivity and the "foreign I" [*fremdes Ich*] (Husserl, 1923–24./2007, pp. 75–81; see also Costa, 2010, 2011). Husserl worked rigorously on empathy, but he did not propose a final definition of it. While the core of the question was very well formulated in his phenomenological perspective, it was addressed in different works to a vast material, scattered and varied, and he never elaborated the theme to the state of a structured discussion. In 1904, he had the good fortune of attending a meeting held by the *Psychologischer Verein.* It was a productive encounter, even though he rejected the "mechanic" character of empirical psychology. This rejection met also Theodor Lipps' research on *Einfühlung* that dealt with aesthetics in terms of applied psychology, because it aimed to investigate an object's faculties as those that exert a certain effect on a subject. Lipps was convinced that looking at an aesthetic object required some degree of emotional involvement from the observer, whose response to the stimulus results from imitating body postures. For Husserl, instead, the *apperception* of the other I is a kind of understanding mediated by empathy and living bodies, such that the other I maintains its *own* value as a primordial phenomenon.

In the second book of *Ideen*, Husserl states that every human being, by virtue of his/her living body, exists in a spatial context among things, and the psyche is constantly fused with the *Leib* through physical connections. That is how the living body and the psyche form a peculiar *unity of experience*, which allows the psyche to (ap)present itself in space and time:

> It is also out of the question that in solipsistic self-experience I encounter all that is subjective about me, along with my perceptually given body, as a reality, i.e., in the form of a perception, although my body has such a multivarious unity with what is subjective. It is only with empathy and the constant orientation of empirical reflection onto the psychic life which is appresented along with the other's body and which is continually taken objectively, together with the body, that the closed unity, man, is constituted, and I transfer this unity subsequently to myself. (Husserl, 1913/1989, p. 175: §46: "Significance of empathy for the constitution of the reality 'I as man'")

According to Husserl, empathy enables the knowledge of the objective world as an *intersubjective one*.

Edith Stein contributes to this philosophico-phenomenological context by imparting a "personalistic turn" at the theme of empathy. In her dissertation of 1916 (first published 1917), she shed light upon the modalities with which personal otherness presents itself to a knowing consciousness. She suggests a proper phenomenology of the empathical act and describes its essence, genesis, and structure. In fact, she is deeply interested in the knowledge of the psycho-physical, cognitive, and spiritual experience of others. She, thus, draws our attention both to the *intersubjectivity* and to the *root of the subjectivity*, that is, the *via individuationis* (see Stein, 1917/2008).

Empathizing means "feeling from within the other". In analysing *Einfühlung*, Edith Stein explains the *ego* and *alter-ego* relationship and investigates the possibility of potential for perceiving an extraneous originary living-experience in a *non-originary way*. She remarks that empathy is a *sui generis Erlebnis*, which allows us to understand the other as a bearer of a psycho-physical, cognitive, and spiritual life *analogous* to our own. In a specular, mirroring way, we are able to perceive our own constitutive structure in relation to another subject, even if these two entities are not identical and do not coincide (Stein, 1917/1989, pp. 10–11). The contact or meeting with the other happens by virtue of the *Leib*, which turns the invisible "inner" into something corporeal that may be perceived sensually. The *medium* of the *Leib* provides the intersubjective relationship to unfold as the presence of a variety of living-experiences constitute a flow of consciousness. The *Leib* is, thus, an unavoidable *medium* for relating: through a fine play of *perception* and *apperception*, it permits us to grasp the real meaning of the living body, the psyche, and the *lógos* of the other "I". On the other hand, as Edith Stein continues, the *alter-ego* shapes our own identity. The *Leib,* thus, grounds the phenomenological description of the human being and gives sense and completeness to its characterization as an intersubjective pole (Manganaro 2010a, pp. 162–164). This intersubjective pole is being individuated as *pure relationship* in its state of being born, in its topological moment, as a "fulfilling explication" (Stein, 1917/1989, p. 10).

Unlike the Platonic view of the body as a prison of the soul, the *Leib* designates the inimitable peculiarity of every human being, who in his/her own corporeality already reveals its unicity, dignity, inviolability, and freedom. The physical body's link with a subject, in fact, cannot be reduced to their simple spatial inseparability; it is rather the *Leib* that feels, perceives, and apperceives. And through empathy, we realize that the other is living a series of different kinds of acts, namely (1) motorial and perceptive ones, which refer to lived corporeality [*Leib*]; (2) reactive, impulsive, and instinctive ones, which refer to the mental or psychical dimension [*Psyche*]; and (3) still additional ones, implying the sphere of values that include freedom (to decide), motivations, responsibility, which refer to a dimension described by Stein with the general term "spiritual"

[*Geist, geistliche*], that is to say, the Aristotelian *logos* (Manganaro, 2007, 2010a, 2012a). In Stein's phenomenological language, personal spirituality means vigilance and openness: Not only am I a living being, but I am actually conscious of my being and living – and all in a single act called *first person experience*. With regard to the *via individuationis*, the nucleus [*Kern*] of a person has a certain interiority that differs from individual to individual. This interior quality further determines the fullness and the vitality of actions. Its width and its depth describe a person's way of being, as "*this*" peculiar, unique, unrepeatable individuality that confers an *original mark* to all that comes from such a nucleus.

Concerning the relationship between the subjective and the intersubjective, it is helpful to remember the Husserlian reflection in the fifth of his *Cartesianische Meditationen,* more precisely in §43: In this world, others are intertwined in ways that are proper to bodies, as psychophysical objects. The "I" experiences the world together with others as part of living consciously, and the sense of such experience implies that others are not synthetic formations lacking an "I", but constitute a world extraneous to the "I" as *intersubjective* – a world that *is there for all* and whose objects are available for all. According to Husserl, the *being-there-for-me* of others is a philosophical problem of a special kind dealt with especially in the transcendental theory of the *experience of the extraneous*, or rather, in the analysis of empathic living-experience (see Husserl, 1929/1950, pp. 122–4, § 43, "The ontic-noematic modes of the other, as transcendental guides for the constitutive theory of the experience of the extraneous").

3 What Empathy Is Not: Edith Stein's Theoretical Stance

3.1 Perception and Apperception

Edith Stein compares empathy with other intentional acts of consciousness. We have already seen that it does not entail outer perception: the living extraneous body is *perceived* as an object that originally offers itself among other objects and is *apperceived* as carrying a psychical life. She states that empathy should not be confused with memory, even though it is similar to remembering because it makes something present interiorly (presentification). But empathy is different; unlike memory, empathy has *non-originary content* and referentially depends on *alterity*. Both are absent in the act of remembering, which is more like a kind of bending back of the "I" on itself (nobody can remember my memories, think my thoughts, or dream my dreams!). In the case of personal remembering, that which was originally experienced is recalled to the present, whereas in the case of empathy you "feel within" that which the other "I" is living *in the first person*. According to Stein, empathy is also *not* identification or imitation. It is not imaginative projection, nor a kind of afterward re-experiencing, nor sympathy or co-feeling. Reading between the lines, we might recognize inexplicit references to Theodor Lipps', Wilhelm Dilthey's, Max Scheler's, and Georg Simmel's ideas that are more tightly linked to historical questions on the faculty of understanding [*Verstehen*] as opposed to the capability of explaining [*Erklären*] in the natural sciences (see Dilthey, 1883/2006; Lipps, 1903, 1903–06; Scheler, 1913, 1923; Simmel, 1918/2000, 1971).

Stein is in search of an *analytical epistemology of conscious living-experiences* and driven by the phenomenological question: How do we attribute conscious life to certain bodies? In her analysis we find that the other "I" partakes in a twofold experience, in which the originally presenting perception is tightly linked to *appresenting empathy*. The other constitutes him/herself in living intentional consciousness by reflecting him/herself in an apperceptive way that is far away from outer perception, as we have seen above. In order to experience another "I" and to attribute a consciousness to that living body, it is necessary to experience it in the intersubjective and *shared space of action*. The "you" constitutes itself as a peculiar, intentional correlate that in turn shows and attests his being in me. But "you" still remains *another "I"* different from my flow of consciousness and from my intentional living. This means that we do not have the same consciousness, while the similarity that connects us nevertheless marks *alterity* as a special shade of the category of difference without opposition and without separation. In this context, we might find further explanations for "individuality", "relation", "singularity", and "community".

3.2 A World of Subject-Bodies

The philosophical problem of the *impossibility of separating what is distinct* is a paradigmatic "cipher" for the phenomenological epistemology of complexity (Manganaro, 2010a, 2010b, 2013, 2014). Here I refer to the fulfilling explications of empathy that constitute the second level of the whole living-experience, as Edith Stein describes it in her dissertation. The intersubjective preconditions of empathy provide an example of this problem: My body is here, now; somebody else's body is there, now. I know that my "here-now" is not his/her "here-now". But the similarity between two living bodies allows us to attribute consciousness to the other and with it the capability of feeling and perceiving from within *like me*. Through this analogic structure intersubjective community is built. For Husserl and Stein, access to the life of the *alter-ego* is possible on the basis of the empathic (*inter*subjective) act, which is completely different from the interior (*intra*subjective) perception, which is originary. A living-experience is filled by contents that do *not* come from me; the experience radiates from a core that is *not* "I" and forces me to lose my centre in order to give room to the extraneous experience.

In the phenomenological analysis, empathy, as this intentional act in present experience, is *primordial*, although its content is *non-primordial*. In *On the Problem of Empathy* (1917), Stein describes three levels or modalities of accomplishment:

> These are (1) the emergence of the experience; (2) the fulfilling explication; and (3) the comprehensive objectifications of the explained experience. On the first and the third level, the representation exhibits the non-primordial parallel to perception, and on the second level it exhibits the non-primordial parallel to the having of the experience. The subject of the empathized experience, however, is not the subject empathizing, but another. And this is what is fundamentally new in contrast with the memory, expectation, or the fantasy of our own experiences. The two

> subjects are separate and not joined together, as previously, by a consciousness of sameness or a continuity of experience. And while I am living in the other's joy, I do not feel primordial joy. It does not issue live from my "I" [. . .]. In my non-primordial experience I feel, as it were, led by a primordial one not experienced by me but still there, manifesting itself in my non-primordial experience. (Stein, 1917/1989, pp. 10–11)

Primordial experience and non-primordial experience explain how the "other" presents him/herself to another consciousness of an "ego" as a phenomenon. Stein's considerations here build upon the Husserlian difference between "own" and "foreign", "ego", and "alter-ego".

3.3 Edith Stein on Theodor Lipps: Why Empathy Is Not a "Feeling of Oneness"

Stein analyses this double dynamism by distinguishing but not separating what is experienced in an "own" way from what is experienced in a "foreign" way (Stein, 1917/1989, pp. 10–11; see Manganaro, 2010b, 2015). Her discussion is especially interesting in relation to other theories and descriptions of empathy. First of all, she engages with Lipps' description of the experience of empathy, noting some points of agreement. Both treat empathy as an *inner participation* in foreign experiences, something that Stein establishes as the highest level of the actuation of empathy, namely to be "at" [*bei*] the foreign subject and turned together with its object. Second, they also share the idea that empathy is akin to memory and expectation. After mentioning these points of commonalty, she then refers to the tendency to full experiencing. In this respect, she argues against Lipps' idea of empathy that he interpreted as a real identification, that is, as the potential to feel what the other is living in the very same way, – a kind of *unipathy*, meaning the identity between the own "I" and the foreign "I". Likewise, Stein does not share Dilthey's idea of *Nach-er-leben*, which he characterizes as the successive re-experiencing of the foreign living-experience in a totalizing way with the same characteristics and intensity. According to Dilthey, internal experience and understanding [*Verstehen*] must be integrated. Since he connects understanding with *Nach-erleben* (literally "re-living") and *Nach-erbilden* (literally "re-constructing"), the basic capacity of his program of humanities [*Geisteswissenschaften*] is very close to the real intersubjective experience of *Einfühlung* (Dilthey, 1883/2006). In contrast, Edith Stein pays particular attention to the phenomenological idea of "present" and "presence", rejecting the notion of any re-duplication of that what has already been lived. On the contrary, she focuses on *Erlebnis* for living-experience, here and now. Stein further claims that it is not possible to understand *Einfühlung* as reflexive sympathy and also contests Max Scheler's concept of *Mit-fühlen* ("to feel with", "to feel together"), which he portrays as an *undifferentiated, neutral* flow of consciousness. She remarks:

> What do "own" and "foreign" mean in the context in which Scheler uses them? If we take his discussion of a neutral stream of experience seriously, we cannot conceive of how a differentiation in this stream can occur. (Stein, 1917/1989, p. 28)

As regards intentional consciousness, she in general upholds the terms of a phenomenological theory and the rigorous elaboration given by her teacher, Husserl.

Although Stein reacts to various philosophers and theorists, the psychologist Lipps remains her main interlocutor throughout her analysis of empathy. He speaks of the fact that every experience about which a subject knows "tends" to be fully experienced, including those remembered and expected as well as those empathized. "Fully experienced", as Lipps puts it, means that nothing in the emphathizing subject opposes against it; it also entails the experience of the self as an "I" that was up until then an object. In this respect, it does not matter if the "I" is past or future, my own or the foreign "I" (Lipps, 1903, p. 192). However, Stein does not think that there is a complete overlap between the remembered, expected, and empathized "I". It is impossible for them to become one. Stein remarks:

> Lipps confuses the following two acts: (1) being drawn into the experience at first given objectively and fulfilling its implied tendencies

> with (2) the transition from non-primordial to primordial experience. (Stein, 1917/1989, p. 13)

Despite this criticism, she was very interested in Lipps' argument. For example, she refers to Lipps' famous case of a spectator watching an acrobat which he uses to illustrate an empathic unity between one's own "I" and a foreign "I" and to claims that as long as empathy is complete, then there is no distinction between them – they are one. But what does it mean to be one with the acrobat and go through his motions inwardly? According to Lipps, a distinction only arises when I step out of complete empathy and reflect on my real "I". Then, the experiences not coming from me appear to belong to "the other" and to his movements. Stein remarks:

> Were this description correct, the distinction between foreign and our own experience, as well as that between the foreign and our own "I", would actually be suspended. This distinction would first occur in association with various real "I's" or psycho-physical individuals. What my body is doing to my body and what the foreign body is doing with the foreign body would then remain completely obscure, since I am living "in" the one in the same way as in the other, experience the movements of the one in the same way as those of the other. This assertion is not only refuted by its consequences, but it is also an evidently false description. I am not one with the acrobat but only "at" (*bei*) him. I do not actually go through his motions but *quasi*. Lipps also stresses, to be sure, that I do not outwardly go through its motions. But neither is what "inwardly" corresponds to the movements of the body, the experience that "I move", primordial; it is non-primordial for me [. . .]. Thus, strictly speaking, empathy is not a feeling of oneness. (Stein, 1917/1989, pp. 16–17)

For Edith Stein, in the very moment when we are interiorly "with" or "at" (that is, "close to") the living-experience of another "I", *the subject of empathy is "we"*. This relationship between the empathizing "I" and the empathized "you" does *not* eliminate the distinction, but allows *the sharing of what is common* – an "intersubjectivity" [*Wirsubjektivität*] without confusion between *ego* and *alter-ego*. For Lipps, on the contrary, the subject of *unipathy* is the "I", since in order to understand the other one has to *project* onto him/her one's own experiences. When a foreign individual shows him/herself, something very unique happens inside of us, an "instinct" [*Instinkt*] as Lipps calls it (see Lipps, 1903). This instinct pushes us to have feelings that we then project onto the other and attribute to his/her psyche. From a phenomenological point of view, and for Stein, what Lipps is describing is a "*psychic contagion*", not empathy.

4 Conclusion – On the Impossibility of Separating What Is Distinct

Through "empathy" and "perception from within" we become clearer to ourselves by *mirroring each other*. Therefore, *intra*subjective experience is not simply introspection because it cannot take place without *inter*subjectivity. In the logic [*lógos*] of the *Leib,* empathy clearly shows that the meaning of social cognition resides in the impossibility of separating what is distinct. And here in lies the deep sense of the human being as a *complexity* that can by no means be split up. This understanding marks a turn in theories of the human subject that proves the dualism approach has been surpassed (Manganaro, 2012a, 2012b, 2016).

Recently, the discovery of *mirror neurons* seems to have confirmed the phenomenological analysis of intersubjectivity, living body, and empathy on neurophysiological basis (see Gallese, 2003, 2006, 2011; Rizzolati & Sinigaglia, 2006). The intersection of phenomenological philosophy and neurosciences takes place in the dimension of *intentional resonance* or consonance, which Vittorio Gallese and others examine and explain from a neurophysiological point of view (Gallese, 2005). This intersection marks a decisive shift of paradigm. Even when we practice science, we must start from an *embodied perspective*, which rather than excluding the *alter-ego's* living body actually includes it in the shared space of action and experience. Gallagher and Zahavi (2008) show how the results of the phenomenological school have become in some way exemplary for cognitive neuroscience and the *mind-body problem*. Given these developments, the social and interrelated theme of a *common world* has become epistemologically relevant in the experimental and "exact" sciences as well. According to Edith Stein, "we" is the real subject of empathy, where the empathizing and empathized "I" are and remain distinct (though not separate). This is the phenomenological sense of *personal and relational identity*, and it is also the sense of a *research community* understood as "co(mm)-unity".

References

Costa, V. (2010). *Fenomenologia dell'intersoggettività. Empatia, socialità, cultura.* Rome: Carocci.

Costa, V. (2011). *Alterità*. Bologna: Il Mulino.

Dilthey, W. (1883/2006). *Einleitung in die Geisteswissenschaften. Versuch einer Grundlegung für das Studium der Gesellschaft und Geschichte. Gesammelte Schriften* [Introduction to the human sciences. An attempt to lay a foundation for the study of society and history. Collected works] (vol. 1). Göttingen: Vandenhoeck & Ruprecht.

Gallagher, S. & Zahavi, D. (2008). *The Phenomenological Mind. An Introduction to philosophy of Mind and Cognitive Science*. New York: Routledge.

Gallese, V. (2003). The roots of empathy: the shared manifold hypothesis and the neural basis of intersubjectivity. *Psychopathology*, *4*, 24–47.

Gallese, V. (2005). Embodied simulation: from neurons to phenomenal experience. *Phenomenology and Cognitive Science*, *4*, 23–48.

Gallese, V. (2006). Corpo vivo, simulazione incarnata e intersoggettività. In M. Cappuccio (Ed.). *Neurofenomenologia. Le scienze della mente e la sfida dell'esperienza coscient* (pp. 293–326). Milan: Bruno Mondadori.

Gallese, V. (2011). Neuroscience and Phenomenology. *Phenomenology & Mind*, *1*, 33–48.

Husserl, E. (1913/1952). *Phänomenologische Untersuchungen zur Konstitution. Ideen zu einer reinen Phänomenologie und phänomenologischen Philosophie* [Phenomenological Investigations on Constitution, Ideas Pertaining to a Pure Phenomenology and to a Phenomenological Philosophy] (vol. 2). Dordrecht: Kluwer Academy Publisher

Husserl, E. (1913/1989). *Phenomenological Investigations on Constitution. Ideas Pertaining to a Pure Phenomenology and to a Phenomenological Philosophy* (vol. 2, R. Rojcewicz & A. Schuwer, Trans.). Dordrecht: Kluwer Academic Publisher.

Husserl, E. (1923–24/2007) *Erste Philosophie. Zweiter Teil: Theorie der Phänomenologischen Reduktion*, Husserliana, vol. 8, Den Haag: Martinus Nijhoff Publisher; transl. it. by A. Staiti, *Filosofia prima. Teoria della riduzione fenomenologica*, introduzione e cura di V. Costa, Soveria Mannelli: Rubbettino.

Husserl, E. (1923–35/1973) *Zur Phänomenologie der Intersubjektivität*, Husserliana, vol. 13–15, The Hague: Martinus Nijhoff Publisher.

Husserl, E. (1929/1950). *Cartesianische Meditationen und Pariser Vorträge* [Cartesian meditations and Paris lectures]. Dordrecht: Kluwer Academy Publisher.

Lipps, Th. (1903). Einfühlung, innere Nachahmung und Organempfindungen [Empathy, inner imitation, and organic sensations]. *Archiv für die gesamte Psychologie, 1*(2–3), 185–204.

Lipps, Th. (1903–06). *Ästhetik: Psychologie des Schönen und der Kunst* [Aesthetics: The psychology of beauty and art]. Hamburg, Leipzig: L. Voss.

Manganaro, P. (2001). 'L'Einfühlung nell'analisi fenomenologica di Edith Stein. Una fondazione filosofica dell'alterità personale. *Aquinas, 1*, 101–121.

Manganaro, P. (2007). Einfühlung e Mind-Body Problem. Dalla svolta linguistica alla svolta cognitiva. *Aquinas, 2*, 465–494.

Manganaro, P. (2010a). Phenomenology and Neuroscience. Living Experience, Empathy and Embodied simulation. *Comprendre. Archive International pour l'Anthropologie et la Psychopathologie Phénoménologiques, 20*, 153–165.

Manganaro, P. (2010b). Sull'impossibilità di separare i distinti. L'armonia nel pensiero di Edith Stein. *Aquinas, 2–3*, 661–668.

Manganaro, P. (2012a). Materia (l) Mente? Le 'ragioni' del corpo e l'empatia. In A. Ales Bello & P. Manganaro (Eds.) ... *e la coscienza? Fenomenologia, Psico-patologia, Neuroscienze* (pp. 241–377). Bari: G. Laterza.

Manganaro, P. (2012b). L'oltre fenomenologico delle neuroscienze. Una via post-moderna al problema difficile della coscienza? *Filosofia e Teologia, 1*, 42–60.

Manganaro, P. (2013) 'Il sentire empatico e l'epistemologia della complessità', *Comprendre. Archive International pour l'Anthropologie et la Psychopathologie Phénoménologiques*, 23, 143–68.

Manganaro, P. (2014). *Empatia*. Padova: EMP.

Manganaro, P. (2015). Materia, mente, coscienza. Fenomenologia e Neurosienze: status quaestionis. In R. Lanfredini (Ed.). *Materia* (pp. 113–132). Sesto S. Giovanni: Mimesis.
Manganaro, P. (2016). *Fenomenologia da Relaçao. A Pessoa Humana em Edith Stein*. Curitiba (Brasil): Juruá.
Pinotti, A. (2011). *Empatia. Storia di un'idea da Platone al post-umano*. Rome-Bari: Laterza.
Rizzolatti, G., & Sinigaglia, C. (2006). *So quel che fai. Il cervello che agisce e i neuroni specchio*. Milan: Raffaello Cortina.
Scheler, M. (1913). *Zur Phänomenologie und Theorie der Sympathiegefühle und von Liebe und Haß* [Phenomenology and theory of the feeling of sympathy and of love and hate]. Halle: Niemeyer.
Scheler, M. (1923). *Wesen und Formen der Sympathie* [The nature of sympathy]. Bonn: Cohen.
Simmel, G. (1918/2000). Vom Wesen des historischen Verstehens [On the nature of historical understanding]. In *Der Krieg und die geistigne Entscheidungen. Grundfragen der Soziologie. Der Konflikt der modernen Kultur* [The war and spiritual decisions. Fundamental questions of sociology. The conflict in modern culture] (pp. 151–79). Frankfurt/Main: Suhrkamp.
Simmel, G. (1971). *On Individual and Social Forms. Selected Writings*. Chicago: The University of Chicago Press.
Stein, E. (1917). *Zum Problem der Einfühlung*. Halle: Buchdruckerei des Waisenhauses.
Stein, E. (1917/1989). *On the Problem of Empathy*. The Collected Works of Edith *Stein* (vol. 3, 3rd revised ed., W. Stein, Trans.). Washington, D.C.: ICS Publications.
Stein, E. (1917/2008). *Zum Problem der Einfühlung, Edith Stein Gesamtausgabe* [On the problem of empathy. The collected works of Edith Stein] (vol. 5, introd. and ed. by M. A. Sondermann OCD). Freiburg im Breisgau: Herder.
Stein, E. (1922/1970). *Beiträge zur philosophischen Begründung der Psychologie und der Geisteswissenschaften* [Contributions to the philosophical foundations of psychology and the human sciences] (2nd ed.). Tübingen: Max Niemeyer Verlag.
Stein, E. (1932–33/2004). *Der Aufbau der menschlichen Person. Vorlesung zur philosophischen Anthropologie.* Edith Stein *Gesamtausgabe* [The structure of the human person. Lectures on philosophical anthropology. The collected works of Edith Stein] (vol. 14). Freiburg et al.: Verlag Herder.

12

Empathy's Translations: Three Paths from *Einfühlung* into Anglo-American Psychology

Susan Lanzoni

In 1945, the social psychologist Gordon Allport lamented the narrow scope of the Americanized notion of empathy:

> *Empathy* arrived in a portmanteau packed in Munich. It was embedded in a whole self-psychology and in an epistemology of *Wissen von fremden Ichen*. Everything went into the ash can save only a greatly oversimplified version of what Lipps originally intended. *Motor mimicry* was all we wanted. What would we be doing with a "mental act that held a guarantee of the objectivity of our knowledge?" (Allport, 1945, p. 118)[1]

Allport was right to note that the complex psychological, epistemological, and aesthetic phenomenon of *Einfühlung*, debated by a generation of German psychologists and philosophers, had become a simple motor

[1] Allport's exposure to *Einfühlung* theory guided him to his own holistic version of personality and social psychology.

S. Lanzoni (✉)
Department of Continuing Education, Harvard University, Cambridge, MA, USA
e-mail: smlanzoni@gmail.com

V. Lux, S. Weigel (eds.), *Empathy*, Palgrave Studies in the Theory and History of Psychology, DOI 10.1057/978-1-137-51299-4_12

imitation for American psychologists by mid-century. Already by the 1920s, American psychologists had been moving towards behaviourism, and were less interested in the rich philosophical and epistemological meanings that had circulated around *Einfühlung*.

As a vaunted aesthetic theory in Germany, *Einfühlung* theory was debated beginning in 1866 by Friedrich Theodor Vischer and his son, Robert Vischer, although its roots extend to Arthur Schopenhauer and Hermann Lotze (Mallgrave & Ikonomou, 1994, p. 20; Vischer, 1873/1994). Robert Vischer described *Einfühlung* as a process of projecting both body and soul into the inner structure or the form of an object; one might feel expansiveness or mental breadth whilst encountering a large form or perceive a cliff as standing at attention and defiant (Vischer, 1873/1994, p. 92, 105). It was most famously depicted by the Munich psychologist and philosopher Theodor Lipps as pleasure objectified or experienced in the object of contemplation itself (Lipps, 1903/1923, 1906/1920; see Allesch, 1987; Jarzombek, 2000; Koss, 2006, Jahoda, 2005). Lipps declared *Einfühlung* the *sine qua non* of aesthetic experience, but he also extended the remit of *Einfühlung* to nature, common objects, and the expressions of others.[2] *Einfühlung* was also closely associated with Dilthey's aesthetic psychological methods of re-experiencing [*Nacherleben*] or putting oneself in the position of another [*sich hineinversetzen*], and *Einfühlung* theory has been called a form of phenomenology *avant la lettre* (Barasch, 1998, p. 117; Friedrich & Gleiter, 2007, p. 9).[3]

[2] Lipps described the forms of *Einfühlung* as general apperceptive *Einfühlung* for common objects; empirical *Einfühlung* of nature; mood *Einfühlung*, and *Einfühlung* with others, achieved through the sensory perception of living beings. See Lipps (1903, Chapter 14, "Die Einfühlung", pp. 187–202). For a definition of aesthetic *Einfühlung* as an unmediated experience in which one's own feelings are experienced in the aesthetic object, see Lipps (1902, p. 368). See also (Lipps, 1903/1960).

[3] Dilthey's 1894 outline of a *verstehende* psychology, or a descriptive psychology in contrast to an explanatory or causal psychology included psychological and historical methods of transferring one's self into expressions of another's life as a way of re-experiencing, a *sich hineinversetzen* (similar to *Einfühlung*) (see Dilthey, 1894/1977; see also Makkreel; 2000; Ringer, 1969, pp. 81–127). Thomas Friedrich and Jörg Gleiter argue that *Einfühlungsästhetik*, as it emerged in the work of the Vischers, found aesthetics to be a special case of everyday sensory experience – a way of perceiving the expressive and soulful content of objects. *Einfühlungsästhetik* also influenced architectural theories of the embodiment of space, exemplified in Heinrich Wölfflin's *Prolegomena zu einer Psychologie der Architektur* (1886) and August Schmarsow's *Über den Werth der Dimensionen im menschlichen Raumgebilde* (1896), both reprinted in Friedrich & Gleiter (2007).

For aestheticians, *Einfühlung* meant "feeling into" art objects and the natural world, or sensing or importing movement into these experiences. But was this process based on a kinaesthetic sense, an inner muscular imitation, an imaginative capacity, or the self's projection into an object or another person? Could the possibility of *Einfühlung* create a higher unity of subject and object, affect and cognition? And significantly for this chapter, how did Anglophone psychologists incorporate, translate, and adapt *Einfühlung* in the first decades of the twentieth century?

1 Translational Paths of *Einfühlung* into Anglo-American Psychology

Einfühlung made the journey into Anglo-American psychology along different paths as initial attempts to systematize and standardize its meaning failed. In 1902, the American psychologist James Mark Baldwin, editor of the comprehensive *Dictionary of Psychology and Philosophy*, noted that no consensus had been reached on the translation, so the loose rendering of "aesthetic sympathy" was adopted. "Empathy" first appeared as a translation of the German *Einfühlung* sometime in 1908, in concurrent, but also divergent translations by Edward B. Titchener, the British psychologist based at Cornell University, and James Ward, the Cambridge trained psychologist at Trinity College.[4] The adoption of this new term reflected the growing importance of the concept to academic psychology in the Anglophone world, but also showcased its polysemy – "empathy" possessed multiple meanings.

[4] The English "empathy" did appear a few years earlier, in 1895 – but not as a translation of *Einfühlung*. It was an energy concept described by E. L. Hinman in his review of a paper written by K. Lasswitz, *Ueber psychophysische Energie und ihre Factoren* ["On Psychophysical Energy and Its Factors"]. He writes, "For the capacity factor of psychophysical energy the name 'empathy' is proposed. Empathy is then a physical quantity, a physiological brain-function, and is defined as the relation of the whole energy at any change of the central organ to the intensity" (Hinman, 1895, p. 673). For details on the initial translation of *Einfühlung* as "enpathy" and its correction in the pages of *The Philosophical Review* in November 1908, see Lanzoni (2012b).

This chapter tracks three directions of *Einfühlung*'s translational paths into Anglo-American scientific psychology beginning with Baldwin's psychology of child's play and the imaginary, moving to experimental introspection and kinaesthetic imagery practiced at the Cornell laboratory, and concluding with Ward's anthropological notion of empathy as personification and animation.

In 1902, James Mark Baldwin sought an acceptable translation for *Einfühlung* for his *Psychological Dictionary*, offering his own translation, "semblance". "Semblance" showcased the connection to play and aesthetic experience, but also stood as a pillar to Baldwin's genetic or developmental epistemology. Children engaged in semblant activity during pretend play, but a similar kind of "as-if" thinking was integral to a higher developmental stage, what Baldwin called the hyperlogical aesthetic stage, in which the distinctions between subject and object were blurred.

Edward B. Titchener, head of the Cornell psychological laboratory minimized *Einfühlung*'s aesthetic significance and identified empathy's basic mental constituent as the kinaesthetic image or an image of movement. He offered his translation of "empathy" sometime in mid-late 1908. Not long afterwards, subjects in his laboratory began to report "empathic kinaestheses" in their introspections, described as imagined bodily feelings of merging with or moving into the experimental stimuli (see Lanzoni, 2012b).

James Ward, based at Trinity College, also suggested the term "empathy" for *Einfühlung* around 1908. He construed it in a mythic or anthropological sense. Ward was a member of an informal anthropological circle of scholars from Cambridge, along with his close friend, the social anthropologist James G. Frazer. Ward explained to Frazer that empathy was akin to a process of personification. It was familiar in mythic and symbolic thinking, but Ward emphasized that it was also common in everyday experience. Ward linked empathy to his evolutionary model of the continuity of conscious life and to his philosophical view that mind permeated nature.

Baldwin's "semblance", linking child's play to its more advanced form of aesthetic appreciation, did not transfer into American psychology in part due to a personal scandal that caused Baldwin to resign his academic post, followed by his expatriation to Paris in 1909. Ward did not use "empathy" regularly in his writings, but highlighted its anthropomorphic meanings, sharing in the popular Anglo-American view of the time that mind extended through nature (Skrbina, 2005). Titchener's emphasis on kinaesthesis was adopted by art psychologists Kate Gordon (Gordon, 1934), Vernon Lee (syn. Violet Paget) (Lee & Anstruther-Thomson, 1897, 1912), Herbert Langfeld (Langfeld, 1920/1967), and Robert Ogden (Ogden, 1909; 1938); it became the most frequent designation of "empathy" in these years. The new term "empathy" had stuck by around 1913, and Baldwin reluctantly adopted it as the preferred translation. Over the next decades, empathy came most often to denote motor mimicry, especially for behaviourist psychologists, who would eventually dominate American psychology. By the post-World War II years, "empathy" lost its connection with things, nature, and the inanimate world and became almost exclusively an interpersonal form of identification, imitation, and understanding.[5]

At the turn of the twentieth century, however, the first tentative translations of *Einfühlung* from "aesthetic sympathy" to "semblance" to "empathy" stressed the mental qualities of movement, emotion, and the imagination. These early formulations comprise an integral part of empathy's complex genealogy. It is therefore not surprising to see some aspects of these early conceptions re-emerge in recent accounts of empathy, from simulation theories to mirror neuron theory to neuroaesthetics, while other meanings have yet to be revived.

2 James Mark Baldwin and the "Semblant"

This story begins at the fin-de-siècle with the psychologist James Mark Baldwin who took up the enormous task of standardizing psychological nomenclature, calling upon the expertise and collaboration of sixty colleagues from the overlapping fields of psychology and philosophy. This

[5] See Chapter 10: Andrea Pinotti, on the history of empathy with inanimate objects, in this volume. See also Pinotti (2010).

project resulted in the publication of the *Dictionary of Philosophy and Psychology* between the years 1901 and 1905, often called "Baldwin's Dictionary" (Wozniak & Santiago-Blay, 2013). As one of the promulgators of the new evolutionary psychology, Baldwin also helped found the *Psychological Review* with James McKeen Cattell in 1894, and became Professor of Psychology and Philosophy at Johns Hopkins in 1903.[6]

Baldwin completed his undergraduate years at Princeton with close advising from University President James McCosh, where he earned a traveling fellowship that took him to Germany. He trained in experimental psychology at Leipzig with Wilhelm Wundt as did most American psychologists of the period, and read Spinoza before returning to Princeton to earn his doctorate. In 1889, he obtained a position at the University of Toronto, where he set up a psychological laboratory. Baldwin is remembered in the eponymously named "Baldwin effect", an evolutionary principle of organic selection that describes individual adaptations and learned behaviour that sufficed to keep individuals alive, adaptations that he believed would eventually be passed on through natural selection.[7]

Baldwin began work on the *Dictionary* in 1898, listing English equivalents and translations for a number of French, German, and Italian psychological and philosophical terms. He was convinced that a new language was necessary for the new science of the mind – psychology – because the older nineteenth-century terms, "soul, reason, cause, creation, vital force", evoked metaphysical and ontological notions and were thus problematic (Baldwin, 1930, p. 26). Strategies for developing a new psychological language ranged from William James's attempt to retool familiar terms for the purposes of the new science to the logician Charles Peirce's call for "a clear and consistent terminology for the mental and moral sciences as had been done for mathematics and symbolic logic" (Baldwin, 1930, p. 26). Baldwin sought a middle ground between the adaptation of the older terminology to the new

---

[6] For biographical information on Baldwin, see Baldwin (1930) and Sokal (1997).

[7] For more on the Baldwin effect and on Baldwin's legacy in psychology, see Wozniak (2004, 2009a) and Richards (1987).

discipline and a whole-scale invention of neologisms. He was convinced that the confusion in the growing field was due in good part to the "lack of well-defined terms", and thought that the *Dictionary* would help forge a professional consensus.

There was, however, no agreement on the translation of *Einfühlung*. Baldwin reported in 1906 that the "committee of the *Dict. of Philos*. failed to find any available term for *Einfühlung*" (Baldwin, 1906/1975a, p. 122). The loose translation "aesthetic sympathy" was offered as a substitute in an entry authored by Baldwin himself. As a collaborative venture, the *Dictionary* demonstrated agreement between multiple psychologists on a given translation by posting their initials at the end of an entry. The translation "aesthetic sympathy" boasted the initials of Wilbur M. Urban (WMU), Baldwin's former student at Princeton and a philosopher at Ursinus College, and E. B. Titchener (EBT), already at Cornell and director of its psychological laboratory. The entry also includes a competing translation: "animation", which to some more accurately rendered the word *Beseelung*, Lipps' synonym for *Einfühlung*. To underline the multiple meanings of *Einfühlung*, the German psychologist Karl Groos complains in an addendum to the entry that the localization of feeling (either in oneself or in the object) was confused in Lipps' theory of *Einfühlung* (Baldwin, 1901–05, p. 679). This entry echoes the contentious voices of psychologists, reflecting not only the lack of agreement on possible translations, but also on the meaning and scope of *Einfühlung*.

Once the *Dictionary* was completed, Baldwin moved on to other projects, in particular a dense four-volume work on genetic (or developmental) logic, entitled *Thought and Things*, the first volume of which was published in 1906 and the final volume, *The Genetic Theory of Reality*, in 1915.[8] In these volumes, Baldwin outlined the scope of his genetic theory of knowledge, beginning with the prelogical modes of the child, progressing into a logical phase, and culminating in a hyperlogical stage. Baldwin stressed the importance of the play sensibility throughout

[8] Volume 1 was entitled *Functional Logic, or Genetic Theory of Knowledge* (1906/1975a), Volume 2 *Experimental Logic, or Genetic Theory of Thought* (1908/1975b), Volume 3 *Interest and Art Being Real Logic. I Genetic Epistemology* (1911/1975c), and Volume 4 *The Genetic Theory of Reality* (1915/1975d). See also Wozniak (1998).

the lifespan: child's play in the prelogical phase transmuted into aesthetic appreciation in the hyperlogical phase. Here, he drew on the writings of German philosopher and psychologist Karl Groos on play, inner imitation, and illusion in animals and children. Baldwin and his wife Elizabeth Baldwin collaborated with Groos to bring his work to English audiences, with Elizabeth's translation, and Baldwin's preface and commentary (Groos, 1901).

For Baldwin, the play ability was best described as "semblance" or the "semblant", terms that he suggests as an apt translation of *Einfühlung* in *Thoughts and Things* (Baldwin, 1906/1975a, p. 122). Already in 1902, in the second volume of the *Dictionary*, he had defined "semblant" as a form of inner imitation with a cross-reference to the entry "Sympathy (aesthetic)", as

> the indulgence in the temporary acceptance of a mental construction as real, with the knowledge, at the same time, that it is not. This is characteristic of much play and art enjoyment; one feature of which is that it throws the observer into a voluntary treatment of an artificial situation as real. Cf. Sympathy (aesthetic). (Baldwin, 1901–05, p. 549)

"To semble" is defined as "to make like by imitation", and Baldwin remarked that after the committee had failed to find a good translation for *Einfühlung*, "the rendering here made has since then occurred to me" (Baldwin, 1906/1975a, p. 122). Sometime around 1902, then, Baldwin generated his own translation of *Einfühlung* as semblance, even as the accepted translation of *Einfühlung* in his *Dictionary* was "aesthetic sympathy" or "inner sympathy".

Semblance was in his view a form of play in the early stage of child development based on a child's inner freedom to create a make-believe situation against the backdrop of the real world: "The play object becomes not the inner or fancy [imaginative] object as such, nor yet the outer present object as such, but both at once, what we are calling the semblant object" (Baldwin, 1906/1975a, p. 116).[9] He also called it

[9] He labelled the play instinct the "lower semblant" (Baldwin, 1911/1975c, part IV, "Semblance and the Aesthetic", p. 157).

an "experimental object", as it is partly under the control and manipulation of the child. Semblance interwove the imagination with objects in the actual world:

> Broadly understood, the process of "sembling" consists in the reading into the object of a sort of psychic life of its own, in such a way that the movement, act, or character by which it is interpreted is thought of as springing from its own inner life. We have considered it as showing the psychic tendency to consider the object as detached from the external, and thus as under inner or subjective control. This leads to the thought of the object as itself having inner control or a spring of action and initiation – in short, a psychic life – of its own. (Baldwin, 1906/1975a, p. 124)

Sembling or *Einfühlung* remakes the object in line with the feelings of the perceiver through a process of inner imitation: "There is a certain feeling-into the given object (*Einfühlung*), now made semblant, of the subject's own personal feeling: an attribution to it of the inner movement which its construction requires" (Baldwin, 1906/1975a, p. 122). The object is subjectivized and seems to possess its own inner life. Sometimes this process results in personification – seeing the object as a person or a sentient being – a primitive notion of semblance. It could also be described as "personalizing", or reshaping an object for personal purposes – "*what it might be*" (Baldwin, 1906/1975a, p. 124).

Semblance not only concerned child's play for Baldwin, but was also regarded as a critical feature of art and aesthetics at higher developmental stages. Art differed from play because play had no inherent restrictions, whereas the semblance of art idealized the object. But both play and art were connected by the notion of the "as if actual", meaning that both were suggestive of reality, but not actual reality. As Baldwin puts it in his third volume of *Thought and Things*: "The aesthetic interest presumes a modicum of suggested actuality, existence, reality, truth." (Baldwin, 1911/1975c, p. 162) This meant that art, like play, makes reference to a realistic situation. Therefore, the abstractions of the "mere ink-spot or the mere noisy crash – loses interest, whether in play or in art" because they do not possess the quality of semblance (Baldwin, 1911/1975c, p. 159).

If semblance was central to Baldwin's developmental theories, his translation never became popular with Anglo-American psychologists. Baldwin's student, Wilbur Urban dedicated his book on *Valuation: Its Nature and Laws* to Baldwin, but saw semblance as only "one stage of the total process" and not broad enough to cover the full range of *Einfühlung* (Urban, 1909, p. 235, fn 1).[10] But the most significant reason Baldwin's work was overlooked is undoubtedly due to the scandal resulting from Baldwin's visit to an African-American brothel and his subsequent arrest. He was forced to resign from Johns Hopkins in 1909, and quickly relocated to Paris (Wozniak & Santiago-Blay, 2013). His direct influence on American psychology declined tremendously. There is some evidence, however, that his developmental theories influenced the psychologists Jean Piaget and Lev Vygotsky (Cahan, 1984; Wozniak, 2009b).

With regard to the translation of *Einfühlung*, Baldwin reported in 1911: "Both Titchener and Ward have suggested 'empathy' as the English translation of *Einfühlung*." (Baldwin, 1911/1975c, p. 167) He repeated this claim in his 1913 *History of Psychology* (Baldwin, 1913, p. 151).[11] Ward is also duly credited with the translation by a number of his contemporaries in Britain. Because Baldwin did not elaborate on the provenance of these translations, it remains unclear whether Titchener and Ward suggested the term independently or in concert. As contributing editors to the journal *Mind*, Titchener and Ward might have discussed the translation together, perhaps during Ward's 1904 visit to Cornell.[12] Historical accounts of the

[10] Urban preferred the German *Einfühlung*: "We shall accordingly use the term to designate the entire process (projection, imitation, and ejection) involved in the activities of characterisation and participation, and shall consider it, more over, in its aspect of affective-conative process" (Urban, 1909, p. 235).

[11] In this book he uses "semblance" and "empathy" as synonyms.

[12] The title page of the journal *Mind*, for October 1908 reads: "Mind, a quarterly review of Psychology and Philosophy, edited by Professor G. F. Stout, with the co-operation of E. B. Titchener, American Editorial Representative, and of Dr. E. Caird, Professor Ward, Professor Pringle-Pattison, and other members of an advisory committee." In this volume, "empathy" is mentioned in the "Philosophical Periodicals" section: "We attain to consciousness of the existence of beings analogous to ourselves by way of empathy, which is based mainly upon the impulse to imitation; we communicate and understand ideas by the gradual

provenance of the term "empathy" only credit Edward B. Titchener with the translation, which he printed in his 1909 book, *Experimental Psychology of the Thought Processes* (Wispé, 1987). Titchener sent Baldwin a copy of this book in 1910, after Baldwin had left his post at Johns Hopkins and had begun his expatriate life in Paris.[13] But both Titchener and Ward had already suggested the term in 1908.

Baldwin eventually conceded that "empathy" had become the accepted term, but continued to doubt its usefulness, underlining the "great confusion" on *Einfühlung* in the German literature. In 1911, he advised waiting until there was consensus on the overall concept, before finding a proper English equivalent. He nonetheless began to use "empathy" more frequently, noting that it was closely connected to his own notion of "semblant". He pointed out that a reversion to the German *Einfühlung* would be useless, as it was equivalent to "animism". In a final bid to retain both the terms "semblant" and "empathy", he suggested that empathy is "the best term for the strictly aesthetic movement", whereas it would be best for a "more general word such as 'semblance' being used for the entire group of analogous imaginative processes" (Baldwin, 1913, p. 152).

Baldwin continued to use his favoured term, semblant, along with empathy in his final 1915 volume on development, *The Genetic Theory of Reality*. Semblance had, in fact, become an integral feature of his entire epistemology. Baldwin saw aesthetic experience as the highest and most integrative experience, one far beyond the immature stage of mere play, but also beyond the strict differentiations of logical thinking. In formulating what he called this pancalist view, Baldwin drew on Aristotle, Kant, and Schelling, as well as on his contemporaries,

growth of the speech-function" (*Mind*, Oct. 1908, p. 593). It is unclear who wrote these periodical sections, as both Ward and Titchener were editorial contributors. Titchener had been paid for writing on periodicals in the journal in the 1890s, evidenced by Stout's letter of thanks to Titchener for penning "fresh Notices of Periodicals" (G.F. Stout to Titchener, May 17, 1894. E. B. Titchener Archive, Cornell University Special Collections). Ward thanks Titchener for his visit in a letter (Ward to Titchener, November 28, 1904, E. B. Titchener Archive 14/23/545).

[13] Baldwin to Titchener, March 10, 1910; E. B. Titchener Archive 14/23/545 Box 2.

Theodor Lipps and Theodule Ribot. Pancalism centred on aesthetic feeling, as he explained: "Feeling finds in the artistic or semblant imagination its instrument as organ of a genuine appreciation of the real" (Baldwin, 1917, p. 599).

The aesthetic or hyperlogical way of knowing the world was, according to Baldwin, the most integrated, encompassing, and balanced. It was achieved through *Einfühlung* or semblance, which bridged mind and matter, affect and cognition, truth and value. By imagining or controlling the inner life of objects, one engaged in the highest synthetic and unified activity. This aesthetic knowing mended the breach between subject and object. Baldwin elaborated on this process, which he called "empathy" in 1915:

> The object is not merely presented to me for my observation or criticism; but in it I find the inner world mirrored; in it I feel my own cognitive and active powers establishing themselves. It is not a world foreign to my own life; for in this world, presently semblantly to my gaze, I find realized my community with other selves. (Baldwin, 1911/1975c, p. 240)

Baldwin dedicated the final volume in his developmental schema to "All those who find in Art the noblest instrument of the spiritual life" (Baldwin, 1911/1975c, p. iv). Even if "semblance" was never adopted by his colleagues, its meaning, enclosed within the term "empathy" had become the apotheosis of his genetic or developmental logic.[14]

[14] Although Baldwin's genetic logic was not of great influence in the United States, Wilbur Urban discussed Baldwin's ideas at Trinity College in Hartford, Connecticut. Urban preferred his own translations of "sympathetic participation" or "affective projection", although he did invoke "empathy" when he analysed how it was "through sympathetic projection of my *own* feeling, I may apprehend the inner life of others, how subjective feeling in me may become the bearer of an objective meaning and reference". To him, feelings had a cognitive character: "feelings have as their presuppositions judgments and assumptions" (Urban, 1917, p, 281).

3 The Kinaesthetic Image, Empathy, and Laboratory Introspection

While Baldwin linked semblance to aesthetic experience, Titchener catalogued "empathy" according to its constitutive elements, discovered through introspection. Titchener was one of the foremost practitioners of structural psychology in North America, and served as director of the Cornell laboratory from 1892 until his death in 1927 (Evans, 1990; Heidbreder, 1933). He studied classics at Oxford, then physiological psychology in Leipzig with Wilhelm Wundt. He was an editor of the *American Journal of Psychology* (with G. Stanley Hall and E. C. Sanford), took over sole editorship in 1921, and served as one of the American editors of the British journal *Mind*. Although his method of pinpointing the elemental structures of the mind faded around the time of World War I with the rise of behaviourist methods and applied psychology, for many years his laboratory methods were standard practice for experimental psychologists (Evans, 1990, pp. 30–32; Hindeland, 1971).

Titchener defined empathy according to his structural psychology as an imagined kinaesthetic entry into various stimulus objects through the mind's capacity to form a kinaesthetic image. Just as the mind housed visual or auditory images, so too could it construct moving images of one's own body, or of other bodies, objects, or elements of nature (See Titchener, 1904). Drawing on these meanings of *Einfühlung* that exemplified movement, striving, or muscular imitation, introspective observers at the Cornell laboratory reported empathy as a manner of imaginative moving into or merging with objects and situations.

Titchener introduced his translation in a series of public lectures held at the University of Illinois at Urbana in March 1909. He argued that complex or "higher" forms of thought such as surprise, expectation, and familiarity, which psychologists at Würzburg claimed were *sui generis*, could in fact be reduced to more elementary sensations, images, and affects (Titchener, 1908, p. 8; Brock, 1991; Kusch, 1999). Titchener declared that the psychologists at the Würzburg laboratory headed by Oswald Külpe, had failed to notice kinaesthetic elements in their thought processes, and thus had erroneously claimed that thought was possible without images.

Titchener declared that the mind was populated by images. He explains, for example, that the verbal description "stately" is, for him, composed of the visual image of a heroine – a tall figure with a hand holding up a steely grey skirt (Titchener, 1909a, p. 13). Just as one could visualize the heroine, one could also kinaesthetically form an image of her movements. The kinaesthetic image of bodily movement read into a situation, object, or stimulus comprises the essence of his understanding of "empathy". In an oft-cited passage, Titchener elaborates, "Not only do I see gravity and modesty and pride and courtesy and stateliness, but I feel or act them in the mind's muscles. This is, I suppose, a simple case of empathy, if we may coin that term as a rendering of *Einfühlung*" (Titchener, 1909a, p. 21).[15]

Once Titchener defined the kinaesthetic image as the core of empathic response, empathic kinaesthetic images began to emerge in introspective reports made by "observers" (or experimental subjects) in a series of studies on belief, conscious attitudes, imagination, and meaning conducted at the Cornell laboratory (Perky, 1910; Rogers, 1917). "Observers" in these early psychological laboratories were graduate students, professors, and laboratory assistants, all highly trained to report on the elementary bits of their thought processes (Danziger, 1990). In laboratory spaces and dark rooms, they fixated lights, watched shadowy shapes appear from projected lantern slides, and narrowed their attention while being prompted verbally or visually with a stimulus word or image. Respiration was measured with a kymograph; responses were timed with a chronometer. Extended introspections or catalogues of the stream of thoughts, feelings, and sensations that took place during an experimental session were carefully recorded. Observers were trained to use the language of descriptive

[15] Titchener's conception of the kinaesthetic image was adapted by Vernon Lee (Violet Paget) to explain aesthetic empathy of the formal-dynamic type (Lee & Anstruther-Thompson, 1912, p. 148; see Lanzoni, 2009).

science to report the perceived colors, images, shapes, and tones of the stimulus object, rather than casually describe the object itself, which would mean falling into the "stimulus error" (Titchener, 1909a; pp. 145–146; see also Henle, 1971; Kroker, 2003).

Kinaesthetic images were sometimes attributed directly to the stimuli, sometimes identified with the observer's own body image, and other times reported as startling images of a bodily fusion or confusion between one's self and the stimuli (Okabe, 1910). In a 1910 study of belief conducted by Titchener's doctoral student Tamekichi Okabe, another student Alma De Vries reported an empathic kinaesthetic response to a "visual image of a trick elephant dancing. Felt big and clumsy myself, as if I were the elephant" (Okabe, 1910, pp. 568–569). A frequent participant in imagery studies in the Cornell laboratory, De Vries earned her doctorate in 1912 and went on to study retinal afterimages with Margaret Washburn at Vassar (Schaub, 1911). She is described in a study by Clarke as having mixed responses to stimuli, including visual, tactual, and verbal images, feelings, and kinaesthetic and organic sensations (Clarke, 1911, p. 216). Another instructor of psychology at Cornell, L. R. Geissler also reported empathic-kinaesthetic responses. While listening to a sentence about drinking alcohol, he records the following empathic-kinaesthetic image:

> [T]here was a very vague, kinaesthetic and motor attitude, representing a woman of the total-abstainer kind, with disgust for drunkards, turning away her face and head and wrinkling her forehead: these things seemed to occur in my own case (feeling of disgust, tendency to turn head and wrinkle forehead). (Okabe, 1910, p. 589)

In this report, an empathic response is described as an imagined bodily imitation.

At the Cornell psychological laboratory, then, empathy brought the scientific observer into the interior life of stimulus objects by means of the kinaesthetic image, a basic mental structure. Whereas Baldwin hewed more closely to the aesthetic character of *Einfühlung/*

semblance, for Titchener, empathy was a broad imaginative kinaesthesis that could be called upon in a variety of circumstances.[16]

4 James Ward and "Personification"

In 1915, the psychologist James Ward at Trinity College at the University of Cambridge, wrote to his close friend, the anthropologist James Frazer, to say that there were affinities between Frazer's conception of personification and what German psychologists called *Einfühlung*. He informed Frazer that he had purposed to translate the German term as "empathy". Demonstrating the close alliance of this new term with sympathy, the typescript reads "sympathy", but directly over the letters "sy" Ward printed the letter "e" as a correction (see Fig. 12.1), evidencing his deliberate choice of the new word "empathy".[17]

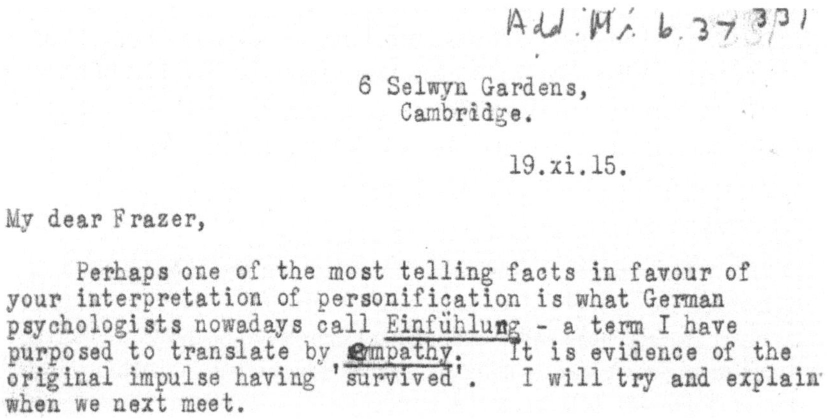

6 Selwyn Gardens,
Cambridge.

19.xi.15.

My dear Frazer,

Perhaps one of the most telling facts in favour of your interpretation of personification is what German psychologists nowadays call Einfühlung - a term I have purposed to translate by empathy. It is evidence of the original impulse having 'survived'. I will try and explain when we next meet.

Fig. 12.1 Letter to Frazer, 1915

[16] Titchener alluded to aesthetic *Einfühlung* theory in 1899 when he spoke of aesthetic sentiments as "one's own emotions, projected into other people or into external nature, and refound there by one's active attention" (Titchener, 1916, p. 330). For more on Titchener's view of empathy see Titchener (1909a, 1910, 1915).

[17] Ward to James Frazer, Nov. 11, 1915 (Add. Ms. b. 37/331), Trinity College Library Master and Fellows of Trinity College Cambridge.

Aside from Ward's own claim that he purposed the translation, others attest to his role in suggesting this new English term. For example, his colleague Charles S. Myers made a similar claim in early 1909 in his textbook on experimental psychology. Explicating Lipps' account, Myers defines *Einfühlung* as "living into" the experience of the object or a process by which "the subject feels in himself the suggestions of strain, movement or rest in the object, and makes them part of himself". He then goes on to use empathy as a translation of *Einfühlung*, commenting in a footnote, "Professor James Ward suggests to me this convenient translation of the German *Einfühlung*." (Myers, 1909, p. 331) In addition to Myers' footnote, the lecturer at St. Andrews, R. F. Hoernle, credited Ward with the translation, along with Ward's student Charles Valentine, and also the psychologist Charles Spearman, who reviewed Myers' textbook in the journal *Mind*.[18]

James Ward was one of the first psychologists in England to embrace physiological principles. After abandoning his post as a congregational minister after only a year, he turned to the study of psychology (Turner, 1974, p. 206). Ward received a scholarship and then a fellowship to study the moral sciences at Trinity College at the University of Cambridge, England, where he wrote a dissertation on the relation of physiology to psychology.[19] He also studied in Carl Ludwig's physiological laboratory in Leipzig and conducted experiments on crayfish in Michael Foster's laboratory (Ward, 1927, pp. 68–72). Ward's exposure to the study of physiology in Germany together with Hermann Lotze's lectures led him to a critique of sensationism and associationism, which dominated philosophy and psychology in Britain in the 1880s. Ward began lecturing in psychology in 1878 and attempted to establish an experimental laboratory in Cambridge, although without success at this time (Ward, 1927, p. 73). Arguing for the active and constructive nature

[18] R.F. Hoernle attributes the translation to Ward in his review of A.C. Macmillan, *The Crowning Phase of the Critical Philosophy; A Study in Kant's Critique of Judgment* (London: Macmillan & Co., 1912) in *Mind New Series*, Vol. 23, No. 92 (Oct. 1914), 597–604, p. 600. See also C. Spearman's review of C. S. Myers, *Text-book of Experimental Psychology*, "New Books" in *Mind New Series*, vol. 18, no. 72, October 1909, 617–18; (Valentine, 1912).

[19] He published a portion of it entitled "An Attempt to interpret Fechner's Law" in the journal *Mind* in 1876 (Ward, 1927, p. 53).

of the mind, Ward put forth his psychological and epistemological ideas in his well-known entry, "Psychology", in the ninth edition of the *Encyclopedia Britannica* in 1886, a description which became a highly influential account of the new psychology (Ward, 1886). In 1897, Ward became the Professor of Mental Philosophy and Logic at Trinity College, and went on to give the Gifford Lectures at Aberdeen as well as St. Andrews (Ward, 1911).

James Ward and the anthropologist James Frazer knew each other since their undergraduate days and became good friends in the early 1880s. Their friendship was sustained by their long mutual connection with Trinity College (Ackerman, 1987, p. 229). Ward recommended Tylor's book on *Primitive Culture* to Frazer before he began his studies in social anthropology. Frazer described Ward as "my friend, James Ward (with whom I have walked and talked on all subjects in earth and heaven on an average once a week for many years)" (Ackerman, 1987, p. 228). Frazer's biographer, Robert Ackerman, reports that Frazer and Ward were members of an informal "Cambridge anthropological circle" at Trinity College that also included Henry Jackson, the philosopher of ancient Greek, Robertson Smith, the biblical scholar and anthropologist, and the classicist W. H. D. Rouse.[20]

The theme of personification appears repeatedly in Frazer's multi-volume work, *The Golden Bough: A Study in Comparative Religion*. It was first published in 1890 and went through many revisions and expansions in later editions. Frazer described anthropomorphic personification as common to many spring and May-day festivals celebrated in diverse cultures in Bavaria, Alsace, Transylvania, and Bengal:

> The names May, Father May, May Lady, Queen of the May, by which the anthropomorphic spirit of vegetation is often denoted, show that the idea

[20] Ackerman describes Robertson Smith as the first "to apply the comparative evolutionary anthropological approach to the study of an entire family of religions, the Semitic" (Ackerman, 1987, p. 58). He cites a letter Frazer wrote to Jackson in 1888, which seems to refer to Ward. Therein Frazer writes that one's way of looking at the world is a product of a long period of cultural growth and change, an idea that a psychologist should be interested in, preferably a modern physiological psychologist (Ackerman, 1987, p. 89).

> of the spirit of vegetation is blent with a personification of the season at which his powers are most strikingly manifested. (Frazer, 1900, p. 212)

Ideas, powers, and spirits were personified or represented by certain individuals i n these rituals.

As Ward explains to Frazer in his letter, empathy could be understood as a kind of personification. His explanation likely formed the beginning of a conversation between the two scholars, which they might have pursued further on one of their weekly walks. In his writings, Ward made clear that the impulse to personify or anthropomorphize was not limited to the primitive mind, nor even to a religious sensibility. It appeared as well in contemporary thinking and philosophizing: "We seem justified then, in maintaining the presence of anthropomorphism or 'poetical metaphysics' not only in the speculation of primitive man but even in those of philosophers down to our own time" (Ward, 1927, pp. 212–213). He was convinced that *Einfühlung* or empathy was a contemporary habit of thinking resonant with anthropomorphic projection or personification, and proof, as he says to Frazer, of the "original impulse having 'survived'".[21]

Psychology was, for Ward, preeminently a science of "experience". The aim of general psychology was "to ascertain, describe, and analyze the invariable factors of psychical life, consciousness, or immediate experience" (Ward, 1906, p. 637). One important aspect of psychological experience was the tendency to project experience outward or to assign one's own attributes to things and concepts. This was true for our everyday perception of unity, change, and striving, as well as for many philosophical concepts. Ward was convinced that one's own psychological experiences modulated the way one perceived entities in the world:

> Few consider that underlying all common-sense thinking there lurks the same natural precipitancy. We attribute to extended things a unity which we know only as the unity of an 'enduring' subject; we attribute to changes among these extended things what we know only when we act

[21] Ward to Frazer, Nov. 11, 1915 (Add. Ms. B. 37/331), Master and Fellows of Trinity College Cambridge.

> and suffer ourselves; and we attribute further to them in their changes a striving for ends which we come to know only because feeling in our case begets appetition and aversion. In asking what they are, how they act, and why they act thus and thus, we naturally tend at first to assimilate things to ourselves, in spite of differences which lead us by and by to find a gulf between mind and matter. (Ward, 1919, pp. 335–336)

Through the attribution of psychological qualities to things in the world, the inner transforms into the outer, but for the most part the subject was unaware of this projection. Over the course of an individual's life, as well as over history, the common perception emerged of a strict divide between mind and matter. Ward saw this type of dualistic thinking as common in the modern world, but nonetheless as deceiving (see Tallon, 1939, pp. 118–121).

In Ward's view, nature is better understood along the same lines as the mind. Nature's laws are akin to psychological habits, as he explains in a 1905 essay entitled "Mechanism and Morals": "All nature is regarded as plastic and evolving like mind: its routine and uniformity being explained on the analogy of habit and heredity in the individual, and of custom and tradition in society" (Ward, 1927, p. 243). He was not alone in this view, as the Anglo-American psychologists and philosophers C. S. Peirce and Josiah Royce also understood nature on the analogy of mind, amounting to a sort of panpsychism (Skrbina, 2005, pp. 141–156; Turner, 1974, pp. 237–239). In his essay, Ward cites both C. S. Peirce, who claims that "matter is effete mind, inveterate habits becoming physical laws", and Josiah Royce, who argues that "evolution would be a vast series of processes suggesting to us various degrees and types of conscious process" (Ward, 1927, p. 244). Ward admits that this philosophical view is not itself science, and yet there is nothing in science that could readily refute this "panpsychic view".

The continuity of evolutionary processes means that no sharp lines could be drawn between animals of a lower and higher order. In a review of Ward's work just after his death, his colleague W. R. Sorley dubbed Ward an evolutionist who "was applying the theory beyond the range of biology; his thought was also dominated by the principle of continuity which he learned from Darwin as well as from Leibniz" (Sorely, 1925, p. 276). If the theory of evolution was first thought to be a levelling down of mankind to his animal origins, Ward argued it might be better understood as a levelling up of the elementary units of life. "At first it appeared as if man were only to be linked with the ape, now it would seem that the atom, if a reality at all, may be linked with man" (Ward, 1927, p. 247). Here, Ward adopts a Leibnizian view that the smallest units, or monads, possess psychical properties and individual peculiarities. Although he does not specify the nature of these monads, Ward cautioned that one should not dismiss the theory out of hand on the basis that chairs or stones were not animated (Ward, 1927, p. 245). The topic of personification reappears in his 1905 essay "Heredity and Memory", where he writes that "all things were animated albeit in diverse degrees" (Ward, 1927, p. 276). As Ward sees it, dualism is a delusion, and inanimate objects possess psychic qualities in some as yet inexplicable fashion. Empathy is therefore much more than a return to mythic thought for Ward, but rather a commonplace phenomenon that discloses a metaphysical truth – the mind's projections are mixed in matter.

5 Conclusion

As Gordon Allport reminds us, *Einfühlung* came to the Anglophone world with a rich set of meanings, most of which were discarded by mid-century (see also Lanzoni, 2012a). By this time, "empathy" lost its connection to things and the world of objects and became exclusively a social phenomenon. Yet in the first decades of the twentieth century, empathy was still closely connected to its origins in *Einfühlung*, and emerged as a polyvalent term. In Titchener's structural psychology, empathy was based on the mind's images of movement, or kinaesthetic images. Baldwin, in contrast, emphasized empathy as a form of semblance, a playful, aesthetic capacity to entertain an "as-if" reality. And finally, Ward's panpsychic vision of empathy offered evidence for the mind's continuity with nature.

Titchener's identification of the kinaesthetic image as the basis for empathy is an approach most similar to recent neuroscientific studies of empathy, both for its attempt to understand empathy's underlying components, and for its coupling of movement and image in consciousness. The perceptual-action theories of mirror neuron empathy, put forward in 1992 by the Parma group of researchers, including Giacomo Rizzolatti, Giuseppe Di Pellegrino, Vittorio Gallese, Luciano Fadiga, and Leonardo Fogassi, have paired perception with motor action in the activity of a single neuron in macaque monkeys (Di Pellegrino, Fadiga, Fogassi, Gallese, & Rizzolatti, 1992; Fadiga, Pavesi, & Rizzolatti, 1996; Gallese, 2001; Gallese & Goldman, 1998; Rizzolatti, Fadiga, Gallese, & Fogassi, 1996). The connections between imagined movement and neuronal activity have been tested in recent neuroscientific studies on viewing art and aesthetic experience. Freedberg and Gallese have shown how abstract art can induce motor images in the viewer of the painterly and artistic gestures that produced such art (Freedberg & Gallese, 2007). The spectator imagines the artist's movements, such as the brush-stroke, for example, that might have created the art piece. In her work on neuroaesthetics, G. Gabrielle Starr finds the "imagery of motion to be at the heart of our capacities for both simulation and aesthetic experience" (Starr, 2013, p. 81). Motor imagery thus plays an important role in contemporary neuroaesthetic theories, as it did more than a century ago.

Yet neuroscientists and philosophers do not agree on the precise meanings of simulation. Does a simulation model of empathy mean that we act out movements internally (at some level), or simply produce an abstract visual image of the movement? Titchener's conception of the kinaesthetic image, or a mental image of movement, challenges us to evaluate the motor and visual qualities of mental images. Relying on evidence from introspection, Titchener disentangled a sensation of movement from an image of movement, a distinction that is still relevant today.[22] We are quick to find neural concomitants for empathic phenomena today, but often do not give enough credence to introspective reports or rich phenomenological accounts of empathic experiences (see Leys, 2014). Titchener's introspective efforts to catalogue images of motion might inspire us to revisit this promising territory of mental imagery.

[22] On the differences that Titchener spelled out between a kinaesthetic image and sensation, see Lanzoni (2012b).

If Titchener's conception of motor imagery resonates with contemporary simulation theories in neuroscience, psychologists today rarely refer to Baldwin's genetic epistemology of semblance or Ward's panpsychism. But these versions of empathy might provoke productive and challenging avenues of research. Does empathy emerge from an early, developmental play instinct, and if so, might it be able to shed light on how children and adults engage with "as-if" or make-believe scenarios as Baldwin describes? And what does empathy look like through the lens of philosophical panpsychism, advocated by Ward and other psychologists at the turn of the twentieth century? Contemplating empathy as a window onto the ways mind inhabits matter might help us imagine a more integrated vision of our world where anthropomorphic empathy is not merely cast off as a perceptual or scientific error. Primatologists have recently argued that a judicious form of anthropomorphism (not to be confused with anthropocentrism) makes it possible for humans to see similarities in other species (De Waal, 2009). Might we also find resonances between early twentieth-century panpsychism and the extended mind thesis as put forth by philosophers Andy Clark and David Chalmers (Clark & Chalmers, 1998; see also Holt, 2007)? This historical excursus into empathy's early Anglophone meanings reminds us of the now almost forgotten aptitude for semblance and personification, which transformed inert things and art objects through the mind's projections. Surprisingly enough, these conceptions of *Einfühlung* and empathy were commonplace a little more than a century ago.

Acknowledgements I would like to thank the Master and Fellows of Trinity College Cambridge for permission to reproduce the image of James Ward's letter of 1915, and the archivist Adam Green for his assistance. I would also like to thank members of my writing group, IWSS, the anonymous reviewers of my manuscript, as well as the editors of this volume for helpful feedback.

References

Ackerman, R. (1987). *J. G. Frazer: His Life and Work*. Cambridge, UK: Cambridge University Press.

Allesch, C. G. (1987). *Geschichte der psychologischen Ästhetik* [History of psychological aesthetics]. Göttingen: Verlag für Psychologie.

Allport, G. (1945). Psychology of Participation. *Psychological Review*, 52(3),117–132.

Baldwin, J. M. (Ed.) (1901–05). *Dictionary of Philosophy and Psychology* (vol. 2). New York: Macmillan.

Baldwin, J. M. (1906/1975a). Functional Logic, or Genetic Theory of Knowledge. In *Thought and Things: A Study of the Development and Meaning of Thought or Genetic Logic* (vol. 1). New York: Arno Press.

Baldwin, J. M. (1908/1975b). Experimental Logic, or Genetic Theory of Thought. In *Thought and Things: A Study of the Development and Meaning of Thought or Genetic Logic* (vol. 2). New York: Arno Press.

Baldwin, J. M. (1911/1975c). Interest and Art Being Real Logic. I. Genetic Epistemology. In *Thought and Things: A Study of the Development and Meaning of Thought or Genetic Logic* (vol. 3). New York: Arno Press.

Baldwin, J. M. (1913). *History of Psychology: A Sketch and an Interpretation* (vol. 2). New York: G.P. Putnam and Sons.

Baldwin, J. M. (1915/1975d). The Genetic Theory of Reality. In *Thought and Things: A Study of the Development and Meaning of Thought or Genetic Logic* (vol. 4). New York: Arno Press.

Baldwin, J. M. (1917). Pancalism. In J. Hastings (Ed.). *Encyclopedia of Religion and Ethics* (vol. 9, pp. 599). New York: Charles Scribner's Sons.

Baldwin, J. M. (1930). James Mark Baldwin. In C. Murchison (Ed.). *A History of Psychology in Autobiography* (vol. 1, pp. 1–30). Washington, D.C.: American Psychological Association.

Barasch, M. (1998). *Modern Theories of Art, 2: From Impressionism to Kandinsky*. New York: NY University Press.

Brock, A. (1991). Imageless Thought or Stimulus Error? The Social Construction of Private Experience. In W. R. Woodward & R. S. Cohen (Eds.). *World Views and Scientific Discipline Formation* (pp. 97–106). Dordrecht: Kluwer.

Cahan, E. D. (1984). The Genetic Psychologies of James Mark Baldwin and Jean Piaget. *Developmental Psychology*, *20*(1), 128–135.

Clark, A. & Chalmers, D. (1998). The Extended Mind. *Analysis*, *58*, 7–19.

Clarke, H. M. (1911). Conscious Attitudes. *The American Journal of Psychology*, *22*(2), 214–249.

Danziger, K. (1990). *Constructing the Subject: Historical Origins of Psychological Research*. Cambridge: Cambridge University Press.

De Waal, F. (2009). *The Age of Empathy: Nature's Lessons For a Kinder Society*. New York: Harmony Books.

Dilthey, W. (1894/1977). Ideas Concerning a Descriptive and Analytic Psychology and The Understanding of Other Persons and Their Expressions of Life. In *Descriptive Psychology and Historical Understanding* (pp. 21–120, Zaner & Heiges, Trans.). The Hague: Martinus Nijhoff.

Di Pellegrino, G., Fadiga, L., Fogassi, L., Gallese, V., & Rizzolatti, G. (1992). Understanding Motor Events: A Neurophysiological Study. *Experimental Brain Research, 91*, 176–180.

Evans, R. B. (1990). The Scientific and Psychological Positions of E.B. Titchener. In R. Leys & R. B. Evans (Eds.). *Defining American Psychology. The Correspondence between Adolf Meyer and E.B. Titchener* (pp. 1–39). Baltimore: Johns Hopkins University Press.

Fadiga, L., Pavesi, L. G., & Rizzolatti, G. (1996). Motor Facilitation during Observation: A Magnetic Simulation Study. *Journal of Neurophysiology, 73*, 2608–2611.

Frazer, J. G. (1900). *The Golden Bough: The King of the Wood, The Perils of the Soul* (2nd ed., vol. 1). London: Macmillan.

Freedberg, D., & Gallese, V. (2007). Motion, Emotion and Empathy in Esthetic Experience. *Trends in Cognitive Sciences, 11*(5), 197–203.

Friedrich, T. & Gleiter, J. (Eds) (2007). *Einfühlung und phänomenologische Reduktion: Grundlagentexte zu Architektur, Design und Kunst* [Empathy and the phenomenological reduction. Basic texts on architecture, design, and fine arts]. Berlin: Lit Verlag Dr. W. Hopf.

Gallese, V. (2001). The 'Shared Manifold' Hypothesis: From Mirror Neurons to Empathy. *Journal of Consciousness Studies, 8*, 33–50.

Gallese, V. & Goldman, A. (1998). Mirror neurons and the simulation theory of mind reading. *Trends in Cognitive Science, 2*, 493–501.

Gordon, K. (1934). A Device for Demonstrating Empathy. *Journal of Experimental Psychology, 17*(6), 892–893.

Groos, K. (1901). *The Play of Man*. New York: D. Appleton.

Heidbreder, E. (1933). *Seven Psychologies*. New York: Appleton-Century Crofts, Inc.

Henle, M. (1971). Did Titchener Commit the Stimulus Error? The Problem of Meaning in Structural Psychology. *Journal of the History of the Behavioral Sciences, 7*(3), 277–282.

Hindeland, M. J. (1971). Edward Bradford Titchener: A Pioneer in Perception. *Journal of the History of the Behavioral Sciences, 7*(1), 23–28.

Hinman, E. L. (1895). Ueber psychophysische Energie und ihre Factoren. K. Lasswitz. *The Philosophical Review, 4*(6), 672–673.
Holt, J. (2007, November 18). Mind of a Rock. *New York Times*. Retrieved from http://www.nytimes.com/2007/11/18/magazine/18wwln-lede-t.html
Jahoda, G. (2005). Theodor Lipps and the Shift from 'Sympathy' to 'Empathy'. *Journal of the History of the Behavioral Sciences, 4*(2), 151–163.
Jarzombek, Mark (2000). *The Psychologizing of Modernity: Art, Architecture and History*. Cambridge, UK: Cambridge University Press.
Koss, J. (2006). On the Limits of Empathy. *The Art Bulletin, 88*(1), 139–157.
Kroker, K. (2003). The Progress of Introspection in America, 1896–1938. *Studies in history and philosophy of biological and biomedical sciences, 34*, 77–108.
Kusch, M. (1999). *Psychological Knowledge: A Social History and Philosophy*. London: Routledge.
Langfeld, H. S. (1920/1967). *The Aesthetic Attitude*. Port Washington, NY: Kennikat Press.
Lanzoni, S. (2009). Practicing Psychology in the Art Gallery: Vernon Lee's Aesthetics of Empathy. *Journal of the History of the Behavioral Sciences, 45*(4), 330–354.
Lanzoni, S. (2012a). Introduction [Special Issue: *Emotions and the Sciences: Varieties of Empathy in Science, Art and History*]. *Science in Context, 25*(3), 287–300.
Lanzoni, S. (2012b). Empathy In Translation: Movement and Image in the Psychological Laboratory. *Science in Context, 25*(3), 301–327.
Lee, V., & Anstruther-Thomson, C. (1897). Beauty and Ugliness. *Contemporary Review, 72*, 544–69; 669–88.
Lee, V., & Anstruther-Thomson, C. (1912). *Beauty and Ugliness and Other Studies in Psychological Aesthetics*. London: John Lane, Bodley Head.
Leys, R. (2014). 'Both of us Disgusted in my Insula': Mirror-Neuron Theory and Emotional Empathy. In F. Biess &D. M. Gross (Eds.). *Science and Emotions after 1945: A Transatlantic Perspective* (pp. 67–95). Chicago: University of Chicago Press.
Lipps, Th. (1902). Von der Form der Aesthetischen Apperception [The form of aesthetic apperception]. In *Philosophische Abhandlungen. Gedenkschrift für Rudolf Haym* (pp. 365–406). Halle: Max Niemeyer.
Lipps, Th. (1903). *Leitfaden der Psychologie* [Guidelines to psychology]. Leipzig: Wilhelm Engelmann.
Lipps, Th. (1903/1923). *Grundlegung der Ästhetik* [The Foundation of Aesthetics] (vol. 1). Leipzig: Leopold Voss.

Lipps, Th. (1903/1960). Empathy, Inner Imitation, and Sense Feelings. In M. Rader (Ed.). *A Modern Book of Esthetics*. New York: Holt, Rinehart and Winston.

Lipps, Th. (1906/1920). *Aesthetik: Psychologie des Schönen und der Kunst* [Aesthetics. Psychology of the beautiful and the arts] (vol. 2). Leipzig: Leopold Voss.

Makkreel, R. (2000). From Simulation to Structural Transposition: A Diltheyean Critique of Empathy and Defense of Verstehen. In H. H. Kögler (Ed.). *Empathy and Agency: The Problem of Understanding in the Human Sciences* (pp. 181–93). Boulder, CO: Westview Press.

Mallgrave, H. F. & Ikonomou, E. (1994). Introduction. In H. F. Mallgrave & E. Ikonomou (Eds.). *Empathy, Form and Space: Problems in German Aesthetics, 1873–1893* (pp. 1–66). Santa Monica, CA: Getty Center.

Myers, C.S. (1909). *Text-Book of Experimental Psychology*. London: Edward Arnold.

Ogden, R. (1909). Reports and Discussion, Sixth International Congress of Psychology. *Psychological Bulletin*, *6*(11), 389–397.

Ogden, R. (1938). *The Psychology of Art*. New York: Charles Scribner's Sons.

Okabe, T. (1910). Experimental Study of Belief. *The American Journal of Psychology*, *21*(4), 563–596.

Perky, C. (1910). An Experimental Study of Imagination. *The American Journal of Psychology*, *21*(3), 422–452.

Pinotti, A. (2010).Empathy.In H. R. Sepp & L. Embree (Eds.).*Handbook of Phenomenological Aesthetics*. Dordrecht: Springer.

Richards, R. J. (1987). James Mark Baldwin: Evolutionary Biopsychology and the Politics of Scientific Ideas. In R. J. Richards. *Darwin and the Emergence of Evolutionary Theories of Mind and Behavior* (pp. 480–496), Chicago: University of Chicago Press.

Ringer, F. (1969). *The Decline of the German Mandarins*. Hanover: Wesleyan University Press.

Rizzolatti, G., Fadiga, L., Gallese, V., & Fogassi, L (1996). Premotor cortex and the recognition of motor actions. *Cognitive Brain Research*, *3*(2), 131–141.

Rogers, A. (1917). An Analytic Study of Visual Perceptions. *American Journal of Psychology*, *28*(4), 519–577.

Schaub, A. D. V. (1911). On the Intensity of Images. *American Journal of Psychology*, *22*, 346–368.

Skrbina, D. (2005). *Panpsychism in the West*. Cambridge, MA: MIT Press.

Sokal, M. M. (1997). Baldwin, Cattell and the *Psychological Review*: a collaboration and its discontents. *History of the Human Sciences, 10*(1), 57–89.

Sorley, W. R. (1925). James Ward. *Mind, New Series, 34*(135), 273–279.

Starr, G. G. (2013). *Feeling Beauty: The Neuroscience of Aesthetic Experience.* Cambridge, MA: MIT Press.

Tallon, H. J. (1939). *The Concept of Self in British and American Idealism: A Dissertation.* Washington, D.C.: The Catholic University of America Press.

Titchener, E. B. (1904). Organic Images. *The Journal of Philosophy, Psychology and Scientific Methods, 1*(2), 36–40.

Titchener, E.B. (1908). *Lectures on the Elementary Psychology of Feeling and Attention.* New York: Macmillan.

Titchener, E. B. (1909a). *Experimental Psychology of the Thought-Processes.* New York: Macmillan.

Titchener, E.B. (1909b). *A Text-book of Psychology.* Part 1. New York: Macmillan.

Titchener, E.B. (1910). *A Text-Book of Psychology.* New York: Macmillan.

Titchener, E.B. (1915). *A Beginner's Psychology.* New York: Macmillan.

Titchener, E.B. (1899/1916). *An Outline of Psychology* (new Edition with Additions). New York: Macmillan.

Turner, F. M. (1974). *Between Science and Religion: The Reaction to Naturalism in Late Victorian England.* New Haven: Yale University Press.

Urban, W. M. (1909). *Valuation: Its Nature and Laws, Being an Introduction to a General Theory of Value.* London: Sonnenschein & Co.

Urban, W. M. (1917). The Knowledge of Other Minds and the Problem of Meaning and Value. *The Philosophical Review, 26*(3), 274–296.

Valentine, C. W. (1912). Psychological Theories of the Horizontal-Vertical Illusion. *The British Journal of Psychology, 5*(1), 8–35.

Vischer, R. (1873/1994). On the Optical Sense of Form. In H. F. Mallgrave & E. Ikonomou (Eds). *Empathy, Form and Space: Problems in German Aesthetics, 1873–1893* (pp. 89–123). Santa Monica, CA: Getty Center.

Ward, J. (1886). Psychology. In *Encyclopedia Britannica: A Dictionary of Arts, Sciences and General Literature* (9th ed., vol. 20, pp. 37–85).

Ward, J. (1906). The Present Problems of General Psychology. In H. J. Rogers (Ed.). *International Congress of Arts and Sciences* (vol. 5). London, New York: University Alliance.

Ward, J. (1911). *The Realm of Ends or Pluralism and Theism: The Gifford Lectures, St. Andrews, 1907–1911.* Cambridge, UK: Cambridge University Press.

Ward, J. (1919). *Psychological Principles.* Cambridge, UK: Cambridge University Press.

Ward, J. (1927). *Essays in Philosophy with a Memoir of the Author by Olwen Ward Campbell.* Cambridge, UK: Cambridge University Press.

Wispé, L. (1987). History of the concept of empathy. In N. Eisenberg & J. Strayer (Eds.). *Empathy and its Development* (pp. 17–37). Cambridge, UK: Cambridge University Press.

Wozniak, R. H. (1998). Thought and Things: James Mark Baldwin and the Biosocial Origins of Mind. In R. W. Rieber & K. D. Salzinger (Eds). *Psychology: Theoretical and Historical Perspectives* (2nd ed., pp. 429–453). Washington, D.C.: American Psychological Association.

Wozniak, R. H. (2004). Lost Classics and Forgotten Contributors: James Mark Baldwin as a Case Study in the Disappearance and Rediscovery of Ideas. In T. C. Dalton & R. B. Evans (Eds.). *The Life Cycle of Psychological Ideas* (pp. 33–58). New York: Kluwer Academic/Plenum.

Wozniak, R. H. (2009a). Consciousness, Social Heredity and Development. *American Psychologist, 64*(2), 93–101.

Wozniak, R. H. (2009b). James Mark Baldwin, professional disaster, and the European connection. *Rassegna di Psicologia, 26,* 111–128.

Wozniak, R. H. & Santiago-Blay, J. A. (2013). Trouble at Tyson Alley: James Mark Baldwin's Arrest in a Baltimore Bordello. *History of Psychology, 16*(2), 227–248.

Index

V. Lux, S. Weigel (eds.), *Empathy*, Palgrave Studies in the Theory and History of Psychology, DOI 10.1057/978-1-137-51299-4

D

E

F